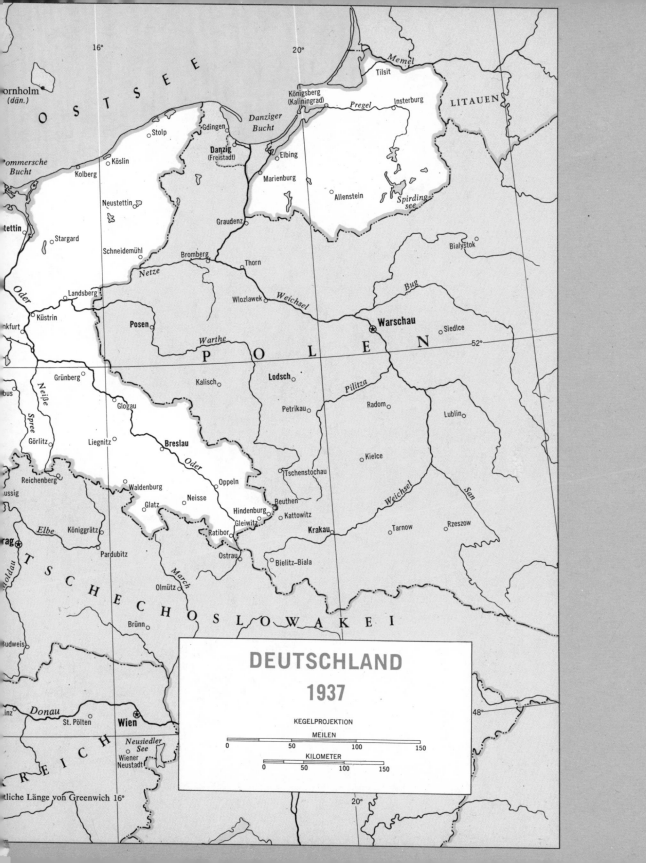

O S T S E E

Bornholm
(dän.)

Pommersche
Bucht

Memel

Tilsit

Königsberg
(Kaliningrad)

Pregel

Insterburg

LITAUEN

Danziger
Bucht

Gdingen

Stolp

Danzig
(Freistadt)

Elbing

Köslin

Kolberg

Marienburg

Allenstein

Spirding-
see

Neustettin

Stettin

Stargard

Graudenz

Schneidemühl

Bromberg

Thorn

Bialystok

Netze

Oder

Landsberg

Küstrin

Frankfurt

Wlozlawek

Weichsel

Bug

Posen

Warschau

Siedlce

Warthe

P O L E N

52°

Grünberg

Neiße

Spree

Lodsch

Kalisch

Pilitza

Radom

Lublin

Glogau

Petrikau

Görlitz

Liegnitz

Breslau

Oder

Kielce

Reichenberg

Waldenburg

Oppeln

Tschenstochau

Aussig

Glatz

Neisse

Weichsel

San

Elbe

Königgrätz

Hindenburg

Gleiwitz

Beuthen

Kattowitz

Rzeszow

Prag

Moldau

Pardubitz

Ratibor

Krakau

Tarnow

Ostrau

Bielitz–Biala

T S C H E C H O S L O W A K E I

Olmütz

March

Brünn

Budweis

DEUTSCHLAND

1937

KEGELPROJEKTION

MEILEN

0   50   100   150

KILOMETER

0   50   100   150

Donau

Linz

St. Pölten

Wien

REICH

Neusiedler
See

Wiener
Neustadt

östliche Länge von Greenwich 16°

16°

20°

20°

48°

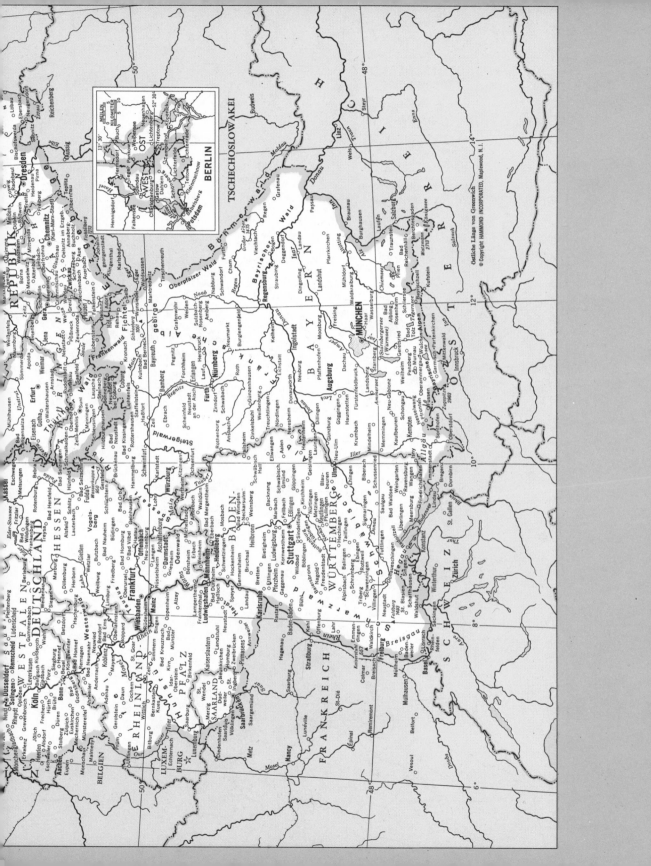

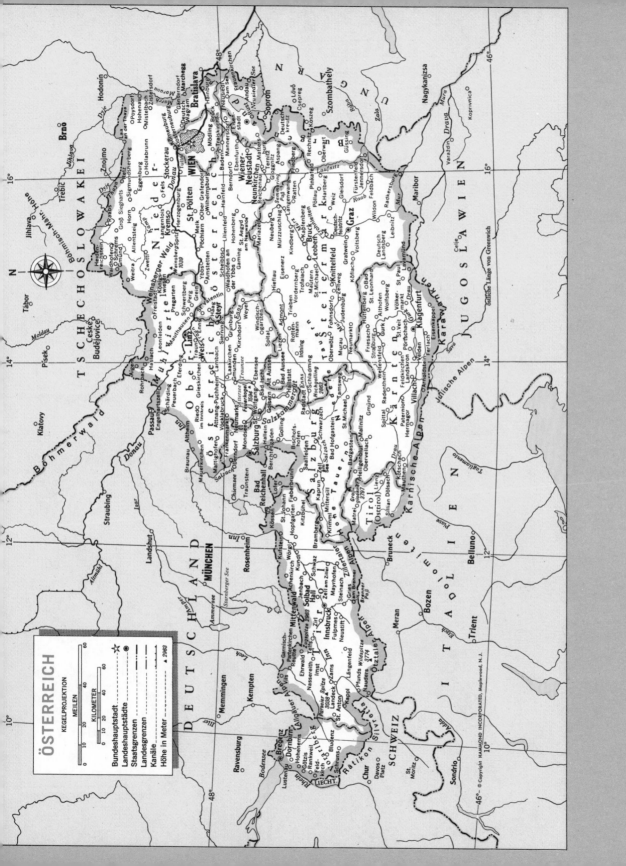

ÖSTERREICH

KEGELPROJEKTION

MEILEN

0 10 20 40 60

KILOMETER

0 20 40 60

Bundeshauptstadt ☆ ◉
Landeshauptstädte ⊙
Staatsgrenzen
Landesgrenzen
Kanäle
Höhe in Meter ▲ 2963

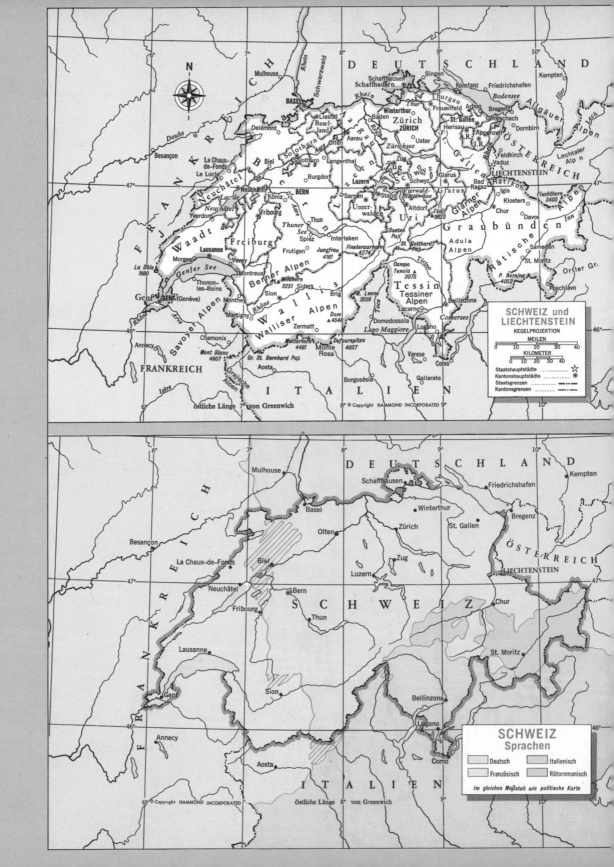

German
Through
Reading

A Basic Text

German Through Reading

A Basic Text

Reinhold K. Bubser
Verne Rudebusch
Texas A & M University

D. VAN NOSTRAND COMPANY

New York • Cincinnati • Toronto • London • Melbourne

D. Van Nostrand Company Regional Offices:
New York   Cincinnati

D. Van Nostrand Company International Offices:
London   Toronto   Melbourne

Copyright © 1978 by Litton Educational Publishing, Inc.

Library of Congress Catalog Card Number: 77-88338
ISBN: 0-442-211430

Published by D. Van Nostrand Company
135 West 50th Street, New York, N.Y. 10020

10 9 8 7 6 5 4 3 2 1

reface

This text is designed for students in the Humanities, Social Sciences, and Natural Sciences who want to acquire a functional proficiency in German, whether for study, research, or personal pleasure. Although intended primarily to teach reading, the book covers all skills by combining a thorough presentation of basic grammar with relevant practice.

The starting point is the student's own knowledge of English. The progression is from structures in English to analogous ones in German. The authors recognize that some students want a textual approach that will develop their reading skill quickly while minimizing materials that do not directly contribute to this skill.

The book presents structural elements in the following cyclic sequences:

1. Pronunciation;
2. Grammatical / structural explanations;
3. Exercises applying these elements;
4. Reading;
5. Vocabulary and structural exercises.

Pronunciation

Pronunciation practice opens each of the first fifteen lessons. Along with the introductory "Reference Guide to German Sounds," these pronunciation exercises and the accompanying tapes / cassettes acquaint the student with the basic sounds of the language. These sounds are presented in a sequence beginning with those most needed for correct pronunciation. The exercises may be used as five-minute "warm-up" at the beginning of each session to attune the student's ear and mind to the language. We have found in our own classes that students exposed to such practice developed excellent speaking proficiency.

Structure and Exercises

The grammatical / structural elements are presented in logical sequences small enough to learn and apply immediately. Frequent programmed practice (called "Self-Preparatory Exercises") allow the students to test their own knowledge. The class exercises that follow afford additional and more intensive practice to enable the instructor to evaluate student progress and, if necessary, review and reinforce structural elements.

Reading

The lesson readings were selected from several major areas and increase in length and difficulty. The topics were chosen in order to cover basic vocabulary in several fields. The readings are from original texts that were modified in accordance with student preparation at particular points in the book.

We believe students will benefit from this approach to reading in that they are given a general exposure to several areas of study other than their major field of interest. Thus an English major may read about logarithms, and a Chemistry student may read Bertolt Brecht or about Gothic architecture. Almost all lessons have two to three reading selections.

Vocabulary

The new vocabulary is listed directly following the reading text. This vocabulary is constantly used and reused in the exercises from that point on. Meanings of words are given only on first occurrence, unless additional meanings are presented. If students encounter a word whose meaning they do not recognize, they may jog their memory by referring to the end vocabulary, where they will find — not an English equivalent — but a page number listing the word's first use in the book.

The goal envisioned by this approach is twofold:

1. to induce the student to infer the meanings of words from context and to rely on memory;
2. to encourage the learning of words in context, rather than by list or by rote.

For example, a student might remember **der Vogel** not only as *the bird* from the vocabulary list, but also in the context of Wilhelm Busch's poem **"Humor"** on page 337, which depicts the bird in the trap, warbling his last bits of gallows humor before succumbing to the cat. Most new native words are learned through a similar process, and the process has obvious merits in learning a new language. Thus, the exercises following the readings test the student's knowledge of the vocabulary and certain structures in the context of concepts and words already known.

ACKNOWLEDGMENTS

Grateful acknowledgment is extended to the following publishers for their permission to reproduce reading selections of which they are the copyright holders (numbers in parentheses refer to pages in this book):

Atrium Verlag, Zürich: Erich Kästner, "Die andere Möglichkeit," from *Ein Mann gibt Auskunft* (414).

Bibliographisches Institut AG, Mannheim: *Schlag nach! 10. Auflage*, 1972 (171, 185, 262, 286, 312, 364, 366).

The Bobbs-Merrill Company, Indianapolis: Howard S. Hirschhorn, *Scientific and Technical German Reader*, 1964 (368, 371).

Deutscher Taschenbuch Verlag, München: *dtv = junior-Lexikon, Band 1*, 1974 (36, 56, 81, 87, 156, 213, 226, 237, 348, 404, 417, 425).

Diesterweg Verlag, Frankfurt am Main: Hans Joachim Störig, *Wirtschaft — Ein Entscheidungsbereich* (358, 361).

Holt, Rinehart and Winston, New York: Wulf Koepke, *Die Deutschen*, 1971 (146).

Max Hueber Verlag, Ismanning / München: Johanna Haarer, *Die Welt des Arztes, 3. Auflage*, 1966 (383).

Ernst Klett Verlag, Stuttgart: *Grundwissen Deutsche Literatur, 2. Auflage*, 1976 (339); *Blick auf Deutschland*, 1974 (207, 266, 317, 325, 330, 342).

Langenscheidt-Verlag, Berlin, München, Wien, Zürich: *Langenscheidts Sprach-Illustrierte, Heft 1, XVIII. Jahrgang* (127).

Verlag des Rheinischen Merkur, Köln: *Rheinischer Merkur, Ausgabe Nr. 2/1968* (397).

Rowohlt Verlag, Reinbek: Sigismund von Radecki, *Das ABC des Lachens* (278).

Scala (Societäts-Druckerei GMBH), Frankfurt am Main: *Scala International* (65, 95, 97, 103, 160, 180, 229, 240, 255).

Schocken Books, Inc., New York: Franz Kafka, *Erzählungen*, Berlin, 1946 (378).

Südwest Verlag, München: *Das will ich wissen, 9. Auflage*, 1974 (245, 390, 395, 401, 421).

Suhrkamp Verlag, Frankfurt am Main: Bertolt Brecht, *Die Dreigroschenoper* (295); Ernst Penzoldt, *Die Liebenden, Prosa aus dem Nachlaß* (426).

ontents

LESSON 11   99

PRONUNCIATION: German **v.** German **w.** German **y.** German **z.** STRUCTURE: 1. Prepositions — Dative and Accusative. 2. Prepositions — Dative and Accusative (continued). 3. Two-Way Prepositions With Fixed Cases. READING: **Die Analyse von Proteinstrukturen.** STRUCTURE: 4. **Der**-Words. 5. **Der**-Words — Accusative. 6. **Der**-Words — Dative. 7. **Der**-Words — Genitive. READING: **Einleitung in die Mathematik.**

LESSON 12   111

PRONUNCIATION: German / ch /. STRUCTURE: 1. Genitive — Indefinite Article. 2. Prepositions with the Genitive Case. READING: **Albert Einstein.** STRUCTURE: 3. Past Tense — Weak Verbs. 4. Past Tense — Verbs Ending in **-ieren.** 5. Contracted Forms of Prepositions. 6. Feminine Nouns Ending in **-in.** READING: **Volkshochschule: Erwachsene auf der Schulbank.**

LESSON 13   122

PRONUNCIATION: German / chs /. German / kn / and / gn /. German / schw /. STRUCTURE: 1. Past Tense — Strong Verbs. 2. Irregular Verbs. READING: **Unser Herz in Zahlen.** STRUCTURE: 3. Past Tense — **haben.** 4. Past Tense — Strong Verb Dictionary Listing. 5. Past Tense — **sein.** 6. Two-Way Prepositions with Fixed Cases. 7. Time. 8. Temperature. READING: **Abitur.**

LESSON 14   135

PRONUNCIATION: German **sp** and **st.** German **pf** and **ps.** German **ß.** Glottal Stop. STRUCTURE: 1. Verb — **nehmen.** 2. Subordinating Conjunctions. READING: **Johann Gutenberg.** STRUCTURE: 3. Word Order — Subordinate Clause. 4. Negation — **kein** (continued). 5. Possessive Adjectives. 6. **Ein**-Word Phrases. 7. Arithmetic. READING: **Das Klima.**

LESSON 15   148

PRONUNCIATION: Contrast Exercises — Vowels. STRUCTURE: 1. Subordinating Conjunctions (continued). 2. Irregular Verb — **wissen.** READING: **Afrika.** STRUCTURE: 3. Verbs — Principal Parts. 4. Past Participle. 5. Weak Past Participle. 6. Stem Ending in **-d, -t,** or **-n.** 7. Stem Ending in **-ier.** READING: **Absoluter Nullpunkt.**

LESSON 22   235

LESSON 23   248

LESSON 24   258

LESSON 25   268

LESSON 26   280

LESSON 27   292

German Through Reading

A Basic Text

# Reference Guide To German Sounds

This section contains a brief description of the German sounds for speakers of American English. The reference guide serves only as an approximate system for the reproduction of the sounds. For further practice with the individual sounds, pronunciation exercises have been provided at the beginning of each chapter. The additional pronunciation exercises are indicated in the boxes preceding each section.

A. VOWELS

ADDITIONAL PRACTICE

Sound	Page
a	14, 15, 148
e	9, 10, 15, 148
i	20, 148
o	38, 148
u	29, 148

German vowels are pronounced either long or short.

GERMAN SOUND		ENGLISH	GERMAN
/ **a** /	pronounced like English long / a / as in	*father*	Saat
	or like English short / o / as in	*rot*	satt
/ **e** /	pronounced like English long / ay / as in	*hay*	Beet
	or like English short / e / as in	*get*	Bett
/ **i** /	pronounced like English long / e / as in	*she*	ihn
	or like English short / i / as in	*did*	in
/ **o** /	pronounced like English long / o / as in	*go*	Sohn
	or like English short / o / as in	*cot*	Sonne
/ **u** /	pronounced like English long / u / as in	*flute*	Huhn
	or like English short / u / as in	*put*	Hund

B. DIPHTHONGS

ADDITIONAL PRACTICE

Sound	Page
ai, ei	48
ay, ey	48
eu, aü	48
au	39

GERMAN SOUND		ENGLISH	GERMAN
/ **ai** / / **ei** / / **ay** / / **ey** /	pronounced like English / i / as in	*like*	m**ei**n
/ **eu** / / **äu** /	pronounced like English / oi / as in	*loiter*	H**eu**
/ **au** /	pronounced like English / ou / as in	*house*	H**au**s

C. UMLAUT

ADDITIONAL PRACTICE

Sound	Page
ä	58, 148
ö	58, 148
ü	59, 148

The word *umlaut* refers to a change in the vowel sound. A diacritical mark (¨) is placed over the sound to indicate the vowel change to an umlaut sound.

GERMAN SOUND		ENGLISH	GERMAN
/ **ä** /	pronounced like English / a / as in	*rare*	H**ä**nde
/ **ö** /	pronounced like English / u / as in	*hurler*	k**ö**nnt
/ **ü** /	pronounced like English / u / as in	*demure*	M**ü**ller

D.   GERMAN WORD ENDINGS

ADDITIONAL PRACTICE

Sound	Page
e	67
en	67
er	67

1.   Ending -e

When a word ends in **-e** in German, this / e / sound is unstressed. The pronunciation of the final unstressed **-e** corresponds closely to the / a / sound in the English word *sofa*. Examples:

Dame
Rede

2.   Ending -en

The pronunciation of final **-en** is also unstressed and may be compared with the pronunciation of final *-en* in English *mitten, hidden*. Examples:

singen
sagen

3.   Ending -er

This ending is unstressed in German, and the pronunciation resembles that of English *-ah* in *Sarah*. Examples:

Mutter
besser

E.   CONSONANTS

ADDITIONAL PRACTICE

Sound	Page
c	77
j	77
l	78
q	89
s	90
v	99
w	99
y	59, 99
z	100

German consonants differ from their English counterparts only as shown below or in the following section on special sounds. For all other consonants, the German pronunciation corresponds closely to English.

1.   German / c /

a.   If it precedes the sounds / e /, / ä /, or / i /, **c** is pronounced like / ts / in the words *tsar, tsetse,* or *rats.* Examples:

Celsius
Cäsar
Circus

b.   If **c** precedes the vowels **a, o,** or **u,** it is pronounced like / k / in the words *coffee* or *Africa.* Examples:

Caracas
Computer
Cuxhaven

2.   German / j /

is pronounced like English / y / as in *yes.*

VIER

3.   German / l /

The German / l / sound is like the babbling sound in *lalala*.

4.   German / q /

This letter occurs only in connection with **u,** and is pronounced like / kv /. Example:

Quelle

5.   German / s /

There are two / s / sounds in German:

voiced (similar to English / s / as in *his*);

voiceless (similar to English / s / as in *sun* or *hiss*).

Generally, **s** is voiced whenever it is single and in front of a vowel. In all other combinations, **s** is voiceless. Examples:

Nase (voiced)
Haus (voiceless)

6.   German / v /

is pronounced like / f / at the beginning of words of German origin. In all other situations, initial **v** is pronounced like English / v /. In the middle of a word **v** is also pronounced like English / v /. Examples:

Vater (v = f)
Vakzin (v = v)
Universität (v = v)

7.   German / w /

is pronounced like English / v / as in *visa*. Example:

wie

8.   German / y /

As a letter of the alphabet it is called **Üpsilon.** The pronunciation of the sound is similar to the umlaut vowel sound / ü /. Example:

Pyramide

FÜNF

9. German / z /

is pronounced like / ts / in *tsar* or *rats*. Example:

Zar

F. SPECIAL SOUNDS

ADDITIONAL PRACTICE

Sound	Page
ch	111
chs	122
kn, gn	123
sch + *cons.*	123
sp, st	135
pf, ps	135
ß	135
r	89

1. German / ch /

This sound is closely related to the / k / sound; but instead of making a complete closure between between the back of the tongue and the soft palate, **ch** is produced by leaving an opening between the back of the tongue and the soft palate. This opening results in an audible friction sound as the breath passes through.

Depending on the vowel sound that precedes or follows **ch**, the production of / **ch** / will shift, in accordance with the vowel, from the front of the mouth to the back and vice versa. Compare:

Dach   **mich**
(back)   (front)

2. German / chs /

After vowels, **chs** is usually pronounced like / x / in English *six*. Example:

Sachsen

SECHS

3. German / kn / and / gn /

The **k** and the **g** are not silent and are pronounced in German like / **k** + **n** / and / **g** + **n** /. Examples:

Knie   **Gnom**

4. German / sch / + Consonant

Imitate the English sound for being quiet or demanding silence / sch! / and add the consonant. Examples:

Schweden   **Schlegel**

5. German / sp / and / st /

The / s / sound before **p** and **t** is pronounced like / sh /. Imitate the English sound / sch! / and add the consonant. Examples:

Spiel   **Stil**

6. German / pf / and / ps /

In German, the / p / sound is pronounced in both clusters. Examples:

Pfad   **Psalm**

7. German / ß /

This special letter indicates an / ss / sound. It is always pronounced like an unvoiced / s / as in *hiss*. The letter **ß** is called **s-z** (ess-tset). It is used in place of **ss:**

a.   between two vowels of which the first is long. Example:

Straße

b.   after a vowel or diphthong and before a consonant. Example:

mußt

c.   in final position. Example:

daß

8. German / r /

a.   The preferred articulation of the / r / sound in German is the uvular / r /. "Uvular" refers to the raising of the tongue toward the uvula and the back of the soft palate. A narrow, slit-shaped opening is formed. The breath stream which escapes through the opening causes the uvula to vibrate against the back of the tongue.

There is a similarity in the articulation of **ch** and **r.** Therefore, in order to produce / r /, say the following:

Buk
Buche

Now pronounce / ch / as far back as possible and say:

Bure

b.   The pronunciation of German / r / sound varies according to its position (initial, medial, final) in the word.

c.   Medial / r / and its articulation have been demonstrated in the sequence above.

d.   Initial / r / may be produced in this sequence. Say:

Aachen

Pronounce / ch / as far back as possible. Say:

Aare

Say:

re

Say:

rat, riet, rot, rum

e.   Final / r / is generally pronounced like the final sound in English Sarah. Example:

bitter

WORD STRESS

German does not have printed or written accents for stressed syllables. The main stress in German words normally falls on the first or root syllable. To help you with words which do not have the stress on the first or root syllable, we will use a dash (e̱) to indicate a stressed long vowel or diphthong and a dot (e̦) to indicate a stressed short vowel. Examples:

Vakzi̱n   **Stude̦nt**

ACHT

esson 1

PRONUNCIATION
Short Vowels — Short / e /

Say the following English words:

get   set   bet   met

The short / e / in these English words closely corresponds to the German short / **e** /.

Now pronounce the following German words containing short / **e** / vowels:

denn   **Bett**   **fett**   **nett**

In general, German vowels are pronounced short when they are followed by:

a. a double consonant

    Bett   **denn**

b. two or more consonants

    Nest   **Heft**

PRACTICE

hell	**fest**	**nett**
Kette	**Feld**	

Long Vowels — Long / e /

German long / e / sounds like English / a / as in *make* or like English / ay / as in *stay*.

German vowels lack the off-glide of English. In the English words *make* and *stay*, at

NEUN

least two recognizable sounds can be heard in the pronunciation of the letters *a* or *ay*. These two sounds together produce off-glide as in *make* and *stay*.

German vowels are spoken as pure vowels, that is, without off-glide. A vowel has only one sound.

Say the following English words without the off-glide:

hay   stay   take   ray

Now pronounce the following German words. Maintain a pure vowel sound without off-glide:

Long / e /

geh   nehmen   den
Tee   gegen

In general, German vowels are pronounced long if

a.   they are followed by a single consonant:

  den   gegen

b.   they are followed by **h:**

  geh   nehmen

c.   they are doubled:

  Beet   Tee

Long / e / vs. Short / e /

Contrast Exercise:

den   denn
wen   wenn
stehlen   stellen
reden   retten

STRUCTURE

1.   Genders

a.   Nouns are words which designate concepts, objects, and living beings.

ZEHN

b. In German, nouns are divided into three genders, which are specified by an article:

der
die } English: *the*
das

c. Each noun has a definite gender:

masculine   feminine   neuter

d. The definite articles designate the genders:

der = masculine
die = feminine
das = neuter

e. All nouns are capitalized in German:

	MASCULINE	FEMININE	NEUTER
LIVING BEINGS	**der Mann** *(the man, husband)*	**die Frau** *(the woman, wife)*	**das Kind** *(the child)*
OBJECTS	**der Tisch** *(the table)*	**die Lampe** *(the lamp)*	**das Haus** *(the house)*
CONCEPTS	**der Gedanke** *(the thought)*	**die Vernunft** *(the reason)*	**das Gefühl** *(the feeling)*

2. Infinitive / Verb

a. The verb is a type of a word which describes an action, a relationship, or a state of being.

b. The basic form of the verb is the infinitive: to sing

c. In German, the infinitive form of the verb usually ends in **-en** (occasionally in **-n**):

singen   **lernen**   **studieren**

d. The part of the verb preceding the ending is called the stem:

STEM	+	INFINITIVE ENDING	=	INFINITIVE
sing	+	**en**	=	**singen**
lern	+	**en**	=	**lernen**
studier	+	**en**	=	**studieren**

f. Most verbs following singular nouns (all genders) add **t** to the verb stem to form the present tense:

NOUN	VERB STEM + ENDING	= SENTENCE
Der Mann **Die Frau** **Das Kind**	**sing** **lernt** } + **t** **studier**	= **Der Mann singt.** = **Die Frau lernt.** = **Das Kind studiert.**

SELF-PREPARATORY EXERCISE

Instructions:

The right column is the verification column. Cover this column.

Look at the words in the left column, and form German sentences in the present tense.

EXAMPLE: Cue: (Der Mann / singen)
 Answer: Say or write: **Der Mann singt.**

(die Frau / singen)	
(das Kind / spielen)	Die Frau singt.
(der Mann / lernen)	Das Kind spielt.
(das Haus / stehen)	Der Mann lernt.
(das Gefühl / bleiben)	Das Haus steht.
(der Tisch / stehen)	Das Gefühl bleibt.
	Der Tisch steht.

singen = *to sing*

spielen = *to play*

lernen = *to learn; to study*

stehen = *to stand*

bleiben = *to remain; to stay*

3. Present Tense

There are three present-tense forms in English:

REGULAR FORM:	The child *sings.*
PROGRESSIVE FORM:	The child *is singing.*
EMPHATIC FORM:	The child *does sing.*

4. Present Tense / German

In contrast to English, there is only one present tense form in German. This single German form corresponds to the three English forms:

The child *sings.*
The child *is singing.* } = Das Kind **singt.**
The child *does sing.*

EXERCISES

A. *Supply the definite article:**

1. _____ Haus steht.   4. _____ Frau lernt.
2. _____ Kind singt.   5. _____ Tisch steht.
3. _____ Vernunft bleibt.

B. *Form sentences using the noun and verb given:**

1. Frau / stehen   4. Gedanke / bleiben
2. Kind / singen   5. Mann / lernen
3. Haus / stehen

C. *Write all three English equivalents:*

1. Die Frau steht.   4. Der Gedanke bleibt.
2. Die Lampe steht.   5. Das Kind lernt.
3. Der Mann singt.

READING

Der Student in Deutschland

Der Student lernt Deutsch. Der Student studiert in Deutschland. Der Student studiert Physik. Der Student lernt viel in Deutschland. Der Student bleibt ein Jahr in Deutschland.

VOCABULARY

der	**Student**	student	die	**Physik**	physics
	lernen	to study, to learn		**viel**	a lot, much
	Deutsch	German		**bleiben**	to stay
	studieren	to study		**ein**	a, an, one
	in	in	das	**Jahr**	year
	Deutschland	Germany			

STRUCTURAL EXERCISE

Underline all verbs in the above reading.

VOCABULARY EXERCISE

Give the English equivalents of the italicized words:

1. Der Student lernt *viel.*
2. Der Student bleibt *ein Jahr* in Deutschland.
3. Der Student *lernt* Deutsch.
4. Der Student *bleibt* ein Jahr in Deutschland.

                                                        DREIZEHN

Lesson 2

PRONUNCIATION

Vowels — Short / a /

Say the following English words:

rot   cot   lot   hot

Now say these German words:

Ball   **Kamm**   **Latte**   **hat**

Vowels — Long / a /

Say the following English words:

father   bother   rather

Now say these German words:

Saat   **Bahn**   **Bad**   **sagen**

Long / a / vs. Short / a /

Contrast Exercise:

mahn	**Mann**
sag	**Sack**
Maat	**matt**
Saat	**satt**

VIERZEHN

Long / a / vs. Long / e /   **Short / a / vs. Short / e /**

Contrast Exercise: Contrast Exercise:

Vater	**Feder**	**Lack**	**Leck**
stahlen	**stehlen**	**Ratte**	**rette**
lagen	**legen**	**fast**	**fest**
sagen	**Segen**	**Latte**	**Lette**

der Bruder = brother; reden = *to talk*

STRUCTURE

1.   Present Tense

a.   Verbs whose stems end in **-d** or **-t** add an **-e-** before the personal ending **-t** in the present tense:

NOUN	+		VERB			=	SENTENCE
		STEM	+		ENDING		
Der Mann	+ **arbeit**	+	**e**	+		**t**	= **Der Mann arbeitet.**
Die Frau	+ **wart**	+	**e**	+		**t**	= **Die Frau wartet.**
Das Kind	+ **red**	+	**e**	+		**t**	= **Das Kind redet.**

SELF-PREPARATORY EXERCISE

(Frau / finden)
(Student / arbeiten)
(Bruder / reden)
(Mann / warten)

Die Frau findet.
Der Student arbeitet.
Der Bruder redet.
Der Mann wartet.

finden = *to find*

arbeiten = *to work*

der Bruder = *brother*; reden = *to talk*

warten = *to wait*

EXERCISE

Form sentences, using the words below: *

1. Bruder / reden
2. Schwester *(sister)* / finden
3. Student / arbeiten
4. Kind / warten
5. Tochter *(daughter)* / reden

2. Personal Pronouns

a. The English personal pronouns *he, she, it,* correspond to German **er, sie, es:**

er = *he*
sie = *she*
es = *it*

b. Verbs conjugated with these pronouns take the ending **-t:**

er singt   **sie singt**   **es singt**

3. Indefinite Pronoun <u>man</u>

a. The German indefinite pronoun **man** is equivalent to English *one,* as in "One has (a house)." Sometimes this pronoun may also mean *you,* as in "You can never predict that. . ." or as *they* or *people,* as in "They will never know. . ." or "People will never know. . ."

Verbs conjugated with the pronoun **man** take the ending **-t:**

man singt { *one sings*
you sing
they sing }

SELF-PREPARATORY EXERCISE

Give the German equivalents of the English sentences:

He sings.	
She stands.	Er singt.
The child is playing.	Sie steht.
It plays.	Das Kind spielt.
She is learning.	Es spielt.
The thought remains.	Sie lernt.
	Der Gedanke bleibt.

EXERCISES

A. *Form sentences, using the words below:**

1. er / singen   4. es / stehen
2. man / lernen   5. man / reden
3. sie / studieren

SECHZEHN

B. *Give the three English equivalents:*

1. Die Frau steht.
2. Er studiert.
3. Der Mann arbeitet.
4. Man lernt.
5. Das Kind redet viel.

C. *Express in German:*

1. The table is standing.
2. One does sing.
3. The feeling remains.
4. She is talking.
5. The lamp does stand.

4. Cognates

a. English and German share many words of common ancestry. These words resemble each other because they have the same root. They are called cognates.

b. The English meaning of the following German nouns is easily recognized without consulting a dictionary:

der Finger   **die Hand**   **der Arm**

c. Unlike the English words, the German nouns have a gender. Not all cognates are as easy to identify as our examples above. Many cognates have undergone changes in spelling:

der Apfel = *apple*   **das Haus** = *house*   **das Schiff** = *ship*

EXERCISE

Identify the following cognates. Changes in spelling that have occurred in English are in heavy type:

1. der Garten
2. **kalt**
3. das Wetter
4. **gut**
5. die **M**aus

5. False Cognates

a. There are some German words that have a spelling similar to familiar English words. The meaning of these German words, however, differs from the English words. Examples:

GERMAN WORD	ENGLISH MEANING
das Labor	*laboratory*
die Hose	*trousers, pants*
die Art	*kind, species*
der Hut	*hat*
der Gang	*hallway*

6.   Pronouns: Noun Replacement

a.   Nouns may be replaced by pronouns.

b.   The personal pronouns **er, sie, es** replace nouns of corresponding gender:

er	=	**der Tisch**	(masculine)	*he* (or *it*)
sie	=	**die Lampe**	(feminine)	*she* (or *it*)
es	=	**das Haus**	(neuter)	*it*

SELF-PREPARATORY EXERCISE

Cover the right column. Substitute the corresponding personal pronoun for the noun. Check your answer in the right column: *

Das Gold bleibt.		
Der Sohn lernt.	Es bleibt.	das Gold = *gold*
Der Chemiker studiert.	Er lernt.	der Sohn = *son*
Der Physiker steht.	Er studiert.	der Chemiker = *chemist*
Der Gedanke bleibt.	Er steht.	der Physiker = *physicist*
	Er bleibt.	

EXERCISE

Replace the nouns by personal pronouns: *

1. Der Chemiker lernt.   _____ lernt.
2. Der Sohn studiert.   _____ studiert.
3. Der Gedanke bleibt.   _____ bleibt.
4. Die Lampe steht.   _____ steht.
5. Das Kind lernt.   _____ lernt.

SUMMARY

1. After **er, sie, es,** and **man,** the ending **t** is added to the verb stem to form the present tense.
2. Verbs whose stems end in **d** or **t** add **e** before the ending **t** in the present tense.
3. The German present tense has three different equivalent meanings in English (sings, is singing, does sing).
4. Pronouns in the nominative case are: **er, sie, es.** Pronouns may replace nouns.

ACHTZEHN

READING

Der Student in Hamburg

Zeit: Montag
Ort: Universität Hamburg

Der Student geht in das Labor. Er arbeitet dort. Er studiert Chemie und Physik. Er lernt viel über Chemie und Physik. Der Professor ist aus Amerika. Er lehrt nur Chemie. Das Studium ist schwer.

VOCABULARY

die	**Zeit**	time		**und**	and
der	**Montag**	Monday		**über**	about
der	**Ort**	place	der	**Professor**	professor
die	**Universität**	university		**ist**	is
	gehen	to go		**aus**	from
das	**Labor**	laboratory		**lehren**	to teach, instruct
	er	he		**nur**	only
	arbeiten	to work	das	**Studium**	study
	dort	there		**schwer**	difficult
die	**Chemie**	chemistry			

STRUCTURAL EXERCISE

Underline all verbs in the present tense in the above reading.

VOCABULARY EXERCISE

Note: Some of the italicized words are from the previous lesson. To find the English equivalent, turn to the Vocabulary in the back of the book, beginning on page 460, and look up the word. You will find a page number next to the word. This number indicates the first page on which the word appears in a Reading with its English meaning.

Give the English equivalents of the italicized words:

1. Der Professor ist *aus* Amerika.
2. Er lernt *viel* über Physik.
3. Er *lehrt* nur Chemie.
4. Das Studium ist *schwer.*
5. Der Professor arbeitet *dort.*

Lesson 3

PRONUNCIATION

Short / i /

Pronounce the following English words:

fit   pit   tip   lick

Pronounce the following German words:

in   bin   mit   dick

Long / i /

Pronounce the following English words:

beak   meet   see

Pronounce the following German words:

die   pi (π)   tief
nie   ihnen   Marie

Long / i / vs. Short / i /

Contrast Exercise:

Lied   litt
Miete   Mitte
ihm   im
Ihnen   innen
bieten   bitten

ZWANZIG

STRUCTURE

1. Verb: <u>sein</u> = to be

The verb **sein** does not follow the conjugation pattern outlined for the other verbs. The third person singular form in the present tense is irregular:

er			he	
sie			she	
es			it	
man	ist		one	is
der Mann			the man	
die Frau			the woman	
das Kind			the child	

EXERCISE

Supply the correct form of **sein:**

1. Der Mann _____ Chemiker.
2. Das Studium _____ schwer.
3. Er _____ Student.
4. Deutschland _____ in Europa.
5. Das Kind _____ dort.

2. Nouns — Definition of Case and Subject

a. Case

The case of a noun indicates its relationship to other words in a sentence.

b. Subject

The subject is the center of attention and activity in a sentence. Together with the verb, the subject establishes relationships with other sentence elements.

c. Nominative

The nominative case is the basic form of the noun as it appears in the dictionary. It is also the case of the subject:

Subject = Nominative Case

Der Mann ist Chemiker.	*The man is (a) chemist.*
Sie spielt Tennis.	*She is playing tennis.*
Die Lampe steht dort.	*The lamp stands there.*

EINUNDZWANZIG

3. Verb: <u>haben</u> = to have

The verb **haben** is irregular in the third person singular form of the present tense:

er		he	
sie		she	
es		it	
man	**hat**	one	*has*
der Mann		the man	
die Frau		the woman	
das Kind		the child	

EXERCISE

Supply the correct form of **haben:**

1. Das Kind _____ Zeit.
2. Man _____ die Lampe.
3. Der Physiker _____ das Labor.
4. Die Frau _____ das Kind.
5. Sie _____ Zeit. *(she)*

4. Nouns — Definition of the Direct Object

a.   Object

The object is a sentence element which receives the action expressed by the verb. The verb determines the form of the object.

b.   Direct object = Accusative case

Most verbs in German use an accusative object. Accusative objects receive the direct action of the verb:

Der Mann hat **die Lampe.**	*The man has the lamp.*
Er findet **das Labor.**	*He finds the laboratory.*
Sie kennt **das Kind.**	*She knows the child.*
Das Kind singt **das Lied.**	*The child sings the song.*

The word **die Lampe** (first example) is the direct object. Since the accusative object receives the immediate or direct action expressed by the verb, it is also referred to as the direct object. Accusative and direct object are synonymous terms.

c.   Accusative case

In German, the direct object can often be recognized by the definite article which precedes the noun; each gender also has an accusative equivalent:

NOMINATIVE   ACCUSATIVE

der Mann   **den** Mann
die Frau   **die** Frau
das Kind   **das** Kind

Note that the feminine and neuter forms of the definite articles are identical in the nominative and accusative. The only new form is the accusative masculine, which is **den.**

EXERCISES

A.   *Supply the appropriate form of the accusative:* *

EXAMPLE: Da ist der Mann. Er kennt den Mann. *(He knows the man.)*

1. Da ist die Frau.   Er kennt _____ Frau.
2. Da ist der Chemiker.   Der Mann kennt _____ Chemiker.
3. Da ist das Labor.   Man kennt _____ Labor.
4. Da ist der Professor.   Die Frau kennt _____ Professor.
5. Da ist die Universität.   Das Kind kennt _____ Universität.

B.   *Supply the definite article for the subject and the direct object in the following sentences:*

1. _____ Professor hat _____ Gefühl.
2. _____ Student kennt _____ Universität.
3. _____ Frau findet _____ Kind.
4. _____ Mann kennt _____ Chemiker.
5. _____ Physiker hat _____ Labor.

READING

Bier

Bier ist in Deutschland und auch in Amerika sehr beliebt. Man produziert es aus Gerste, Hopfen, Hefe und Wasser. Das Bier hat gewöhnlich 4% (vier Prozent) Alkohol. Man braut das Bier in Brauereien.

DREIUNDZWANZIG

VOCABULARY

das	**Bier**	beer		die	**Hefe**	yeast
	auch	also, too			**gewöhnlich**	usually
	sehr	very			**vier**	four
	beliebt	popular		das	**Prozent (%)**	per cent
	man	one		der	**Alkohol**	alcohol
	produzieren	to produce			**brauen**	to brew
	es	it		die	**Brauerei**	brewery
die	**Gerste**	barley			**Brauereien**	breweries
der	**Hopfen**	hop				

STRUCTURAL EXERCISE

Underline all the subjects (= nominative case) and all the nouns in the accusative case (= direct object) in the above reading.

VOCABULARY EXERCISE

Note: Some of the italicized words are from previous lessons. To find the English equivalent, turn to the Vocabulary in the back of the book, beginning on page 460, and look up the word. You will find a page number next to the word. This number indicates the first page on which the word appears in a Reading with its English meaning.

Give the English equivalents of the italicized words:

1.   Das Studium ist *schwer.*
2.   Es hat *gewöhnlich* 4% (vier Prozent) Alkohol.
3.   Er *bleibt* ein Jahr in Deutschland.
4.   Bier ist *sehr* beliebt.
5.   Er *lehrt* nur Chemie.

STRUCTURE

5.   Compound Words

a.   Some German compound words have been assimilated by the English language:

   Kindergarten   Hausfrau   Zeitgeist   Hinterland

b.   Compound words consist of two or more components. The meaning of many compound words can be derived from the individual elements:

   Kinder + garten = der Garten für Kinder *(the garden for children)*

VIERUNDZWANZIG

c. Each compound word consists of a limiting word (= first element) and a base word (= second element):

LIMITING WORD   BASE WORD

| Kinder | + | garten |

d. The base word determines the gender of the compound noun:

der Garten   **der Kindergarten**

e. To deduce the meaning of the compound noun, start with the base word:

| garten | = | **der Garten** *(the garden)* |

f. The limiting word is added with the help of a preposition or prepositional phrase:

| Kinder | = | **die Kinder** *(for the children)* |

EXERCISES

A. *Match the following German compound nouns with the English nouns in the right column. One of the elements in the compound noun is a cognate word:*

1. das Handtuch   (a) milk can (the can for the milk)
2. der Backofen   (b) people's car (the car for the people)
3. das Vaterhaus   (c) hand towel (the towel for the hands)
4. die Milchkanne   (d) baking oven (the oven for baking)
5. der Volkswagen   (e) the father's house (the house of the father)

B. *Complete the English phrases by supplying the missing cognate; then supply the English equivalent of the German compound noun:*

1. der Rucksack (the _____ for the back) =
2. der Zeitgeist (the spirit of the _____) =
3. die Weltansicht (the view of the _____) =
4. das Krankenhaus (the _____ for the sick) =

6. Cardinal Numbers 1 – 12

Cardinal numbers are used in counting and in answering the question "how many?":

0	**null**	5	**fünf**	9	**neun**
1	**eins**	6	**sechs**	10	**zehn**
2	**zwei**	7	**sieben**	11	**elf**
3	**drei**	8	**acht**	12	**zwölf**
4	**vier**				

7. Noun Genders

a. German divides nouns into three genders, which can be identified by the definite article: masculine — **der,** feminine — **die,** neuter — **das.**

b. These grammatical genders do not necessarily agree with the natural gender of the noun.

c. The gender of many nouns can be determined by their suffixes.

8. Feminine Nouns

a. Nouns which end in the following suffixes:

-ei	-heit
-schaft	-keit
-t	-ung
-d	

Examples:

die Metzgerei	*butcher shop*	**die Fahrt**	*drive, journey*
die Krankheit	*illness*	**die Jagd**	*hunt*
die Fröhlichkeit	*happiness*	**die Versicherung**	*insurance*
die Freundschaft	*friendship*		

b. Nouns which have suffixes of French, Greek, or Latin origin:

-age	-enz	-esse
-euse	-ie	-ik
-ion	-itis	-tät
-ur		

Examples:

die Massage	*massage*	**die Politik**	*politics, policy*
die Potenz	*power*	**die Station**	*station*
die Delikatesse	*delicacy*	**die Rachitis**	*rickets*
die Friseuse	*beautician*	**die Universität**	*university*
die Sinfonie	*symphony*	**die Natur**	*nature, essence*

c. Female persons and female animals are usually (but not always) of feminine gender; often the suffix **-in** is added to the noun. Examples:

die Frau	*woman*	**die Kuh**	*cow*
die Tochter	*daughter*	**die Hündin**	*(female) dog*
die Mutter	*mother*	**die Wölfin**	*(female) wolf*

SECHSUNDZWANZIG

| die Tante | aunt | die Studentin | (female) student |
| die Schwester | sister | die Ärztin | (female) physician |

Exceptions:

| das Mädchen | girl | das Huhn | chicken |
| das Fräulein | young woman | | |

EXERCISE

*Give the gender (use **der, die, das**) of the following nouns:**

1. _____ Krankheit		6. _____ Abdichtung	
2. _____ Politik		7. _____ Kind	
3. _____ Mädchen		8. _____ Kuh	
4. _____ Mann		9. _____ Geschwindigkeit	
5. _____ Natur		10. _____ Huhn	

9. Sentence Structure — Statements

a. Words are arranged within a sentence to convey a specific idea of the speaker or writer.

b. The simplest word arrangement in German is a statement using a subject and a verb: **Der Mann arbeitet.**

c. Only the agreement of subject and verb provides the reader or listener with an intelligible idea:

Der Mann (what is he doing?)
arbeitet.

The verb **arbeiten** requires no additional information to form a meaningful sentence. There are many verbs, however, that require other sentence elements so that the intended information is comprehensible:

Die Frau findet (?)
The woman finds (what? or whom?)

In order to convey sufficient information, this sentence must have a direct object. The completed sentence could, therefore, read:

Die Frau findet den Mann.
Die Frau findet das Labor.
Die Frau findet die Universität.

German word order usually adheres to this sequence:

SUBJECT	VERB	DIRECT OBJECT
Die Frau	**findet**	**den Mann.**

SIEBENUNDZWANZIG

EXERCISES

A. *Write the following numbers in German:*

1. (8)   3. (5)   5. (1)
2. (12)   4. (7)

B. *Provide the gender of the following nouns* **(der, die, das):**

1. _____ Haus   6. _____ Gefühl
2. _____ Energie   7. _____ Statistik
3. _____ Tisch   8. _____ Professor
4. _____ Nation   9. _____ Fräulein
5. _____ Konsequenz   10. _____ Brauerei

READING

Bildende Kunst

Bildende Kunst ist ein Sammelbegriff. Es ist der Sammelbegriff für Baukunst, Bild-hauerkunst, Malerei, Graphik und das Kunsthandwerk.

VOCABULARY

	bilden	to form; to educate; to develop	das	**Bild**	picture
	bildend	plastic, graphic; educational	die	**Baukunst**	architecture
			der	**Bildhauer**	sculptor
die	**Kunst**	art	die	**Bildhauerkunst**	sculpture
	bildende Kunst	fine arts	die	**Malerei**	painting
	sammeln	to collect, gather	die	**Graphik**	graphic arts
der	**Begriff**	idea, concept, term	das	**Handwerk**	craft, trade, guild
	für	for	das	**Kunsthandwerk**	skilled craft

STRUCTURAL EXERCISE

In the above reading, underline all base words of the compound nouns.

VOCABULARY EXERCISE

Give the English equivalents of the italicized words:

1. Bildende *Kunst* ist ein Sammelbegriff.
2. Der Student *geht* in das Labor.
3. *Man* braut Bier in Brauereien.
4. Der Professor *lehrt* Physik.
5. Bildende Kunst ist *ein Sammelbegriff.*

ACHTUNDZWANZIG

Lesson 4

PRONUNCIATION

Short Vowels — Short / u /

Say the following English words:

book   cook   look   foot

Now pronounce these German words:

Busse   dumm   spucken   Schuft

Long Vowels — Long / u /

Pronounce the following English words:

noon   soon   tune   toot

Say these German words:

tun   Huhn   Hut   gut   Schub

Long / u / vs. Short / u /

Huhn	Hunne
du	dumm
Mut	Mutter
Kuh	Kutte

STRUCTURE

1.   Verb: Stem-Vowel Change

a.   Some verbs change the stem vowel in the third person singular of the present
tense. In a number of these verbs, the stem vowel **e** changes to **i (e → i):**

INFINITIVE   THIRD-PERSON VOWEL CHANGE

sprechen   Der Mann **spricht.**
helfen   Er **hilft.**
essen   Das Kind **ißt.**
vergessen   Sie **vergißt.**
geben   Es **gibt.**

b.   Other **e** stem verbs change the stem vowel to **ie (e → ie):**

lesen   Man **liest.**
sehen   Die Tochter **sieht.**

SELF-PREPARATORY EXERCISES

Cover the right column and form sentences with the words in the left column: *

EXAMPLE: (Kind / geben)
                  Das Kind gibt.

(Mann / sprechen)		
(Es / helfen)	Der Mann spricht.	sprechen = *to speak*
(Man / vergessen)	Es hilft.	helfen = *to help*
(Student / lesen)	Man vergißt.	vergessen = *to forget*
(Kind / sehen)	Der Student liest.	lesen = *to read*
(Er / geben)	Das Kind sieht.	sehen = *to see*
(Amerikaner / essen)	Er gibt.	geben = *to give*
	Der Amerikaner ißt.	essen = *to eat*

EXERCISES

A. *Supply the correct form of the verb in parentheses:*

1. Der Professor _____ viel. (lesen)
2. Der Student _____ das Labor. (sehen)
3. Man _____ viel. (helfen)
4. Sie *(she)* _____ Deutsch. (sprechen)
5. Er _____ die Zeit. (vergessen)

DREISSIG

B.   *Form sentences, using the words below:**

1.   Mann / essen / viel
2.   Er / sehen / Professor
3.   Sie (*she*) / lesen / ,,Die Zeit"
4.   Kind / sprechen / viel
5.   Es / helfen

C.   *Supply the correct form of the verb in parentheses:*

1.   Der Student _____ schwer.   (arbeiten)
2.   Er _____ Deutsch.   (sprechen)
3.   Die Frau _____ Chemie.   (studieren)
4.   Man _____ viel.   (vergessen)
5.   She (*she*) _____ in das Labor.   (gehen)

2.   Cardinal Numbers 13 – 20

13	**dreizehn**	16	**sechzehn**	19	**neunzehn**
14	**vierzehn**	17	**siebzehn**	20	**zwanzig**
15	**fünfzehn**	18	**achtzehn**		

Note: (16)   **sechzehn** (loses **-s** from **sechs**)
             (17)   **siebzehn** (loses **-en** from **sieben**)

READING

Biologie

Biologie ist das griechische Wort für die ,,Lehre von dem Leben". Die Biologie hat verschiedene Teilgebiete: Botanik, Zoologie und Anthropologie.

Die Botanik behandelt Pflanzen, die Zoologie behandelt Tiere, und die Anthropologie behandelt den Menschen.

VOCABULARY

die	**Biolog<u>ie</u>**	biology
	griechisch	Greek
das	**Wort**	word
	für	for
die	**Lehre**	teaching, science, theorie
	von	of
das	**Leben**	life
	von dem Leben	of life
	verschieden	different, various
der	**Teil**	part, section, component
das	**Gebiet**	area, domain, region

das	**Teilgebiet**	branch, division
die	**Botanik**	botany
die	**Zoolog<u>ie</u>**	zoology
die	**Anthropolog<u>ie</u>**	anthropology
	behandeln	to treat, deal with
die	**Pflanze**	plant
	Pflanzen	plants
das	**Tier**	animal
	Tiere	animals
der	**Mensch**	human being, man
den	**Menschen**	the human being, man *(accusative singular)*

STRUCTURAL EXERCISE

Underline all direct objects (accusative objects) in the above reading.

VOCABULARY EXERCISE

Give the English equivalents of the italicized words:

1. Die Botanik *behandelt* Pflanzen.
2. Bildende Kunst ist ein *Sammelbegriff.*
3. Das Studium ist *schwer.*
4. Die Biologie hat *verschiedene* Teilgebiete.
5. Biologie: ,,Die *Lehre* von dem Leben''.
6. Die Zoologie behandelt *Tiere.*
7. Er arbeitet *dort.*
8. Die Anthropologie behandelt *den Menschen.*

STRUCTURE

3. Indefinite Article — Nominative

a. Declension

The article in front of a noun enables one to recognize the gender of a noun. The form of the article shows whether the noun is used in the singular or plural and also its case. The change in the article in the four cases and the singular or plural is called declension.

b. Indefinite article

The indefinite article is used when we refer to a noun which we do not define specifically:

A car is in the driveway.
I see *a car.*

The reference here is to a car in general, not to a specific car.

c. Declensional endings

In German, the different genders and cases use different declensional endings for the indefinite article.

d. Indefinite article — nominative

The indefinite articles in the nominative case are:

MASCULINE	**ein**	
FEMININE	**eine**	= *a, an*
NEUTER	**ein**	

Example:

Da ist **ein Mann.**	*(There is a man.)*
Da ist **eine Lampe.**	*(There is a lamp.)*
Da ist **ein Haus.**	*(There is a house.)*

EXERCISES

A. *Change the following definite articles to indefinite articles:* *

1. Das ist die Brauerei.   Das ist _____ Brauerei.
2. Das ist der Begriff.   Das ist _____ Begriff.
3. Das ist das Gebiet.   Das ist _____ Gebiet.
4. Das ist der Mensch.   Das ist _____ Mensch.
5. Das ist die Pflanze.   Das ist _____ Pflanze.

B. *Change the following indefinite articles to definite articles:* *

1. Das ist ein Wort.   Das ist _____ Wort.
2. Das ist eine Lehre.   Das ist _____ Lehre.
3. Das ist ein Labor.   Das ist _____ Labor.
4. Das ist ein Student.   Das ist _____ Student.
5. Das ist ein Professor.   Das ist _____ Professor.

4.   Prepositions

Prepositions are functional elements of the sentence. They indicate the relation-ship between a noun and a verb, an adjective, or another noun:

He goes *into the house.*

In this example sentence, *into* is the preposition. It relates the verb—subject—unit *(He goes)* to *the house; into* shows the direction of the subject's movement: *into the house.*

5.   Prepositions — Accusative

a.   In German, each preposition is associated with a certain case, such as the accu-sative. This case is reflected in the form of the article:

Das Kind geht **um das Haus.**
The child goes (is going) around the house.

b.   Prepositions using only the accusative case in German are:

durch	*through*	**ohne**	*without*
für	*for*	**um**	*around*
gegen	*against*		

EXERCISES

A. *Supply the appropriate preposition:*

    1. Er geht _____ das Haus. (around)
    2. Das ist gut _____ das Studium. (for)
    3. Man arbeitet _____ das Labor. (without)
    4. Er spricht _____ die Lehre. (against)
    5. Sie geht _____ die Brauerei. (through)

B. *Supply the appropriate definite articles:*

    1. Das ist ein Sammelbegriff für _____ Kunst.
    2. Das ist gegen _____ Natur.
    3. Er geht durch _____ Universität.
    4. Sie liest ohne _____ Lampe.
    5. Das Kind geht um _____ Tisch.

C. *Give the German equivalents:*

    1. He has the animal for the laboratory.
    2. The professor speaks against the theory.
    3. She is reading without the lamp.
    4. He is going through the house.
    5. The child is going around the table.

SUMMARY

1. Some verbs change their stem vowels in the third person singular, present tense:

    (e → i)   **sprechen** → **er spricht**
    (e → ie)   **lesen**   → **er liest**

2. The indefinite articles, nominative case, are:

    ein   (masculine)
    eine   (feminine)
    ein   (neuter)

3. Prepositions using only the accusative case are:

    durch   *through*   **ohne**   *without*
    für   *for*   **um**   *around, at*
    gegen   *against*

STRUCTURE

6. Compound Words (continued)

Compound words may consist of two different grammatical elements; the limiting word and the base word are not always nouns.

a. The limiting word may be:

AN ADJECTIVE	**der Vollmond** = *full moon*
A VERB	**der Schreibtisch** = *writing table / desk*
A PREPOSITION	**die Vorstadt** = *the city in front of a city / suburb*
A NAME	**der Marshallplan**

b. The base word may be:

AN ADJECTIVE	**schneeweiß** = *white as snow*
A VERB	**warmmachen** = *to make warm*

EXERCISES

A. *Match the following German compound words with the English words:*

1. die Tiefsee
2. butterweich
3. weitergehen
4. der Gebrauchtwagen
5. der Singvogel

(a) a used car
(b) the deep sea
(c) the bird which sings   (songbird)
(d) to continue to go   (to walk)
(e) soft as butter

B. *Give the English equivalents of the following compound words used in the reading exercises:*

1. das Teilgebiet
2. der Sammelbegriff
3. die Baukunst
4. der Bildhauer
5. das Handwerk
6. die Bildhauerkunst
7. das Kunsthandwerk

7. Neuter Nouns

The following are basic groups of neuter nouns:

a. Nouns designating metals and chemical elements:

das Eisen (*iron*)
das Kupfer (*copper*)
das Zinn (*tin*)
das Zink (*zinc*)
das Gold (*gold*)
das Silber (*silver*)

das Uran (*uranium*)
das Plutonium (*plutonium*)
das Kalzium (*calcium*)
das Kalium (*potassium*)
das Natrium (*sodium*)
das Helium (*helium*)

das **Magnesium** (magnesium)   das **Neon** (neon)
das **Blei** (lead)   das **Oxyd** (oxide)

b.   Exceptions:

der **Wasserstoff** (hydrogen)   der **Stahl** (steel)
der **Sauerstoff** (oxygen)   der **Schwefel** (sulfur)

c.   Nouns which describe collectives:

das **Volk** (people)   das **Gewebe** (tissue)
das **Gebirge** (mountain range)   das **Gemisch** (mixture, compound)

EXERCISES

A.   Give the gender (**der, die, das**) of the following nouns:*

1. _____ Eisen   6. _____ Schwefel
2. _____ Gewebe   7. _____ Mädchen
3. _____ Natur   8. _____ Bier
4. _____ Wasserstoff   9. _____ Sinfonie
5. _____ Begriff   10. _____ Jagd

B.   Match the German words with the English cognates:

1. das Schiff   (a) school
2. fallen   (b) often
3. die Schule   (c) the ship
4. oft   (d) to come
5. kommen   (e) to fall

READING

Basilika

Basilika ist ein griechisches Wort. Es bedeutet Königsbau. Die Basilika hat eine rechteckige Halle. Die Halle hat Säulen und eine halbrunde Apsis. Die Basilika ist eine Urform für die christlichen Kirchen.

VOCABULARY

die **Basilika** basilica
bedeuten to mean, signify
der **König** king
der **Bau** building, structure
der **Königsbau** royal palace
haben / hat to have / has
rechteckig rectangular
die **Halle** hall, nave
die **Säule** column, pillar
Säulen columns, pillars
halb half

rund round
die **Apsis** apse
Ur German noun prefix meaning original, primitive
die **Form** form, shape
die **Urform** original form, prototype, archetype
christlich Christian
die **Kirche** church
Kirchen churches

SECHSUNDDREISSIG

STRUCTURAL EXERCISE

Underline all direct objects (accusative objects) in the above reading.

VOCABULARY EXERCISE

Give the English equivalents of the italicized words:

1. Die Anthropologie *behandelt* den Menschen.
2. Die Basilika hat eine *rechteckige* Halle.
3. Es *bedeutet* Königsbau.
4. Die Halle hat *Säulen.*
5. Die Lehre von dem *Leben.*
6. Die Basilika ist eine *Urform.*
7. Das Bier hat *gewöhnlich* 4% (Prozent) Alkohol.

Für die kleinsten Feste der Welt.

esson 5

PRONUNCIATION

Vowels — Short / o /

Say the following English words:

box   top   lock

Say the following German words:

komm   Gott   Bonn
ob   Sonne   hoffen

Vowels — Long / o /

Say the following English words:

low   go   so   no

Now say these German words:

Lohn   Ton   Hof   wohne   Boot

Long / o / vs. Short / o /

Bohne   Bonn
wohne   Wonne
Hof   hoffen
Sohn   Sonne
Oder   Otter

ACHTUNDDREISSIG

Diphthong / au /

Pronounce the following English words:

mouse   house   plough   now   how

Say these German words:

Maus   Haus   blau   Sau   Bau

STRUCTURE

1.   Nouns — Plural

a.   Most English nouns form plurals by adding **s** to the singular form:

SINGULAR: *the book*
PLURAL: *the books*

b.   In contrast, German plurals are formed by:

1.   a vowel change of the noun;
2.   various endings on the noun.

c.   These changes and endings are not predictable, but they do follow general patterns.

d.   One group of nouns adds **e** to the singular noun to form the plural:

SINGULAR: **der Tag** *(the day)*
PLURAL: **die Tage** *(the days)*

Note that the definite article also changes in the plural. All three genders **(der, die, das)** have the same plural nominative form **(die).**

SELF-PREPARATORY EXERCISE

Give the plurals of the following nouns. All nouns in this exercise add -e to form the plural:*

das Bier	
der Tag	die Biere
der Beruf	die Tage
der Tisch	die Berufe
der Freund	die Tische
	die Freunde

der Tag = *day*

der Beruf = *job, profession*

der Freund = *friend*

2.   Nouns — Plural (continued)

Other nouns form plurals by adding an umlaut (¨) to the stem vowel:

SINGULAR: **der Vater** *(the father)*
PLURAL: **die Väter** *(the fathers)*

SELF-PREPARATORY EXERCISE

Give the plurals of the following nouns. All nouns in this exercise add ¨ to form the plural:*

der Vater	
die Mutter	die Väter
der Garten	die Mütter
der Bruder	die Gärten
der Mantel	die Brüder
	die Mäntel

der Vater = *father*

die Mutter = *mother*

der Bruder = *brother*

der Mantel = *coat*

EXERCISE

Give the plurals of the following nouns:*

1. der Tag   4. der Bruder
2. der Vater   5. der Garten
3. der Beruf

3.   Verbs — Plural / Present Tense

Most verbs add **en** to the stem to form the third person plural of the present tense. This form of the verb is identical to the infinitive:

INFINITIVE: **singen**

THIRD PERSON PLURAL PRESENT TENSE: **singen**

Note: Verbs with a stem vowel change in the singular (third person, present tense) do not change that vowel in the plural:

SINGULAR: Der Vater **spricht.**
PLURAL: Die Väter **sprechen.**

VIERZIG

SELF-PREPARATORY EXERCISE

Transform the sentences into plural. Make all necessary changes in the nouns, definite articles, and verbs:

Der Freund geht.	
Der Bruder spricht.	Die Freunde gehen.
Der Vater liest.	Die Brüder sprechen.
Die Mutter singt.	Die Väter lesen.
Der Tisch steht.	Die Mütter singen.
	Die Tische stehen.

4.   Nouns — Plural (continued)

Some German nouns form their plural by adding **er** to the singular stem:

SINGULAR: **das Kind** *(the child)*
PLURAL: **die Kinder** *(the children)*

SELF-PREPARATORY EXERCISE

Give the plural of the following nouns. All nouns in this exercise add **-er** *to form the plural:**

das Feld	
das Lied	die Felder
das Bild	die Lieder
das Brett	die Bilder
	die Bretter

das Feld = *field*

das Lied = *song*

das Bild = *picture*

das Brett = *board*

5.   Nouns — Plural (continued)

Other noun plurals are formed by adding an umlaut (¨) to the stem vowel and **er** to the singular form of the noun:

SINGULAR: **der Mann** *(the man, husband)*
PLURAL: **die Männer** *(the men, husbands)*

SELF-PREPARATORY EXERCISE

Give the plurals of the following nouns. All nouns in this exercise add ¨ to the stem vowel and **-er** *to form the plural:* *

der Mann	
das Buch	die Männer
das Glas	die Bücher
das Haus	die Gläser
das Land	die Häuser
	die Länder

das Buch = *book*

das Glas = *glass*

das Land = *state, country, land*

EXERCISES

A. *Give the plural forms of the following nouns:* *

1. der Tisch   4. das Haus
2. das Bild   5. das Feld
3. die Mutter

B. *Transform the sentences into plural. Make all the necessary changes in the nouns, articles, and verbs:*

1. Der Mann spricht.   4. Die Frau liest das Buch.
2. Das Kind singt das Lied.   5. Der Freund sieht das Bild.
3. Das Haus steht dort.

READING

Atheismus

Atheismus ist ein griechisches Wort. Es bedeutet Gottesleugnung oder Gottlosigkeit. Ein Atheist glaubt überhaupt nicht an Gott und leugnet alle religiösen Glaubensbekenntnisse.

Der Agnostiker bezweifelt nur die Existenz Gottes, denn der Agnostiker ist skeptisch gegenüber Beweisen für die Existenz Gottes.

VOCABULARY

der **Atheismus**	atheism	die **Gottlosigkeit**	ungodliness
der **Gott**	god	der **Atheist**	atheist
die **Leugnung**	denial, disavowal	**glauben**	to believe; to think
die **Gottesleugnung**	atheism	**überhaupt**	altogether, generally
oder	or		

ZWEIUNDVIERZIG

	nicht	not	der	**Agnostiker**	agnostic

nicht — not
überhaupt nicht — not at all
an — at, by, near
glauben an — to believe in
leugnen — to deny, disavow
alle — all
religiös — religious
der Glauben — belief, faith, trust
das Bekenntnis — confession, avowal
das Glaubensbekenntnis — creed, denomination
Glaubensbekenntnisse — religious beliefs

der Agnostiker — agnostic
bezweifeln — to doubt; to question
nur — only
die Existenz — existence
die Existenz Gottes — the existence of God
denn — because, for
skeptisch — sceptical
gegenüber — toward, facing, vis-à-vis
der Beweis — proof, evidence
Beweise — proofs

STRUCTURAL EXERCISE

Underline all verbs used in the third person singular (present tense) in the reading above.

VOCABULARY EXERCISE

Give the English equivalents of the italicized words:

1. Atheismus ist ein griechisches *Wort*.
2. Der Agnostiker bezweifelt *nur* die Existenz Gottes.
3. Die Basilika hat eine *rechteckige* Halle.
4. Der Atheist *glaubt* überhaupt nicht an Gott.
5. Die Botanik *behandelt* Pflanzen.
6. Er *leugnet* alle religiösen Glaubensbekenntnisse.
7. Die Biologie hat *verschiedene* Teilgebiete.

STRUCTURE

6. Indirect Object — Dative Case

a. An accusative object (direct object) receives the direct action expressed by the verb. It answers the question "whom?" or "what?" and names the object of the action.

b. The dative object (indirect object) answers the question "to whom?" or "to what?" and tells us to or for whom (or to or for what) an action is performed.

c. There are several verbs in German which use only the dative case for their objects:

helfen *(to help)*   **antworten** *(to answer)*
folgen *(to follow)*   **vertrauen** *(to entrust, believe, trust)*

d. Nouns used as indirect objects (dative case) are preceded by the following definite articles:

SINGULAR

MASCULINE NOUNS:	**dem**
FEMININE NOUNS:	**der**
NEUTER NOUNS:	**dem**

PLURAL

ALL GENDERS:	**den**

e. All nouns add **n** to their plural form when used in the dative plural, with the exception of those nouns which end in **n** or **s** already:

DATIVE PLURAL: **den Häusern**
              den Autos   (**das Auto** = *car*)
              den Freunden

Examples with verbs using the dative case:

Der Student hilft **dem Professor.**   *(The student helps the professor.)*
Der Chemiker antwortet **dem Freund.**   *(The chemist answers the friend.)*
Man folgt **dem Wagen.**   *(One follows the car.)*
Die Mutter vertraut **den Kindern.**   *(The mother trusts the children.)*

EXERCISES

A. *Supply the definite article:*

1. Das Kind vertraut _____ Mutter.
2. Er antwortet _____ Freunden. (plural)
3. Der Student folgt _____ Professor in das Labor.
4. Er hilft _____ Frau.
5. Das Kind antwortet _____ Vater.

B. *Supply the correct form of the verb:*

1. Sie _____ dem Bruder. (she / to answer)
2. Es _____ dem Freund. (to follow)
3. Die Kinder _____ den Müttern. (to trust)
4. Der Student _____ dem Professor. (to help)
5. Man _____ dem Chemiker in das Labor. (to follow)

VIERUNDVIERZIG

7.   Neuter Nouns (continued)

The following basic groups exist for neuter nouns:

a.   Nouns which add the suffixes **-chen** or **-lein** are neuter:

das Mädchen *(girl)*   **das Hühnchen** *(little chicken)*
das Fräulein *(young woman)*   **das Brötchen** *(roll)*

b.   Nouns with the suffixes **-ett, -ment,** and **-um** are neuter:

das Parkett *(parquet)*   **das Natrium** *(sodium)*
das Sextett *(sextet)*   **das Helium** *(helium)*
das Sakrament *(sacrament)*   **das Medium** *(medium)*
das Parlament *(parliament)*   **das Kambrium** *(Cambrian Period)*

c.   Names of continents, countries, and cities are usually neuter:

CONTINENTS: **das Amerika** *(America)*
              das Europa *(Europe)*
              das Afrika *(Africa)*
              das Australien *(Australia)*
              das Asien *(Asia)*

COUNTRIES: **das Spanien** *(Spain)*   Exceptions:
              das Italien *(Italy)*
              das Rußland *(Russia)*   **die Schweiz** *(Switzerland)*
              das Frankreich *(France)*   **die Turkei** *(Turkey)*
              das Deutschland *(Germany)*   **die Tschechoslowakei** *(Czechoslovakia)*
              das England *(England)*   **die Vereinigten Staaten** *(United States)*

CITIES: **das Berlin von 1920** *(the Berlin of 1920)*
              das moderne Chicago *(the modern Chicago)*
              das alte Frankfurt *(the old Frankfurt)*

EXERCISES

A.   *Give the appropriate definite article* **(der, die, das)** *for the following nouns:* *

1. _____ Eisen   6. _____ Sinfonie
2. _____ Bruder   7. _____ Europa
3. _____ Türkei   8. _____ Deutschland
4. _____ Tag   9. _____ Mädchen
5. _____ Wasserstoff 10. _____ Parlament

B.   *Supply the appropriate form of the verb:*

1. Der Mann _____ das Lied.   (singen)
2. Das Wort _____ Gottlosigkeit.   (bedeuten)
3. Der Student _____ das Buch.   (lesen)
4. Sie *(she)* _____ dort.   (arbeiten)

C. *Give the German equivalents:*

1. He answers the man.
2. The children read the books.
3. She has time.

4. A student reads a lot (= much).
5. The tables stand there.

8. Verb: haben

The third person plural (present tense) form of the verb **haben** *(to have)* is identical with the infinitive:

INFINITIVE

THIRD PERSON PLURAL PRESENT TENSE

> **haben**

Example:

Die Kinder **haben** die Bücher.   *(The students have the books.)*

9. Verb: sein

The third person plural (present tense) form of **sein** *(to be)* is:

> **sind**

Example:

Die Bücher **sind** schwer.   *(The books are heavy.)*

EXERCISES

A. *Supply the correct form of* **sein** *or* **haben:**

1. Der Mann _____ Zeit. (has)
2. Das Studium _____ schwer. (is).
3. Die Brüder _____ die Bilder. (have)
4. Die Kinder _____ dort. (are)
5. Er _____ aus Amerika. (is)

B. *Supply the correct form of the verb in parentheses:*

1. Die Mutter _____ dem Kind. (to help)
2. Der Student _____ die Bücher. (to read)
3. Er _____ das Labor. (to find)
4. Die Lampen _____ dort. (to be)
5. Bildende Kunst _____ ein Sammelbegriff. (to be)

C. *Supply the correct definite article:*

1. Er kennt _____ Mann.
2. Das Mädchen antwortet _____ Freund.

3. Der Student liest _____ Buch.
4. Sie vertraut _____ Professor.
5. Der Vater sieht _____ Bild.

10. Cardinal Numbers 20 – 31

20	zwanzig	26	sechsundzwanzig
21	einundzwanzig	27	siebenundzwanzig
22	zweiundzwanzig	28	achtundzwanzig
23	dreiundzwanzig	29	neunundzwanzig
24	vierundzwanzig	30	dreißig
25	fünfundzwanzig	31	einunddreißig

READING

Archäologie

Man nennt Archäologie in der deutschen Sprache auch Altertumskunde. Die Archäologie ist eine Wissenschaft. Sie behandelt alte Kulturen.

VOCABULARY

	nennen	to call, name, term	die	**Altertumskunde**	science of antiquity, archaeology
die	**Archäologie**	archaeology			
	deutsch	German	die	**Wissenschaft**	science
die	**Sprache, -n**[1]	language		**sie**	it (see page 18)
das	**Altertum**	antiquity		**alt**	old
die	**Kunde**	knowledge, science, information	die	**Kultur, -en**	culture

STRUCTURAL EXERCISE

Underline all direct objects (accusative objects) in the above reading.

VOCABULARY EXERCISE

Give the English equivalent of the italicized words:

1. Sie behandelt *alte* Kulturen.
2. Er *bezweifelt* die Existenz Gottes.
3. Sie spricht die deutsche *Sprache*.
4. Die Archäologie ist eine *Wissenschaft*.
5. Sie *behandelt* alte Kulturen.
6. Er ist skeptisch gegenüber *Beweisen*.
7. Man nennt Archäologie *auch* Altertumskunde.

1. Starting with this lesson, vocabularies indicate plural endings: **die Sprache, -n = die Sprache, die Sprachen.**

Lesson 6

PRONUNCIATION

Diphthongs / ei / / ey / / ai / / ay /

Say the following English words:

my   tile   mine   fine   by

The English sounds / i / and / y / in the words above closely resemble the pronunciation of the German diphthongs / **ei** /, / **ey** /, / **ai** /, and / **ay** /.

Say these German words:

/ ei /	/ ey /	/ ai /	/ ay /
Teil	Meyer	Main	Mayer
mein	Geysir	Maid	Bayer
fein	Frey	Hain	Haydn
bei		Mais	

Diphthongs / eu / / äu /

Say the following English words:

toy   boy   coy

The English sound / oy / in the words above closely resembles the pronunciation of the German diphthongs / **eu** / and / **äu** /.

ACHTUNDVIERZIG

Say these German words:

/ eu /	/ äu /
neu	Säure
deutsch	Mäuse
leugnen	Häuser
Beute	Säule

STRUCTURE

1. Verbs — Stem-Vowel Changes

a. Previously we observed that some verbs change the stem vowel in the singular of the present tense. Some verbs change the stem vowel from **e** to **i**, others change from **e** to **ie**.

b. Other verbs with **a** or **au** as the stem vowel add an umlaut (**ü**) to that stem vowel:

fahren:	er fährt	*(to drive, travel)*
schlafen:	er schläft	*(to sleep)*
lassen:	er läßt	*(to let, allow, cause)*
wachsen:	er wächst	*(to grow)*
laufen:	er läuft	*(to run)*

EXERCISES

A. *Supply the correct form of the verb:*

    1. Er _____ durch das Land. (fahren)
    2. Die Kinder _____ viel. (schlafen)
    3. Die Universität _____. (wachsen)
    4. Der Volkswagen _____ und _____. (laufen)
    5. Die Mutter _____ das Kind schlafen. (lassen)

B. *Give the German equivalent of the verb in parentheses:*

    1. Der Vater _____ den Motor laufen. (to let)
    2. Die Wissenschaft _____. (to grow)
    3. Der Motor _____. (to run)
    4. Die Kinder _____ dort. (to sleep)
    5. Der Wagen _____ gegen das Haus. (to drive)

2. Nouns — Plural (continued)

Another group of nouns forms plurals by adding **-n** or **-en** to the singular. Remember that the plural article is **die** for all genders (**der, die, das**):

SINGULAR:	**der Professor**	SINGULAR:	**die Karte**
PLURAL:	**die Professoren**	PLURAL:	**die Karten**

SELF-PREPARATORY EXERCISE

*Form the plurals of the following nouns. Add **-n** to nouns that end in **-e** and **-en** to all others:* *

die Adresse	
die Karte	die Adressen
die Frau	die Karten
der Professor	die Frauen
die Zeitung	die Professoren
	die Zeitungen

die Adresse = *address*

die Karte = *card, map*

die Zeitung = *newspaper*

3.   Nouns — Plural (continued)

The following group of nouns retains the singular form for the plural:

SINGULAR: **das Mädchen**
PLURAL: **die Mädchen**

SELF-PREPARATORY EXERCISE

Form the plurals of the following nouns. All nouns in this exercise retain the singular form for the plural: *

der Amerikaner	
der Lehrer	die Amerikaner
der Schüler	die Lehrer
das Fräulein	die Schüler
das Zimmer	die Fräulein
das Mädchen	die Zimmer
	die Mädchen

der Amerikaner = *American (citizen)*

der Lehrer = *teacher*

der Schüler = *pupil*

das Fräulein = *young woman, girl*

das Zimmer = *room*

das Mädchen = *girl*

4.   Nouns — Plural (continued)

Nouns in this group form their plurals like most English nouns by adding **-s** to the singular:

SINGULAR: **das Hotel**
PLURAL: **die Hotels**

FÜNFZIG

SELF-PREPARATORY EXERCISE

Form the plurals of the following nouns. All nouns in this exercise add **-s** *to form the plural:**

das Hotel	
das Restaurant	die Hotels
der Chef	die Restaurants
das Büro	die Chefs
	die Büros

der Chef = *boss*

das Büro = *office*

EXERCISE

Form the plurals of the following nouns:*

1. der Vater
2. der Tag
3. der Mann
4. der Lehrer
5. das Bier
6. das Feld
7. das Hotel
8. der Amerikaner

READING

Baumwolle

Baumwolle wächst in Asien, Afrika, Australien und Amerika. Der Baumwollstrauch ist 1–2 (eins bis zwei) Meter hoch. Die Samenhaare sind weiß und 5 (fünf) Zentimeter lang. Baumwolle ist ein Malvengewächs. Man spinnt die Samenhaare zu Garn. Baumwolle ist ein wichtiger Textilrohstoff.

VOCABULARY

die **Baumwolle**	cotton	**weiß**	white
wachsen (ä)[1]	to grow	**fünf**	five
Asien	Asia	der **Zentimeter, -**	centimeter
Afrika	Africa	**lang**	long
Australien	Australia	das **Gewächs, -e**	plant, herb, vegetable
der **Strauch, ̈-er**	bush, shrub	die **Malve, -n**	mallow
eins	one	das **Malvengewächs, -e**	mallow plant
zwei	two	**spinnen**	to spin, twist
der **Meter, -**	meter	**zu**	to, into
hoch	high	das **Garn**	yarn
der **Same, -n**	seed, grain, sperm, semen	**wichtig**	important
		textil	textile
das **Haar, -e**	hair	der **Rohstoff, -e**	raw material
das **Samenhaar, -e**	seed hair	der **Textilrohstoff, -e**	textile raw material

1. Indicates vowel change in singular, present tense.

EINUNDFÜNFZIG

STRUCTURAL EXERCISE

Underline all verbs in the third person singular (present tense) in the above reading.

VOCABULARY EXERCISE

Give the English equivalents of the italicized words:

1. Baumwolle ist ein wichtiger *Textilrohstoff.*
2. Er spricht die deutsche *Sprache.*
3. Baumwolle ist ein *Malvengewächs.*
4. Die Basilika ist die *Urform* für die christlichen Kirchen.
5. Man spinnt die Samenhaare zu *Garn.*
6. Man braut Bier aus *Gerste.*
7. Die *Samenhaare* sind weiß.

STRUCTURE

5.   Verb: <u>werden</u>

a.   The verb **werden** *(to become, to get)* is unlike any other in its conjugation of the third person singular, present tense:

INFINITIVE | **werden** | THIRD PERSON
SINGULAR, | **wird** |
          PRESENT TENSE

Example: Er **wird** alt. *(He is getting old.)*

b.   The plural form of **werden** is identical to the infinitive form:

PLURAL | **werden** |

Example: Die Männer **werden** alt. *(The men are getting old.)*

EXERCISE

Supply the correct form of **werden:**

1. Die Kinder _____ alt.
2. Die Samenhaare _____ weiß.
3. Das Haus _____ hoch.
4. Die Sträucher _____ zwei Meter hoch.
5. Das Bier _____ auch in Amerika beliebt.

ZWEIUNDFÜNFZIG

6. Indefinite Articles — Accusative Case

a. We have already dealt with indefinite articles in the nominative case, that is, with nouns serving as subjects.

b. Indefinite articles also occur in the accusative case. They function like definite articles in relation to other parts of the sentence.

c. The indefinite articles in the accusative case are:

MASCULINE	**einen**
FEMININE	**eine**
NEUTER	**ein**

Examples:

Er sieht **einen Lehrer.**   *(He sees a teacher.)*
Er sieht **eine Basilika.**   *(He sees a basilica.)*
Er sieht **ein Buch.**   *(He sees a book.)*

Note that only the masculine article differs between the accusative and the nominative case **(ein → einen)**.

EXERCISES

A. *Give the appropriate forms of the indefinite article:**

1. Er sieht die Tochter.
    Er sieht _____ Tochter.
2. Sie kennt das Buch.
    Sie kennt _____ Buch.
3. Der Student kennt den Amerikaner.
    Der Student kennt _____ Amerikaner.
4. Der Lehrer trinkt das Bier.
    Der Lehrer trinkt _____ Bier.
5. Die Frauen singen das Lied.
    Die Frauen singen _____ Lied.

B. *Supply the definite articles:**

1. Er sieht ein Mädchen.
    Er sieht _____ Mädchen.
2. Das Kind hat einen Mantel.
    Das Kind hat _____ Mantel.
3. Die Mutter kauft eine Lampe.
    Die Mutter kauft _____ Lampe.
4. Er kennt einen Lehrer.
    Er kennt _____ Lehrer.
5. Er trinkt ein Bier.
    Er trinkt _____ Bier.

DREIUNDFÜNFZIG

7. Cardinal Numbers 30–100

30	**dreißig**	21	**einundzwanzig**
40	**vierzig**	32	**zweiunddreißig**
50	**fünfzig**	43	**dreiundvierzig**
60	**sechzig**	54	**vierundfünfzig**
70	**siebzig**	65	**fünfundsechzig**
80	**achtzig**	76	**sechsundsiebzig**
90	**neunzig**	87	**siebenundachtzig**
100	**hundert, einhundert**	98	**achtundneunzig**

EXERCISE

Give the following cardinal numbers:

21	12	13	30	29
9	40	15	7	70

8. Indefinite Articles — Dative Case

The indefinite articles in the dative case are:

MASCULINE	**einem**
FEMININE	**einer**
NEUTER	**einem**

Examples:

Er hilft **einem Mann.**	*(He helps a man.)*
Er antwortet **einer Frau.**	*(He answers a woman.)*
Sie folgt **einem Kind.**	*(She follows a child.)*

EXERCISES

A. *Give the indefinite article:**

1. Der Lehrer antwortet dem Schüler.
   Der Lehrer antwortet _____ Schüler.
2. Die Frau folgt dem Kind.
   Die Frau folgt _____ Kind.
3. Er vertraut der Tochter.
   Er vertraut _____ Tochter.
4. Der Vater hilft dem Sohn.
   Der Vater hilft _____ Sohn.
5. Der Student folgt dem Professor.
   Der Student folgt _____ Professor.

VIERUNDFÜNFZIG

B. *Give the definite article:* *

1. Er antwortet einem Freund.
    Er antwortet _____ Freund.
2. Man hilft einer Frau.
    Man hilft _____ Frau.
3. Das Kind vertraut einer Mutter.
    Das Kind vertraut _____ Mutter.

4. Der Student hilft einem Professor.
    Der Student hilft _____ Professor.
5. Das Kind antwortet einem Bruder.
    Das Kind antwortet _____ Bruder.

9. Masculine Nouns

The following groups of nouns usually are masculine:

a. Names of days, months, and seasons

der Montag	*Monday*	**der Freitag**	*Friday*
der Dienstag	*Tuesday*	**der Samstag**	*Saturday*
der Mittwoch	*Wednesday*	**der Sonntag**	*Sunday*
der Donnerstag	*Thursday*		

der Januar	**der April**	**der Juli**	**der Oktober**
der Februar	**der Mai**	**der August**	**der November**
der März	**der Juni**	**der September**	**der Dezember**

der Frühling	**der Herbst**	**der Sommer**	**der Winter**
(spring)	(fall)	(summer)	(winter)

b. Points of the compass

der Norden (north)	**der Westen** (west)	**der Südwesten** (southwest)
der Süden (south)	**der Osten** (east)	**der Nordosten** (northeast)

c. Names of rocks

der Basalt	**der Gneis**	**der Quarz**	**der Granit**
(basalt)	(gneiss)	(quartz)	(granite)

d. Names for winds and precipitation

der Monsun	**der Taifun**	**der Orkan**	**der Hurrikan**
(monsoon)	(typhoon)	(gale)	(hurricane)

der Regen *(rain)*	**der Schnee** *(snow)*	**der Hagel** *(hail)*

e. Nouns ending with the suffixes **-er, -ling, -el, -s**

-er	**der Meister**	(master)
	der Bäcker	(baker)
	der Kenner	(expert, connoisseur)

-el	der Schlüssel	(key)
	der Rüssel	(trunk, snout)
	der Säbel	(sabre)
	der Kiesel	(pebble)

-ling	der Fremdling	(foreigner)
	der Feigling	(coward)
	der Findling	(foundling; drift boulder)
	der Rohling	(ruffian, brute)

-s	der Gips	(plaster)
	der Schlips	(tie, necktie)
	der Knirps	(little fellow)

f.   Names for male persons and animals

der Mann	(man, husband)	der Wissenschaftler	(scientist)
der Bruder	(brother)	der Elefant	(elephant)
der Sohn	(son)	der Fisch	(fish)
der Vater	(father)	der Hund	(dog, hound)
der Lehrer	(teacher)	der Kater	(tomcat)
der Chemiker	(chemist)	der Vogel	(bird)
der Arzt	(doctor, physician)	der Käfer	(beetle)

EXERCISE

Give the articles **(der, die, das)** for the following nouns:*

1. _____ Gold   5. _____ Fahrt   8. _____ Kenner
2. _____ Herbst   6. _____ Sinfonie   9. _____ Mantel
3. _____ Mädchen   7. _____ Nation   10. _____ Feigling
4. _____ Taifun

READING

Bikini

Man nennt Bikini den zweiteiligen Damenbadeanzug mit sehr wenig Stoff. Der Bikini hat den Namen angeblich von dem Bikini-Atoll in dem Südpazifik.

VOCABULARY

der	**Bikini**	bathing suit	der	**Badeanzug, ̈-e**	bathing suit
	zweiteilig	two-piece	der	**Damenbadeanzug, ̈-e**	woman's bathing suit
	baden	to bathe			
die	**Dame, -n**	lady, woman		**mit**	with
der	**Anzug, ̈-e**	suit		**wenig**	little

SECHSUNDFÜNFZIG

der **Stoff, -e**	material, sub-stance	**angeblich**	alleged(ly)
		das **Atoll**	atoll
der **Name, -n**	name	**süd-**	southern
den **Namen**	name (accusative singular)	der **Pazifik**	Pacific
		der **Südpazifik**	South Pacific

STRUCTURAL EXERCISE

Underline all subjects in the above reading.

VOCABULARY EXERCISE

Give the English equivalents of the italicized words.

1. Es ist ein *zweiteiliger* Badeanzug.
2. Er hat sehr wenig *Stoff*.
3. Er hat den Namen *angeblich* von dem Atoll.
4. Baumwolle *wächst* in Amerika.
5. Der *Strauch* ist zwei Meter hoch.
6. Baumwolle ist ein *wichtiger* Textilrohstoff.
7. Archäologie ist eine *Wissenschaft*.

„Warten auf Godot"

PRONUNCIATION

Umlaut

There are three umlaut sounds in German: / **ä** /, / **ö** /, and / **ü** /.

Umlaut / ä /

Say the following German words:

Short / ä /	Long / ä /
Bälle	Säbel
Kämme	Käfer
Hände	Käse
Länder	Däne

Umlaut / ö /

Say the following German words:

Short / ö /	Long / ö /
Köln	schön
öfter	Öl
Töchter	Söhne
Löffel	Töne

ACHTUNDFÜNFZIG

Umlaut / ü /

Say the following German words:

Short / ü /   **Long** / ü /

Mücke   Süden
Hülle   kühl
fünf   Güte
füttern   Schüler

In German, the letter **y** is pronounced like the umlaut sound / ü /.

Say the following German words:

Short / ü /   **Long** / ü /

Hymne   Lyrik
Physik   typisch
Pyramide   zynisch

STRUCTURE

1. Verbs — Two Objects

a.   Some verbs take only one object, either a direct object (accusative) or an indirect object (dative).

b.   Some verbs may take two objects: both a direct and an indirect object:

   Er gibt **dem Mann die Zeitung.**
   (He gives the man the paper; or He gives the paper to the man.)

c.   The direct object (accusative) answers the question "whom?" or "what?" and names the object of the action.

d.   The indirect object (dative) answers the question "to whom?" or "to what?" and tells us to or for whom (what) the action is performed.

e.   Preliminary list of verbs which can take both direct and indirect objects:

zeigen	*to show*	**bringen**	*to take to, bring*
sagen	*to say*	**kaufen**	*to buy*
schicken	*to send*	**geben (gibt)**	*to give*

f.   Word order

   When two noun objects, direct and indirect, are present in a sentence, the indirect object (dative) usually comes first:

   Sie zeigt **der Frau   das Bild.**   *(She shows the woman the picture; or*
              DATIVE   ACCUSATIVE   *She shows the picture to the woman.)*

SELF-PREPARATORY EXERCISE

In the following sentences:

a. *give the direct object (accusative),*
b. *give the indirect object (dative),*
c. *give the English equivalent.*

EXAMPLE: **Er kauft dem Sohn das Buch.**
    a. **das Buch** — direct object — accusative
    b. **dem Sohn** — indirect object — dative
    c. He buys the son the book.

Der Mann sagt der Frau die Addresse.	
Der Lehrer zeigt dem Schüler das Labor.	a. die Adresse = direct object b. der Frau = indirect object c. The man tells the woman the address.
Er bringt dem Amerikaner das Buch.	a. das Labor = direct object b. dem Schüler = indirect object c. The teacher shows the pupil the laboratory.
Sie schickt dem Freund eine Karte aus Berlin.	a. das Buch = direct object b. dem Amerikaner = indirect object c. He brings the American the book.
Er kauft der Frau den Badeanzug.	a. eine Karte = direct object b. dem Freund = indirect object c. She sends the friend a card from Berlin.
Sie gibt dem Kind einen Hund.	a. den Badeanzug = direct object b. der Frau = indirect object c. He buys the woman the bathing suit.
	a. einen Hund = direct object b. dem Kind = indirect object c. She gives a dog to the child.

EXERCISES

A. *Supply the correct article in the dative or accusative case:*

1. Er zeigt _____ Mutter das Buch. (the)
2. Die Tochter schickt dem Vater _____ Hund. (a)

SECHZIG

    3. Der Vater kauft _____ Sohn einen Volkswagen.   (the)
    4. Der Hund bringt dem Mann _____ Zeitung.   (the)
    5. Sie schickt _____ Freund eine Karte.   (the)

B. *Give the correct German equivalents of the words in parentheses:*

    1. Der Sohn zeigt _____ (the father) die Universität.
    2. Die Mutter kauft dem Sohn _____ (a suit).
    3. Er sagt _____ (the professor) das deutsche Wort.
    4. Der Wissenschaftler gibt _____ (the plant) einen Namen.
    5. Sie bringt _____ (the mother) das Bier.

C. *Give the German equivalents of the following sentences:*

    1. He buys the woman the bathing suit.
    2. The dog brings the man the newspaper.
    3. He tells the teacher the word.
    4. The girl shows the father the university.
    5. The scientist gives the plant a name.

2. Impersonal Verb: <u>es gibt</u>

a. In German, impersonal verbs occur only in the third person singular and do not designate any particular person as subject.

b. The German expression **es gibt** corresponds to English "there is," "there are"; **gibt** is used as an impersonal verb:

Es gibt ein Wort für den Stoff.   *(There is a word for the material.)*

SELF-PREPARATORY EXERCISE

Give the English equivalents of the following sentences:

Es gibt ein Theater in Hamburg.		das Theater = *the theater*
Es gibt Öl in dem Atlantik.	There is a theater in Hamburg.	
Es gibt Bier in München.	There is oil in the Atlantic Ocean.	das Öl = *oil*
Es gibt einen Gott.	There is beer in München.	der Atlantik = *Atlantic*
	There is a God.	

3. Prepositions — Dative Case

a. Prepositions indicate relationships between elements of a sentence.

b. The following prepositions use only the dative case:

aus	*out of, from (a place of residence or birth, or the geographical source of mail)*
bei	*at, with*
mit	*with, by means of*
nach	*after* (time aspect)
	to (geographical locations)
von	*from (a place of departure or the sender of mail)*
seit	*since, for*
zu	*to* (persons, buildings)

EXAMPLE: Er kommt **aus dem Haus.** *He is coming out of the house.*

EXERCISES

A. *Supply the appropriate prepositions:*

1. Er fährt _____ dem Wagen.   (with, by means of)
2. Sie geht _____ der Universität.   (to)
3. Das Kind kommt _____ dem Haus.   (out of)
4. Die Familie fährt _____ Berlin.   (to)
5. Die Karte kommt _____ Nürnberg.   (from)

B. *Supply the definite articles:*

1. Die Schüler fahren mit _____ Lehrer.
2. Die Frau geht zu _____ Basilika.
3. Der Student kommt aus _____ Universität.   (kommen = *to come*)
4. Er wohnt bei _____ Vater.   (wohnen = *to live*)
5. Biologie ist die Lehre von _____ Leben.

READING

Arithmetik

Das Wort Arithmetik stammt aus der griechischen Sprache. Die Arithmetik ist ein Teilgebiet in der Mathematik. Sie bezeichnet die Gesetze für die verschiedenen Rechenarten (Addition, Subtraktion, Division und Multiplikation).

ZWEIUNDSECHZIG

VOCABULARY

die	**Arithmetik**	arithmetic	die	**Art, -en**	kind, species
	stammen	to stem	die	**Rechenart, -en**	kind of arithmetic
	aus	from	die	**Addition**	addition
die	**Mathematik**	mathematics	die	**Subtraktion**	subtraction
	sie	it (= **die Arithmetik**)	die	**Division**	division
	bezeichnen	to denote, to designate	die	**Multiplikation**	multiplication
das	**Gesetz, -e**	law			
	für	for			

STRUCTURAL EXERCISE

Underline all direct objects in the above reading.

VOCABULARY EXERCISE

Give the English equivalents of the italicized words:

1. Das Wort Arithmetik *stammt* aus der griechischen Sprache.
2. Baumwolle ist ein wichtiger Textil*rohstoff.*
3. Sie bezeichnet die *Gesetze* für die verschiedenen Rechenarten.
4. Sie *behandelt* alte Kulturen.
5. Sie *bezeichnet* die Gesetze für die verschiedenen Rechenarten.
6. Die Biologie hat *verschiedene* Teilgebiete.
7. Das Wort *bedeutet* Königsbau.

STRUCTURE

4. Personal Pronouns — Nominative

a. A personal pronoun may be substituted for a noun:

Der Lehrer antwortet dem Kind.   **Er** antwortet dem Kind.
The teacher answers the child.   *He answers the child.*

In this example, the subject of the sentence, **der Lehrer,** has been replaced by the personal pronoun, **er.** Both the noun subject and the personal pronoun subject are in the nominative case.

b. A pronoun has the same gender, case, and number as the noun it replaces. There are, therefore, separate personal pronouns for each of the four cases, the three genders, and for singular and plural.

c. The following personal pronouns may replace nouns in the nominative case:

SINGULAR: **er** = *he* (masculine)
            sie = *she* (feminine)
            es = *it* (neuter)

PLURAL: **sie** = *they* (all genders)

SELF-PREPARATORY EXERCISE

*Replace the noun subject with a pronoun:**

Der Wagen fährt.	
Die Lampe ist dort.	Er fährt.
Das Kind spielt.	Sie ist dort.
Der Lehrer antwortet dem Kind.	Es spielt.
Der Vater sieht den Sohn.	Er antwortet dem Kind.
Das Kind spielt im Garten.	Er sieht den Sohn.
Der Professor liest.	Es spielt im Garten.
Die Mutter arbeitet.	Er liest.
	Sie arbeitet.

EXERCISES

A. *Replace the nouns with nominative pronouns:**

    1. Der Professor liest.   _____ liest.
    2. Das Mädchen spielt.   _____ spielt.
    3. Die Mutter arbeitet.   _____ arbeitet.
    4. Der Student lernt.   _____ lernt.
    5. Das Büro ist hier.   _____ ist hier.

B. *Replace the pronouns with the German equivalents of the nouns in parentheses:**

    1. Er fährt.   _____ fährt.   (The car)
    2. Sie lernt.   _____ lernt.   (The daughter)
    3. Es hilft.   _____ hilft.   (The child)
    4. Er spielt.   _____ spielt.   (The son)
    5. Sie arbeitet.   _____ arbeitet.   (The mother)

C. *Express in German:*

    1. The man walks around the house. He walks. (to walk = to go)
    2. The suit is here. It is here.
    3. The car is good. It is good.
    4. The child learns. It learns.
    5. The woman works. She works.

VIERUNDSECHZIG

5. Cardinal Numbers 100 – 1000

100	**(ein) hundert**	102	**(ein) hundertzwei**
200	**zweihundert**	203	**zweihundertdrei**
300	**dreihundert**	374	**dreihundertvierundsiebzig**
400	**vierhundert**	518	**fünfhundertachtzehn**
500	**fünfhundert**	956	**neunhundertsechsundfünfzig**
600	**sechshundert**	1004	**(ein) tausendvier**
700	**siebenhundert**	1017	**(ein) tausendsiebzehn**
800	**achthundert**		
900	**neunhundert**		
1000	**(ein) tausend**		

1978   **(ein) tausendneunhundertachtundsiebzig**
        or: **neunzehnhundertachtundsiebzig**

EXERCISES

A. *Give the German numbers:*

537   867   429   1945   1979

B. *Give the German equivalents:*

1.   37 houses
2.   148 animals
3.   457 pictures
4.   842 restaurants
5.   1767 newspapers

C. *Give the English equivalents of the German compound words:*

1.   die Bildhauerkunst
2.   das Teilgebiet
3.   der Textilrohstoff
4.   die Rechenart
5.   der Sammelbegriff

READING

Nahrung

Eine neue Getreidesorte erscheint auf dem Markt. Sie trägt nach einmaliger Aussaat mehrere Jahre Ähren. Die neue Roggenart spart dem Bauer viel Arbeit. Ein Forschungsinstitut in Braunschweig (Deutschland) erprobt jetzt die neue Getreidesorte.

VOCABULARY

	neu	new	der **Bauer, -n**	farmer, peasant
das	**Getreide**	grain	**viel**	much, a lot
die	**Sorte, -n**	sort, kind, variety	die **Arbeit**	work
	erscheinen	to appear	die **Forschung**	research
	auf	on	das **Institut, -e**	institute
der	**Markt, ⸚e**	market	das **Forschungsinstitut**	research institute
	tragen (ä)	to carry, to wear; *here*: to bear	**Braunschweig**	*city in Germany* (Brunswick)
	nach	after	**erproben**	to test, try out; to probe
	einmalig	a single		
die	**Aussaat**	seeding	**jetzt**	now, at the present time
	mehrer	several		
die	**Ähre, -n**	ear (of grain)		
der	**Roggen**	rye		
	sparen (+ *dative*)	to save; to spare		

STRUCTURAL EXERCISE

Underline all direct objects (accusative) in the above reading.

VOCABULARY EXERCISE

Give the English equivalents of the *italicized* words:

1. Die neue Roggenart *spart* dem Bauer viel Arbeit.
2. Baumwolle ist ein *wichtiger* Textilrohstoff.
3. Ein Forschungsinstitut erprobt *jetzt* die neue Getreidesorte.
4. Das Wort Arithmetik stammt aus der griechischen *Sprache.*
5. Sie *trägt* mehrere Jahre Ähren.
6. Sie ist ein *Teilgebiet* der Mathematik.
7. Eine neue Getreidesorte *erscheint* auf dem Markt.

esson 8

PRONUNCIATION

German Word Endings

The ending -e

When a word ends in **-e,** this / e / is unstressed. The pronunciation of the final unstressed **e** corresponds closely to the / a / sound in the English word *sofa.*

Pronounce the following German words:

Affe   bitte   Tanne   hatte

The ending -en

The pronunciation of this ending is also unstressed and may be compared with the pronunciation of English final *-en* as in *mitten* and *hidden.*

Pronounce the following German words:

kamen   hatten   singen   oben

The ending -er

This ending is unstressed in German, and the pronunciation resembles that of the final sound in English *Sarah.*

Pronounce the following German words:

mager   immer   Peter   Müller

STRUCTURE

1. Personal Pronouns — Accusative

a.   Direct object nouns (accusative) may also be replaced by personal pronouns:

> Das Kind fragt **den Lehrer.**   **(den Lehrer** = direct object noun)
> *The child asks the teacher.*

> Das Kind fragt **ihn.**   **(ihn** = direct object pronoun)
> *The child asks him.*

b.   The direct object (accusative case) personal pronouns are:

> SINGULAR: **ihn** = *him* (masculine)
>   **sie** = *her* (feminine)
>   **es** = *it* (neuter)

> PLURAL: **sie** = *them* (all genders)

Note that only the masculine singular pronoun is different from the nominative forms.

SELF-PREPARATORY EXERCISE

Replace the direct object noun with an accusative pronoun:*

Das Kind fragt den Lehrer.	
Die Schüler singen das Lied.	Das Kind fragt ihn.
Die Studenten lesen die Bücher.	Die Schüler singen es.
Das Kind besucht den Freund.	Die Studenten lesen sie.
Er findet das Haus.	Das Kind besucht ihn.
Sie hat eine Zeitung.	Er findet es.
Die Frauen kaufen einen Wagen.	Sie hat sie.
Der Professor vergißt das Wort.	Die Frauen kaufen ihn.
	Der Professor vergißt es.

besuchen = *to visit*

EXERCISE

A.   *Replace the direct object nouns with pronouns:**

> 1. Er sieht den Professor.   Er sieht _____.
> 2. Das Kind kennt die Mutter.   Das Kind kennt _____.
> 3. Der Vater liest das Buch.   Der Vater liest _____.

ACHTUNDSECHZIG

4. Der Mann kauft den Tisch.   Der Mann kauft _____.
5. Der Schüler liest die Zeitungen.   Der Schüler liest _____.

B. *Express in German:*

1. The student reads the books. He reads them.
2. The children ask the teacher. They ask him.
3. She has the newspaper. She has it.
4. The pupil sings the songs. He sings them.
5. The mother buys the table. She buys it.

2. Negation: <u>nicht</u>

a. The common way of negating a statement in German is through **nicht** *(not)*:

Er studiert **nicht** viel.
He does not study much.
Die Frau sieht das Kind **nicht**.
The woman does not see the child.
Man kennt den Sammelbegriff **nicht**.
One does not know the collective term.

b. Word order with **nicht**

Generally **nicht** stands at the end of the clause:

Die Frau sieht das Kind **nicht**. *(The woman does not see the child.)*
Er antwortet dem Lehrer **nicht**. *(He does not answer the teacher.)*

Exceptions:

1. The negation **nicht** precedes place expressions:
   Er studiert **nicht** in Heidelberg. *(He does not study in Heidelberg.)*
2. The negation **nicht** precedes expressions of manner:
   Der Wagen fährt **nicht** schnell. *(The car does not drive fast.)*

SELF-PREPARATORY EXERCISE

Negate the following sentences, using **nicht:***

Er sieht den Vater.	
Sie hilft der Mutter.	Er sieht den Vater nicht.
Der Sohn studiert in Berlin.	Sie hilft der Mutter nicht.
Sie hat die Zeitung.	Der Sohn studiert nicht in Berlin.
Die Kinder sind hier.	Sie hat die Zeitung nicht.
	Die Kinder sind nicht hier.

EXERCISES

A. *Negate the following sentences:* *

1. Sie gehen in das Büro.
2. Vater kennt ihn.   (kennen = *to know*)
3. Die Getreidesorte erscheint auf dem Markt.
4. Baumwolle wächst in Europa.
5. Sie vertraut der Tochter.

B. *Express in German:*

1. She is not in Berlin.
2. The student does not buy the book.
3. He does not have the car.
4. Mother does not know her.
5. He does not go to Germany.

READING

Der Karpfen

Der Karpfen ist ein Wirbeltier. Er ist braungrau und blaugrau. Er vermeidet schnelle Gewässer. Der Karpfen lebt in schlammigen Gewässern. Er frißt Würmer, Larven, kleine Krebse und auch Pflanzen. Das Weibchen legt im Mai oder Juni 500 000 bis 700 000 (fünfhunderttausend bis siebenhunderttausend) Eier.

VOCABULARY

der **Karpfen, -**	carp	**in**	in
der **Wirbel, -**	vertebra	**schlammig**	muddy
das **Wirbeltier, -e**	vertebrate	**fressen (frißt)**	to eat *(of animals)*
braun	brown	der **Wurm, ̈-er**	worm
grau	gray	die **Larve, -n**	larva
blau	blue	der **Krebs, -e**	crab, crayfish
vermeiden	to avoid, shun	das **Weibchen, -**	female
schnell	fast	**legen**	to lay
das **Gewässer, -**	(body of) water(s)	das **Ei, -er**	egg
leben	to live		

STRUCTURAL EXERCISE

Underline all plural nouns in the above reading.

SIEBZIG

VOCABULARY EXERCISE

Give the English equivalents of the italicized words:

1. Er *vermeidet* schnelle Gewässer.
2. Die Biologie hat *verschiedene* Teilgebiete.
3. Ein Atheist *glaubt* nicht an Gott.
4. Der Karpfen ist ein *Wirbeltier.*
5. Er *frißt* Würmer und Larven.
6. Die Archäologie *behandelt* alte Kulturen.
7. Der Karpfen lebt in schlammigen *Gewässern.*

STRUCTURE

3. Conjunctions

a. Conjunctions connect two or more sentence elements and thereby establish a relationship between these elements. There are two types of conjunctions in German:

1. coordinating conjunctions;
2. subordinating conjunctions.

b. Coordinating conjunctions connect expressions of equal rank, such as two independent clauses, without changing the word order in either clause.

c. Subordinating conjunctions connect expressions of unequal rank and affect the word order of the clause introduced by a subordinating conjunction:

1. Er bleibt zu Hause, **denn er hat kein Auto.**
2. Er bleibt zu Hause, **weil er kein Auto hat.**
   He stays at home, because he doesn't have a car.

Sentence 1 uses a coordinating conjunction — **denn.** Sentence 2 uses a subordinating conjunction — **weil.** In sentence 1, the word order of the second clause remains unchanged; in sentence 2, the word order of the second clause places the conjugated verb **hat** at the end of the clause:

> . . . . , weil er kein Auto **hat.**

d. Coordinating conjunctions

denn	*because, since, for*	**aber**	*but, however*
oder	*or*	**sondern**	*but, rather, on the contrary*
und	*and*		

SELF-PREPARATORY EXERCISE

Combine the following sentences with the indicated conjunctions:*

Der Mann ist arm. (aber) Der Mann ist glücklich.	arm = *poor* glücklich = *happy*
Der Schüler liest das Buch. (oder) Er liest das Buch nicht.	Der Mann ist arm, aber er ist glücklich.
Der Karpfen wächst schnell. (denn) Er frißt viel.	Der Student liest das Buch oder er liest das Buch nicht.
Er ist in Deutschland. (und) Er studiert Biologie.	Der Karpfen wächst schnell, denn er frißt viel.
Ein Atheist glaubt nicht an Gott. (aber) Ein Agnostiker bezweifelt nur die Existenz Gottes.	Er ist in Deutschland, und er studiert Biologie.
	Ein Atheist glaubt nicht an Gott, aber ein Agnostiker bezweifelt nur die Existenz Gottes.

4.   Coordinating Conjunction <u>sondern</u>

Sondern is used instead of **aber** when the preceding clause is negative and *"but"* has the value of *rather* or *on the contrary*:

Der Direktor arbeitet nicht viel, **sondern er spielt viel Tennis.**
The director does not work much, but he plays a lot of tennis.

SELF-PREPARATORY EXERCISE

Give the English equivalent of the German sentences:

Er gibt dem Schüler das Buch nicht, sondern er liest es.	
Der Karpfen ist nicht blau, sondern braungrau.	He does not give the book to the student, but he reads it.
Der Student lernt nicht, sondern er spielt nur.	The carp is not blue, but brownish gray.
	The student does not study, but he only plays.

ZWEIUNDSIEBZIG

5. Coordinating Conjunctions — Omission of Repeated Element

a.   English and German may drop elements repeated in the second clause: *Bill* goes to the university and *he* studies math.

The second reference to *Bill (he)* may be eliminated: Bill goes to the university and studies math.

In German, both sentences are also possible:

Willi geht zur Universität und **er** studiert Mathematik.
Willi geht zur Universität und studiert Mathematik.

b.   The omission of the repeated element is possible with the following conjunctions: **und, oder, sondern.**

The omission is rare with the conjunction **aber.** It never occurs with the conjunction **denn.**

SELF-PREPARATORY EXERCISE

*Combine the following sentences. Omit repeated elements whenever possible:**

Der Mann ist arm. (aber) Der Mann ist glücklich.	
Er geht in das Büro. (und) Er liest ein Buch.	Der Mann ist arm aber glücklich.
Der Baumwollstrauch ist nicht 30 cm hoch. (sondern) Er ist 90 cm hoch.	Er geht in das Büro und liest ein Buch.
Die Basilika hat eine rechteckige Halle. (und) Sie ist eine Urform für die christlichen Kirchen.	Der Baumwollstrauch ist nicht 30 cm hoch, sondern 90 cm hoch.
	Die Basilika hat eine rechteckige Halle und ist eine Urform für die christlichen Kirchen.

EXERCISES

A.   *Combine the sentences using the conjunctions indicated:**

   1.   Der Schüler lernt nicht.   (sondern)
        Er spielt nur Tennis.

2. Die Botanik behandelt Pflanzen.   (und)
   Die Zoologie behandelt Tiere.
3. Der Agnostiker bezweifelt die Existenz Gottes.   (aber)
   Der Atheist glaubt nicht an Gott.
4. Die neue Getreidesorte ist wichtig.   (denn)
   Sie spart dem Bauer viel Arbeit.
5. Der Karpfen ist ein Wirbeltier.   (und)
   Er vermeidet schnelle Gewässer.

B. *Give the German equivalents of the following sentences:*

1. The cotton plant is not 30 cm high, but 90 cm high.
2. The pupil studies mathematics and plays tennis.
3. The carp grows fast because it eats a lot (much).
4. He is in Germany and he learns German.
5. The student reads the newspaper or the book.

SUMMARY

Personal Pronouns

Personal pronouns may be substituted for nouns. The personal pronouns in the nominative and accusative cases are:

SINGULAR	NOMINATIVE	ACCUSATIVE
MASCULINE	**er**	**ihn**
FEMININE	**sie**	**sie**
NEUTER	**es**	**es**
PLURAL		
ALL GENDERS	**sie**	**sie**

Coordinating Conjunctions

Coordinating conjunctions connect two independent clauses without changing the word order of either clause. Coordinating conjunctions are:

aber	*but, however*
denn	*because, since, for*
oder	*or*
sondern	*but, rather, on the contrary*
und	*and*

DIE DEUTSCHE SPRACHE

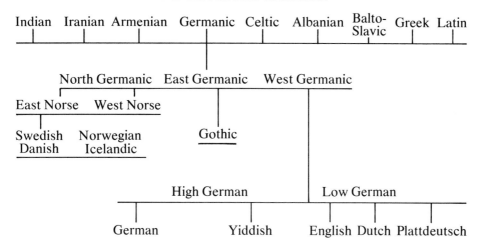

READING

Die deutsche Sprache

119 (einhundertneunzehn) Millionen Menschen sprechen Deutsch als Muttersprache in der Welt. Rund 18 (achtzehn) Millionen Menschen lernen Deutsch als Fremdsprache. Jedes 10. (zehnte) Buch erscheint in deutscher Sprache. Man spricht Deutsch als Muttersprache in diesen europäischen Ländern: Österreich, Schweiz, Bundesrepublik Deutschland und Deutsche Demokratische Republik.

VOCABULARY

die	**Million, -en**	million		**zehn**	ten
	sprechen (spricht)	to speak		**zehnt-**	tenth
die	**Mutter, ⁓**	mother	das	**Buch, ⁓er**	book
die	**Muttersprache, -n**	native language		**erscheinen**	to appear; *here:* to
die	**Welt, -en**	world			be published
	in der Welt	in the world		**diesen**	these
	rund	about, approxi-		**europäisch**	European
		mately, around	das	**Land, ⁓er**	country, state, land
	lernen	to learn, study		**Österreich**	Austria
	als	as	(die)	**Schweiz**	Switzerland
	fremd	foreign		**Bundesrepublik**	Federal Republic
die	**Fremdsprache, -n**	foreign language		**demokratisch**	democratic
	jedes	every	die	**Republik, -en**	republic

STRUCTURAL EXERCISE

Underline all plural nouns in the above reading.

VOCABULARY EXERCISE

Give the English equivalents of the italicized words:

1. Jedes 10. (zehnte) Buch *erscheint* in deutscher Sprache.
2. Rund 18 (achtzehn) Millionen Menschen lernen Deutsch als *Fremdsprache*.
3. Der Karpfen *lebt* in schlammigen Gewässern.
4. Ein Forschungsinstitut erprobt jetzt die *neue* Getreidesorte.
5. Die Arithmetik *bezeichnet* die Gesetze für die verschiedenen Rechenarten.
6. Man *spricht* Deutsch als Muttersprache in Österreich.
7. Basilika *bedeutet* Königsbau.

esson *9*

PRONUNCIATION

Consonants

Some German consonants differ considerably from their English counterparts. We will deal with these particular German sounds in the following sections. Most German consonants, however, correspond closely to the English pronunciation.

German c

If the letter **c** precedes the vowels **a, o, u,** it is pronounced like / k / as in English *coffee* or *Africa.*

Pronounce the following words:

Caracas   Cuxhaven   Computer

If the letter **c** precedes the sounds / **e** /, / **ä** /, / **i** /, **c** is pronounced like / ts / as in *tsar, tsetse,* or *rats.*

Pronounce the following words:

Celsius   Cäsar   Circus

German j

The German letter **j** is pronounced like English **y** in *yes.*

Pronounce the following words:

ja   je   Jo-Jo   Judo

In words of English origin, the consonant **j** is pronounced like English *j.* Pronounce the following words:

Jet   Jockei   Job

German l

The German consonant **l** is pronounced like the / l / sound of the babbling word "lalala."

Pronounce the following words:

Land   Leben   Liebe   lügen

STRUCTURE

1.   Personal Pronouns — Dative Case

For nouns used in the dative case (indirect object), the following personal pronouns may be substituted:

SINGULAR: **ihm**   *(to) him* (masculine)
            ihr   *(to) her* (feminine)
            ihm   *(to) it* (neuter)

PLURAL: **ihnen**   *(to) them* (all genders)

Examples:

Man glaubt **ihm.** *(One believes him.)*
Er antwortet **ihr.** *(He answers her.)*
Der Mann gibt **ihr** die Zeitung. *(The man gives her the newspaper.)*

SELF-PREPARATORY EXERCISE

*Substitute the appropriate personal pronoun for the indirect object:**

Er hilft **den Männern.**	
Der Lehrer antwortet **dem Schüler.**	Er hilft **ihnen.**
Er gibt **dem Professor** das Buch.	Der Lehrer antwortet **ihm.**
Die Frau folgt **dem Kind.**	Er gibt **ihm** das Buch.
Er vertraut **der Tochter.**	Die Frau folgt **ihm.**
	Er vertraut **ihr.**

EXERCISES

A.   *Substitute the appropriate personal pronoun for the indirect object:**

1.   Er zeigt dem Bauer das Getreide. Er zeigt _____ das Getreide.
2.   Sie kauft der Tochter das Buch. Sie kauft _____ das Buch.
3.   Er gibt den Kindern einen Hund. Er gibt _____ einen Hund.

ACHTUNDSIEBZIG

4. Der Schüler antwortet dem Lehrer. Der Schüler antwortet _____.
5. Sie schicken dem Freund eine Karte aus Berlin. Sie schicken _____ eine Karte aus Berlin.

B. *Substitute the German equivalent of the noun in parentheses for the personal pronoun in the dative case:**

1. Tom gibt ihm die Zeitung.   (the friend)
2. Er kauft ihr den Badeanzug.   (the daughter)
3. Sie antwortet ihr.   (the mother)
4. Der Lehrer zeigt ihnen des Labor.   (the pupils)
5. Der Sohn hilft ihm.   (the father)

C. *Express in German:*

1. They give him the newspapers.
2. The teacher answers the pupils.
3. He sends her a card from Berlin.
4. He helps them.
5. The father buys her a car.

2.   Word Order of Direct and Indirect Objects

a.   There are several German verbs that can take both direct and indirect objects, like **geben, zeigen, sagen, schicken, bringen, kaufen.**

b.   The direct object (accusative) follows the indirect object (dative) if both objects are nouns:

Er gibt   **der Frau   die Zeitung.** *(He gives the woman the newspaper.)*
         (dative)   (accusative)

c.   If both objects — direct and indirect — are pronouns, the direct object (accusative) precedes the indirect object (dative):

Er gibt   **sie   ihr.** *(He gives it to her.)*
         (accusative) (dative)

ihr = die Frau   sie = die Zeitung

d.   If one of the two objects is a pronoun, it precedes the noun, regardless of case:

Er gibt   **sie   der Frau.**
Er gibt   **ihr   die Zeitung.**
         (pronoun) (noun)

SELF-PREPARATORY EXERCISE

Substitute personal pronouns for the direct objects (accusative case): *

Er zeigt den Schülern das Labor.	
Man bringt dem Chef die Bücher.	Er zeigt es den Schülern.
Sie schicken den Kindern die Karte.	Man bringt sie dem Chef.
Er zeigt dem Bauer das Getreide.	Sie schicken sie den Kindern.
Sie kaufen dem Sohn den Anzug.	Er zeigt es dem Bauer.
	Sie kaufen ihn dem Sohn.

EXERCISES

A. *Substitute personal pronouns for the direct objects:* *

1. Er gibt dem Mann die Zeitung.   Er gibt _____ dem Mann.
2. Man bringt dem Mädchen das Buch.   Man bringt _____ dem Mädchen.
3. Sie zeigt dem Sohn den Anzug.   Sie zeigt _____ dem Sohn.
4. Er schickt den Kindern die Bilder.   Er schickt _____ den Kindern.
5. Man kauft dem Bruder das Haus.   Man kauft _____ dem Bruder.

B. *Substitute personal pronouns for indirect objects (dative case):* *

1. Er zeigt den Schülern das Labor.   Er zeigt _____ das Labor.
2. Sie kaufen der Tochter das Bild.   Sie kaufen _____ das Bild.
3. Man bringt dem Chef die Bücher.   Man bringt _____ die Bücher.
4. Sie schicken den Kindern die Karte.   Sie schicken _____ die Karte.
5. Man gibt der Pflanze einen Namen.   Man gibt _____ einen Namen.

C. *Substitute personal pronouns for both the direct and indirect object and make the necessary changes in the word order:* *

1. Die Mutter kauft dem Sohn den Anzug.   Die Mutter kauft _____.
2. Er zeigt den Schülern das Labor.   Er zeigt _____.
3. Sie sagt dem Professor das Wort.   Sie sagt _____.
4. Man bringt dem Chef die Bücher.   Man bringt _____.
5. Der Professor gibt der Pflanze einen Namen.   Der Professor gibt _____.

ACHTZIG

Niederdeutsches Bauernhaus

D. *Express in German:*

1. They show the animal to the children.
2. He sends them to the boss.
3. One buys him the house.
4. He gives the plant a name.
5. She tells him the word.

READING

Bauernhäuser I

Die alten deutschen Bauernhäuser haben verschiedene Bauformen. Die Bauform variiert mit der Landschaftsform, aber auch das Klima, die Bodenverhältnisse und die Wirtschaftweise beeinflussen die Bauweise. Man unterscheidet drei Grundformen in der Bauweise: Das „Niederdeutsche Bauernhaus" (in Niedersachsen, Schleswig-Holstein, Westfalen und Mecklenburg[1]) ist ein Fachwerkbau. In dem 5 Bauernhaus sind Wohnräume und Ställe.

1. States **(Länder)** in Germany (see map).

VOCABULARY

das **Haus**, ⸚er	house	
das **Bauernhaus**, ⸚er	farmhouse	
die **Form**, -en	form, shape, condition	
die **Bauform**, -en	building style	
variieren	to vary	
die **Landschaft**, -en	landscape	
die **Landschaftsform**, -en	form of the landscape	
aber	but, however	
das **Klima**	climate	
der **Boden**	ground, soil, bottom	
das **Verhältnis**, -se	relationship, condition	
das **Bodenverhältnis**, -se	soil condition	
die **Wirtschaft**	economy	
die **Weise**, -n	method, style, custom, kind	

die **Wirtschaftsweise**, -n	farming, management	
beeinflussen	to influence	
die **Bauweise**, -n	guilding method, building style	
man	one, people	
unterscheiden	to differentiate, to distinguish	
die **Grundform**, -en	basic form	
niederdeutsch	lower German	
Niedersachsen	Lower Saxony	
Schleswig-Holstein	Schleswig-Holstein	
Westfalen	Westphalia	
Mecklenburg	Mecklenburg	
das **Fachwerk**	framework	
der **Raum**, ⸚e	room, space	
der **Wohnraum**, ⸚e	living space, room	
der **Stall**, ⸚e	stall	

STRUCTURAL EXERCISE

Underline all direct objects (accusative case) in the above reading.

VOCABULARY EXERCISE

Give the English equivalents of the italicized words:

1. Man *unterscheidet* drei Grundformen in der Bauweise.
2. Die Arithmetik ist ein *Teilgebiet* in der Mathematik.
3. In dem Bauernhaus sind *Wohnräume* und Ställe.
4. 119 (einhundertneunzehn) Millionen Menschen sprechen Deutsch als Muttersprache in der *Welt*.
5. Die Bodenverhältnisse *beeinflussen* die Bauweise.
6. Das alte *Bauernhaus* ist ein Fachwerkbau.
7. Die *Wirtschaftsweise* beeinflußt die Bauweise.

STRUCTURE

3.   Negation: kein

German uses a form of **kein** where English uses *not a* or *not any*. The word **kein** assumes the same endings as the indefinite article **ein**:

Er sieht **einen** Mann.   *(He sees a man.)*
Er sieht **keinen** Mann.   *(He doesn't see a man.)*

		MASCULINE	FEMININE	NEUTER	PLURAL (ALL GENDERS)
NOM.		kein Mann	keine Frau	kein Buch	keine Männer
ACC.		keinen Mann	keine Frau	kein Buch	keine Männer
DAT.		keinem Mann	keiner Frau	keinem Buch	keinen Männern

SELF-PREPARATORY EXERCISE

Negate the following sentences with a form of **kein:** *

Er sieht ein Bild.	
Sie kauft einen Wagen.	Er sieht kein Bild.
Es gibt eine Zeitung.	Sie kauft keinen Wagen.
Er ist ein Lehrer.	Es gibt keine Zeitung.
Der Student kauft ein Haus.	Er ist kein Lehrer.
	Der Student kauft kein Haus.

EXERCISES

A. *Supply the correct form of* **kein:**

1. Es gibt _____ Bier in Deutschland.
2. Man hat _____ Fachwerkhäuser in Amerika.
3. Zwei Millionen Menschen haben _____ Arbeit.
4. Das Getreide trägt _____ Ähren.
5. Die Basilika hat _____ Wohnräume.

B. *Express in German:*

1. He is not a teacher.
2. They are not buying a house.
3. The university doesn't have any teachers.
4. The farmer does not have any work.
5. The farmhouse does not have any stalls.

4. Question Words

a. Questions

Questions may be formed by using question words:

Was kauft der Mann? *(What does the man buy?)*

b. The most frequent question words in German are:

wann	*when*	**wie**	*how*
wer	*who*	**wo**	*where*
wen	*whom* (accusative of **wer**)	**warum**	*why*
wem	*to whom* (dative of **wer**)	**was**	*what*
		wieviel	*how much*

c. Questions — word order

The word order of a question with a question word has the following sequence:

QUESTION WORD	VERB	SUBJECT	OBJECT
Was	**kauft**	**der Mann?**	
Wer *(who)*	**kennt**		**den Mann?**
Wen *(whom)*	**kennt**	**der Mann?**	
Wem *(to whom)*	**gibt**	**er**	**das Buch?**

EXERCISES

A. *Supply the correct question word:*

1. _____ kommt sie?   (when)
2. _____ studiert er?   (where)
3. _____ Zeit hat er?   (how much)
4. _____ bedeutet das Wort?   (what)
5. _____ ist der Chef?   (who)
6. _____ wächst die Pflanze?   (how)
7. _____ variiert die Bauform?   (why)

B. *Form German sentences from the following elements:**

1. Wo / das Bauernhaus / stehen?
2. Was / das Wort / bedeuten?
3. Wer / der Mann / kennen?
4. Wie / die Bauform / variieren?
5. Was / der Karpfen / vermeiden?

C. *Express in German:*

1. When does he work?
2. Who is learning German?
3. What does the carp eat?
4. Where is the book being published?
   (= Where does the book appear?)
5. How does the economy vary?

5. Questions Without Question Words

Questions may also be formed without a question word by beginning the sentence with the conjugated verb:

VIERUNDACHTZIG

> **Kauft er** das Haus? *(Is he buying the house?)*
> **Kommt sie** jetzt? *(Is she coming now?)*

The subject follows the verb directly.

SELF-PREPARATORY EXERCISE

Form questions without question words from the following statements: *

EXAMPLE: (Statement)   **Er arbeitet** hier.
               (Question)   **Arbeitet er** hier?

Er wartet dort.	
Sie redet viel.	Wartet er dort?
Sie singen die Lieder.	Redet sie viel?
Das Kind spielt Tennis.	Singen sie die Lieder?
Die Kinder sehen den Vater.	Spielt das Kind Tennis?
	Sehen die Kinder den Vater?

EXERCISES

A. *Form questions without question words from the following statements:* *

1. Er hat keine Zeit.
2. Sie kennt den Chef.
3. Der Sohn hilft dem Vater.
4. Er spricht viel.
5. Die Tochter gibt der Mutter das Buch.

B. *Express in German:*

1. Does the son play tennis?
2. Does he sing songs?
3. Does the child see the brother?
4. Does she have time?
5. Do they know the plant?

C. *Supply the definite articles of the following nouns:* *

1. _____ Station
2. _____ Natur
3. _____ Taifun
4. _____ Hotel
5. _____ Zeitung
6. _____ Krankheit
7. _____ Sauerstoff
8. _____ September
9. _____ Elefant
10. _____ Mädchen

D. *Give the English equivalents of the following compound words:*

1. die Fremdsprache
2. die Grundform
3. die Wirtschaftsweise
4. die Landschaftsform
5. das Wirbeltier

Oberdeutsches Bauernhaus

Fränkisches Bauernhaus

SECHSUNDACHTZIG

SUMMARY

Personal Pronouns

Nouns may be replaced by pronouns in the different cases:

		MASCULINE	FEMININE	NEUTER	PLURAL (ALL GENDERS)
	NOM.	er	sie	es	sie
	DAT.	ihm	ihr	ihm	ihnen
	ACC.	ihn	sie	es	sie

Word Order of Objects

a. When the direct and indirect object are nouns, the sequence is:

dative (indirect object) — accusative (direct object)

b. When the direct and indirect are pronouns, the sequence is:

accusative (direct object) — dative (indirect object)

c. When there is a combination of noun and pronoun, the pronoun precedes the noun.

READING

Bauernhäuser II

Das „Fränkische Bauernhaus" (in Mitteldeutschland) ist auch ein Fachwerkbau. Das Wohnhaus, die Ställe und die Scheune sind nicht unter einem Dach. Alle sind Einzelgebäude. Sie stehen um einen viereckigen geschlossenen Hof. Das „Oberdeutsche Bauernhaus" (in Bayern, in dem Schwarzwald) ist ein mehrstöckiger Baukörper mit inneren Trennwänden zwischen Wohn-, Stall- und Speicherräumen. Der Unterbau ist meistens aus Stein, der Oberbau ist aus Holz. 5

VOCABULARY

	fränkisch	Franconian	
	Mitteldeutschland	Central Germany	
	wohnen	to live, dwell	
das	**Wohnhaus, ⁔er**	residence, dwelling unit	
die	**Scheune, -n**	barn	
	unter	under, among	
	einem	*here:* one	

das	**Dach, ⁔er**	roof	
	alle	all	
	einzel	individual, single	
das	**Gebäude, -**	building	
	stehen	to stand, be located	
	um	around	
	viereckig	rectangular	
	geschlossen	inclosed	

SIEBENUNDACHTZIG

der **Hof, ⸚e**	court, courtyard	
oberdeutsch	upper German (South)	
Bayern	Bavaria	
schwarz	black	
der **Wald, ⸚er**	forest, woods	
der **Schwarzwald**	Black Forest	
mehrstöckig	multiple-story	
der **Körper,**	body, unit, structure	
der **Baukörper, -**	building structure	
inner	inner, interior	
trennen	to separate	
die **Wand, ⸚e**	wall	

die **Trennwand, ⸚e**	dividing, separating wall	
zwischen	between	
der **Speicher, -**	attic, loft	
der **Speicherraum, ⸚e**	storeroom, granary	
der **Unterbau**	substructure	
meistens	mostly, generally, in most cases	
aus	of, made of	
der **Stein, -e**	stone	
der **Oberbau**	superstructure	
das **Holz, ⸚er**	wood	

STRUCTURAL EXERCISE

Underline all prepositions that use only the dative case.

VOCABULARY EXERCISE

Give the English equivalents of the italicized words:

1. Es ist ein Baukörper mit *inneren* Trennwänden.
2. Der Unterbau ist *meistens* aus Stein.
3. Alle sind *Einzelgebäude.*
4. Sie stehen um einen *viereckigen* Hof.
5. Man *nennt* Archäologie in der deutschen Sprache auch Altertumskunde.
6. Der Student *bleibt* ein Jahr in Deutschland.
7. Das Bauernhaus hat *Trennwände.*

esson 10

PRONUNCIATION

German q

This letter occurs only in combination with the vowel **u.** It is then pronounced like / kv / : **Quelle.**

Pronounce the following words:

Qual   quer   Quiz   Quartett

German r

a. The preferred articulation of the / r / sound in German is the uvular / r / . "Uvular" refers to the raising of the tongue toward the uvula and the back of the soft palate. A narrow, slit-shaped opening is formed. The breath stream which escapes through the opening causes the uvula to vibrate against the back of the tongue.

There is a similarity in the articulation of / **ch** / and / **r** /; therefore, in order to produce / **r** /, say the following: **Buk, Buche.**

Now pronounce / **ch** / as far back as possible and say: **Bure**

b. The pronunciation of German / r / varies according to its position (initial, medial, final) in the word.

c. Medial / **r** / and its articulation have been demonstrated in the sequence above. Pronounce the following words:

lernen   breit   warten   Chrom

d. Initial / **r** / may be produced in this sequence. Say: **Aachen.** Pronounce / ch / as far back as possible.

Say: Aare
Say: re
Say: rat, riet, rot, rum.

Pronounce the following words:

Rand   Rest   Rom   Raum

e. Final / **r** / is generally pronounced like the final sound in English *sofa.*

Pronounce the following words:

Liter   Chlor   Vater   Natur

German s

There are two / **s** / sounds in German:

Voiced (similar to English / s / as in *his*).

Voiceless (similar to English / s / as in *sun* or *hiss*).

Generally **s** is voiced whenever it is single and in front of a vowel. In all other combinations, **s** is voiceless:

Nase   (voiced / s /)   **Haus**   (voiceless / s /)

Pronounce the following German words:

VOICED / s /

Samen   Mäuse   suchen   Faser

VOICELESS / s /

Kasse   dreißig   Skandinavien   Gas

STRUCTURE

1. Genitive Case

a. In general, the genitive in German designates a distinctive aspect of a noun:

POSSESSION	**das Auto meines Bruders** *(the car of my brother; my brother's car)*
BELONGING TO, ASSOCIATION WITH	**die Studenten der Universität** *(the students of the university)*
PART OF	**die Farbe des Tisches** *(the color of the table)*
ACCESSORIES CONCRETE ABSTRACT	 **der Reifen des Autos** *(the tire of the car)* **das Gefühl der Liebe** *(the feeling of love)*

b. The genitive case has two special forms of the definite article: **des** and **der**:

des

masculine, singular	=	**(des Direktors)**
neuter, singular	=	**(des Zimmers)**

der

feminine, singular	=	**(der Frau)**
all genders, plural	=	**(der Frauen, der Männer)**

c. Masculine and neuter nouns consisting of two or more syllables usually add -s to their nominative in order to form the genitive singular:

NOMINATIVE: **der Begriff**   GENITIVE: **des Begriffs**
            das Leben   **des Lebens**

d. Masculine and neuter nouns consisting of one syllable usually add **-es** to their nominative stem in order to form the genitive singular:

NOMINATIVE: **der Mann**   GENITIVE: **des Mannes**
            das Kind   **des Kindes**

e. Feminine nouns do not add endings in the genitive singular:

NOMINATIVE: **die Frau**   GENITIVE: **der Frau**
            die Liebe   **der Liebe**

SELF-PREPARATORY EXERCISES

Supply the endings for the definite articles and nouns.

Was ist das Gebiet d_____ Professor _____ ? (singular)	
Er kennt die Form d_____ Kirche. (singular)	Was ist das Gebiet des Professors?
Sie ist die Tochter d_____ Freund _____ . (singular)	Er kennt die Form der Kirche.
Dort ist das Buch d_____ Lehrer _____ . (singular)	Sie ist die Tochter des Freundes.
Das Klima d_____ Welt variiert. (singular)	Dort ist das Buch des Lehrers.
	Das Klima der Welt variiert.

EXERCISES

A. *Supply the endings of the definite articles and nouns:*

1. Ist Zoologie ein Teilgebiet d_____ Biologie? (singular)
2. Die Apsis d_____ Basilika ist halbrund. (singular)
3. Das Dach d_____ Gebäude_____ ist hoch. (singular)
4. Der Unterbau d_____ Baukörper_____ ist meistens aus Stein. (singular)
5. Wer spricht die Sprache d_____ Land_____? (singular)

B. *Express in German:*

1. He knows the climate of the land.
2. Who is the father of the child?
3. He shows him the roof of the house.
4. She is the daughter of the director.
5. The pupil has the teacher's book.

2. Numbers — Fractions

a. Thus far, we have learned the numbers from 1 to 1000. These numbers, which are used in counting and in indicating quantity, are called cardinal numbers.

b. To express fractions, the cardinal number is used for the numerator:

$$\text{Fraction} = \frac{\text{Numerator}}{\text{Denominator}}$$

c. The denominator is formed by adding **-tel** to a cardinal number:

$$3/5 = \frac{\textbf{drei}}{\textbf{Fünftel}}$$

The denominator is capitalized because it is a neuter noun: **das Fünftel.**

d. Fractions involving one half, thirds, and sevenths are irregular:

1/2	**ein halb**		1/7	**ein Siebtel**	2/5	**zwei Fünftel**
1/3	**ein Drittel**		1/8	**ein Achtel**	7/9	**sieben Neuntel**
1/4	**ein Viertel**		1/9	**ein Neuntel**		
1/5	**ein Fünftel**		1/10	**ein Zehntel**		
1/6	**ein Sechstel**					

SELF-PREPARATORY EXERCISE

Read the following fractions in German:

1/2	
1/3	ein halb
2/3	ein Drittel
5/9	zwei Drittel
7/8	fünf Neuntel
	sieben Achtel

5/6	
4/7	fünf Sechstel
9/14	vier Siebtel
15/19	neun Vierzehntel
2/17	fünfzehn Neunzehntel
	zwei Siebzehntel

EXERCISES

A. *Read and write out the following fractions in German:*

1. 1/2   4. 2/5   7. 11/19   10. 9/11
2. 1/4   5. 5/11   8. 3/8   11. 2/16
3. 1/7   6. 5/13   9. 2/3   12. 3/7

B. *Replace both the nominative and accusative nouns by pronouns:**

1. Der Mann kauft das Haus.
2. Die Frauen kaufen den Wagen.
3. Das Kind sieht die Mutter.
4. Der Schüler liest die Zeitungen.
5. Die Tochter liest die Bücher.

C. *Negate the following sentences, using **nicht.***

1. Er ist hier.
2. Er sieht den Vater.
3. Sie singen das Lied.
4. Das Kind kennt sie.
5. Der Schüler lebt in Bayern.

READING

Biologische Welle

500 (fünfhundert) Bauernhöfe in der Bundesrepublik Deutschland schwimmen auf
der „biologischen Welle". Die Bauern verwenden nur natürliche Düngemittel.
Mineraldünger und Pflanzenschutzmittel sind tabu. Die Erträge sind etwas niedriger,
aber die Ernte erzielt höhere Preise.

VOCABULARY

der	**Bauernhof, ⸚e**	farm(house)	das	**Pflanzenschutzmittel, -**	insecticide (*literally:* means of protecting plants)
	schwimmen	to swim			
	biologisch	biological			
die	**Welle, -n**	wave			
	verwenden	to use, employ		**tabu**	taboo
	natürlich	natural	der	**Ertrag, ⸚e**	yield, production
	düngen	to spread fertilizer			
das	**Mittel, -**	means, agent		**etwas**	somewhat
das	**Düngemittel, -**	fertilizer, manure		**niedriger**	lower
			die	**Ernte**	harvest, crop
das	**Mineral, -ien**	mineral		**erzielen**	to produce, obtain, realize
der	**Dünger, -**	fertilizer			
der	**Mineraldünger**	mineral fertilizer		**höher**	higher
			der	**Preis, -e**	price, rate
der	**Schutz**	protection			

STRUCTURAL EXERCISE

Underline all nouns used in the plural in the above reading.

VOCABULARY EXERCISE

Give the English equivalents of the italicized words:

1. Die Bauern *verwenden* nur natürliche Düngemittel.
2. Die Ernte *erzielt* höhere Preise.
3. Der Student bleibt *ein Jahr* in Deutschland.
4. Das Studium ist *schwer*.
5. Die Erträge sind *etwas* niedriger.
6. *Pflanzenschutzmittel* sind tabu.
7. Das Bier *enthält* Alkohol.

STRUCTURE

3. Word Order — Subject and Verb

a.   In German, there are three basic kinds of sentence structures:

    statements   questions   imperatives (commands)

b. In English statements, the subject precedes the first verb.

c. In German statements, the subject has two possible positions:

either directly < before / or > the conjugated verb / after

1. Subject before verb:

   Er kauft heute einen Wagen. *(He buys a car today.)*

   Word Order Analysis

SUBJECT:	**Er**
VERB:	**kauft**
ADVERB:	**heute**
DIRECT OBJECT:	**einen Wagen**

2. Subject after verb:

   Heute **kauft er** einen Wagen. *(Today he buys a car.)*

   Word Order Analysis

ADVERB:	**Heute**
VERB:	**kauft**
SUBJECT:	**er**
DIRECT OBJECT:	**einen Wagen**

Note that the position of the verb is fixed in second place. Only the subject and adverb exchange places.

SELF-PREPARATORY EXERCISE

Begin each sentence with the italicized element and make the necessary changes in the word order:*

Er kauft *heute* einen Wagen.	
Der Chemiker fährt *jetzt* nach Berlin.	Heute kauft er einen Wagen.
Viele Menschen sprechen Deutsch *in der Welt.*	Jetzt fährt der Chemiker nach Berlin.
Der Karpfen lebt *in schlammigen Gewässern.*	In der Welt sprechen viele Menschen Deutsch.
Eine neue Getreidesorte erscheint *auf dem Markt.*	In schlammigen Gewässern lebt der Karpfen.
	Auf dem Markt erscheint eine neue Getreidesorte.

EXERCISES

A. *Begin each sentence with the italicized word and make the necessary changes in the word order:*

1. Die Arithmetik ist ein Teilgebiet *in der Mathematik.*
2. Der Bikini hat den Namen *angeblich* von dem Bikini-Atoll.
3. Die Baumwolle ist *ein wichtiger Textilrohstoff.*
4. Man nennt Archäologie *in der deutschen Sprache* auch Altertumskunde.
5. Bier ist *in Deutschland* sehr beliebt.

B. *Give the English equivalents of the following sentences:*

1. In Brauereien braut man das Bier.
2. In der Welt sprechen viele Menschen Deutsch.
3. Angeblich hat der Bikini den Namen von dem Bikini-Atoll.
4. Chemie und Physik studiert er und nicht Biologie oder Mathematik.
5. Auf dem Markt erscheint eine neue Getreidesorte.

4. Days of the Week

All days of the week are masculine:

der Montag	*Monday*	**der Freitag**	*Friday*
der Dienstag	*Tuesday*	**der Samstag**	*Saturday*
der Mittwoch	*Wednesday*	**der Sonntag**	*Sunday*
der Donnerstag	*Thursday*		

EXERCISES

A. *Give the German equivalents of the days of the week:*

1. Wednesday   4. Tuesday   6. Monday
2. Friday   5. Saturday   7. Thursday
3. Sunday

B. *Supply the appropriate prepositions:*

1. Das Kind kommt _____ dem Haus. (out of)
2. Er findet das Hotel _____ den Freund. (without)
3. Er fährt _____ die Wand des Hauses. (against)
4. Der Professor kommt _____ Deutschland. (from = residence)
5. Biologie ist das griechische Wort _____ die ,,Lehre von dem Leben''. (for)

C. *Supply the appropriate preposition and definite article:*

1. Sie kauft das Buch _____ Professor. (for the)
2. Er geht _____ halbrunde Apsis. (around the)
3. Der Bikini hat den Namen _____ Bikini-Atoll. (from the)
4. Die Bauform variiert _____ Landschaftsform. (with the)
5. Die Gebäude stehen _____ viereckigen Hof. (around the)

SECHSUNDNEUNZIG

D. *Supply the correct definite article in the dative or accusative case:*

1. Der Chef zeigt _____ Frau das Büro.
2. Der Sohn schickt dem Mädchen _____ Bild.
3. Er kauft _____ Kind das Buch.
4. Sie bringen _____ Freunden die Zeitungen.
5. Sie schicken dem Forschungsinstitut _____ Beweise.

SUMMARY

Genitive

a. The definite articles for the genitive are:

SINGULAR:

MASCULINE NOUNS	**des**	nouns add **-s** or **-es**
NEUTER NOUNS		

FEMININE NOUNS   **der**   nouns add no endings

PLURAL:

ALL GENDERS   **der**   nouns add plural endings

b. The most frequent English equivalent of the German genitive form is *of the:*

Ich kenne das Haus **des Freundes.**
I know the house of the friend. I know the friend's house.

Word Order — Subject and Verb

The position of the German verb in statements is fixed in second place. The subject either directly precedes or follows the verb in statements.

READING

Nur für Nichtraucher

Das Zigarettenrauchen vermindert die Strömungsgeschwindigkeit des Blutes. Sie sinkt nach einer Zigarette um 40 (vierzig) bis 60 (sechzig) Prozent. Das ist das Resultat von Ultraschallmessungen der Blutzirkulation.

VOCABULARY

	rauchen	to smoke	das	**Resultat, -e**	result
der	**Raucher**	smoker,		**von**	of
		person who		**ultra**	ultra, super
		smokes	der	**Schall**	sound
	vermindern	to reduce,	der	**Ultraschall**	supersonic
		lower,		**messen**	to measure
		lessen	die	**Messung, -en**	measurement
die	**Strömung, -en**	flow, stream	die	**Ultraschallmessung, -en**	supersonic
die	**Geschwindigkeit**	speed, ve-			measure-
		locity			ment
das	**Blut**	blood	die	**Zirkulation**	circulation
	sinken	to sink, fall	die	**Blutzirkulation**	blood circula-
	nach	after			tion
die	**Zigarette, -n**	cigarette			
	um	around, at;			
		here: by			

STRUCTURAL EXERCISE

Underline all nouns in the genitive case in the above reading.

VOCABULARY EXERCISE

Give the English equivalents of the italicized nouns:

1. Sie sinkt *nach* einer Zigarette um 40 (vierzig) bis 60 (sechzig) Prozent.
2. Die Bauern verwenden nur *natürliche* Düngemittel.
3. Das Zigarettenrauchen *vermindert* die Strömungsgeschwindigkeit des Blutes.
4. Die *Erträge* sind etwas niedriger.
5. Die Archäologie ist eine *Wissenschaft.*
6. Sie *behandelt* alte Kulturen.
7. Die Strömungs*geschwindigkeit* sinkt nach einer Zigarette.

ACHTUNDNEUNZIG

esson 11

PRONUNCIATION

German v

The German consonant **v** is pronounced like / f / at the beginning of words of Germanic origin: **Vater** (v = f), **Vieh.**

Pronounce the following words:

viel   vier   voll   vor   Volk

In words of non-Germanic origin, **v** is pronounced like English / v /; in the middle of a word, **v** is also pronounced like / v /: **Vakzin** (v = v), **Universität.**

Pronounce the following words:

Vulkan	Vokabel	Lava	Malve
Volt	Vitamin	Navigator	Java

German w

The German consonant **w** is pronounced like English / v / as in *visa:* **was, Löwe.**

Pronounce the following words:

wie   jawohl   wer   Juwel

German y

As a letter of the alphabet, y is called **Üpsilon.** The pronunciation of **y** is similar to the / **ü** / umlaut vowel: **Mythos** (y = ü), **Lyrik.** Compare with the section about / **ü** / on page 59.

Pronounce the following words:

LONG **y**	SHORT **y**
typisch	Physik
Lyrik	Syntax
Mythos	Dynastie

German z

The German consonant **z** is pronounced like / ts / as in *tsar* or *rats:* **Zar** (z = ts), **Bazillus.**

Pronounce the following words:

Zeit   Bazar   Zigarette   dazu

STRUCTURE

1.   Prepositions — Dative and Accusative

a.   So far, you have encountered prepositions that use either the dative or the accusative case.

b.   There are nine prepositions that can take either the dative or accusative case, depending on the function of the preposition in the clause:

an	*at, to, on*	**über**	*over, above, across*
auf	*on, to, at*	**unter**	*under, among*
hinter	*behind*	**vor**	*in front of, before, ago*
in	*in, into, to*	**zwischen**	*between*
neben	*next to, besides*		

SELF-PREPARATORY EXERCISE

Give the English equivalents of the prepositions:

Er geht in das Labor	
Der Wagen steht hinter dem Haus.	into
Der Bauer fährt über das Land.	behind
Sie steht an der Wand.	over
Das Kind läuft zwischen den Gebäuden.	at, next to
	between

HUNDERT

EXERCISE

Supply the correct preposition:

1. Die Bauernhöfe schwimmen _____ der „biologischen Welle". (on)
2. Das Wohnhaus und die Ställe sind _____ einem Dach. (under)
3. Das Bauernhaus hat Trennwände _____ den Wohn- und Stallräumen. (between)
4. Eine neue Getreidesorte erscheint _____ dem Markt. (on)
5. Der Mann steht _____ dem Haus. (in front of)

2. Prepositions — Dative and Accusative (continued)

Two-way prepositions use either the dative or the accusative depending on the following situations:

a. Two-way prepositions with the dative case:

1. The prepositional phrase expresses location and answers the question "where . . .?":

    Der Mann steht **vor dem Haus.** *(The man stands in front of the house.)*

    Wo steht der Mann? *(Where does the man stand?)*

    Vor dem Haus. *(In front of the house.)*

2. An action or motion happens in a confined or defined area and the prepositional phrase answers the question "where . . .?":

    Das Kind läuft **zwischen den Gebäuden.** *(The child is running between the buildings.)*

    Wo läuft das Kind? *(Where is the child running?)*

    Zwischen den Gebäuden. *(Between the buildings.)*

c. Two-way prepositions with the accusative case:

1. The prepositional phrase expresses motion toward a destination or in a defined direction;
2. The prepositional phrase answers the question "where (to) . . .?" or "in what direction . . .?":

    Sie geht **in die Universität.** *(She is going [in]to the university.)*

    Wohin geht sie? [or] **Wo** geht sie **hin?** *(Where [to] is she going?)*

    In die Universität. *([In]to the university.)*

SELF-PREPARATORY EXERCISE

Supply the correct definite article:

Das Buch ist auf _____ Tisch.	
Sie läuft in _____ Haus.	Das Buch ist auf dem Tisch.
Der Bauer fährt in _____ Scheune.	Sie läuft in das Haus.
Das Bild ist an _____ Wand.	Der Bauer fährt in die Scheune.
Der Freund lebt in _____ Schweiz.	Das Bild ist an der Wand.
	Der Freund lebt in der Schweiz.

EXERCISES

A. *Supply the correct two-way prepositions:*

1. Er arbeitet _____ dem Labor. (in)
2. Man behandelt das Tier _____ der Zoologie. (in)
3. _____ Biologie studiert er auch Mathematik. (besides)
4. Der Wagen steht _____ der Scheune. (behind)
5. Er fährt den Wagen _____ das Haus. (in front of)

B. *Supply the correct definite article:*

1. 119 (einhundertneunzehn) Millionen Menschen sprechen Deutsch als Muttersprache in _____ Welt.
2. Der Freund lebt jetzt auf _____ Speicher.
3. Das Mädchen läuft in _____ Haus.
4. Der Professor lehrt an _____ Universität.
5. Der Bauer arbeitet auf _____ Land.

3. Two-Way Prepositions With Fixed Cases

Following is a selected listing of verbs with two-way prepositions. Note that these two-way prepositions have assumed one definite case with the particular verb:

studieren an	+	dative	*to study at*
glauben an	+	accusative	*to believe in*
schicken an	+	accusative	*to send to*
antworten auf	+	accusative	*to answer*
warten auf	+	accusative	*to wait for*

EXERCISES

A. *Supply the correct prepositions:*

1. Er wartet _____ das Mädchen. (for)
2. Sie glauben _____ einen Gott. (in)
3. Er schickt die Karte _____ den Freund. (to)
4. Der Student studiert _____ der Universität. (at)
5. Man antwortet _____ die Karte.

B. *Supply the correct definite article:*

1. Die Mutter wartet auf _____ Sohn.
2. Er studiert an _____ Forschungsinstitut.
3. Sie glauben an _____ Existenz Gottes.
4. Sie antwortet auf _____ Karte.
5. Die Kinder schicken die Bilder an _____ Freunde.

READING

Die Analyse von Proteinstrukturen

Man analysiert jetzt Proteinstrukturen mit Hilfe des Computers. Röntgen-Kristallographe ermitteln die Ergebnisse in wenigen Stunden mit Hilfe des Computers.

Dieses neue Verfahren gehört zu den sogenannten direkten Methoden. Diese Methoden benutzen als Grundlage die mathematischen Relationen unter den Faktoren der Kristallstruktur. Diese Relationen definieren die Verteilung von Materie   5
innerhalb des Moleküls. Man errechnet die Molekularstrukturen nach physikalischen Prinzipien.

Man richtet einen gebündelten Röntgenstrahl auf ein Material. Eine Streuung der Strahlung erfolgt an den Bausteinen der Materie.

Man registriert das Röntgenstrahl-Brechungsmuster auf einem Film. Dieses Muster   10
dient als Grundlage für die genaue Berechnung der Atomanordnung.

VOCABULARY

die	**Analyse, -n**	analysis
das	**Protein, -e**	protein
die	**Struktur, -en**	structure
	analysieren	to analyse
die	**Hilfe**	help
	mit Hilfe von	with the help of
der	**Computer,**	computer

Röntgen *name derived from the discoverer of X-rays, the German physicist Wilhelm Röntgen (1845–1923)*

HUNDERTDREI

der	**Kristallogr**a**ph, -e**	diffractometer	
	ermitteln	to determine, to ascertain	
das	**Ergebnis, -se**	result	
	wenig	few	
die	**Stunde, -n**	hour	
	dies	this	
das	**Verfahren, -**	method, procedure, process	
	gehören	to belong	
	gehören zu + *dative*	to belong to	
	sogenannt	so called	
	dire**kt**	direct	
die	**Meth**o**de, -n**	method	
	benutzen	to use, employ	
die	**Grundlage, -n**	basis, foundation	
	mathema**tisch**	mathematical	
die	**Relati**o**n, -en**	relationship	
	unter	under, among, between	
der	**Faktor, -en**	factor	
der	**Krist**a**ll, -e**	crystal	
die	**Krist**a**llstrukt**u**r, -en**	crystalline structure	
	definie**ren**	to define	
die	**Verteilung**	distribution	
die	**Mat**e**rie**	matter, substance	
	innerhalb + *genitive*	within, inside of	
das	**Molek**ü**l, -e**	molecule	
	errechnen	to calculate, compute	
die	**Molekularstrukt**u**r, -en**	molecular structure	

	nach	here: according to	
	physika**lisch**	physical	
das	**Prinz**i**p, -ien**	principle	
	richten	to direct; to aim	
	richten auf + *accusative*	to direct at, aim at	
	gebü**ndelt**	concentrated, fasciculated	
der	**Strahl, -en**	ray, beam	
der	**Röntgenstrahl, -en**	X-ray	
das	**Material, -ien**	material, substance	
die	**Streuung, -en**	diffusion, dispersion	
	erfolgen	to ensue, occur	
	erfolgen an + *dative*	to result in, occur in	
der	**Baustein, -e**	building block	
	registrie**ren**	to register, record	
die	**Brechung, -en**	refraction	
das	**Muster, -**	pattern	
das	**Brechungsmuster, -**	refractional pattern	
der	**Film, -e**	film	
	dienen	to serve	
	genau	precise, exact	
die	**Berechnung, -en**	calculation, computation	
das	**At**o**m, -e**	atom	
die	**Anordnung, -en**	arrangement, order	
die	**At**o**manordnung, -en**	atomic structure	

STRUCTURAL EXERCISE

Underline all nouns used in the genitive case in the above reading.

VOCABULARY EXERCISE

Give the English equivalents of the italicized words:

1. Dieses neue Verfahren ist eine *direkte* Methode.
2. Man analysiert jetzt Proteinstrukturen *mit Hilfe* des Computers.
3. Man ermittelt die *Ergebnisse* in wenigen Stunden.
4. Dieses Muster *dient* als Berechnungsgrundlage.
5. Man *errechnet* die Molekularstrukturen nach physikalischen Prinzipien.

HUNDERTVIER

6. Ein Forschungsinstitut *erprobt* jetzt die neue Methode.
7. Man *richtet* einen gebündelten Röntgenstrahl auf ein Material.

STRUCTURE

4. Der-Words

a. The following words are declined like definite articles:

dies-	*this*	**welch-**	*which*
jed-	*each, every*	**solch-**	*such*
jen-	*that*	**manch-**	*some, many a*

b. These words take "strong endings," that is, endings similar to the definite articles:

NOMINATIVE SINGULAR	DEFINITE ARTICLE	DER-WORD
MASCULINE	**der**	**dieser**
FEMININE	**die**	**diese**
NEUTER	**das**	**dieses**
PLURAL		
ALL GENDERS	**die**	**diese**

SELF-PREPARATORY EXERCISE

Supply the correct nominative ending:

jed_____ Mann	
solch_____ Bücher	jeder Mann
dies_____ Frau	solche Bücher
manch_____ Kind	diese Frau
jen_____ Bauer	manches Kind
	jener Bauer

EXERCISE

Supply the correct nominative endings:

1. Dies_____ Buch ist neu.
2. Jen_____ Bauernhof ist aus Holz.
3. Manch_____ Menschen glauben ihm.
4. Jed_____ Student studiert viel.
5. Welch_____ Methode ist das?

5. Der-Words — Accusative

SINGULAR	DEFINITE ARTICLE	DER-WORD
MASCULINE FEMININE NEUTER	den die das	diesen diese dieses
PLURAL		
ALL GENDERS	die	diese

SELF-PREPARATORY EXERCISE

Supply the correct accusative endings:

Er sieht dies_____ Material	
Der Mann kauft jed_____ Anzug.	Er sieht dieses Material.
Sie arbeitet für jen_____ Chef.	Der Mann kauft jeden Anzug.
Welch_____ Schüler (*sing.*) kennt der Lehrer?	Sie arbeitet für jenen Chef.
Sie analysiert dies_____ Struktur.	Welchen Schüler kennt der Lehrer?
	Sie analysiert diese Struktur.

EXERCISE

Supply the correct accusative endings:

1. Welch_____ Tisch kauft sie?
2. Er kennt dies_____ Prinzip nicht.
3. Für welch_____ Institut arbeiten sie?
4. Er sieht jed_____ Film.
5. Der Wagen fährt gegen dies_____ Wand.

6. Der-Words — Dative

SINGULAR	DEFINITE ARTICLE	DER-WORD
MASCULINE FEMININE NEUTER	dem der dem	diesem dieser diesem
PLURAL		
ALL GENDERS	den	diesen

SELF-PREPARATORY EXERCISE

Supply the correct dative endings:

Die Brechung erfolgt an dies_____ Bausteinen.	
Es gehört zu jen_____ Methode.	Die Brechung erfolgt an diesen Bausteinen.
Welch_____ Bruder schickt er die Karte?	Es gehört zu jener Methode.
Nach jed_____ Messung errechnet er die Struktur der Kristalle.	Welchem Bruder schickt er die Karte?
Mit welch_____ Landschaftsformen variiert die Bauweise?	Nach jeder Messung errechnet er die Struktur der Kristalle.
	Mit welchen Landschaftsformen variiert die Bauweise?

EXERCISE

Supply the correct dative endings:

1. Er hilft dies_____ Frau.
2. Jen_____ Professor bringt er das Buch.
3. An welch_____ Universität studiert sie?
4. Jen_____ Kindern zeigt er die Bilder.
5. Mit welch_____ Methoden ermittelt man die Kristallstruktur?

7. Der-Words — Genitive

SINGULAR	DEFINITE ARTICLE	DER-WORD
MASCULINE	**des**	**dieses**
FEMININE	**der**	**dieser**
NEUTER	**des**	**dieses**
PLURAL		
ALL GENDERS	**der**	**dieser**

SELF-PREPARATORY EXERCISE

Supply the correct genitive endings:

Man analysiert die Struktur mit Hilfe dies_____ Computers.	
Es dient als Grundlage für die Berechnung jed_____ Atomanordnung.	Man analysiert die Struktur mit Hilfe dieses Computers.
Diese Relationen zeigen die Verteilung jen_____ Materie in dem Molekül.	Es dient als Grundlage für die Berechnung jeder Atomanordnung.
	Diese Relationen zeigen die Verteilung jener Materie in dem Molekül.

EXERCISE

Supply the correct genitive endings:

1. Was ist das Gebiet jen_____ Professors?
2. Er kennt die Tochter dies_____ Freundes.
3. Dieses Verfahren dient als Grundlage für die Berechnung jed_____ Atomanordnung.
4. Wer spricht die Sprachen jen_____ Länder?
5. Wer ist der Vater dies_____ Kinder?

SUMMARY

Der-Words

dies-	*this*	**welch-**	*which*	
jed-	*each, every*	**solch-**	*such*	
jen-	*that*	**manch-**	*some, many a*	

Declension of Der-Words

The declension of the **der**-words is similar to that of the definite articles:

SINGULAR	MASCULINE	FEMININE	NEUTER	PLURAL
NOMINATIVE	**dieser**	**diese**	**dieses**	**diese**
GENITIVE	**dieses**	**dieser**	**dieses**	**dieser**
DATIVE	**diesem**	**dieser**	**diesem**	**diesen**
ACCUSATIVE	**diesen**	**diese**	**dieses**	**diese**

HUNDERTACHT

Two-Way Prepositions

an	*at, to, on, next to*	**über**	*over, above, across*
auf	*on, to, at*	**unter**	*under, among*
hinter	*behind*	**vor**	*in front of, before, ago*
in	*in, into, to*	**zwischen**	*between*
neben	*next to, besides*		

READING

Einleitung in die Mathematik

Mathematik ist ein griechisches Wort und bedeutet die Lehre von den Zahlen- und Raumgrößen. Das heutige technische Zeitalter ist ohne die Mathematik nicht denkbar, deshalb ist sie die Grundlage für alle technischen Berufe. Die Bausteine der Mathematik sind also die Zahlen- und Raumgrößen. Die Lehre von den Zahlengrößen (Arithmetik) zerfällt in: 5

1. das Rechnen mit Ziffern (1, 2, 3, 4, . . .)
2. das Rechnen mit Buchstaben (a, b, c, . . .)
3. das Rechnen mit Gleichungen (Algebra)

Die Lehre von den Raumgrößen (Geometrie) zerfällt in:

1. die Lehre von den Flächen (Planimetrie)   10
2. die Lehre von den Körpern (Stereometrie)

Die Trigonometrie verbindet Raum- und Zahlengrößen. Sie verknüpft Zahlen, Winkel und Strecken.

VOCABULARY

die **Einleitung, -en**	introduction	**denkbar**	conceivable
die **Zahl, -en**	number	**deshalb**	for that reason, therefore
die **Größe, -n**	size, quantity		
die **Zahlengröße, -n**	number, numerical quantity	der **Beruf, -e**	profession
		also	consequently, therefore
die **Raumgröße, -n**	volumetric quantity		
		zerfallen (zerfällt) in *+ accusative*	to break down into
heutig	present-day, current		
		das **Rechnen**	counting, calculus
technisch	technological, technical		
		die **Ziffer, -n**	number, digit
das **Alter**	age	der **Buchstabe, -n**	letter
das **Zeitalter**	age, era, epoch, generation	die **Gleichung, -en**	equation
		die **Algebra**	algebra
ohne *+ accusative*	without	die **Geometrie**	geometry
denken	to think	die **Fläche, -n**	plane, surface

HUNDERTNEUN

die **Planimetrie**	plane geometry	**verknüpfen**	to tie, to join, to bind
die **Stereometrie**	solid geometry		
die **Trigonometrie**	trigonometry	der **Winkel,-**	angle
verbinden	to combine, to join, to connect	die **Strecke, -n**	distance, line

STRUCTURAL EXERCISE

Underline the following items in the above reading:

1. all direct objects (solid line);
2. all prepositions using the accusative case only (dotted line).

VOCABULARY EXERCISE

Give the English equivalents of the italicized words:

1. Mathematik *bedeutet* die Lehre von den Zahlen- und Raumgrößen.
2. Die Trigonometrie *verbindet* Raum- und Zahlengrößen.
3. Sie ist die *Grundlage* für alle technischen Berufe.
4. Die Bausteine der Mathematik sind *also* die Zahlen- und Raumgrößen.
5. Sie *ermitteln* die Ergebnisse in wenigen Stunden.
6. Das *heutige* Zeitalter ist ohne die Mathematik nicht denkbar.
7. *Einleitung* in die Mathematik.

esson 12

PRONUNCIATION

German / ch /

This sound is closely related to the / **k** / sound; but instead of making a complete closure between the back of your tongue and the soft palate, **ch** is produced by leaving an opening between the back of the tongue and the soft palate. This opening results in an audible friction sound as the breath passes through.

Depending on the vowel sound that precedes or follows **ch**, the production of / **ch** / will shift, in accordance with the vowel, from the front of the mouth to the back and vice versa. Compare the two / **ch** / sounds:

Dach   **mich**
(back)   (front)

Pronounce the following words:

Back / **ch** /

mach	lach	Buch	hoch

Contrast Exercise: / k / versus / ch /

nackt	Nacht	Lack	lach
Dock	doch	back	Bach

Front / **ch** /

mich	Bücher	Pech	Löcher	euch

Contrast Exercise: / k / versus / ch /

dick	dich	bücken	Bücher
Leck	Lech	lecker	Löcher

HUNDERTELF

/ ch / after n, l, r

| manch | solch | durch | Dolch |
| Milch | Arche | München | Kelch |

/ ch / in the diminutive ending -chen

Mädchen   Weibchen   Märchen   Häuschen

STRUCTURE

1. Genitive — Indefinite Article

The indefinite article **ein** takes exactly the same endings in the genitive as the definite article and the **der**-words:

SINGULAR	DEFINITE ARTICLE	DER-WORD	INDEFINITE ARTICLE
MASCULINE	**des**	dieses	eines
FEMININE	**der**	dieser	einer
NEUTER	**des**	dieses	eines
PLURAL			
ALL GENDERS	**der**	dieser	**keiner**[1]

SELF-PREPARATORY EXERCISE

Supply the genitive endings of the indefinite articles:

Er kennt den Sohn ein_____ Freundes.	
Man analysiert die Struktur mit Hilfe ein_____ Computers.	Er kennt den Sohn eines Freundes.
Man behandelt das Leben ein_____ Pflanze.	Man analysiert die Struktur mit Hilfe eines Computers.
Die Basilika ist die Urform ein_____ Kirche.	Man behandelt das Leben einer Pflanze.
Es ist die Lehre ein_____ Kultur.	Die Basilika ist die Urform einer Kirche.
	Es ist die Lehre einer Kultur.

1. Since there is no plural form for the indefinite article, the negation **kein** is used to indicate the plural endings for **ein**-words.

HUNDERTZWÖLF

EXERCISE

Supply the genitive endings of the indefinite articles:

1. Er spricht die Sprache ein_____ Landes.
2. Bikini ist der Name ein_____ Atolls.
3. Es ist das Resultat ein_____ Messung.
4. Man behandelt das Leben ein_____ Tieres.
5. Er kennt die Arbeit ein_____ Instituts in Berlin.

2. Prepositions with the Genitive Case

trotz	*in spite of*	**innerhalb**	*inside of, within*
während	*during*	**außerhalb**	*outside of*
wegen	*because of, on account of*	**diesseits**	*on this side of*
(an)statt	*instead of*	**jenseits**	*on the other side of*

SELF-PREPARATORY EXERCISE

Supply the correct preposition:

_____ der niedrigen Ernte erzielt man höhere Preise. *(because of)*	
Sie definieren die Verteilung der Materie _____ des Moleküls. *(within)*	Wegen der niedrigen Ernte erzielt man höhere Preise.
_____ des Tages hat er keine Zeit. *(during)*	Sie definieren die Verteilung der Materie innerhalb eines Moleküls.
	Während des Tages hat er keine Zeit.

EXERCISES

A. *Supply the genitive preposition:*

1. _____ des Studiums hat er keine Zeit. (during)
2. _____ der hohen Preise kauft er das Getreide. (in spite of)
3. Er arbeitet _____ des Jahres in Washington. (during)
4. Diese Relationen definieren die Verteilung der Materie _____ des Moleküls. (inside of)
5. _____ der Gesetze lebt sie jetzt in Amerika. (because of)

B. *Supply the correct form of the definite articles:*

1. _____ Mann fährt nach Berlin.
2. Er gibt _____ Schwester das Buch.
3. Das Kind geht zu _____ Vater.
4. Der Wagen fährt gegen _____ Wand.
5. Grau ist die Farbe _____ Wagen _____.

C. *Change all nouns in the sentences to singular and make the necessary changes in the verbs:**

    1. Die Männer sprechen viel.   4. Die Lehrer lesen keine Bücher.
    2. Die Kinder schlafen nicht.   5. Die Mütter sind alt.
    3. Die Chefs arbeiten in den Büros.

D. *Express the following in accordance with the examples given:*

    EXAMPLES: (1 / Buch)   ein Buch
              (12 / Mann)   zwölf Männer

    1. (5 / Lied)   6. (4 / Mädchen)
    2. (2 / Glas)   7. (1 / Frau)
    3. (6 / Mantel)   8. (25 / Zimmer)
    4. (14 / Tag)   9. (10 / Vater)
    5. (2 / Karte)   10. (3 / Büro)

E. *Change the definite articles to indefinite articles:**

    1. Er gibt dem Mann das Buch.
        Er gibt _____ Mann das Buch.
    2. Der Lehrer kauft das Buch.
        Der Lehrer kauft _____ Buch.
    3. Der Wagen fährt gegen den Baum.
        Der Wagen fährt gegen _____ Baum.
    4. Man sagt es der Frau.
        Man sagt es _____ Frau.

F. *Supply the question words:*

    1. _____ ist in dem Gebäude? (who)
    2. _____ fährt er nach Berlin? (why)
    3. _____ liest der Student? (how much)
    4. _____ bleiben sie nicht hier? (why)
    5. _____ ist der Wagen? (where)

G. *Write out the following fractions:*

    1. 2/3   3. 5/7   5. 3/16
    2. 1/2   4. 15/20

H. *Substitute pronouns for direct and indirect objects:**

    1. Der Schüler liest die Zeitung.
        Der Schüler liest _____.
    2. Der Vater gibt dem Kind das Buch.
        Der Vater gibt _____ _____.
    3. Er fährt mit den Kindern nach Deutschland.
        Er fährt mit _____ nach Deutschland.

HUNDERTVIERZEHN

4. Sie kennt die Bilder nicht.
    Sie kennt _____ nicht.
5. Der Mann hilft der Frau in dem Labor.
    Der Mann hilft _____ in dem Labor.

READING

Albert Einstein

1879   geboren in Ulm, Süddeutschland.

1905   Einstein beendet seine Dissertation in Zürich. Die Arbeit an der Dissertation
        führt ihn zu der Relativitätstheorie. Er erklärt auch den photoelektrischen
        Effekt und untersucht die Bewegung der Atome.

1910   Professor für theoretische Physik an der Technischen Hochschule Zürich.   5

1913   Direktor für theoretische Physik am Kaiser Wilhelm Institut in Berlin.

1921   Verleihung des Nobelpreises für Physik.

1933   Emigration in die Vereinigten Staaten. Er arbeitet am Institut für „Ad-
        vanced Studies" an der Princeton Universität.

1955   Gestorben in Princeton.   10

VOCABULARY

geboren	born	die **Bewegung, -en**	movement, motion
Ulm	*city in Southern*	**theoretisch**	theoretical
	Germany	die **Schule, -n**	school
süd-	southern	die **Hochschule, -n**	university
beenden	to finish, complete	der **Direktor, -en**	director
die **Dissertation, -en**	dissertation, thesis	**am (= an dem)**	at the
Zürich	*city in Switzerland*	der **Kaiser, -**	emperor
führen	to lead	die **Verleihung, -en**	bestowal, granting
die **Theorie, -n**	theory	der **Nobelpreis**	Nobel Prize
die **Relativität**	relativity	die **Emigration**	emigration
die **Relativitätstheorie**	theory of	die **Vereinigten Staaten**	United States
	relativity	**sterben (stirbt)**	to die
erklären	to explain	**gestorben**	died (*past par-*
photoelektrisch	photoelectric		*ticiple of* **sterben**)
der **Effekt, -e**	effect		
untersuchen	to investigate,		
	examine		

STRUCTURAL EXERCISE

Underline all two-way prepositions in the above reading.

HUNDERTFÜNFZEHN

Albert Einstein

HUNDERTSECHZEHN

VOCABULARY EXERCISE

Give the English equivalents of the italicized words:

1. Die Arbeit an der Dissertation *führt* ihn zu der Relativitätstheorie.
2. Einstein *erklärt* den photoelektrischen Effekt.
3. Er *untersucht* die Bewegung der Atome.
4. Die Ernte *erzielt* höhere Preise.
5. Das heutige technische Zeitalter ist ohne die Mathematik nicht *denkbar.*
6. *Deshalb* ist die Mathematik die Grundlage für alle technischen Berufe.
7. Eine Streuung der Strahlen *erfolgt* an den Bausteinen der Materie.

STRUCTURE

3. Past Tense — Weak Verbs

a. Many German verbs have a single basic verb stem in all tenses. These verbs are called regular or weak verbs.

b. Weak verbs form their past tense by adding endings to the infinitive stem:

INFINITIVE: **sagen** *(to say)*

INFINITIVE STEM: **sag-**

PAST TENSE
THIRD PERSON   **er sagte** *(he said)*
SINGULAR

The past tense of weak verbs is formed by adding **-te** to the infinitive stem in the third person singular. In the third person plural, the ending **-ten** is added to the infinitive stem:

SINGULAR:		
er fragte	*he asked*	
sie sagte	*she said*	
es machte	*it made*	(**machen** = *to make, do*)
die Frau fragte	*the woman asked*	
man sagte	*one said*	

PLURAL:		
sie fragten	*they asked*	
die Männer sagten	*the men said*	

c. If the infinitive stem ends in **-d** or **-t,** an **-e** is inserted between the stem and the ending:

INFINITIVE: **warten** *(to wait)*

INFINITIVE STEM: **wart-**

THIRD PERSON ⎫
SINGULAR   ⎬   **er wartete** *(he waited)*
PAST TENSE   ⎭

THIRD PERSON ⎫
PLURAL   ⎬   **sie warteten** *(they waited)*
PAST TENSE   ⎭

SELF-PREPARATORY EXERCISE

Form the past tense of the following verbs:*

EXAMPLE: (er / sagen)   er sagte

(er / fragen)	
(Der Mann / sagen)	Er fragte.
(Der Mann / warten)	Der Mann sagte.
(Die Männer / warten)	Der Mann wartete.
(Das Kind / spielen)	Die Männer warteten.
(Heinz und Johann / sammeln)	Das Kind spielte.
(Der Lehrer / antworten)	Heinz und Johann sammelten.
	Der Lehrer antwortete.

EXERCISE

Supply the past tense form of the verbs:

1. Sie *(she)* _____ dem Lehrer.   (antworten)
2. Die Mutter _____ dem Kind.   (folgen)
3. Die Kinder _____ in dem Garten.   (spielen)
4. Der Student _____ viel.   (lernen)
5. Der Chef _____ in dem Büro.   (arbeiten)

HUNDERTACHTZEHN

4. Past Tense — Verbs Ending in -ieren

Verbs with the infinitive ending **-ieren** also form the past tense by adding **-te** (singular) and **-ten** (plural) to the verb stem:

| INFINITIVE: | **studieren** *(to study)* |
| INFINITIVE STEM: | **studier-** |

THIRD PERSON SINGULAR PAST TENSE **er studierte** *(he studied)*

THIRD PERSON PLURAL PAST TENSE **sie studierten** *(they studied)*

EXERCISE

Form the past tense of the following verbs:

1. Der Student _____ ein Jahr in Deutschland.   (studieren)
2. Die Bauform _____ mit der Landschaftsform.   (variieren)
3. Man _____ die Proteinstruktur mit Hilfe des Computers.   (analysieren)
4. Sie *(they)* _____ die Verteilung von Materie innerhalb des Moleküls. (definieren)
5. Man _____ das Brechungsmuster auf einem Film.   (registrieren)

5. Contracted Forms of Prepositions

a.   Many of the prepositions you have learned so far may occur in a contracted form. Contraction refers to the combining of a preposition and a definite article; for example: The preposition **zu** may be combined with the definite article **dem** (dative singular, masculine or neuter) to form the contracted form **zum.**

b.   Not all prepositions lend themselves to the formation of contracted forms. Following is a list of possible contractions:

Prepositions with the accusative:

für + das = fürs   **um + das = ums**

Prepositions with the dative:

zu + dem = zum   **bei + dem = beim**
zu + der = zur

Two-way prepositions:

an + dem = am   in + das = ins
an + das = ans   in + dem = im
auf + das = aufs

Note that these contractions of prepositions are not mandatory. Whenever they are used, however, they do not alter the meaning of the prepositional phrase.

6. Feminine Nouns Ending in -in

a. There are many German nouns which can form a feminine counterpart to the masculine noun by simply adding **-in** to the masculine noun:

der Student   die Studentin

b. The plural of the feminine noun is formed by adding **-innen** to the masculine noun:

der Student   die Studentin   PLURAL: **die Studentinnen**
(male)   (female)

EXERCISES

A. *Form the feminine noun from the masculine noun (singular):**

1. der Freund   die _____   5. der Chemiker   die _____
2. der Professor   die _____   6. der Physiker   die _____
3. der Lehrer   die _____   7. der König   die _____
4. der Chef   die _____

B. *Give the plurals of the feminine nouns in exercise A.*

C. *Give the English equivalents of the German compound words:*

1. das Zeitalter   3. der Röntgenstrahl   5. die Ultraschallmessung
2. der Buchstabe   4. die Grundlage

READING

Volkshochschule: Erwachsene auf der Schulbank

Jeden Herbst beginnt eine neue Saison für Volkshochschulen. Immer mehr Bürger gehen in die Volkshochschule: In Wuppertal, im Haus der Erwachsenenbildung, lernen sie Steuerrecht und Arbeitsrecht, höhere Mathematik und Experimentalphysik, Ökologie und Geologie. In einer anderen Schule hören sie Betriebswirtschaftslehre und Kostenrechnung.

In Landshut, im Land Bayern, gibt es im Meditationszentrum eine Einführung in die Meditation. Insgesamt studieren rund 8 Millionen Erwachsene an den Volkshochschulen in Deutschland.

HUNDERTZWANZIG

VOCABULARY

das	**Volk, ̈-er**	people	
die	**Volkshochschule, -n**	adult education, evening school, university extension	
der	**Erwachsene, -n**	(male) adult	
die	**Erwachsene, -n**	(female) adult	
die	**Bank, -ë**	bench, seat	
	auf der Schulbank	attending school, at school	
der	**Herbst**	fall, autumn	
	beginnen	to begin, to start	
die	**Saison**	season; *here:* schoolyear	
	immer	always	
	immer mehr	more and more	
der	**Bürger, -**	citizen	
	Wuppertal	*city in West Germany*	
das	**Haus, ̈-er**	house	
die	**Bildung**	education, formation	
die	**Steuer, -n**	tax, duty	
das	**Recht, -e**	law, right	
	höher	higher	
	experimental	experimental	
die	**Ökologie**	ecology	
die	**Geologie**	geology	
	ander-	other	

	hören	to hear, to listen to
der	**Betrieb, -e**	plant, operation, management
die	**Wirtschaft**	economy
die	**Lehre, -n**	theory, doctrine, teaching, subject
die	**Betriebswirtschaftslehre**	(theory of) economic management
die	**Rechnung, -en**	calculation, account, bill
die	**Kostenrechnung**	cost accounting
	Landshut	*city in West Germany*
das	**Land, ̈-er**	*state (a "Land" is similar to a state in America as part of the Federal Republic)*
	es gibt	there is, there are
die	**Meditation**	meditation
das	**Zentrum, die Zentren**	center
	insgesamt	altogether, in total

STRUCTURAL EXERCISE

Underline all two-way prepositions in the above reading.

VOCABULARY EXERCISE

Give the English equivalents of the italicized words:

1. Dort gibt es eine *Einführung* in die Meditation.
2. In einer *anderen* Schule hören sie Betriebswirtschaftslehre.
3. Jeden *Herbst* beginnt eine neue Saison.
4. *Immer mehr* Bürger gehen in die Volkshochschule.
5. Die Bauern *verwenden* nur natürliche Düngemittel.
6. Er *vermeidet* schnelle Gewässer.
7. Sie trägt nach einmaliger Aussaat *mehrere* Jahre Ähren.

esson 13

PRONUNCIATION

German / chs /

a. Genitive

Masculine and neuter nouns ending in **-ch** sometimes simply add **-s** to form the genitive singular; **-chs** is pronounced like / ch / + / s /.

Pronounce the following words:

des Reichs   des Mönchs   des Kelchs   des Dolchs

b. Superlative

Most German adjectives and adverbs add **-st** (+ ending) to form the superlative. In adjectives and adverbs ending in **-ch,** the superlative is pronounced like / ch / + / s /.

Pronounce the following words:

am reichsten   am höchsten   der Reichste   der Ehrlichste

c. Verbs

Most German verbs add **-st** to the stem to form the second person singular. The second person singular form of verbs ending in **-ch** is pronounced like / ch / + / st /.

Pronounce the following verbs:

du *(you)* machst   du wächst   du gleichst   du keuchst

HUNDERTZWEIUNDZWANZIG

d. Exception

In words where the consonant cluster **-chs** is not a result of the genitive formation, the superlative, or the personal ending, but part of the word stem, **-chs** is pronounced like / ks / as in English *six*.

Pronounce the following words:

Wachs	sechs	wechseln
Fuchs	wachsen	Sachsen

German / kn / and / gn /

The **k** and the **g** are not silent and are pronounced in German like **k + n** and **g + n**. Examples: **Knie, Gnom.**

Pronounce the following words:

Knall	Knick	Knochen	Knüller
Gnade	Gneis	Gnostik	Gnu

German / sch / + Consonant

This cluster is pronounced like / sch /. Imitate the English sound for being quiet or demanding silence / sh! / and add the consonant. Example: **Schwan.**

Pronounce the following words:

Schwalbe	schwimmen	Schlegel	schlimm

STRUCTURE

1. Past Tense — Strong Verbs

a. The characterization "strong" refers to the fact that verbs in this category change their stem vowel completely when forming the past tense.

b. Both English and German have "strong" verbs.

English (i–o):

INFINITIVE	*to drive*
PRESENT TENSE	*he drives*
PAST TENSE	*he drove*

German **(a– u)**

INFINITIVE	**fahren**	*(to drive)*
PRESENT TENSE	**er fährt**	*(he drives, is driving, does drive)*
PAST TENSE	**er fuhr**	*(he drove, was driving, did drive)*

c.   The third person singular form of the strong verb does not add any ending to the past stem:

er		*he*	
sie		*she*	
es	**fuhr**	*it*	*drove*
man		*one*	
der Mann		*the man*	

d.   In the third person plural, strong verbs add **-en** to the past stem:

sie	**fuhren**	*they*	*drove*
die Frauen		*the women*	

e.   There is no logical way to determine what the vowel change will be. To facilitate learning, strong verbs are grouped according to their stem-vowel changes. Strong verbs use one of five stem-vowel changes (**a, o, u, ie, i**) to form the past tense:

GROUP I (past-tense stem vowel **a**):

INFINITIVE STEM VOWEL		PAST-TENSE STEM VOWEL
e		**a**
geben	*to give*	**gab**
sprechen	*to speak*	**sprach**
helfen	*to help*	**half**
fressen	*to eat*	**fraß**
sehen	*to see*	**sah**
lesen	*to read*	**las**
stehen	*to stand*	**stand**

i		**a**
finden	*to find*	**fand**
singen	*to sing*	**sang**

ie		**a**
liegen	*to lie*	**lag**

HUNDERTVIERUNDZWANZIG

GROUP II (past-tense stem vowel **o**):

INFINITIVE STEM VOWEL	PAST-TENSE STEM VOWEL
ie	**o**
fliegen *to fly*	**flog**

GROUP III (past-tense stem vowel **u**):

INFINITIVE STEM VOWEL	PAST-TENSE STEM VOWEL
a	**u**
fahren *to drive*	**fuhr**

GROUP IV (past-tense stem vowel **ie**):

INFINITIVE STEM VOWEL	PAST-TENSE STEM VOWEL
ei	**ie**
bleiben *to stay*	**blieb**

a	**ie**
schlafen *to sleep*	**schlief**
lassen *to let*	**ließ**

au	**ie**
laufen *to run*	**lief**

GROUP V (past-tense stem vowel **i**):

INFINITIVE STEM VOWEL	PAST-TENSE STEM VOWEL
e	**i**
gehen *to go*	**ging**

ä	**i**
hängen *to hang*	**hing**

SELF-PREPARATORY EXERCISE

Give the past tense of the verbs:*

EXAMPLE: Er **bleibt** hier.   Er **blieb** hier.

Sie liest das Buch.	
Der Motor läuft.	Sie las das Buch.
Er spricht nicht.	Der Motor lief.
Man sieht ihn.	Er sprach nicht.
Sie fliegen hoch.	Man sah ihn.
	Sie flogen hoch.

EXERCISES

A.   *Change the following sentences to past tense:**

1. Der Schüler schläft in der Schule.
2. Er liest das Buch.
3. Die Frau hilft der Chefin.
4. Die Maschine läuft nicht.
5. Das Haus steht in dem Garten.

B.   *Give the German equivalents:*

1. He drove to Berlin.
2. The animal ate the grain.
3. The (female) chemist found the laboratory.
4. The man saw the film.
5. She ran around the house.

2.   Irregular Verbs

There are a few verbs which undergo changes both in their stem vowels and in their consonants. In addition, they add the endings of weak verbs **-te** (singular), **-ten** (plural). These verbs are called irregular verbs. Following is a list of the most frequent irregular verbs:

INFINITIVE		PAST TENSE
denken	*to think*	**er dachte**
bringen	*to bring; to take*	**er brachte**
kennen	*to know*	**er kannte**
nennen	*to call; to name*	**er nannte**
rennen	*to run*	**er rannte**

HUNDERTSECHSUNDZWANZIG

SELF-PREPARATORY EXERCISE

Supply the past-tense forms of these irregular verbs: *

Der Student denkt nicht.	
Sie nennt den Namen.	Der Student dachte nicht.
Die Kinder rennen um das Haus.	Sie nannte den Namen.
Sie bringen ihm das Buch.	Die Kinder rannten um das Haus.
Man kennt das Resultat.	Sie brachten ihm das Buch.
	Man kannte das Resultat.

EXERCISES

A. *Supply the past-tense forms of the verbs in parentheses:*

1. Er _____ die Chemikerin. (to know)
2. Man _____ das Pflanzenschutzmittel in das Labor. (to bring)
3. Die Studentin _____ nicht. (to think)
4. Man _____ ihr den Namen des Mannes. (to name)
5. Die Kinder _____ aus der Schule. (to run)

B. *Supply the past-tense forms of the verbs in parentheses:*

1. Der Schüler _____ Deutsch. (lernen)
2. Er _____ im Labor. (arbeiten)
3. Immer mehr Menschen _____ dieses Buch. (lesen)
4. Sie *(she)* _____ ihm den Beweis. (bringen)
5. Der Chef _____ im Büro. (warten)

C. *Give the German equivalents:*

1. The children played here.
2. She knew the film.
3. They brought him the picture.
4. One saw her in the house.
5. She read the book.

READING

Unser Herz in Zahlen

Die Größe des menschlichen Herzens entspricht etwa der Größe der Faust seines Besitzers. Ein Menschenherz wiegt durchschnittlich nicht viel mehr als ein halbes Pfund. Es besteht fast ganz aus Muskulatur. Dieser Muskel hat eine große Leistungsfähigkeit. Der Herzmuskel arbeitet Tag und Nacht pausenlos. Der Hohlmuskel vollbringt an einem Tag die Leistung von 12 700 mkg. (Meterkilogram). 5

Das Herz preßt mit jedem Herzschlag 60 ccm (Kubikzentimeter) Blut in das
Röhrennetz des Blutgefäßsystems. Das geschieht 4 200mal in der Stunde, am Tag
100 800mal! Die gesamte Blutmenge des Menschen beträgt etwa 5 Liter. Das Herz
befördert am Tag 5 760 Liter Blut. Der Herzschlag erteilt der Pulswelle eine
Geschwindigkeit von 5 bis 6 Metern in der Sekunde.   10

VOCABULARY

	unser	our	
das	**Herz**	heart	
	menschlich	human	
	entsprechen (entspricht),	to correspond,	
	entsprach (*past*)	be equivalent to	
	etwa	about, approximately	
die	**Faust, ̈e**	fist	
der	**Besitzer, -**	owner, possessor, proprietor	
die	**Besitzerin, -nen**	(female) owner	
	wiegen, wog (*past*)	to weigh	
	durchschnittlich	on the average	
	als	than	
	halb	half	
das	**Pfund**	pound	
	bestehen, bestand (*past*)	to consist	
	bestehen . . . aus	to consist of	
	fast	almost	
	ganz	complete(ly), entire(ly)	
die	**Muskulatur, -en**	musculature, muscular system	
der	**Muskel, -n**	muscle	
	groß	large, big	
die	**Leistung, -en**	achievement, performance, work	
die	**Fähigkeit, -en**	ability, capacity, talent	
die	**Leistungsfähigkeit**	work capacity	
der	**Tag, -e**	day	
die	**Nacht, ̈e**	night	
	pausenlos	uninterrupted, without a break	
	hohl	hollow	
der	**Hohlmuskel**	hollow muscle; *here:* heart	
	bringen, brachte (*past*)	to bring, to take to	

	vollbringen	to achieve; to perform; to carry out	
	an einem Tag	in one day	
	pressen	to force, press, push	
der	**Schlag, ̈e**	beat, hit, stroke	
der	**Meter, -**	meter	
der	**Kubikzentimeter, -**	cubic centimeter	
die	**Röhre, -n**	pipe, tube, canal	
das	**Netz, -e**	net, network	
das	**Röhrennetz**	veins, arteries, capillaries	
das	**Gefäß, -e**	vessel, container	
das	**Blutgefäß, -e**	blood vessel	
das	**Blutgefäßsystem,**	vascular system	
	geschehen (geschieht), geschah (*past*)	to happen, occur	
	mal	times	
die	**Stunde, -n**	hour	
	am Tag	per day, during the day	
	gesamt	total, entire	
die	**Menge, -n**	amount, mass, quantity	
	betragen (beträgt), betrug (*past*)	to amount to, come to	
der	**Liter, -**	liter	
	befördern	to transport, haul, carry	
	erteilen (+ *dative*)	to give; to impart	
der	**Puls**	pulse	
die	**Welle, -n**	wave	
die	**Pulswelle, -n**	pulse wave, pulse stream	
	von . . . bis	from . . . to	
die	**Sekunde, -n**	second	
	in der Sekunde	per second	

HUNDERTACHTUNDZWANZIG

STRUCTURAL EXERCISE

A. Underline all prepositions used in the above reading.

B. Identify the cases in which these prepositions are used.

VOCABULARY EXERCISE

Give the English equivalents of the italicized words:

1. Das Herz *besteht* fast ganz aus Muskulatur.
2. Der Hohlmuskel *vollbringt* an einem Tag die Leistung von 12 700 mkg.
3. Das Herz *befördert* am Tag 5 760 Liter Blut.
4. Das Herz wiegt nicht viel mehr *als* ein halbes Pfund.
5. *Insgesamt* studieren etwa 8 Millionen Erwachsene an den Volkshochschulen in Deutschland.
6. Der Herzschlag erteilt der Pulswelle eine Geschwindigkeit *von 5 bis 6* Metern in der Sekunde.
7. Mathematik *bedeutet* die Lehre von den Zahlen- und Raumgrößen.

STRUCTURE

3. Past Tense — haben

The verb **haben** changes its stem in the past tense to **hatt-:**

INFINITIVE	PAST TENSE	
haben *to have*	**er hatte**	*he had*
	sie hatten	*they had*

Examples:

Die Frau **hatte** den Wagen. *(The woman had the car.)*
Die Menschen **hatten** keine Zeit. *(The people did not have any time.)*

EXERCISES

A. *Change the following sentences to past tense:**

1. Er hat den Beweis.
   Er _____ den Beweis.
2. Sie haben viel Zeit.
   Sie _____ viel Zeit.
3. Er hat kein Buch.
   Er _____ kein Buch.
4. Sie hat den Film nicht.
   Sie _____ den Film nicht.
5. Die Chefs haben große Büros.
   Die Chefs _____ große Büros.

B.   *Give the German equivalents:*

1.   She had a lot of time.
2.   They had the newspapers.
3.   The teacher had the pictures.
4.   The farmer had a lot of work.
5.   One had the proof.

4.   Past Tense — Strong Verb Dictionary Listing

Dictionaries and tables of strong verbs usually list only the third person singular form of the strong verb. Add **-en** to the singular form to obtain the plural form of the third person in the past tense:

INFINITIVE: **fahren**
PRESENT: **fährt**
PAST: **fuhr** (3rd person singular)
                fuhren (3rd person plural)

5.   Past Tense — sein

The verb **sein** forms its past tense by using the stem **war-**:

INFINITIVE		PAST TENSE	
sein	to be	**er war**	he was
		sie waren	they were

Examples:

Das Kind **war** in der Schule.
The child was at school.
Die Erwachsenen **waren** in der Volkshochschule.
The adults were in the adult evening school.

EXERCISES

A.   *Supply the past tense form of* **sein:***

1.   Er ist Direktor des Instituts.
2.   Sie sind Schüler.
3.   Die Studentin ist aus Amerika.
4.   Das Resultat der Messung ist in diesem Buch.
5.   Es ist ein Sammelbegriff.

B.   *Give the German equivalents:*

1.   The professor was from America.
2.   Next to the farmhouse were stalls and the barn.
3.   The substructure was mostly of stone.

HUNDERTDREISSIG

    4.   The film was new.
    5.   The study was difficult.

C. *Change to past tense:**

    1.   Die Studentinnen gehen in die Universität.
        Die Studentinnen _____ in die Universität.
    2.   Sie sehen das Haus in Wuppertal.
        Sie _____ das Haus in Wuppertal.
    3.   Er fährt nach Deutschland.
        Er _____ nach Deutschland.
    4.   Sie laufen um die Kirche.
        Sie _____ um die Kirche.
    5.   Sie liest die Zeitung.
        Sie _____ die Zeitung.

D. *Give the German equivalents:*

    1.   He stood in front of the house.   4.   She brought it to him.
    2.   They helped her.   5.   He knew the result.
    3.   He followed them.

E. *Give the dative or accusative definite article:*

    1.   Er ging in _____ Haus.
    2.   Es lag auf _____ Tisch.
    3.   Der Wagen stand neben _____ Gebäude.
    4.   Sie liefen in _____ Labor.
    5.   Das Buch war unter _____ Zeitung.

6.   Two-Way Prepositions with Fixed Cases

Below are three verbs which require the accusative case from otherwise two-way prepositions:

denken an + accusative	*to think of, about*
sprechen über + accusative	*to talk about*
hören auf + accusative	*to listen to, obey someone*

Examples:

Er **spricht über das** Forschungsinstitut.
He is talking about the research institute.
Das Kind **hört auf die** Mutter.
The child listens to the mother.
Er **denkt an die** Freundin.
He is thinking of the girl friend.

SELF-PREPARATORY EXERCISE

Supply the correct preposition:

Sie sprechen _____ die Studentin.	
Er denkt _____ das Mädchen.	Sie sprechen über die Studentin.
Man hört _____ den Chef.	Er denkt an das Mädchen.
	Man hört auf den Chef.

EXERCISES

A. *Supply the correct present tense verb form and preposition:*

1. Der Bauer _____ die Arbeit.   (to think about)
2. Der Sohn _____ den Vater.   (to listen to)
3. Der Professor _____ die Baukunst.   (to talk about)

B. *Give the English equivalents of the following sentences:*

1. Der Physiker sprach über die Analyse von Proteinstrukturen.
2. Der Bauer dachte an die Ernte und die Preise.
3. Die Kinder hörten auf die Erwachsenen.

7.   Time

a.   In Germany, the twenty-four-hour system is used for official records, timetables, and broadcasting and entertainment programs.

b.   German uses the prepositions **nach** and **vor** to indicate minutes after and before the hour:

Es ist **zehn Minuten vor acht.**   (7:50)
Es ist **drei Minuten nach sieben.**   (7:03)

c.   To express a point in time, German uses the preposition **um,** which corresponds to English *at:*

Er kommt **um vier Uhr.** *(He is coming at four o'clock.)*

d.   There are several ways of expressing English *quarter after, quarter to,* and *half past:*

1.   Using minutes:

Es ist **fünfzehn Minuten nach zwölf.**   (12:15)
Es ist **fünfzehn Minuten vor eins.**   (12:45)
Es ist **dreißig Minuten vor / nach eins.**   (12:30 / 1:30)

HUNDERTZWEIUNDDREISSIG

2. Using fractions:

   Es ist **Viertel nach zwölf.**   (12:15)
   Es ist **Viertel eins.**   (12:15)
   Es ist **Viertel vor eins.**   (12:45)
   Es ist **drei Viertel eins.**   (12:45)
   Es ist **halb eins.**   (12:30)

3. Using **Uhr** *(o'clock)*:

   Es ist **12 Uhr 15.**   (12:15)
   Es ist **12 Uhr 30.**   (12:30)
   Es ist **12 Uhr 45.**   (12:45)

EXERCISE

Express in German:

11:45   9:10   2:30   8:40   4:15

8. Temperature

The most commonly asked questions and answers for temperature are:

Questions:

Wie warm ist es?	*How warm is it?*
Wie kalt ist es?	*How cold is it?*
Wie heiß ist es?	*How hot is it?*

Answer:

Es ist 10 Grad (Celsius).   *It is 10 degrees (Centigrade).*

READING

Abitur

Das Abitur ist die Reifeprüfung an höheren Schulen. Der Schüler beendet mit dem Abitur seine Erziehung am Gymnasium. Es berechtigt zum Studium an Universitäten oder Technischen Hochschulen. Das Abitur heißt auch Matura in Österreich.

VOCABULARY

das **Abitur**	comprehensive final exam	die **Reifeprüfung, -en**	certificate examination, comprehensive exam (synonym of **das Abitur**)
die **Reife**	maturity		
die **Prüfung, -en**	examination, test		

höher	here: secondary	berechtigen	to entitle, qualify for
sein	his	heißen, hieß	to be called, be
die Erziehung	education	*(past)*	named
das Gymnasium,	secondary school	die Mat**u**ra	*synonym of* **das**
die Gymnasien			**Abitur**

STRUCTURAL EXERCISE

Underline all contracted forms of prepositions in the above reading.

VOCABULARY EXERCISE

Give the English equivalents of the italicized words:

1. Es *berechtigt* zum Studium an Universitäten.
2. Das Abitur *heißt* auch Matura in Österreich.
3. Der Schüler beendet mit dem Abitur seine *Erziehung* am Gymnasium.
4. Das Abitur ist die *Reifeprüfung* an höheren Schulen.
5. Das Herz besteht *fast* ganz aus Muskulatur.
6. Der Schüler *beendet* mit dem Abitur seine Erziehung am Gymnasium.
7. Die Trigonometrie *verbindet* Zahlen- und Raumgrößen.

esson 14

PRONUNCIATION

German sp and st

These clusters are pronounced like / **sch** / + / **p** / and / **sch** / + / **t** /. Examples: **Spiel,
Stil.**

Pronounce the following words:

sparen	spät	Specht	Spion	sprechen
stehen	Stich	Stoff	Stuhl	Struktur

German pf and ps

In German, the / **p** / sound has to be pronounced in both clusters. Examples: **Pfad,
Psalm.**

Pronounce the following words:

Pfeffer	Pfiff	Pflege	Pflug	pfui
psi	Pseudologie	Psychologie	Psalter	

German ß

This special letter indicates an / **ss** / sound. It is pronounced like a voiceless / **s** / sound as in *hiss*.

The letter **ß** is usually called **s-z** (ess-tset). It is used in place of **ss** either:

a.   between two vowels of which the first is long. Example: **Straße.**

b.   before the letter **t**. Example: **heißt.**

c.   in final position. Example: **muß.**

Glottal Stop

The glottal stop involves a temporary closing off of the air flow through the throat passage. When the glottis is reopened, a sudden rush of air occurs. Although the glottal stop is not common in English, it can be heard between the two sounds signaling apprehension:

oh - oh

or in the admonition:

uh - uh - uh

The glottal stop accompanies initial vowel sounds in words. Say these words:

aus   ob   ein   ist

Often words are separated by glottal stops. Say the following phrases, while keeping the words separate with the glottal stop:

ein Affe   aus Ulm   er aber ist alt
ist es   an ihm

STRUCTURE

1.   Verb — nehmen

a.   The verb **nehmen** *(to take)* changes the stem vowel and the consonant in the present tense singular (third person):

INFINITIVE: **nehmen**   *to take*

THIRD PERSON ⎫
SINGULAR   ⎬ **er nimmt** ⎰ *he is taking*
PRESENT TENSE ⎭   ⎱ *he takes*
                                   he does take

b.   The plural forms of the present tense retain the infinitive stem:

Die Kinder **nehmen** den Wagen.

c.   In the past tense of **nehmen** the stem vowel **e** changes to **a** in the singular and plural forms:

Sie **nahm** das Buch. *(She took the book.)*
Die Studentinnen **nahmen** die Bücher. *(The students took the books.)*

HUNDERTSECHSUNDDREISSIG

EXERCISES

A. *Supply the correct form of* **nehmen** *in the tense indicated:*

1. Der Mann _____ die Zigarette. (past)
2. _____ die Studentinnen den Wagen? (present)
3. Der Bauer _____ die neue Getreidesorte. (present)
4. Warum _____ man es nicht? (present)
5. Welchen Wagen _____ die Chefs? (past)

B. *Give the German equivalents:*

1. Is he taking the newspaper?
2. He did not take it.
3. When are they going to take them?
4. They took them.
5. Why does he take the cigarette?

2.   Subordinating Conjunctions

a. Coordinating conjunctions connect two independent clauses without changing the word order in either clause:

Sie bleiben zu Hause, denn sie haben kein Auto.
They stay home because they don't have a car.

b. Subordinating conjunctions affect the word order of the clause introduced by a subordinating conjunction.

Sie bleiben zu Hause, **weil sie kein Auto haben.**
They stay home because they don't have a car.

c. Subordinating conjunctions move the conjugated verb form to the end of the subordinate clause:

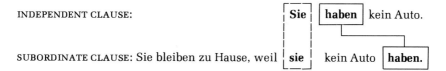

INDEPENDENT CLAUSE: **Sie** | **haben** | kein Auto.

SUBORDINATE CLAUSE: Sie bleiben zu Hause, weil **sie** kein Auto **haben.**

d. The most frequent subordinating conjunctions are:

weil	*because, since*	**bis**	*until*
daß	*that*	**ob**	*whether, if*
damit	*so that, in order that*	**als ob**	*as if*

SELF-PREPARATORY EXERCISE

Combine the following sentences using the conjunctions:*

Er fragte sie. (ob) Sie geht in die Schule.	
Die Kinder bleiben hier. (bis) Der Vater kommt.	Er fragte sie, ob sie in die Schule geht.
Sie arbeitet viel. (damit) Sie kennt das Resultat in wenigen Stunden.	Die Kinder bleiben hier, bis der Vater kommt.
Man hat errechnet. (daß) Die Strömungsgeschwindigkeit sinkt nach einer Zigarette.	Sie arbeitet viel, damit sie das Resultat in wenigen Stunden kennt.
	Man hat errechnet, daß die Strömungsgeschwindigkeit nach einer Zigarette sinkt.

EXERCISES

A. *Give the English equivalents of the subordinating conjunctions:*

1. Er wartet in der Halle, bis man ihm das Bild bringt.
2. Die Ultraschallmessung zeigt, daß die Strömungsgeschwindigkeit des Blutes nach einer Zigarette sinkt.
3. Er hilft ihnen, weil er Zeit hat.
4. Man wartete, bis man die Brechung auf dem Film registrierte.
5. Der Bauer verwendet nur natürliche Düngemittel, weil Pflanzenschutzmittel und Mineraldünger tabu sind.

B. *Combine the two sentences using the German equivalents of the indicated conjunctions:**

1. Er wartet vor dem Hotel.   (until)   Das Mädchen kommt.
2. Er untersucht. (whether, if)   Die Strömungsgeschwindigkeit des Blutes sinkt.
3. Sie helfen dem Freund.   (because, since)   Er hat viel Arbeit.
4. Der Film zeigte. (that)   Die Streuung erfolgt an den Bausteinen der Materie.
5. Die Kinder blieben in der Schule.   (until)   Die Mutter kam.

READING

Johann Gutenberg (1394–1468)

Johann Gutenberg entwickelte das Druckverfahren mit gegossenen, beweglichen Lettern. Das Verfahren ermöglichte die Herstellung von gegossenen Lettern in großen Mengen und auf schnelle Weise.

HUNDERTACHTUNDDREISSIG

Johann Gutenberg

Gutenberg Museum:
Die Druckpresse von Gutenberg

HUNDERTNEUNUNDREISSIG

Zwischen 1450 und 1455 druckte Gutenberg die erste Bibel mit Hilfe der neuen Methode. Diese Bibel hatte 42 Zeilen pro Spalte und zwei Spalten pro Seite.   5

Das neue Verfahren vereinfachte den Buchdruck. Am Ende des 15. (fünfzehnten) Jahrhunderts gab es schon zwischen 15 und 20 Millionen Bücher. Der Einfluß des vereinfachten Druckverfahrens auf das Wissen und Denken folgender Generationen ist schwer zu bestimmen.

VOCABULARY

	entwickeln	to develop
der	Druck, -e	printing; pressure, thrust
	gießen (gießt), goß gegossen	to pour, cast cast, molded (*past participle of gießen*)
	beweglich	movable
die	Letter, -n	letter, type, character
	möglich	possible
	ermöglichen	to enable, make possible
die	Herstellung	production, manufacture
die	Weise, -n	fashion, way
	zwischen	between
	drucken	to print
	erst	first
die	Bibel, -n	bible
die	Methode, -n	method
die	Zeile, -n	line
	pro	per
die	Spalte, -n	column

die	Seite, -n	page, side
	einfach	simple, simply
	vereinfachen	to simplify
der	Buchdruck	printing
das	Ende	end, conclusion
	am Ende	at the end
	fünfzehnt-	fifteenth
das	Jahrhundert, -e	century
	schon	already
der	Einfluß, ⸚sse	influence
	vereinfacht	simplified
das	Wissen	knowledge, learning
	wissen (weiß), wußte	to know
das	Denken	thought, thinking, reflection
	denken (denkt), dachte	to think
	folgend	following
	folgen	to follow
die	Generation, -en	generation
	schwer	difficult, hard
	bestimmen	to determine, to ascertain

STRUCTURAL EXERCISE

Underline all past-tense forms of weak verbs in the above reading.

VOCABULARY EXERCISE

Give the English equivalents of the italicized words:

1. Johann Gutenberg *entwickelte* das Druckverfahren mit gegossenen, beweglichen Lettern.
2. Der Einfluß auf folgende Generationen ist *schwer* zu bestimmen.
3. Gutenberg *druckte* die *erste* Bibel.
4. Das Verfahren *ermöglichte* die Herstellung von gegossenen Lettern in großer Menge.

HUNDERTVIERZIG

5. Das heutige technische *Zeitalter* ist ohne die Mathematik nicht denkbar.
6. Jeden *Herbst* beginnt eine neue Saison für die Volkshochschulen.
7. Das neue Verfahren *vereinfachte* den Buchdruck.

STRUCTURE

3. Word Order — Subordinate Clauses

Thus far, all of our examples have demonstrated the word order of main and subordinate clauses when appearing in this sequence:

MAIN CLAUSE: **Sie bleiben zu Hause,**
SUBORDINATE CLAUSE: **weil sie kein Auto haben.**

This sequence may also be reversed. The sentence then begins with the subordinate clause, which retains its established word order. The main clause, however, now begins with the inflected verb:

SUBORDINATE CLAUSE: **Weil sie kein Auto haben,**
MAIN CLAUSE: **bleiben sie zu Hause.**

SELF-PREPARATORY EXERCISE

Combine the two sentences with the German equivalents of the subordinating conjunctions:

(until) Der Vater kommt. Die Kinder bleiben hier.	
(because) Er hat Zeit. Er hilft ihnen.	Bis der Vater kommt, bleiben die Kinder hier.
(that) Er lernt viel Deutsch. Der Professor glaubt.	Weil er Zeit hat, hilft er ihnen.
	Daß er viel Deutsch lernt, glaubt der Professor.

EXERCISE

Combine the two sentences, using the German equivalents of the subordinating conjunctions:*

1. (because)   Er hat viel Arbeit. Sie helfen dem Freund.
2. (until)   Die Mutter kam. Die Kinder blieben in der Schule.
3. (because)   Pflanzenschutzmittel sind tabu. Der Bauer verwendet nur natürliche Düngemittel.
4. (that)   Sie gab ihm das Buch. Er glaubt (es) nicht.

4.   Negation — <u>kein</u> (continued)

a.   There are two basic ways to negate a sentence in German, using either **nicht** or **kein.**

b.   **Kein** is used only before a noun and is equivalent to English *not a* or *not any.* **Nicht** is used in all other situations to negate a statement:

Er hat **keinen Freund.** *(He does not have any friend.)*
Er kennt den Mann **nicht.** *(He does not know the man.)*

c.   **Kein** uses the same endings as the indefinite article **ein,** according to the gender, number, and case of the noun which it precedes:

	SINGULAR			PLURAL
	MASCULINE	FEMININE	NEUTER	ALL GENDERS
NOMINATIVE	kein	keine	kein	keine
GENITIVE	keines	keiner	keines	keiner
DATIVE	keinem	keiner	keinem	keinen
ACCUSATIVE	keinen	keine	kein	keine

d.   Remember that all nouns add the ending **-n** in the dative plural, except when the nominative plural already ends in **-n (die Frauen)** or in **-s (die Autos).**

EXERCISES

A.   *Supply the correct ending for* **kein:**

1.   Er hat kein_____ Haus.
2.   Die Schüler haben kein_____ Bücher.
3.   Sie schickt ihm kein_____ Karte.
4.   Viele Menschen haben kein_____ Zeit.
5.   Man liest kein_____ Zeitung in diesem Büro.

B.   *Give the German equivalents:*

1.   The children do not sing any songs.
2.   There are not any pictures in this book.
3.   The farmer does not use any mineral fertilizers.
4.   He does not have any work.
5.   She did not buy him a suit.

HUNDERTZWEIUNDVIERZIG

5.   Possessive Adjectives

a.   Possessive adjectives express a possessive relationship:

That is *his car.*
That is *her sister.*

In these examples, *his* and *her* are possessive adjectives. They establish the owner of the car (first example) and a possessive relationship (second example).

b.   The German equivalents for the following English possessive adjectives are:

sein = *his, its*
ihr = *her, their*

c.   In German, the possessive adjectives use the same declensional endings as the indefinite articles and **kein:**

	SINGULAR			PLURAL
	MASCULINE	FEMININE	NEUTER	ALL GENDERS
NOMINATIVE	-	**-e**	-	**-e**
GENITIVE	**-es**	**-er**	**-es**	**-er**
DATIVE	**-em**	**-er**	**-em**	**-en**
ACCUSATIVE	**-en**	**-e**	-	**-e**

d.   Possessive adjectives modify nouns. Consequently, their endings must correspond to the case, gender, and number of the nouns they modify:

Er gibt **seinem Vater** das Buch.

seinem is a possessive adjective, singular, masculine (gender of the noun / **der Vater**), and is used in the dative case.

e.   Note that there are no endings on the possessive adjectives and in the following cases:

NOMINATIVE SINGULAR: MASCULINE AND NEUTER:

Das ist **sein Wagen.**   *(That is his car.)*
Das ist **sein Haus.**   *(That is his house.)*

ACCUSATIVE SINGULAR: NEUTER:

Sie zeigt mir **ihr Buch.**   *(She shows me her book.)*

HUNDERTDREIUNDVIERZIG

EXERCISES

A. *Supply the possessive adjective endings:*

1. Sie kennt sein_____ Bruder.
2. Sie liest in ihr_____ Buch.
3. Er fährt mit ihr_____ Wagen.
4. Wegen sein_____ Arbeit bleibt er in Berlin.
5. Er fragte nach ihr_____ Studium.

B. *Supply the possessive adjectives in German:*

1. Sie singen _____ Lieder.   (their)
2. Er lief um _____ Haus.   (his)
3. Der Student kennt _____ Schwester nicht.   (her)
4. _____ Wagen ist hier.   (his)
5. Sie denkt an _____ Mutter.   (her)

C. *Give the German equivalents:*

1. The professor reads in his book.
2. Her child is playing.
3. They know their chidren.
4. He shows the picture to his friend.
5. She is waiting for her boyfriend.

6. Ein-Word Phrases

a. The **ein**-words of the following phrases use the same endings as the possessive adjectives and **kein**. The endings are determined by the gender, number, and case of the noun they describe:

was für ein	*what a, what kind of a*
solch ein	*such a*
welch ein	*what a*

Examples:

Was für eine Zeitung ist das?	*(What kind of a newspaper is that?)*
Solch ein schöner Tag!	*(Such a beautiful day!)*
Welch eine Überraschung!	*(What a surprise!)*

b. The most frequently used phrase is **was für ein**. Note that these phrases may also be used in the dative or accusative case:

Was für einen Wagen fährt er?	*(What kind of a car does he drive?)* (accusative)
An was für einer Universität studiert er?	*(At what kind of a university does he study?) (dative)*

EXERCISES

A. *Supply the correct endings of the* **ein**-*words:*

1. Was für ein_____ Getreidesorte verwendet der Bauer?
2. Solch ein_____ Buch!
3. Was für ein_____ Methode verwendet er?
4. Solch ein_____ Wagen fährt er!
5. In was für ein_____ Labor geht er?

B. *Give the German equivalents:*

1. What kind of a newspaper is he reading?
2. Such a day!
3. What kind of a table are they buying?
4. Such a world!
5. What kind of a book is he talking about?

7. Arithmetic

Following are the basic German arithmetic expressions:

+	**plus, und**
−	**minus, weniger**
×, •	**mal, multipliziert mit**
:, /	**geteilt durch, dividiert durch**

Examples:

$3 + 4 = 7$ **Drei plus (und) vier ist sieben.**

$5 - 3 = 2$ **Fünf weniger (minus) drei ist zwei.**

$\left.\begin{array}{l} 2 \times 6 = 12 \\ 2 \cdot 6 = 12 \end{array}\right\}$ **Zwei mal sechs ist zwölf.**

$\left.\begin{array}{l} 12 : 3 = 4 \\ 12 / 3 = 4 \end{array}\right\}$ **Zwölf geteilt durch drei ist vier.**

EXERCISE

Write out the following arithmetic expressions:

$2 + 3 =$	$25 - 21 =$	$2 \cdot 2 =$	$16 : 4 =$
$7 + 16 =$	$22 - 12 =$	$5 \times 5 =$	$21 : 4 =$
$11 + 17 =$	$19 - 12 =$	$27/3 =$	

READING

Das Klima

Deutschland hat ein kühles, gemäßigtes Klima. Die Temperaturunterschiede zwischen Sommer und Winter sind geringer als in Nordamerika. Durch den warmen Golfstrom und die Landschaftsformen ist das Klima wärmer als in den gleichen Breitengraden der USA. Die durchschnittlichen Temperaturen im Sommer sind um 18° (Grad) Celsius (64° Fahrenheit). Die wärmsten Temperaturen sind am Rhein, am   5
Main, am Neckar und am Bodensee. Im Januar liegt die Temperatur durchschnittlich bei – 2° (minus zwei Grad Celsius) (29° Fahrenheit). Die kältesten Temperaturen sind in den Gebirgen; dort fällt auch der meiste Schnee und Regen. Deutschlands Klima ist vorwiegend maritim, nach Osten wird es kontinental. Im Osten Deutschlands sind also die Sommer wärmer und die Winter kälter.   10

VOCABULARY

	kühl	cool	
	gemäßigt	moderate, temperate	
die	**Temperatur, -en**	temperature	
der	**Unterschied, -e**	variation, difference	
der	**Sommer**	summer	
der	**Winter**	winter	
	gering	small, little	
	geringer als	less than, smaller than	
	nord	north	
	durch	through, because of, as a result of	
der	**Golf, -e**	gulf	
der	**Strom, ̈e**	stream	
der	**Golfstrom, ̈e**	gulf stream	
	warm	warm	
	wärmer als	warmer than	
	gleich	same, equal	
	breit	wide	
der	**Grad, -e**	degree	
der	**Breitengrad, -e**	degree of latitude	
	durchschnittlich	(on the) average	
	Celsius	centigrade	
der	**Rhein**	Rhine river	

der	**Main**	Main river	
der	**Neckar**	Neckar river	
der	**Bodensee**	Lake Constance	
	liegt bei	*here:* is at	
	kalt	cold	
	kälter	colder	
	kältest	coldest	
das	**Gebirge, -**	mountain range, mountains	
	dort	there	
	fallen (fällt), fiel	to fall	
	meist	most	
der	**meiste**	most of the	
der	**Schnee**	snow	
der	**Regen**	rain	
	vorwiegend	predominantly, primarily	
	maritim	maritime	
der	**Osten**	east	
	nach Osten	towards the east	
	kontinental	continental	
	also	consequently, therefore	

STRUCTURAL EXERCISE

Underline the following items in the above reading:

1. Dative prepositions (solid line).
2. Accusative prepositions (dotted line).
3. Two-way prepositions (wavy line).

HUNDERTSECHSUNDVIERZIG

VOCABULARY EXERCISE

Give the English equivalents of the italicized words:

1. Die kältesten Temperaturen sind in den *Gebirgen.*
2. Deutschlands Klima ist *vorwiegend* maritim.
3. Im Januar liegt die Temperatur *durchschnittlich* bei −2° Grad Celsius.
4. Die *gesamte* Blutmenge des Menschen beträgt etwa 5 Liter.
5. Das Herz *befördert* am Tag etwa 5 760 Liter Blut.
6. Das Klima in Deutschland ist wärmer als in den *gleichen* Breitengraden der USA.
7. Einstein *erklärte* den photoelektrischen Effekt.

Lesson 15

PRONUNCIATION

Contrast Exercises — Vowels

Long / a / versus short / a /

| Wahn | wann | Made | Matte |
| lasen | lassen | Saat | satt |

Long / e / versus short / e /

| Heer | Herr | Beet | Bett |
| Wesen | wessen | legen | Lecken |

Long / i / versus short / i /

| Lied | litt | ihn | in |
| Miene | Minne | Stil | still |

Long / o / versus short / o /

| Mode | Motte | Oder | Otter |
| Sohn | Sonne | Polen | Pollen |

Long / u / versus short / u /

| Huhn | Hunne | Mus | muß |
| Mut | Mutter | Luv | Luft |

Long / ä / versus short / ä /

| wähle | Wälle | käme | Kämme |
| Hähne | Hände | wähnte | Wände |

Long / ö / versus short / ö /

| Goethe | Götter | mögen | möchte |
| Öfen | öffnen | König | können |

HUNDERTACHTUNDVIERZIG

Long / ü / versus short / ü /

Sühne	Sünde	Düse	düster
Mühle	Müller	lügen	Lücken

Sound Sequence

mit Rat und Tat	Spott und Hohn
Knall und Fall	Zug um Zug
auf Hieb und Stich	kurz und gut
auf Schritt und Tritt	in Hülle und Fülle
Sonne und Mond	hüben und drüben

STRUCTURE

1.   Subordinating Conjunctions (continued)

a.   As we have seen, the subordinating conjunction moves the verb to the end of the subordinate clause:

MAIN CLAUSE: Sie bleiben zu Hause,
SUBORDINATE CLAUSE: weil sie kein Auto **haben.**

b.   Following is a list of other subordinating conjunctions:

während	*while*	**obgleich**	
da	*because, since*	**obschon**	*although, even though*
wie	*as, how*	**obwohl**	

SELF-PREPARATORY EXERCISE

Combine the sentences, using the subordinating conjunction indicated:*

Die Kinder blieben zu Hause. (während) Die Mutter ging in das Büro.	
Der Bauer verwendet nur Mineraldünger. (obwohl) Die Ernte ist niedriger.	Die Kinder blieben zu Hause, während die Mutter in das Büro ging.
Der Student arbeitet viel. (da) Er hat eine Prüfung.	Der Bauer verwendet nur Mineraldünger, obwohl die Ernte niedriger ist.
Der Herz befördert am Tag 5 760 Liter Blut. (wie) Man errechnete (es).	Der Student arbeitet viel, da er eine Prüfung hat.
	Das Herz befördert am Tag 5 760 Liter Blut, wie man errechnete.

EXERCISES

A. *Give the English equivalents of the subordinating conjunctions:*

1. Der Mann arbeitet schnell, obwohl er viel Zeit hat.
2. Immer mehr Erwachsene gehen zur Volkshochschule, wie man errechnete.
3. Seine Frau ist im Büro, während er im Labor arbeitet.
4. Die Herstellung von beweglichen Lettern war wichtig, da sie den Buchdruck vereinfachte.
5. Das Klima in Deutschland ist gemäßigt, weil es den Golfstrom gibt.

B. *Combine the sentences with the German equivalents of the subordinating conjunctions:* *

1. Im Osten Deutschlands sind die Winter kälter. (because) Das Klima ist vorwiegend kontinental.
2. Der Bauer erzielt eine hohe Ernte. (although) Er hat nicht viel Land.
3. Einstein untersuchte den photoelektrischen Effekt. (as) Man weiß (es).
4. Das heutige technische Zeitalter ist ohne die Mathematik nicht denkbar. (since) Sie ist die Grundlage für alle technischen Berufe.
5. Man richtet einen gebündelten Röntgenstrahl auf ein Material. (because) Eine Streuung erfolgt an den Bausteinen der Materie.

C. *Subordinating and coordinating conjunctions. Combine the sentences with the respective conjunction:* *

1. Er ist kein Student. (sondern) Er ist Lehrer.
2. Die Ernte ist etwas niedriger. (aber) Sie erzielt höhere Preise.
3. Die Studentin arbeitet schnell. (da) Sie hat keine Zeit.
4. Gutenberg entwickelte das Druckverfahren mit beweglichen Lettern. (und) Er vereinfachte mit diesem Verfahren den Buchdruck.
5. Der Schüler bleibt auf dem Gymnasium. (bis) Er beendet seine Erziehung mit dem Arbitur.

SELF-PREPARATORY EXERCISE

Combine the two sentences with the subordinate clause in first position: *

(da) Er arbeitet in dem Büro. Er ist der Chef.	
(obwohl) Sie hat keine Zeit. Sie hilft ihnen.	Da er in dem Büro arbeitet, ist er der Chef.
(wie) Man weiß (es). Einstein untersuchte den photoelektrischen Effekt.	Obwohl sie keine Zeit hat, hilft sie ihnen.
	Wie man weiß, untersuchte Einstein den photoelektrischen Effekt.

HUNDERTFÜNFZIG

EXERCISE

*Combine the two sentences with the subordinate clause in first position:**

1. (obwohl)   Der Bauer hat nicht viel Land. Er erzielt eine große Ernte.
2. (da)   Die Studentin hat eine Prüfung. Sie arbeitet viel.
3. (während)   Die Mutter ging ins Büro. Die Kinder blieben zu Hause.
4. (wie)   Man errechnete (es). Das Herz befördert am Tag 5 760 Liter Blut.
5. (da)   Das Klima ist vorwiegend kontinental. Die Winter im Osten Deutschlands sind kälter.

2.   Irregular Verb — <u>wissen</u>

a.   The verb **wissen** *(to know)* is an irregular verb. It does not follow the normal conjugational patterns:

b.   In the present tense singular, the stem vowel shifts from **i** to **ei**:

INFINITIVE   **wissen**

PRESENT TENSE	**Das Kind weiß.**	*The child knows.*
THIRD PERSON	**Er weiß.**	*He knows.*
SINGULAR	**Sie weiß.**	*She knows.*
	Es weiß.	*It knows.*
	Man weiß.	*One knows.*

c.   The present-tense plural form retains the infinitive stem:

PRESENT TENSE:	**Sie wissen.**	*They know.*
THIRD PERSON PLURAL:	**Die Menschen wissen.**	*People know.*

d.   The past tense of **wissen** is irregular. The infinitive stem vowel **i** shifts to the past tense form **u**. In addition, **wissen** adds the weak past-tense ending **-te**:

PAST TENSE	**Er wußte.**	*he knew*
THIRD PERSON	**Sie wußte.**	*she knew*
SINGULAR	**Es wußte.**	*it knew*
	Man wußte.	*one knew*
	Das Kind wußte.	*The child knew.*

PAST TENSE		
THIRD PERSON	**Sie wußten.**	*They knew*
PLURAL	**Die Kinder wußten.**	*The children knew.*

SELF-PREPARATORY EXERCISE

Supply the correct form of **wissen:**

He knew it.	
They knew the results.	Er wußte es.
She knows the word.	Sie wußten die Ergebnisse.
One does not know it.	Sie weiß das Wort.
How did he know it?	Man weiß es nicht.
	Wie wußte er es?

EXERCISE

Supply the correct form of **wissen:**

1. Er _____ den Namen nicht.   (present tense)
2. _____ sie *(she)* das Wort?   (past tense)
3. Warum _____ sie *(they)* es nicht?   (past tense)
4. Immer mehr Menschen _____ es.   (present tense)
5. Er _____ nicht, was für ein Klima Deutschland hat.   (past tense)

READING

Afrika

Afrika ist der drittgrößte Erdteil. Dort leben rund 350 Millionen Menschen.

Der Äquator verläuft mitten durch den Kontinent. Afrika ist ein tropischer Erdteil und ist reich an Bodenschätzen: Kupfer, Diamanten, Gold, Uran, Erdöl, Erdgas, Baumwolle, Kakao, Bananen, Kaffee, Erdnüsse, Sisal und Kautschuk. Trotz des natürlichen Reichtums sind die meisten Länder Afrikas Entwicklungsländer. Die in- industrielle Entwicklung Afrikas ist noch nicht auf dem Niveau der Industrieländer.   5

VOCABULARY

drittgrößt-	third largest	der **Kontinent, -e**	continent
die **Erde**	earth, globe, soil	**tropisch**	tropical
der **Erdteil, -e**	continent	**reich**	rich
der **Äquator**	equator	**reich an**	rich in, abundant in
verlaufen (verläuft), verlief	to pass; to run; to take its course	der **Boden, ⸚**	soil, bottom, ground, floor, base
mitten	midway		
mitten durch	through the middle, right through	der **Schatz, ⸚e**	treasure, wealth
		die **Bodenschätze** *(pl.)*	mineral wealth, mineral resources

das **Kupfer**	copper	der **Kautschuk**	rubber
der **Diamant, -en**	diamond	**trotz**	despite, in spite of
das **Gold**	gold		
das **Uran**	uranium	der **Reichtum, ⸚er**	wealth
das **Erdöl**	oil, petroleum, mineral oil	die **Entwicklung, -en**	development
		das **Entwicklungsland, ⸚er**	developing country
das **Erdgas**	natural gas		
der **Kakao**	cocoa	**industriell**	industrial
die **Banane, -n**	banana	**noch nicht**	not yet
der **Kaffee**	coffee	das **Niveau**	level, standard, niveau
die **Erdnuß, ⸚sse**	peanut		
der **Sisal**	sisal	die **Industrie, -n**	industry

VOCABULARY EXERCISE

Give the English equivalents of the italicized words:

1. Afrika ist der drittgrößte *Erdteil.*
2. Afrika ist reich an *Bodenschätzen.*
3. Die industrielle *Entwicklung* ist noch nicht auf dem Niveau der Industrieländer.
4. Die *meisten* Länder sind Entwicklungsländer.
5. Das Abitur *berechtigt* zum Studium an den Universitäten.
6. Die *durchschnittlichen* Temperaturen sind um 18° (achtzehn Grad) Celsius.
7. Deutschlands Klima ist *vorwiegend* maritim.

STRUCTURE

3. Verbs — Principal Parts

a.   Each verb in German has four principal parts or components:

infinitive
present tense (third person singular)
past tense (third person singular)
past participle

b.   The first three components are familiar to you:

	WEAK VERB	STRONG VERB
INFINITIVE	**fragen**	**sehen**
PRESENT TENSE	**fragt**	**sieht**
PAST TENSE	**fragte**	**sah**

4.   Past Participle

A past participle is used to form compound tenses, the present perfect and past perfect:

He has asked.
He has seen.

In the above example, *asked* and *seen* are past participles used to form the present perfect tense.

5.   Weak Past Participle

In German, the past participle of weak verbs is usually formed by:

> **ge** + verb stem + **t**

Example:

> **ge + frag + t**   = **gefragt**

SELF-PREPARATORY EXERCISE

Give the past participle of the following weak verbs:

folgen	
lernen	gefolgt
suchen	gelernt
spielen	gesucht
machen	gespielt
glauben	gemacht
haben	geglaubt
	gehabt

suchen = *to look for, to seek*

6.   Stem Ending in -d, -t, or -n

Weak verbs whose stems end in **-d**, **-t**, or **-n** add **e** between the verb stem and the final **-t**:

> **ge** + verb stem + **e** + **t**

HUNDERTVIERUNDFÜNFZIG

Example:

ge + wart + e + t	= gewartet
ge + bild + e + t	= gebildet
ge + leugn + e + t	= geleugnet

7. Stem Ending in -ier

Verbs with stems ending in **-ier** do not add **ge-** to form the past participle:

verb stem + **t**

Example:

studier + t	= **studiert**

SELF-PREPARATORY EXERCISE

*Give the past participle of the following verbs:**

antworten	
definieren	geantwortet
arbeiten	definiert
bilden	gearbeitet
variieren	gebildet
	variiert

EXERCISES

A. *Give the past participle:**

1. legen   3. führen   5. rauchen
2. sparen   4. hören

B. *Give the past participle:**

1. bilden   3. arbeiten   5. warten
2. leugnen   4. richten

C. *Give the past participle:**

1. analysieren   3. registrieren   5. studieren
2. definieren   4. variieren

READING

Absoluter Nullpunkt

Absoluter Nullpunkt bedeutet: es ist die tiefste, theoretisch mögliche Temperatur von 273,16 (zweihundertdreiundsiebzig Komma sechzehn) Grad unter Null, bezogen auf das Celsius Thermometer.

VOCABULARY

absolut	absolute	**beziehen (auf),**	to base (upon)
die **Null, -en**	zero	**bezog**	
der **Punkt, -e**	point	**bezogen**	based (*past*
der **Nullpunkt, -e**	zero point		*participle*)
tief	deep, low		
tiefst-	deepest,		
	lowest		

VOCABULARY EXERCISE

Give the English equivalents of the italicized words:

1. Der absolute Nullpunkt ist die tiefste, theoretisch *mögliche* Temperatur.
2. Afrika ist *reich* an Bodenschätzen.
3. Die industrielle Entwicklung ist *noch nicht* auf dem Niveau der Industrieländer.
4. Die kältesten Temperaturen sind in den *Gebirgen*.
5. Das neue Verfahren *vereinfachte* den Buchdruck.
6. Der *Einfluß* auf das Wissen und Denken ist schwer zu bestimmen.
7. Das Abitur *heißt* auch Matura in Österreich.

Lesson 16

STRUCTURE

1. Present Perfect Tense — Weak Verbs

a. German weak verbs form the present perfect tense, as in English, with two components — the verb **haben** or **sein** as auxiliary and a past participle:

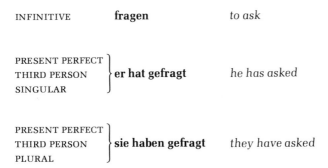

INFINITIVE	**fragen**	*to ask*

PRESENT PERFECT THIRD PERSON SINGULAR **er hat gefragt** — *he has asked*

PRESENT PERFECT THIRD PERSON PLURAL **sie haben gefragt** — *they have asked*

The German present perfect has two meanings in English, depending on the context: **Er hat gefragt** may mean *He asked* or *He has asked.*

SELF-PREPARATORY EXERCISE

Form the present perfect tense with the elements given: *

EXAMPLE: (er / fragen) Er hat gefragt.

(er / suchen)	
(man / lernen)	Er hat gesucht.
(es / arbeiten)	Man hat gelernt.
(sie [pl.] / antworten)	Es hat gearbeitet.
(die Studentin / warten)	Sie haben geantwortet.
(sie [sing.] / suchen)	Die Studentin hat gewartet.
(der Student / studieren)	Sie hat gesucht.
(das Kind / spielen)	Der Student hat studiert.
	Das Kind hat gespielt.

EXERCISES

A. *Supply the past participle of the verb indicated by the English equivalent:*

  1. Man hat _____.   (to wait)
  2. Die Männer haben _____.   (to smoke)
  3. Die Kinder haben _____.   (to play)
  4. Der Physiker hat _____.   (to analyse)
  5. Sie hat _____.   (to answer)

B. *Form sentences in the present perfect with the elements given:* *

  1. man / glauben   4. der Professor / definieren
  2. der Chef / antworten   5. zehn Tiere / legen
  3. die Schüler / lernen

C. *Give the German equivalents:*

  1. The man has smoked.   3. She has believed.   5. He has defined.
  2. The farmer has answered. 4. They have denied.

2.   Word Order — Present Perfect Tense

In statements, the auxiliary verb **haben** occupies the second position, that is, after the subject or another sentence element in first position. The past participle is in last position:

Er **hat** den Lehrer nicht **gefragt.** *(He has not asked the teacher.)*

HUNDERTACHTUNDFÜNFZIG

SELF-PREPARATORY EXERCISE

Form sentences in the present perfect tense using the elements given:

EXAMPLE: (Er / seinem Freund / es / sagen)
Er hat es seinem Freund gesagt.

man / glauben / dem Kind / nicht	
er / die Bibel / drucken	Man hat dem Kind nicht geglaubt.
sie *(pl.)* / den Wagen / hier / suchen	Er hat die Bibel gedruckt.
die Schüler / in der Schule / warten	Sie haben den Wagen hier gesucht.
die Studentin / Deutsch / studieren	Die Schüler haben in der Schule gewartet.
	Die Studentin hat Deutsch studiert.

EXERCISES

A. *Change the following sentences to present perfect:**

    1. Der Student studiert in Deutschland.
    2. Gutenberg druckt die erste Bibel.
    3. Man analysiert Proteinstrukturen.
    4. Die Filme registrieren das Brechungsmuster.
    5. Sie raucht keine Zigaretten.

B. *Form sentences in the present perfect with the elements given:**

    1. der Chef / das Resultat / nicht / hören
    2. man / glauben / dem Kaiser / immer
    3. der Mann / schwer / arbeiten
    4. die Wand / trennen / den Speicher / und / den Wohnraum
    5. die Schüler / eine Fremdsprache / in der Schule / lernen

3. Word Order — Present Perfect Tense (continued)

a. Questions without question words in the present perfect tense have the following word order: The auxiliary verb **haben** is in first position; the past participle is in last position:

Hat der Student in Deutschland **studiert?**
Has the student studied in Germany?
Did the student study in Germany?

b. Questions with question words form the present perfect tense with the auxiliary **haben** in second position and the past participle in last position:

Wo **hat** der Student **studiert?**
Where has the student studied?
Where did the student study?

c. Subordinate clauses (clauses introduced by a subordinating conjunction) form the present perfect tense with the past participle and the auxiliary verb **haben** in last position:

Er weiß, daß Gutenberg die erste Bibel **gedruckt hat.**
He knows that Gutenberg (has) printed the first bible.

EXERCISES

A. *Change the following statements and questions to present perfect:**

1. Lernt sie eine Fremdsprache?
2. Wie leben die Menschen in Österreich?
3. Er weiß, daß sie es leugnet.
4. Hört der Chef das Resultat?
5. Wo leben die Tiere?

B. *Give the German equivalents in the present perfect:*

1. When did he smoke?
2. Has she heard it?
3. He has analyzed the structure.
4. They know that she (has) waited in school.
5. When did he define it?

READING

Kreislaufkollaps

Die Regenwälder am Amazonas sind mit ihrer Vielfalt an Pflanzen und Tierarten ein Dorado für Wissenschaftler. Dieses äußerst komplizierte Ökosystem reagiert empfindlich auf Eingriffe durch die Zivilisation. Der Mensch zerstört das Ökosystem durch eine Unterbrechung des natürlichen Kreislaufs.

Ökologen plädieren für die Erhaltung der urwüchsigen amphibischen Landschaft   5
und ihres einmaligen Innenlebens.

VOCABULARY

der **Kreis, -e**	circle	der **Kreislauf**	cycle, circulation
der **Lauf, ⁼e**	circulation course, flow, pace	der **Kollaps**	breakdown
		der **Regen**	rain

HUNDERTSECHZIG

der **Wald, -er**	forest, woods	der **Eingriff, -e**	interference, intervention
der **Regenwald, -er**	rain forest		
der **Amazonas**	*Amazon river in South America*	die **Zivilisation**	civilization
		zerstören	to destroy
die **Vielfalt**	multitude	die **Unterbrechung, -en**	interruption, break
das **Dorado**	*short for Eldorado, the land of fabulous wealth*	der **Ökologe, -n**	ecologist
		plädieren	to plead
		die **Erhaltung**	preservation, conservation
der **Wissenschaftler, -**	scientist		
äußerst	extremely, highly	**urwüchsig**	original, native
kompliziert	complex, complicated	**amphibisch**	amphibious
		die **Landschaft, -en**	landscape
das **System, -e**	system	**einmalig**	unique
das **Ökosystem, -e**	ecosystem, ecological system	das **Leben**	life
		das **Innenleben**	interior life, inner life; *here:* specific environment, life cycle
reagieren auf	to react to, respond to		
empfindlich	sensitively *(adverb)*		

STRUCTURAL EXERCISES

A. *Underline all two-way prepositions in the above reading.*

B. *Give the English equivalents of the following idiomatic expressions:*

1. reagieren auf   4. berechtigen zu   6. führen zu
2. plädieren für   5. bestehen aus   7. zerfallen in
3. beziehen auf

VOCABULARY EXERCISE

Give the English equivalents of the italicized words:

1. Der Mensch *zerstört* das Ökosystem.
2. Man plädiert für die *Erhaltung* der urwüchsigen Landschaft.
3. Das *äußerst* komplizierte Ökosystem reagiert empfindlich auf Eingriffe.
4. Man plädiert für die Erhaltung des *einmaligen* Innenlebens.
5. Der Äquator *verläuft* mitten durch den Kontinent.
6. Das System reagiert *empfindlich* auf Eingriffe.
7. Das Klima Deutschlands ist wärmer als in den *gleichen* Breitengraden in den USA.

STRUCTURE

4. Past Participle — Strong Verbs

a. The changes in the stem vowels and consonants that we observed in some past-tense forms also occur in most past participles of these same strong verbs.

b. English also has strong past participle forms:

INFINITIVE: to drive   PAST PARTICIPLE: driven
           to buy   bought
           to sing   sung

c. In German, the strong past participle is usually formed by:

> **ge** + past participle stem + **en**

Example:

> **ge + fund + en**   = gefunden   INFINITIVE: **finden**

d. From now on, it will help you to memorize the four principle parts of strong verbs:

INFINITIVE		**geben**	*to give*
PRESENT TENSE THIRD PERSON SINGULAR	(er)	**gibt**	*(he) gives*
PAST TENSE THIRD PERSON SINGULAR	(er)	**gab**	*(he) gave*
PAST PARTICIPLE THIRD PERSON SINGULAR	(er hat)	**gegeben**	*(he has) given*

e. This stem vowel variation in principle parts may be summarized as follows: **fahren (ä), u, -.**

These abbreviated forms indicate:

INFINITIVE:	**fahren**	*to go, drive*
PRESENT TENSE THIRD PERSON SINGULAR	**(er) fährt**	*(he) goes, drives*
PAST TENSE THIRD PERSON SINGULAR	**(er) fuhr**	*(he) went, drove*
PAST PARTICIPLE	**(er ist) gefahren**	*(he has) gone, driven*

HUNDERTZWEIUNDSECHZIG

f.   Depending on the changes the strong verb undergoes in the formation of the past participle, it can be grouped into one of three categories:

     1.   No change in the stem vowel or stem consonant: the infinitive stem and the past participle stem are identical;

     2.   Only the stem vowel changes;

     3.   The stem vowel and in some instances the stem consonant change; these verbs also use the weak verb participle ending **(-t)** for the past participle; the verb is irregular.

g.   Note that Appendix 2 of this book contains a list of the most frequent strong and irregular verbs in German.

h.   The following strong verbs from previous lessons retain their infinitive stem in the formation of the past participle:

GROUP A

INFINITIVE	PAST PARTICIPLE	ENGLISH MEANING
fahren	**gefahren**	*to go, to drive*
fallen	**gefallen**	*to fall*
fressen	**gefressen**	*to eat*
geben	**gegeben**	*to give*
halten	**gehalten**	*to hold, to stop*
heißen	**geheißen**	*to be called*
kommen	**gekommen**	*to come*
lassen	**gelassen**	*to let*
messen	**gemessen**	*to measure*
schlafen	**geschlafen**	*to sleep*
sehen	**gesehen**	*to see*
tragen	**getragen**	*to carry; to wear*
wachsen	**gewachsen**	*to grow*

i.   The following group of strong verbs change the stem vowel from the infinitive to the past participle:

GROUP B

INFINITIVE	PAST PARTICIPLE	ENGLISH MEANING
ei	**ie**	
bleiben	**geblieben**	*to stay, to remain*
schreiben	**geschrieben**	*to write*

HUNDERTDREIUNDSECHZIG

INFINITIVE	PAST PARTICIPLE	ENGLISH MEANING

ie	**e**

| liegen | gelegen | *to lie* |

ie	**o**

fliegen	geflogen	*to fly*
gießen	gegossen	*to pour*
wiegen	gewogen	*to weigh*

e	**o**

helfen	geholfen	*to help*
sprechen	gesprochen	*to speak, talk*
sterben	gestorben	*to die*

i	**o**

| spinnen | gesponnen | *to spin* |
| schwimmen | geschwommen | *to swim* |

i	**u**

finden	gefunden	*to find*
singen	gesungen	*to sing*
sinken	gesunken	*to sink; to decrease*

ä	**a**

| hängen | gehangen | *to hang* |

j. The following group of verbs show changes in the stem vowel and in some instances in the stem consonant; they will also use the weak verb participle ending (**-t**) to form the past participle:

GROUP C

e	**a**

kennen	gekannt	*to know*
nennen	genannt	*to call*
rennen	gerannt	*to run*

HUNDERTVIERUNDSECHZIG

INFINITIVE	PAST PARTICIPLE	ENGLISH MEANING

Stem-consonant change

denken	**gedacht**	*to think*
stehen	**gestanden**	*to stand*
gehen	**gegangen**	*to go*

i	a

bringen	**gebracht**	*to bring; to take*

i	u

wissen	**gewußt**	*to know*

i	o

ziehen	**gezogen**	*to pull*

SELF-PREPARATORY EXERCISE

Form the past participles of the following strong verbs. The stem-vowel changes are indicated in parentheses:*

finden (u)	
singen (u)	gefunden
helfen (o)	gesungen
sprechen (o)	geholfen
fliegen (o)	gesprochen
fahren (-)	geflogen
hängen (a)	gefahren
bleiben (ie)	gehangen
schreiben (ie)	geblieben
geben (-)	geschrieben
lesen (-)	gegeben
schlafen (-)	gelesen
liegen (e)	geschlafen
sehen (-)	gelegen
	gesehen

Abraham Lincoln

THE BETTMAN ARCHIVE, INC.

HUNDERTSECHSUNDSECHZIG

EXERCISE

Give the past participle forms of the following strong verbs:*

1. fahren	5. denken	8. wissen
2. lesen	6. finden	9. stehen
3. helfen	7. sprechen	10. bringen
4. geben		

READING

Abraham Lincoln (1809–1865)

Lincoln war der 16. (sechzehnte) Präsident der Vereinigten Staaten (1861–1865). Er stammte aus einer armen Familie. Er war Advokat und Abgeordneter im Parlament von Illinois (1834–1841) und im Kongreß (1847–1849). Von 1856 an begann sein schneller Aufstieg in der Republikanischen Partei. Er vertrat eine gemäßigte Ansicht in der Sklavenfrage. Er war ein glänzender, volkstümlicher Redner und ein 5 gewandter Parteitaktiker. Man nominierte ihn 1860 in Chicago als Präsidentschaftskandidat. Die Grundsätze seiner Politik formulierte Lincoln in seiner Rede auf dem Schlachtfeld von Gettysburg (1863): „Eine Regierung des Volkes durch das Volk für das Volk." Nach dem Ende des Bürgerkrieges zielte Lincolns Politik auf eine schnelle Wiedereingliederung der besiegten Südstaaten, aber er stieß auf den Wider- 10 stand des radikalen Segments der Partei.

Seine Gegner verhinderten jedoch nicht seine Wiederwahl (1864). Der Fanatiker J. W. Booth ermordete Lincoln im Jahre 1865.

VOCABULARY

der	**Präsident, -en**	president	der **Sklave, -n**	slave
	stammen aus	to come from, stem from, originate	die **Frage, -n**	question
			glänzend	splendid, brilliant
	arm	poor	**volkstümlich**	popular
die	**Familie, -n**	family	der **Redner, -**	speaker, orator
der	**Advokat, -en**	lawyer	**gewandt**	skillful, versatile
der	**Abgeordnete, -n**	representative	der **Taktiker, -**	tactician
das	**Parlament, -e**	parliament	**nominieren**	to nominate
der	**Kongreß, -sse**	congress	**als**	as, for
	schnell	fast, rapid	die **Präsidentschaft**	presidency
der	**Aufstieg, -e**	rise, ascent	der **Kandidat, -en**	candidate, applicant
	republikanisch	republican		
die	**Partei, -en**	party	der **Präsidentschafts-kandidat**	presidential candidate
	vertreten (vertritt), vertrat, vertreten	to represent; to advocate; to plead	der **Grundsatz, ̈-e**	principle, maxim, rule of conduct
	gemäßigt	moderate	die **Politik**	politics, policy
die	**Ansicht, -en**	view, opinion	**formulieren**	to formulate

die **Rede, -n**	speech, talk, words		**besiegen**	to defeat, conquer
die **Schlacht, -en**	battle, fight		**besiegt**	defeated
das **Feld, -er**	field, area, domain	der **Staat, -en**	state, country
das **Schlachtfeld, -er**	battle field	der **Südstaat, -en**	southern state
die **Regierung, -en**	government, administration, rule		**stoßen (auf)**	to encounter, hit upon, meet upon
das **Volk**	people	der **Widerstand**	resistance
das **Ende**	end, finish, conclusion		**radikal**	radical
der **Bürger, -**	citizen	das **Segment, -e**	segment
der **Krieg, -e**	war	der **Gegner, -**	opponent, adversary
der **Bürgerkrieg, -e**	civil war		**verhindern**	to prevent, hinder
zielen auf	to aim at		**jedoch**	however
wieder-	again, re-	die **Wahl, -en**	election
die **Eingliederung**	insertion, incorporation	die **Wiederwahl**	re-election
die **Wiedereingliederung**	reunification	der **Fanatiker, -**	fanatic
			ermorden	to murder, assassinate

STRUCTURAL EXERCISE

A. *Underline all subjects in the above reading (straight line).*
B. *Underline all direct objects in the above reading (dotted line).*

VOCABULARY EXERCISE

Give the English equivalents of the italicized words:

1. Lincoln formulierte die *Grundsätze* seiner Politik in Gettysburg.
2. Er stieß auf den *Widerstand* des radikalen Segments seiner Partei.
3. Er vertrat eine *gemäßigte* Ansicht in der Sklavenfrage.
4. Er *stammte aus* einer armen Familie.
5. Lincolns Politik *zielte auf* eine schnelle Wiedereingliederung der besiegten Südstaaten.
6. Die Regenwälder am Amazonas haben *eine Vielfalt* an Pflanzen- und Tierarten.
7. Seine Gegner *verhinderten* seine Wiederwahl *nicht*.

esson 17

STRUCTURE

1. Present Perfect Tense — Strong Verbs

a. Remember that most weak verbs form their present perfect tense with two components:

> conjugated form of **haben** or **sein** + past participle

b. Most strong verbs use **haben** as an auxiliary verb:

Er **hat** das Haus **gesehen.** *(He has seen the house.)*

c. Verbs that use **sein** as an auxiliary must fulfill two conditions simultaneously:

1. The verb must be intransitive, that is, it does not take a direct object;
2. The verb must express motion, a change of state, or a change of condition:

Er **ist** nach Berlin **gefahren.**   (verb indicates motion)
He has gone to Berlin.

Der Baum **ist gewachsen.**   (verb indicates change of condition)
The tree has grown.

d.   Following is a list of verbs which use **sein** as an auxiliary to form the present perfect tense. The verbs are listed with their principal parts to facilitate memorization:

INFINITIVE	PRESENT	PAST	PRESENT PERFECT	ENGLISH
fahren	fährt	fuhr	ist gefahren	to go
fallen	fällt	fiel	ist gefallen	to fall
fliegen	fliegt	flog	ist geflogen	to fly
gehen	geht	ging	ist gegangen	to go
kommen	kommt	kam	ist gekommen	to come
laufen	läuft	lief	ist gelaufen	to run
rennen	rennt	rannte	ist gerannt	to run
schwimmen	schwimmt	schwamm	ist geschwommen	to swim
sinken	sinkt	sank	ist gesunken	to sink
sterben	stirbt	starb	ist gestorben	to die
wachsen	wächst	wuchs	ist gewachsen	to grow

e.   There are also a few verbs which do not fit the above description but use the auxiliary **sein:**

INFINITIVE	PRESENT	PAST	PRESENT PERFECT	ENGLISH
sein	ist	war	ist gewesen	to be
bleiben	bleibt	blieb	ist geblieben	to stay
werden	wird	wurde	ist geworden	to become

EXERCISES

A.   *Supply the correct form of* **haben** *or* **sein:**

1.   Sie _____ nach Chicago geflogen.
2.   Man _____ das Buch nicht gefunden.
3.   Wo _____ die Freunde gewesen?
4.   Wann _____ er in das Büro gegangen?
5.   _____ der Student die Zeitung gelesen?

B.   *Supply the correct form of the past participle:*

1.   Er hat es ihr _____.   (to give)
2.   Wann haben sie es _____?   (to see)
3.   Die Kinder haben das Lied _____.   (to sing)
4.   Sie hat nicht an den Freund _____.   (to think)
5.   Wo hat der Tisch _____?   (to stand)

C.   *Form sentences in the present perfect, using the indicated elements:**

1.   Er / fahren / zur Universität
2.   Der Student / bleiben / ein Jahr in Deutschland

HUNDERTSIEBZIG

3. Der Mann / bringen / ihr die Zeitung
4. Die Familie / fliegen / nach Chicago
5. Er / sehen / das Haus

D. *Give the German equivalents of the English sentences in the present perfect:*

1. We did not find the book.
2. She did not think of the friend.
3. He brought her the newspaper.
4. Where has the family been?
5. The children ran into the house.

READING

Romanische Baukunst (750–1250)

Die romanische Bauweise bezeichnet man häufig als Rundbogenstil, denn der
Rundbogen ist ein Merkmal des romanischen Stils. Andere Merkmale sind: die
langgestreckte horizontale Gliederung, die starken Mauern mit verhältnismäßig
kleinen Fenstern und die gedrungene Form der Turmspitzen, des Dachgiebels
und der Grundrißgestaltung.   5

   Die Basilika ist die Keimzelle des romanischen Kirchenbaus. Der Mittelbau der
Basilika ist wesentlich höher als die Seitenschiffe. Das Licht fällt durch Fenster
unterhalb der Decke. Der Querschnitt einer Basilika zeigt eine stufenförmige
Konstruktion. Durch diese Bauweise erhält das Mittelschiff den Charakter von fest
zusammenhängenden Wänden. Freistehende Säulen (anstatt Wände) tragen die   10
Gewölbe der späteren Hallenkirchen, z. B. in der Gotik.

   Der Grundriß der romanischen Kirche zeigt die folgenden charakteristischen
Merkmale: Die drei Langschiffe enden in einer halbkreisförmigen Apsis (Altar-
nische), ebenso jedes Querschiff; die Zwischenräume zwischen je vier Säulen oder
Pfeilern des Mittelschiffes (Joche) sind stets quadratisch; in den Winkeln der   15
Apsiden stehen zwei kleinere Seitentürme, ebenso an den Eingangsflanken.

VOCABULARY

romanisch	Romanesque	**langgestreckt**	elongated, extended, stretched
bezeichnen	to designate, describe	**horizontal**	horizontal
häufig	frequently	die **Gliederung**	arrangement, structure
als	as		
rund	round	**stark**	strong, thick, heavy
der **Bogen, ¨e**	arch		
der **Stil, -e**	style, manner	die **Mauer, -n**	wall
der **Rundbogenstil**	Romanesque style	**verhältnismäßig**	relatively
das **Merkmal, -e**	characteristic, feature	**klein**	small
		das **Fenster, -**	window
ander-	other	**gedrungen**	stocky, squat
lang	long	der **Turm, ¨e**	tower, steeple

Romanischer Baustil

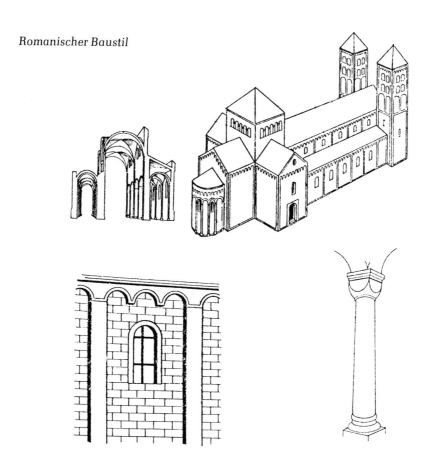

die	**Spitze, -n**	peak, top, point, summit
die	**Turmspitze, -n**	spire
das	**Dach, ¨er**	roof
der	**Giebel, -**	gable
der	**Grundriß, -sse**	groundplan, design
die	**Gestaltung**	modelling, shaping, arrangement
der	**Keim, -e**	germ, bud, shoot, embryo
die	**Zelle, -n**	cell
die	**Keimzelle**	germ cell
die	**Kirche, -n**	church
der	**Mittelbau**	nave (center portion of building)
	wesentlich	essentially, considerably
	als	than
das	**Seitenschiff, -e**	side aisle (next to the nave)
das	**Licht, -er**	light
	unterhalb	beneath, underneath
die	**Decke, -n**	ceiling
	quer	cross, across
der	**Schnitt, -e**	cut
der	**Querschnitt**	cross section
	zeigen	to show, exhibit, display
die	**Stufe, -n**	step
	stufenförmig	graduated
	erhalten (erhält), erhielt, erhalten	to obtain, get, receive
der	**Charakter**	character
	fest	solid(ly), stable
	zusammen	together
	zusammenhängend	cohesive, connected
	freistehend	detached, free-standing, isolated
	anstatt	instead of
	tragen (trägt), trug, getragen	to carry, bear, support
das	**Gewölbe, -**	vault
	spät	late
	später	later
die	**Hallenkirche, -n**	church with several naves
die	**Gotik**	Gothic style
das	**Langschiff, -e**	nave, main hall
	enden	to end, to terminate, close
	halbkreisförmig	semicircular
die	**Apsis, die Apsiden**	apse
der	**Altar, -e**	altar
die	**Nische, -n**	niche, recess
die	**Altarnische**	chancel, location of altar
	ebenso	likewise, also, just so
das	**Querschiff, -e**	transept (crosses the nave)
der	**Zwischenraum, ¨e**	space in between, interval, gap
	je	every
der	**Pfeiler, -**	pillar, jamb
das	**Joch, -e**	yoke, crossbeam
	stets	always
	quadratisch	square
der	**Winkel, -**	corner, nook, angle
die	**Seite, -n**	side, page
der	**Seitenturm, ¨e**	side tower
der	**Eingang, ¨e**	entrance
die	**Flanke, -n**	side, flank
die	**Eingangsflanke, -n**	entrance side

STRUCTURAL EXERCISE

Underline all definite articles in the genitive case.

VOCABULARY EXERCISE

Give the English equivalents of the italicized words:

1. Der Mittelbau der Basilika ist *wesentlich* höher als die Seitenschiffe.
2. Man *bezeichnet* die romanische Bauweise auch als Rundbogenstil.
3. Der *Querschnitt* einer Basilika zeigt eine stufenförmige Konstruktion.
4. Das Licht fällt durch das Fenster *unterhalb* der Decke.

5. Der Rundbogen ist ein *Merkmal* des romanischen Stils.
6. Die starken Mauern haben *verhältnismäßig* kleine Fenster.
7. Das Mittelschiff *erhält* durch diese Bauweise den Charakter von fest zusammenhängenden Wänden.

EXERCISES

A. *Supply the correct forms of* **haben** *or* **sein:**

1. Sie _____ die romanische Kirche gefunden.
2. Wann _____ die Erwachsenen zur Volkschochschule gegangen?
3. Sie *(she)* _____ ihm wesentlich geholfen.
4. Der Wagen _____ verhältnismäßig schnell gefahren.
5. Der Student _____ drei Stunden am Tag geschrieben.

B. *Supply the past participle:*

1. Sein Einfluß ist kleiner _____. (to become, get)
2. Wann ist sie in der Stadt _____? (to be)
3. Ich weiß nicht, wann er _____ hat. (to sleep)
4. Wie hat diese Bauweise _____? (to be called)
5. Hat der Karpfen die Larven _____? (to eat)

C. *Supply the past participle; strong and weak verbs are mixed:*

1. Der Chemiker hat die Lösung _____. (to find)
2. Man hat die Proteinstrukturen _____. (to analyse)
3. Er hat ihn _____. (to ask)
4. Der Vater hat dem Sohn _____. (to answer)
5. Der Student hat schwer _____. (to work)

D. *Change the following sentences to present perfect:**

1. Ihr Freund fliegt nach Rom.
2. Er half seinem Freund.
3. Die Temperaturen waren um 20 Grad Celsius.
4. Sie studierte in Deutschland.
5. Er wartet auf seine Freundin.

E. *Give the German equivalents of the following sentences in the present perfect:*

1. He stayed in Germany.
2. The president flew to Berlin.
3. She came late.
4. They found the book.
5. The teacher read three newspapers.

F. *Give the English equivalents of the following compound words:*

1. der Temperaturunterschied
2. das Entwicklungsland
3. die Wiedereingliederung
4. die Regierungspolitik
5. der Kongreßabgeordnete

STRUCTURE

2.   Relative Clauses

The relative clause is a type of subordinate clause using a relative pronoun to connect the relative clause with the main clause:

That is the man *who gave me the book.*

The relative pronoun *who* relates the relative clause to the main clause. It refers to one element (the antecedent) in the main clause. The antecedent here is *the man.*

3.   German Relative Pronouns

a.   The same set of relative pronouns is used for persons and objects:

	SINGULAR			PLURAL
	MASCULINE	FEMININE	NEUTER	ALL GENDERS
NOMINATIVE	**der**	**die**	**das**	**die**
GENITIVE	**dessen**	**deren**	**dessen**	**deren**
DATIVE	**dem**	**der**	**dem**	**denen**
ACCUSATIVE	**den**	**die**	**das**	**die**

b.   The declension of relative pronouns in German is closely related to that of the definite articles. As you can see in the table above, only the dative plural form and the genitive forms are different from the definite article declensions.

c.   Relative pronouns agree in gender and number with their antecedent. Their case is determined by their function in the relative clause.

d.   The determining factors for the relative pronoun are:

1.   The antecedent (in the main clause), which determines gender and number of the relative pronoun;
2.   The function of the relative pronoun (in the relative clause), which determines its case:

EXAMPLE A:

Das ist	**der Mann, der**	ihr das Buch gegeben hat.[1]
That is	*the man who*	*has given her the book.*

1.   The antecedent in the main clause is: **der Mann;** the antecedent is masculine singular.

1.   Note that German relative clauses are always set off by commas.

2. The relative pronoun replaces the antecedent in the relative clause, that is, it functions as a substitute for the antecedent and consequently assumes the role of the antecedent:

Relative Clause: **der ihr das Buch gegeben hat**

replaces

Der Mann hat ihr das Buch gegeben.

Der Mann is the antecedent subject (= nominative). The substituting relative pronoun is: **der**

EXAMPLE B:

Das ist ⎢ **der Chef, für den** ⎢ er arbeitet.
That is ⎢ *the boss   for whom* ⎢ *he is working.*

1. The antecedent in the main clause is: **der Chef;** the antecedent is masculine singular.
2. The relative pronoun (in the relative clause) assumes the function of its antecedent.

Two independent sentences with a common element:

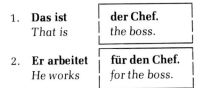

1. **Das ist** ⎢ **der Chef.**
    That is ⎢ *the boss.*

2. **Er arbeitet** ⎢ **für den Chef.**
    He works ⎢ *for the boss.*

Sentences 1 & 2 combined:

Das ist ⎢ **der Chef, für den** ⎢ er arbeitet.
That is ⎢ *the boss for whom* ⎢ *he works.*

für den Chef is a prepositional phrase (accusative). The substituting relative pronoun is **den.**

SELF-PREPARATORY EXERCISE

Supply the relative pronoun and identify the three factors you used in choosing the relative pronoun:

Das ist der Lehrer, _____
an der Universität lehrt.

Das ist der Lehrer, der   MASC.
an der Universität lehrt.   SING. NOM.

Das ist die Frau, _____ Deutsch spricht.		
Wer ist der Mann, _____ er gesehen hat?	Das ist die Frau, die Deutsch spricht.	FEM. SING. NOM.
Wo sind die Kinder, mit _____ wir fahren?	Wer ist der Mann, den er gesehen hat.	MASC. SING. ACC.
Ist das der Bus, _____ nach München fährt?	Wo sind die Kinder, mit denen wir fahren?	PLUR. DAT.
Die Frau, _____ er es gegeben hat, ist nicht gekommen.	Ist das der Bus, der nach München fährt?	MASC. SING. NOM.
Das ist die Frau, _____ Kind man sah.	Die Frau, der er es gegeben hat, ist nicht gekommen.	FEM. SING. DAT.
	Das ist die Frau, deren Kind man sah.	FEM. SING. GEN.

EXERCISES

A. *Complete the sentences with the correct relative pronoun. Circle the gender, number, and case of the relative pronoun and indicate the reason for that case:*

EXAMPLE:

Das ist das Buch, _____ er gelesen hat.		MAIN CLAUSE			RELATIVE CLAUSE		
Answer: **das**	M F (N)		(S) Pl		N G D (A)		
Reason: direct object neuter singular							
	GENDER		NUMBER		CASE		
1. Wo ist das Haus, _____ er gekauft hat?	M F N		S Pl		N G D A		
2. Er ist der Mann, _____ sie es gegeben hat.	M F N		S Pl		N G D A		
3. München ist die Stadt, in _____ er wohnt.	M F N		S Pl		N G D A		
4. Das sind die Studenten, _____ sie sieht.			S Pl		N G D A		

	MAIN CLAUSE			RELATIVE CLAUSE
	GENDER	NUMBER		CASE
5. Das ist die Studentin, _____ sie sieht.	M F N	S Pl		N G D A
6. Es ist das Kind, _____ Mutter hier war.	M F N	S Pl		N G D A
7. Wo ist die Familie _____ Wagen sie gekauft haben?	M F N	S Pl		N G D A
8. Wie heißt der Sohn, zu _____ er ging?	M F N	S Pl		N G D A
9. Löwenbräu ist das Bier, _____ er gekauft hat.	M F N	S Pl		N G D A
10. Das sind die Kinder, _____ sie es gegeben hat.		S Pl		N G D A

B. *Supply the relative pronoun:*

1. Der Freund, _____ er geholfen hat, heißt Willi.
2. Der Student, mit _____ sie spricht, ist aus Amerika.
3. Das Haus, in _____ die Familie wohnt, ist alt.
4. Das ist der Professor, bei _____ er studiert.
5. Lincoln, _____ aus einer armen Familie stammte, war Advokat und Abgeordneter.

C. *Form sentences with the following elements in the present perfect tense:**

1. der Bruder / schreiben / eine Karte
2. der Schüler / sprechen / kein Deutsch
3. der Vater / helfen / dem Kind
4. Er / werden / alt
5. die Studentin / sein / in London

D. *Change the following sentences to past tense:**

1. Er wird alt.
2. Sie sind in die Stadt gefahren.
3. Man analysiert Proteinstrukturen.
4. Wo spielt das Kind?
5. Er hat der Tochter ein Buch geschickt.

HUNDERTACHTUNDSIEBZIG

E. *Change the nouns to plural and make the necessary changes in the verbs:*

1. Die Studentin lernt.
2. Das Bild ist hier.
3. Dort ist das Hotel.
4. Er spricht die Sprache.
5. Der Mann arbeitet.

4. Word Order — Relative Pronouns

a. Relative pronouns, like subordinating conjunctions, affect the word order in the clause. Both relative pronouns and subordinating conjunctions introduce subordinate clauses.

b. The inflected verb form stands at the end of a clause introduced by a relative pronoun:

Das ist der Professor, **für den er gearbeitet hat.**
That is the professor, for whom he has worked.

MAIN CLAUSE: **Das ist der Professor,**
SUBORDINATE CLAUSE: **für den er gearbeitet hat.**

EXERCISES

A. *Complete the relative clause in the tense indicated:*

1. Wie heißt die Frau, mit der er / sprechen /?   (present perfect)
2. Dort sind die Mädchen, mit denen die Lehrerin / sprechen /.   (past)
3. Er zeigt ihm das Buch, das er / kaufen /.   (present perfect)
4. Wo findet man die Zigaretten, die er / rauchen /?   (present)
5. Ist das der Chef, für den er / arbeiten /?   (present perfect)

B. *Complete the following sentences by giving the German equivalents of the relative clause:*

1. Wo steht der Wagen, _____ (which he is driving)?
2. Das sind die Kinder, _____ (with whom they play).
3. Das sind die Proteine, _____ (whose structures he analyses).
4. Er kennt die Universität, _____ (at which she is studying).
5. Der Mann, _____ (who has printed the bible), heißt Gutenberg.

C. *Change the following sentences to past tense:* *

1. Der Karpfen frißt Würmer und Larven.
2. Der Ökologe plädiert für die Erhaltung der Landschaft.
3. Das Buch liegt auf dem Tisch.
4. Er denkt an seine Freundin.
5. Lincoln stammt aus einer armen Familie.

HUNDERTNEUNUNDSIEBZIG

D. *Change the following sentences to present perfect:**

1. Der Atheist glaubt nicht an Gott.
2. Der Student studiert in Hamburg.
3. Das Studium ist schwer.
4. Die Kinder singen die Lieder.
5. Man sieht das Bild an der Wand.

E. *Give the English equivalents of the following compound words:*

1. die Wiederwahl
2. die Sklavenfrage
3. die Kreislaufstörung
4. die Herstellungsmethode
5. die Leistungsfähigkeit

READING

Malaria

Das Wechselfieber Malaria bedroht immer noch viele Menschen in tropischen Regionen. Eine Art von Stechmücke (anopheles) verbreitet diese Infektionskrankheit. Die Forschung sucht schon seit Jahrzehnten nach einem geeigneten Bekämpfungsmittel zur Dezimierung dieser Stechmücken. Man verwendet DDT zur chemischen Bekämpfung. Die Insekten entwickeln schnell Resistenz gegen dieses Insektizid. 5

Eine andere Möglichkeit ist die genetische Bekämpfung. Sie verhindert die Fortpflanzung der Insekten. Die genetische Kontrolle beruht auf der sogenannten Inkompatibilitätsmethode. Inkompatibilität bedeutet in diesem Falle die Unvereinbarkeit von Männchen und Weibchen. 10

VOCABULARY

die **Malaria**	malaria	**verbreiten**	to spread, disseminate
der **Wechsel, -**	change, alternation, fluctuation	die **Infektion, -en**	infection
		die **Krankheit, en**	disease, sickness
das **Fieber**	fever	die **Infektionskrankheit**	infectious disease
das **Wechselfieber**	intermittent fever, malaria	**suchen nach**	to search for, look for
bedrohen	to threaten, to menace	**seit**	since
immer noch	still, yet	das **Jahrzehnt, -e**	decade
tropisch	tropical	**seit Jahrzehnten**	for decades
die **Region, -en**	region, area	**geeignet**	suitable, suited
die **Art, -en**	species, kind	die **Bekämpfung**	control, combat
stechen (sticht), stach, gestochen	to sting, bite, prick	das **Mittel, -**	means, substance
die **Mücke, -n**	fly	das **Bekämpfungsmittel**	control substance, pesticide
die **Stechmücke**	biting fly		

HUNDERTACHTZIG

die **Dezimierung**	decimation
zur **Dezimierung**	for the decimation
chemisch	chemical
das **Insekt, -en**	insect
die **Resistenz**	resistance, immunity
gegen	against
das **Insektizid, -e**	insecticide
die **Möglichkeit, -en**	possibility
genetisch	genetic
verhindern	to prevent

die **Fortpflanzung**	reproduction, propagation
die **Kontrolle, -n**	control, supervision
beruhen auf	to be based on; to depend upon
die **Inkompatibilität**	incompatibility
der **Fall, ⁻e**	case, situation
die **Unvereinbarkeit**	incompatibility
das **Männchen, -**	male

STRUCTURAL EXERCISE

A. Underline all direct objects in the above reading (straight line).

B. Underline all definite articles used in the genitive in the above reading (dotted line).

VOCABULARY EXERCISE

Give the English equivalents of the italicized words:

1. Die *Forschung* sucht nach einem Bekämpfungsmittel.
2. Die genetische Bekämpfung *beruht auf* der sogenannten Inkompatibilitätsmethode.
3. Die Insekten *entwickeln* schnell Resistenz.
4. Die Stechmücke *verbreitet* diese Krankheit.
5. Malaria bedroht *immer noch* viele Menschen.
6. Das Wort bedeutet *in diesem Falle* die Unvereinbarkeit von Männchen und Weibchen.
7. *Seit Jahrzehnten* sucht man nach einem geeigneten Bekämpfungsmittel.

SUMMARY OF STRONG AND IRREGULAR VERB FORMS

INFINITIVE	PRESENT	PAST	PRESENT PERFECT	ENGLISH
bleiben	bleibt	blieb	ist geblieben	*to stay*
bringen	bringt	brachte	hat gebracht	*to bring*
denken	denkt	dachte	hat gedacht	*to think*
fahren	fährt	fuhr	ist gefahren	*to drive*
fallen	fällt	fiel	ist gefallen	*to fall*
finden	findet	fand	hat gefunden	*to find*
fliegen	fliegt	flog	ist geflogen	*to fly*
fressen	frißt	fraß	hat gefressen	*to eat*
geben	gibt	gab	hat gegeben	*to give*
gehen	geht	ging	ist gegangen	*to go*
gießen	gießt	goß	hat gegossen	*to pour*

INFINITIVE	PRESENT	PAST	PRESENT PERFECT	ENGLISH
halten	hält	hielt	hat gehalten	to hold
hängen	hängt	hing	hat gehangen	to hang
heißen	heißt	hieß	hat geheißen	to be called
helfen	hilft	half	hat geholfen	to help
kennen	kennt	kannte	hat gekannt	to know
kommen	kommt	kam	ist gekommen	to come
lassen	läßt	ließ	hat gelassen	to let
laufen	läuft	lief	ist gelaufen	to run
lesen	liest	las	hat gelesen	to read
liegen	liegt	lag	hat gelegen	to lie
messen	mißt	maß	hat gemessen	to measure
nehmen	nimmt	nahm	hat genommen	to take
nennen	nennt	nannte	hat genannt	to call
rennen	rennt	rannte	ist gerannt	to run
schlafen	schläft	schlief	hat geschlafen	to sleep
schließen	schließt	schloß	hat geschlossen	to close
schneiden	schneidet	schnitt	hat geschnitten	to cut
schreiben	schreibt	schrieb	hat geschrieben	to write
schwimmen	schwimmt	schwamm	ist geschwommen	to swim
sehen	sieht	sah	hat gesehen	to see
sein	ist	war	ist gewesen	to be
singen	singt	sang	hat gesungen	to sing
sinken	sinkt	sank	ist gesunken	to sink
spinnen	spinnt	spann	hat gesponnen	to spin
sprechen	spricht	sprach	hat gesprochen	to speak
stechen	sticht	stach	hat gestochen	to sting
stehen	steht	stand	hat gestanden	to stand
sterben	stirbt	starb	ist gestorben	to die
tragen	trägt	trug	hat getragen	to carry, wear
trinken	trinkt	trank	hat getrunken	to drink
wachsen	wächst	wuchs	ist gewachsen	to grow
waschen	wäscht	wusch	hat gewaschen	to wash
werden	wird	wurde	ist geworden	to become, get
wissen	weiß	wußte	hat gewußt	to know
ziehen	zieht	zog	hat gezogen	to pull

esson **18**

STRUCTURE

1. Indefinite Relative Pronouns and Relative Adverb

a. Relative pronouns relate a relative clause to a main clause. A definite relative pronoun has a specific antecedent in the main clause:

Das ist **der Mann, den** sie kennt.
That is the man (whom) she knows.

b. Indefinite relative pronouns do not refer to a specific person or object in the main clause.

c. Indefinite relative pronouns are:

was	*what*	**wem**	*(to) whom*
wer	*who*	**wen**	*whom*

d. Relative adverb

wo	*where*

2. Use of <u>was</u>

The indefinite relative pronoun **was** is used:

1. After the following indefinite pronouns:

alles	*all, everything*	**nichts**	*nothing*
etwas	*something*	**wenig**	*little*

These indefinite pronouns are used as antecedents in the main clause:

Das ist | **alles, was** | er gemacht hat.
That is | *all (that)* | *he has done.*

2.   When the antecedent is an entire clause:

Der Professor hatte keine Zeit, **was der Student nicht wußte.**
The professor did not have any time, (a fact) which the student did not know.

3.   Use of wer, wem, wen

a.   The indefinite relative pronouns **wer, wem,** and **wen** are used to refer to persons who are not specified in the main clause:

Wer viel Geld hat, ist nicht immer glücklich.
He who (Whoever) has a lot of money is not always happy.
Wem er das Geld gegeben hat, ist nicht bekannt.
(To) Whom he gave the money is not known.
Wen man kennt, ist wichtig.
Whom one knows is important.

b.   **Wem** and **wen** are also used with prepositions:

Mit wem er nach München fährt, hat er nicht gesagt.
With whom he is going to Munich he did not say.
Für wen sie den Wagen gekauft hat, weiß man nicht.
For whom she bought the car we don't know.

4.   Use of wo

The relative adverb **wo** is used in relative clauses referring to geographical locations:

Er fährt morgen **nach Heidelberg, wo** er vor drei Jahren studiert hat.
Tomorrow he is going to Heidelberg, where he studied three years ago.

5.   Word Order — Indefinite Relative Pronouns and Relative Adverbs

a.   Relative clauses introduced by indefinite relative pronouns or by a relative adverb are subordinate clauses, that is, the conjugated verb is in last position:

Wen man kennt, . . .

HUNDERTVIERUNDACHTZIG

b. When the relative clause precedes the main clause, the conjugated verb introduces the main clause. The word order of the relative clause is not affected by this sequence:

Wem er geholfen hat, **weiß ich** nicht.

EXERCISES

A. *Supply the German relative pronoun or adverb indicated in parentheses:*

1. Er weiß, _____ der Mann ist. (who)
2. Das ist alles, _____ er gesagt hat. (that)
3. _____ ihm geholfen hat, weiß man nicht. (whoever)
4. Zu _____ sie gegangen ist, das hat sie nicht gesagt. (whom)
5. Hans bleibt in Ulm, _____ er eine Freundin hat. (where)

B. *Supply the correct relative clause:*

1. _____ (to whom she has said it), weiß man nicht.
2. Er sagt ihr alles, _____ (that he knows).
3. Er zeigt ihnen die Schule, _____ (where he is learning German).
4. Sie kauft alles, _____ (that she sees).
5. Karl fährt nach Berlin, _____ ([a fact] which his friends did not know).

C. *Supply the definite or indefinite relative pronoun:*

1. Sie kennt die Frau, _____ sie es gegeben hat. (to whom)
2. Er hat nicht gesagt, _____ er nach München fährt. (with whom)
3. Wo ist der Wagen, _____ er gekauft hat? (which)
4. Sie gibt ihm alles, _____ sie hat. (that)
5. Sie las das Buch, _____ er ihr gegeben hat. (which)

D. *Give the German equivalents:*

1. She tells him everything (that) she hears.
2. Frieda is in Freiburg, where she has a friend.
3. Is that all (that) he is saying?
4. Where is the brewery in which he is working?
5. He knows **(wissen)** who the scientist is.

READING

Gotische Baukunst (1200–1525)

Der gotische Stil entstand unabhängig in verschiedenen europäischen Ländern. Man spricht deswegen auch von einer deutschen, italienischen, französischen und englischen Gotik. Die gotische Architektur zeigt die Lebensauffassung der damaligen Menschen. Viele Menschen hatten damals weniger Interesse an dem weltlichen Leben und mehr Interesse für das Jenseits. Die gotische Baukunst beweist dieses ⁵

Gotische Baukunst: Der Dom in Aachen

HUNDERTSECHSUNDACHTZIG

Streben nach dem Jenseits in der aufstrebenden senkrechten Gliederung. Die gotische Architektur verlief in mehreren Abschnitten, d.h. Frühgotik, Hochgotik und Spätgotik. Man erkennt den gotischen Stil sehr leicht an dem Spitzbogen der Fenster, Türen und Gewölbe.

VOCABULARY

	entstehen (entsteht), entstand, ist entstanden	to arise; to begin; to develop	das	**Jenseits**	the next world, the hereafter
	unabhängig	independently		**beweisen (beweist), bewies, bewiesen**	to prove, show, demonstrate
	europäisch	European	das	**Streben**	strive, aspiration, longing
	Europa	Europe			
	deswegen	therefore, for that reason		**aufstrebend**	aspiring, upward striving
	italienisch	Italian		**senkrecht**	vertical
	Italien	Italy	der	**Abschnitt, -e**	section, segment, period
	französisch	French			
	Frankreich	France		**d.h. (= das heißt)**	that is (to say), in other words
	englisch	English			
	England	England	die	**Frühgotik**	early Gothic
die	**Architektur**	architecture	die	**Hochgotik**	high Gothic
die	**Auffassung, -en**	view, concept, comprehension	die	**Spätgotik**	late Gothic
				erkennen . . . an (erkennt), erkannte, erkannt	to recognize . . . by, know . . . by
die	**Lebensauffassung**	view of life, life philosophy			
	damalig	then, at that time (*adjective*)	der	**Spitzbogen**	pointed (Gothic) arch
	damals	then, at that time (*adverb*)	die	**Tür, -en**	door
			das	**Gewölbe, -**	vault, arched ceiling
das	**Interesse an / für**	interest in / for			
	weltlich	wordly, mundane, secular			

STRUCTURAL EXERCISE

Underline all direct objects in the above reading.

VOCABULARY EXERCISE

Give the English equivalents of the italicized words:

1. Man *erkennt* den gotischen Stil sehr leicht an dem Spitzbogen.
2. Viele Menschen hatten *damals* weniger Interesse an dem weltlichen Leben.
3. Man spricht *deswegen* auch von einer deutschen, italienischen oder französischen Gotik.
4. Die gotische Architektur *verlief* in mehreren Abschnitten.
5. Die gotische Architektur zeigt die *Lebensauffassung* der damaligen Menschen.
6. Die gotische Architektur *beweist* dieses Streben nach dem Jenseits in der aufstrebenden senkrechten Gliederung.
7. Die gotische Architektur verlief in *mehreren* Abschnitten.

STRUCTURE

6.   Verb Prefixes

a.   Verb prefixes often change the meanings of the verbs to which they are attached:

sprechen	*to speak; to talk*	**besprechen**	*to discuss*
stehen	*to stand*	**verstehen**	*to understand*
		entstehen	*to come about, occur, develop*

7.   Inseparable Prefixes

a.   Inseparable prefixes always remain attached to the main verb stem.

b.   Inseparable prefixes do not affect the basic verb conjugation:

INFINITIVE: **besprechen**   *to discuss*
PAST TENSE: (er) **besprach**   *(he) discussed*

Note that the word stress remains on the verb stem or root syllable: **bespre̜chen, bespra̲ch.**

c.   Past participles of verbs with inseparable prefixes do not add the usual **ge-**:

INFINITIVE: **besprechen**   *to discuss*
PRESENT PERFECT: (er hat) **besprochen**   *(he has) discussed*

d.   The most common inseparable prefixes are:

be-	**ge-**	**emp-**	**miß-**
ent-	**ver-**	**er-**	**zer-**

8.   Weak Verbs with Inseparable Prefixes[1]

INFINITIVE	ENGLISH MEANING	INFINITIVE	ENGLISH MEANING
be-		**be-**	
bedeuten	*to mean*	**befördern**	*to transport*
bedrohen	*to threaten*		
beenden	*to finish, end, complete*	**behandeln**	*to treat, deal with*

1.   The verbs in this list have occurred in the first eighteen lessons.

HUNDERTACHTUNDACHTZIG

INFINITIVE	ENGLISH MEANING	INFINITIVE	ENGLISH MEANING
be-		**be-**	
benutzen	*to use, employ*	**bestimmen**	*to determine*
beruhen (auf)	*to be based (on)*	**bezeichnen**	*to term, designate*
besiegen	*to defeat*	**bezweifeln**	*to doubt*
er-		**-er**	
erfolgen	*to ensue, happen*	**erreichen**	*to reach, achieve*
erklären	*to explain*	**erteilen**	*to impart, give*
ermorden	*to assassinate, murder*	**erzielen**	*to obtain, realize*
erproben	*to test, try*		
errechnen	*to calculate*		
ver-		**ver-**	
verhindern	*to prevent*	**verbreiten**	*to spread, disseminate*
verknüpfen	*to join, link*	**vermindern**	*to reduce, lower*
ent-			
entwickeln	*to develop*		

SELF-PREPARATORY EXERCISE

Change the following sentences to past tense:*

Er benutzt den Computer.	
Sie beendet das Studium.	Er benutzte den Computer.
Man erzielt eine gute Ernte.	Sie beendete das Studium.
Er benutzt natürliche Düngemittel.	Man erzielte eine gute Ernte.
Das Rauchen vermindert die Strömungsgeschwindigkeit.	Er benutzte nur natürliche Düngemittel.
	Das Rauchen verminderte die Strömungsgeschwindigkeit.

EXERCISES

A. *Change the following sentences to past tense:**

1. Kristallographe ermitteln die Ergebnisse.
2. Man errechnet die Molekularstrukturen nach physikalischen Prinzipien.
3. Diese Methode benutzt als Grundlage die mathematischen Relationen unter den Faktoren der Kristallstruktur.
4. Eine Streuung der Strahlung erfolgt an den Bausteinen der Materie.
5. Der Bauer benutzt keine Mineraldünger.

B. *Supply the correct past-tense equivalents of the verbs in parentheses:*

1. Einstein _____ seine Dissertation in Zürich.   (to complete)
2. Er _____ den photoelektrischen Effekt.   (to explain)
3. Der Herzschlag _____ der Pulswelle eine Geschwindigkeit von 5 bis 6 Metern in der Sekunde.   (to impart)
4. Die Insekten _____ schnell Resistenz gegen dieses Insektizid.   (to develop)
5. Der Fanatiker J. W. Booth _____ Lincoln im Jahre 1865.   (to assassinate)

SELF-PREPARATORY EXERCISE

Change the following sentences to present perfect:*

Die Anthropologie behandelt den Menschen.	
Das Wort bedeutet Königsbau.	Die Anthropologie hat den Menschen behandelt.
Der Agnostiker bezweifelt die Existenz Gottes.	Das Wort hat Königsbau bedeutet.
Man erprobt die neue Getreidesorte.	Der Agnostiker hat die Existenz Gottes bezweifelt.
Die Ernte erzielt höhere Preise.	Man hat die neue Getreidesorte erprobt.
	Die Ernte hat höhere Preise erzielt.

EXERCISES

A. *Change the following sentences to present perfect:**

1. Die Bauern erproben eine neue Getreidesorte.
2. Das Herz befördert am Tag 5 760 Liter Blut.
3. Der Schüler beendet mit dem Abitur seine Erziehung am Gymnasium.
4. Man bezeichnet die romanische Bauweise häufig als Rundbogenstil.
5. Malaria bedroht viele Menschen in tropischen Regionen.

HUNDERTNEUNZIG

B. *Supply the German equivalents of the indicated verbs in the present perfect tense:*

1. Die genetische Kontrolle _____ die Fortpflanzung der Insekten _____. (to prevent)
2. Die Insekten _____ schnell Resistenz gegen dieses Insektizid _____. (to develop)
3. Man _____ DDT zur chemischen Bekämpfung _____. (to use)
4. Die Ernte _____ höhere Preise _____. (to realize)
5. Einstein _____ seine Dissertation in Zürich _____. (to complete)

READING

Martin Luther

1483	geboren in Eisleben (Stadt im heutigen Ostdeutschland).
1501	Studienbeginn an der Universität Erfurt.
1512	Doktor der Theologie.
1517	Anschlag der 95 Thesen an der Schloßkirche in Wittenberg.
1518	Einleitung des kanonischen Prozesses gegen Luther in Rom.
1520	Werke: „An den christlichen Adel deutscher Nation." „Von der babylonischen Gefangenschaft der Kirche." „Von der Freiheit eines Christenmenschen."
1521	Beginn der deutschen Übersetzung des Neuen Testaments.
1521	Wormser Edikt: Reichsacht gegen Luther.
1534	Bibelübersetzung beendet. Erste Gesamtausgabe der Deutschen Bibel.
1545	Werk: „Wider das Papsttum zu Rom. Vom Teufel gestiftet."
1546	Tod in Eisleben.

VOCABULARY

die	**Stadt, ⸚e**	city	das **Schloß, ⸚sser**	castle
	Ostdeutschland	East Germany	die **Einleitung**	*here:* beginning, preparation
der	**Beginn**	beginning, start		
der	**Studienbeginn**	beginning of studies, education	**kanonisch**	canonical
			der **Prozeß, -sse**	process, proceedings, trial
der	**Doktor**	doctor		
die	**Theologie**	theology	**Rom**	Rome
der	**Anschlag, ⸚e**	posting, attachment	das **Werk, -e**	work, publication
die	**These, -n**	thesis, assertion	**christlich**	Christian (*adjective*)

Martin Luther

Martin Luther in Worms

HUNDERTZWEIUNDNEUNZIG

der **Adel**	aristocracy, nobility	die **Reichsacht**	imperial ban
die **Nation, -en**	nation	**gesamt**	complete, total
babylonisch	babylonian	die **Ausgabe, -n**	edition, issue
die **Gefangenschaft**	captivity, imprison-	die **Gesamtausgabe**	complete edition
	ment	**wider**	against, in opposition
die **Freiheit**	freedom, liberty		to
der **Christ, -en**	Christian	der **Papst, -̈e**	pope
die **Übersetzung, -en**	translation	das **Papsttum**	papacy
das **Testament, -e**	testament	der **Teufel, -**	devil
Worms	*city in Germany*	**stiften**	to found, institute,
Wormser	of Worms		initiate
das **Edikt, -e**	edict, order, decree	der **Tod**	death
das **Reich, -e**	empire	**Eisleben**	*city in East Germany*
die **Acht**	ban, excommunica-		
	tion		

STRUCTURAL EXERCISE

Underline all definite articles used in the genitive case in the above reading.

VOCABULARY EXERCISE

Give the English equivalents of the italicized words:

1. Im Jahre 1521 begann Luther mit der *Übersetzung* des Neuen Testaments.
2. ,,Von der *Freiheit* eines Christenmenschen.''
3. Im Jahre 1534 erscheint die erste *Gesamtausgabe* der Deutschen Bibel.
4. Die gotische Architektur verlief in mehreren *Abschnitten*.
5. Die Menschen hatten damals weniger Interesse an dem *weltlichen* Leben.
6. Im Jahre 1534 hat Luther die Bibelübersetzung *beendet*.
7. Die Regenwälder am Amazonas haben ein *äußerst* kompliziertes Ökosystem.

STRUCTURE

9. Strong Verbs with Inseparable Prefixes

INFINITIVE	ENGLISH MEANING	PRINCIPAL PARTS OF BASIC VERB
be-		

bestehen (aus)	*to consist (of)*	**stehen (steht), stand, gestanden**
betragen	*to amount (to)*	**tragen (trägt), trug, getragen**
beweisen	*to prove*	**weisen (weist), wies, gewiesen**
beziehen (auf)	*to refer (to)*	**ziehen (zieht), zog, gezogen**

INFINITIVE	ENGLISH MEANING	PRINCIPAL PARTS OF BASIC VERB
ent-		

enthalten	*to contain*	**halten (hält), hielt, gehalten**
entsprechen	*to correspond*	**sprechen (spricht), sprach, gesprochen**
entstehen	*to arise, develop*	**stehen (steht), stand, gestanden**

er-		

erhalten	*to receive, get*	**halten (hält), hielt, gehalten**
erkennen	*to recognize*	**kennen (kennt), kannte, gekannt**
erscheinen	*to appear; to be published*	**scheinen (scheint), schien, geschienen**

unter-		

unterscheiden	*to differentiate*	**scheiden (scheidet), schied, geschieden**

ver-		

verbinden	*to combine*	**binden (bindet), band, gebunden**
verlaufen	*to pass, procede*	**laufen (läuft), lief, ist gelaufen**
vermeiden	*to avoid*	**meiden (meidet), mied, gemieden**
verwenden[1]	*to use, employ*	**wenden (wendet), wandte, gewandt**
vertreten	*to represent*	**treten (tritt), trat, getreten**

voll-		

vollbringen	*to perform, complete*	**bringen (bringt), brachte, gebracht**

zer-		

zerfallen	*to break down into*	**fallen (fällt), fiel, ist gefallen**

1. **Verwenden** may be used as a weak as well as a strong verb.

HUNDERTVIERUNDNEUNZIG

Note that the following verbs use **sein** in the present perfect tense:

entstehen	(er) **ist entstanden**	**verlaufen**	(er) **ist verlaufen**
erscheinen	(er) **ist erschienen**	**zerfallen**	(er) **ist zerfallen**

SELF-PREPARATORY EXERCISE

*Change the following sentences to past tense:**

Die Größe des Herzens entspricht der Faust seines Besitzers.	
Die Blutmenge beträgt etwa 5 Liter.	Die Größe des Herzens entsprach der Faust seines Besitzers.
Der Muskel vollbringt eine große Leistung.	Die Blutmenge betrug etwa 5 Liter.
Die Trigonometrie verbindet Raum- und Zahlengrößen.	Der Muskel vollbrachte eine große Leistung.
Die Bauern verwenden nur natürliche Düngemittel.	Die Trigonometrie verband Raum- und Zahlengrößen.
	Die Bauern verwandten nur natürliche Düngemittel.

EXERCISES

A. *Change the following sentences to past tense:**

   1. Man unterscheidet drei Grundformen in der Bauweise.
   2. Jedes zehnte Buch erscheint in deutscher Sprache.
   3. Der Äquator verläuft mitten durch Afrika.
   4. Das Bier enthält Alkohol.
   5. Der Karpfen vermeidet schnelle Gewässer.

B. *Supply the correct past-tense equivalents of the verbs in parentheses:*

   1. Die Lehre der Mathematik _____ in verschiedene Teilgebiete. (to break down into)
   2. Der Äquator _____ mitten durch den Kontinent. (to pass)
   3. Lincoln _____ eine gemäßigte Ansicht in der Sklavenfrage. (to represent)
   4. Das Mittelschiff _____ den Character von fest zusammenhängenden Wänden. (to get)
   5. Der gotische Stil _____ unabhängig in verschiedenen Ländern Europas. (to develop)

SELF-PREPARATORY EXERCISE

*Change the following sentences to present perfect:**

Man erkennt den Stil sehr leicht.	
Sie verlief in mehreren Abschnitten.	Man hat den Stil sehr leicht erkannt.
Die Bibel erscheint im Jahre 1534.	Sie ist in mehreren Abschnitten verlaufen
Man beweist die Existenz Gottes nicht.	Die Bibel ist im Jahre 1534 erschienen.
Der Karpfen vermeidet schnelle Gewässer.	Man hat die Existenz Gottes nicht bewiesen.
	Der Karpfen hat schnelle Gewässer vermieden.

EXERCISES

A. *Change the following sentences to present perfect:**

1. Die Lehre der Mathematik zerfällt in verschiedene Teilgebiete.
2. Der Muskel vollbringt eine große Leistung.
3. Ein neues Buch erscheint auf dem Markt.
4. Die Blutmenge beträgt etwa 5 Liter.
5. Das Mittelschiff erhält den Charakter von zusammenhängenden Wänden.

B. *Supply the German equivalents of the verbs in the present perfect tense:*

1. Die Bauern _____ nur natürliche Düngemittel _____. (to use)
2. Der Muskel _____ eine große Leistung _____. (to perform)
3. Man _____ drei Grundformen in der Bauweise _____. (to differentiate)
4. Die Schüler _____ den gotischen Stil sehr leicht _____. (to recognize)
5. Jedes zehnte Buch _____ in deutscher Sprache _____. (to appear)

C. *Weak and strong verbs mixed. Supply the correct German equivalents of the verbs in the past tense:*

1. Das Bier _____ Alkohol. (to contain)
2. Einstein _____ seine Dissertation in Zürich. (to finish)
3. Die Trigonometrie _____ Raum- und Zahlengrößen. (to combine)
4. Der Student _____ den Computer. (to use)
5. Der Bauer _____ eine gute Ernte. (to obtain)

D. *Form sentences with the given elements in the present perfect tense. Weak and strong verbs mixed:*

1. Das Rauchen / vermindern / die Strömungsgeschwindigkeit des Blutes.
2. Eine neue Getreidesorte / erscheinen / auf dem Markt

HUNDERTSECHSUNDNEUNZIG

3. Der Muskel / vollbringen / eine große Leistung
4. Lincoln / vertreten / eine gemäßigte Ansicht in der Sklavenfrage
5. Die Ernte / erzielen / höhere Preise

READING

Der Planet Merkur

Der Planet Merkur hat ein Magnetfeld. Das ist das Ergebnis des Fluges der amerikanischen Raumsonde „Mariner 10". Im Jahre 1974 passierte „Mariner" zweimal den Planeten. Das Magnetfeld von Merkur ist noch ein Rätsel: der Magnetismus der Erde entsteht durch den „Dynamoeffekt", d.h., die Rotation der Flüssigkeit im Erdinnern erzeugt das Magnetfeld. Die Rotation von Merkur aber ist   5 zu langsam. Ein Merkurtag ist 53 Tage lang.

VOCABULARY

der **Planet, -en**	planet	der **Magnetismus**	magnetism
Merkur	Mercury	die **Erde**	earth
der **Magnet**	magnet	**entstehen . . . durch (entsteht), entstand, ist entstanden**	to be generated . . . by, produced . . . by
das **Feld, -er**	field		
das **Magnetfeld**	magnetic field		
das **Ergebnis, -se**	result		
der **Flug, ⁃e**	flight	der **Dynamo**	dynamo
amerikanisch	American (adjective)	der **Effekt, -e**	effect
		der **Dynamoeffekt**	dynamo effect
der **Raum, ⁃e**	space, room	die **Rotation**	rotation
die **Sonde, -n**	probe, capsule, ship	die **Flüssigkeit, -en**	liquid
		das **Erdinnere**	interior of the earth
die **Raumsonde**	space capsule		
passieren	to pass; to go by	**erzeugen**	to produce; to generate
zweimal	two times		
noch	still, yet	**zu**	too
das **Rätsel, -**	puzzle	**langsam**	slow(ly)

STRUCTURAL EXERCISE

Underline all direct objects in the above reading.

VOCABULARY EXERCISE

Give the English equivalents of the italicized words:

1. Die Rotation ist *zu langsam.*
2. Das Magnetfeld von Merkur ist *noch* ein Rätsel.
3. Das ist *das Ergebnis* des Fluges der amerikanischen Raumsonde.
4. Die Raumsonde passierte *zweimal* den Planeten.
5. Das Magnetfeld von Merkur ist noch *ein Rätsel.*
6. Der Magnetismus der Erde *entsteht durch* den „Dynamoeffekt".
7. Die Rotation *der Flüssigkeit* im Erdinnern erzeugt das Magnetfeld.

esson **19**

STRUCTURE

1. Prefixes (continued)

a. Prefixes alter the meaning of the basic verb.

b. Inseparable prefixes remain attached to the basic verb.

2. Separable Prefixes

a. In the present and in past tenses, separable prefixes separate from the basic verb in main clauses.

b. When separated, the prefix always stands at the end of the clause:

Der Bus **fährt ab.** (present tense)
The bus is leaving.

Der Bus **fuhr ab.** (past tense)
The bus left / was leaving.

c. In a subordinate clause, the prefix is not separated from the verb.

Er weiß, daß der Bus **abfährt.** (present tense)
He knows that the bus is leaving.

Er wußte, daß der Bus **abfuhr.** (past tense)
He knew that the bus was leaving.

d. In the present perfect tense, the separable prefix is attached to the past participle of the verb. Note that **ge** is not omitted:

INFINITIVE: **abfahren** *to leave, depart*
PAST PARTICIPLE: **abgefahren**

HUNDERTACHTUNDNEUNZIG

Der Bus ist **abgefahren.**   (present perfect)
The bus has left.

Er weiß, daß der Bus **abgefahren** ist.
He knows that the bus has left.

e.   The separable prefix does not affect the conjugation of the basic verb:

Der Bus	**fährt**	**ab.**
Der Bus	**fuhr**	**ab.**
Der Bus	**ist**	**ab**gefahren.

f.   The most common separable prefixes are:

ab-	**dar-**	**hin-**	**vorbei-**
an-	**ein-**	**mit-**	**weg-**
auf-	**fort-**	**nach-**	**zu-**
aus-	**her-**	**vor-**	**zurück-**
bei-			

g.   Separable prefixes may be prepositions, adverbs, verbs, adjectives, or nouns.

3.   Weak Verbs with Separable Prefixes[1]

INFINITIVE	ENGLISH MEANING
ab-nutzen	*to use up, wear out*
an-deuten	*to point out, hint, indicate*
auf-zeichnen	*to record; to draw, sketch*
aus-rechnen	*to figure out, compute*
bei-stimmen	*to concur in, agree to, accede to*
dar-stellen	*to describe, represent, display*
ein-teilen	*to divide, classify, calibrate*
fort-setzen	*to carry on, continue, pursue*
her-stellen	*to produce; to establish*
hin-stellen	*to place down; to represent*
mit-teilen	*to inform, notify*
nach-prüfen	*to check, verify; to control*
vorbei-sprechen	*to talk around a subject*
vor-führen	*to present, show, demonstrate*
weg-legen	*to put away, put aside*
zu-machen	*to close, shut*
zurück-legen	*to cover a distance; to lay aside*

1.   These verbs will occur in subsequent lessons.

SELF-PREPARATORY EXERCISE

*Change the following sentences to past tense:**

Er zeichnet das Muster auf.	
Sie rechnet die Gleichung aus.	Er zeichnete das Muster auf.
Man führt den Film vor.	Sie rechnete die Gleichung aus.
Sie legen einen Kilometer zurück.	Man führte den Film vor.
Sie macht das Fenster zu.	Sie legten einen Kilometer zurück.
	Sie machte das Fenster zu.

EXERCISES

A. *Change the following sentences to past tense:**

1. Der Physiker prüft das Experiment nach.
2. Die Brauerei stellt Bier her.
3. Man setzt den Kirchenbau fort.
4. Der Freund deutet an, daß er nicht kommt.
5. Man teilt die Mathematik in verschiedene Teilgebiete ein.

B. *Supply the present-tense equivalents of the verbs in parentheses:*

1. Er _____ ihr _____, daß er nicht kommt. (to inform)
2. Nicht alle Menschen _____ der These Luthers _____. (to concur in)
3. Die schnelle Rotation _____ den Dynamo _____. (to wear out)
4. Der Präsidentschaftskandidat _____ seine Politik _____. (to describe)
5. Der Redner _____ an der Grundsatzfrage _____. (to talk around the subject)

SELF-PREPARATORY EXERCISE

*Change the following sentences to present perfect:**

Sie macht das Fenster zu.	
Man setzt den Kirchenbau fort.	Sie hat das Fenster zugemacht.
Die Brauerei stellt Bier her.	Man hat den Kirchenbau fortgesetzt.
Er führt den Film vor.	Die Brauerei hat Bier hergestellt.
Sie zeichnet das Muster auf.	Er hat den Film vorgeführt.
	Sie hat des Muster aufgezeichnet.

ZWEIHUNDERT

EXERCISES

A. *Change the following sentences to present perfect:* *

1. Sie rechnet die Gleichung aus.
2. Der Physiker prüft das Ergebnis nach.
3. Sie legen einen Kilometer in 10 Minuten zurück.
4. Man teilt die Mathematik in verschiedene Teilgebiete ein.
5. Was deutet der Freund an?

B. *Give the German equivalents of the following sentences:*

1. Einstein continued his work in America.   (present perfect)
2. She notified him that she had the result.   (past tense)
3. Gutenberg produced a bible.   (past tense)
4. They are checking the magnetic field.   (present tense)
5. The computer recorded the pattern.   (present perfect)

READING

Albrecht Dürer (1471–1528)

Albrecht Dürer war ein deutscher Maler, Graphiker und Kunsttheoretiker. Er unternahm Kunstreisen in Deutschland, nach Italien und in die Niederlande. Seine großen Werke schuf er in seiner Vaterstadt Nürnberg. Sehr bekannte Werke von ihm sind Ölgemälde (,,Adam und Eva''; ,,Die Apostel''), zahlreiche Porträts, Holzschnitte (,,Apokalypse''; ,,Ritter, Tod und Teufel'') und Kupferstiche, daneben aber auch   5 theoretische Werke über Anatomie und Perspektive.

VOCABULARY

der	**Maler, -**	painter, artist	das **Öl**	oil
der	**Graphiker, -**	graphic artist, illustrator	das **Ölgemälde**	oil painting
			der **Apostel, -**	apostle
die	**Kunst, ⸚e**	art	**zahlreich**	numerous
der	**Theoretiker, -**	theorist	das **Porträt, -s**	portrait
	unternehmen		das **Holz, ⸚er**	wood, lumber
	(unternimmt),		der **Schnitt, -e**	cut, cutting
	unternahm,		der **Holzschnitt**	wood cutting
	unternommen	to undertake	die **Apokalypse**	apocalypse
die	**Reise, -n**	travel, trip, journey	der **Ritter, -**	knight
die	**Niederlande**	Netherlands	der **Tod**	death
	schaffen		der **Stich, -e**	*here:* engraving, cut
	(schafft), schuf,		der **Kupferstich**	(copperplate) engraving
	hat geschaffen	to create, produce		
der	**Vater, ⸚**	father	**daneben**	besides, moreover, also
die	**Vaterstadt**	hometown		
	Nürnberg	Nuremberg	**theoretisch**	theoretical
	bekannt	well-known, famous, noted	die **Anatomie**	anatomy
			die **Perspektive, -n**	perspective
das	**Gemälde, -**	painting		

Albrecht Dürer: Selbstbildnis 1493   GERMAN INFORMATION CENTER

ZWEIHUNDERTZWEI

STRUCTURAL EXERCISE

Underline all nouns used in the plural in the above reading.

VOCABULARY EXERCISE

Give the English equivalents of the italicized words:

1. Dürer *unternahm* Kunstreisen in Deutschland, nach Italien und in die Niederlande.
2. Dürer schuf *zahlreiche* Portraits.
3. *Daneben* schuf er aber auch theoretische Werke.
4. Die Rotation der Flüssigkeit im Erdinnern *erzeugt* das Magnetfeld.
5. Seine Ölgemälde sind sehr *bekannt.*
6. Der gotische Stil entstand *unabhängig* in verschiedenen europäischen Ländern.
7. Eine andere Möglichkeit ist die genetische *Bekämpfung.*

STRUCTURE

4. Strong Verbs with Separable Prefixes[1]

INFINITIVE	ENGLISH MEANING	PRINCIPAL PARTS OF BASIC VERBS
ab-fahren	*to leave, depart*	**fahren (fährt), fuhr, ist gefahren**
an-kommen	*to arrive*	**kommen (kommt), kam, ist gekommen**
auf-stehen	*to get up*	**stehen (steht), stand, hat gestanden**
aus-halten	*to endure*	**halten (hält), hielt, hat gehalten**
bei-stehen	*to assist*	**stehen (steht), stand, hat gestanden**
dar-bringen	*to present, offer*	**bringen (bringt), brachte, hat gebracht**
ein-sehen	*to understand*	**sehen (sieht), sah, hat gesehen**
fort-fahren	*to continue, leave*	**fahren (fährt), fuhr, ist gefahren**
her-kommen	*to originate*	**kommen (kommt), kam, ist gekommen**
hin-gehen	*to go there*	**gehen (geht), ging, ist gegangen**
mit-nehmen	*to take along*	**nehmen (nimmt), nahm, hat genommen**
nach-denken	*to reflect, ponder*	**denken (denkt), dachte, hat gedacht**
vor-ziehen	*to prefer*	**ziehen (zieht), zog, hat gezogen**
vorbei-fliegen	*to fly by*	**fliegen (fliegt), flog, ist geflogen**

1. These verbs will occur in subsequent lessons.

INFINITIVE	ENGLISH MEANING	PRINCIPAL PARTS OF BASIC VERBS
weg-nehmen	*to take away*	**nehmen (nimmt), nahm, hat genommen**
zu-geben	*to admit*	**geben (gibt), gab, hat gegeben**
zurück-kommen	*to come back, return*	**kommen (kommt), kam, ist ge-kommen**

Note that the following verbs with separable prefixes take **sein** in the present perfect tense:

ab-fahren	(er) **ist abgefahren**
an-kommen	(er) **ist angekommen**
auf-stehen	(er) **ist aufgestanden**
fort-fahren	(er) **ist fortgefahren**
her-kommen	(er) **ist hergekommen**
vorbei-fliegen	(er) **ist vorbeigeflogen**
zurück-kommen	(er) **ist zurückgekommen**

SELF-PREPARATORY EXERCISE

*Change the following sentences to past tense:**

Der Bus fährt nicht ab.	
Er nimmt das Buch mit.	Der Bus fuhr nicht ab.
Wann kommt der Vater zurück?	Er nahm das Buch mit.
Der Student denkt nicht nach.	Wann kam der Vater zurück?
Wo kommt der Wagen her?	Der Student dachte nicht nach.
	Wo kam der Wagen her?

EXERCISES

A. *Change the following sentences to past tense:**

1. Die Raumsonde fliegt am Mars vorbei.
2. Sie zieht das Gemälde von Dürer vor.
3. Man sieht das Problem ein.
4. Der Lehrer nimmt dem Schüler das Buch weg.
5. Wann steht sie auf?

B. *Supply the present-tense equivalents of the verb in parentheses:*

1. Er _____ die Gefangenschaft _____. (to endure)
2. Der Mann _____ seiner Frau _____. (to assist)
3. Wo _____ diese Karte _____? (to originate)
4. Sie _____ zur Mutter _____. (to go there)
5. Der Maler _____ eine Reise nach Italien _____. (to prefer)

ZWEIHUNDERTVIER

SELF-PREPARATORY EXERCISE

Change the following sentences to present perfect: *

Der Präsident denkt über die Politik nach.	
Er hält den Widerstand aus.	Der Präsident hat über die Politik nachgedacht.
Die Raumsonde fliegt zweimal am Mars vorbei.	Er hat den Widerstand ausgehalten.
Wann kommt der Bus in Ulm an?	Die Raumsonde ist zweimal am Mars vorbeigeflogen.
Sie gibt zu, daß sie es noch nicht gemacht hat.	Wann ist der Bus in Ulm angekommen?
	Sie hat zugegeben, daß sie es noch nicht gemacht hat.

EXERCISES

A. *Change the following sentences to present perfect:* *

   1. Sie denkt über die Kostenrechnung nach.
   2. Die Erwachsenen stehen den Kindern bei.
   3. Sie nimmt das Buch mit.
   4. Er gibt zu, daß er die Übersetzung nicht schrieb.
   5. Wann fliegt die Raumsonde am Mars vorbei?

B. *Give the German equivalents of the English sentences:*

   1. When did she get up? (present perfect)
   2. The student does not reflect on the word.   (present)
   3. He admitted that he was in Ulm. (past tense)
   4. When did the father come back? (present perfect)
   5. She closed the window. (present perfect)

C. *Form sentences from the elements below in the tenses indicated. Separable and inseparable prefixes mixed:*

   1. Gutenberg / benutzen / bewegliche Lettern   (present perfect)
   2. Die Frau / fortsetzen / ihre Reise   (present)
   3. Der Schüler / bestehen / die Prüfung   (present perfect)
   4. Wann / abfahren / der Bus / nach Berlin?   (present)
   5. Der Chemiker / herstellen / die Flüssigkeit   (past)

D. *Change the following sentences to the tenses indicated. Separable and inseparable prefixes mixed:* *

   1. Der Professor hat das neue Buch erhalten.   (past)
   2. Die Stechmücke verbreitete Malaria.   (present perfect)

3. Der Bauer benutzte kein Insektizid.   (present perfect)
4. Damals haben die Menschen die Gefangenschaft ausgehalten.   (past)
5. Man erkennt die gotische Bauweise an dem Spitzbogen.   (past)

5. Impersonal Pronoun Subject <u>es</u>

a.   There are several verbs in German used only with the impersonal pronoun **es** as subject or in place of the subject.

b.   Phenomena in nature:

Es regnet.	**Es schneit.**	**Es donnert.**	**Es blitzt.**
It's raining.	*It's snowing.*	*It's thundering.*	*It's lightening.*

c.   When the cause of the action is unknown:

Es klopft an die Tür.   *(Someone's knocking on the door.)*
Es lärmt auf der Straße.   *(There is noise on the street.)*

d.   Certain fixed expressions:

Es geht seinem Vater **gut.**   *(His father is doing well / is okay.)*
Es gefällt ihr in dieser Stadt.   *(She likes this* city. / This city pleases her.)

e.   Adjective-verb combinations expressing feelings:

Es ist ihnen kalt.   *(They feel cold. / It's cold here.)*
Es wird ihr schlecht.   (She feels sick. / She is getting sick.)

f.   **Es** used in place of the subject:

Es sind   *There are*
Es waren   *There were*

Es waren viele Studenten da.   *There were a lot of students there.*

SELF-PREPARATORY EXERCISE
Give the English equivalents:

Es regnet.	
Es geht dem Lehrer gut.	It's raining.
Es klopft an die Tür.	The teacher is doing well.
Es gibt viele Probleme.	Someone's knocking on the door.
Es gefällt ihm in Berlin.	There are many problems.
	He likes Berlin.

ZWEIHUNDERTSECHS

EXERCISE

Supply the missing **es** *+ verb combination to give the equivalents of the English sentences:*

1. _____ der Frau kalt.   (The woman feels cold.)
2. _____ ihm schlecht.   (He feels sick.)
3. _____.   (It's snowing.)
4. _____ ihr in Zürich.   (She likes Zürich.)
5. _____ viele Menschen da. (There were a lot of people there.)

READING

Deutschland — Ein Überblick

Deutschland ist heute zugleich ein historischer, kultureller und geographischer Begriff. Politisch gibt es auf dem Gebiet des früheren Deutschen Reiches seit 1949 zwei deutsche Staaten: die Bundesrepublik Deutschland (BRD) und die Deutsche Demokratische Republik (DDR). Oft spricht man einfach von ,,Westdeutschland'' und ,,Ostdeutschland''.   5

   Die Bundesrepublik hat ungefähr 62 Millionen Einwohner, die DDR etwa 17 Millionen. Die größte Stadt Deutschlands, Berlin, hat rund 3,2 (drei Komma zwei) Millionen Einwohner, davon 2,1 (zwei Komma eins) Millionen in West- und 1,1 (eins Komma eins) Millionen in Ost-Berlin. Dann folgt die Handels- und Hafenstadt Hamburg mit 1,8 Millionen Einwohnern. Die bayrische Hauptstadt München ist mit   10
1,3 Millionen Einwohnern die drittgrößte Stadt. Die Entfernung von Hamburg nach München ist ungefähr 800 Kilometer.

   Geographisch gliedert man Deutschland in vier große Gebiete: die norddeutsche Tiefebene, die Mittelgebirge, das Alpenvorland, und das Hochgebirge (die Alpen). Die wichtigsten Flüsse sind der Rhein, die Weser, die Elbe, die Oder und die Donau.   15
Der Rhein, die Weser und die Elbe fließen von Süden nach Norden in die Nordsee. Die Oder mündet in die Ostsee. Die Donau fließt von Westen nach Osten durch Österreich, Ungarn und den Balkan in das Schwarze Meer.

VOCABULARY

der	**Überblick**	survey, synopsis		**nord-**	north
	zugleich	at the same time	das	**Deutsche Reich**	German Empire
	historisch	historical		**einfach**	simply
	kulturell	cultural		**west-**	west
	geographisch	geographical		**ost-**	east
der	**Begriff, -e**	concept, idea		**ungefähr**	approximately
	politisch	politically	der	**Einwohner, -**	inhabitant, resident
das	**Gebiet, -e**	area, region		**größt-**	largest, biggest
	früher	earlier, former, prior			

das **Komma**	comma (German decimals are set off by a comma)	das **Hochgebirge**	high mountains, high mountain range
davon	of those, thereof, of that	**wichtigst-**	most important
der **Handel**	trade, commerce	der **Fluß, ̈-sse**	river, stream
die **Handelsstadt**	commerce city	der **Rhein**	Rhine river
der **Hafen, ̈-**	harbor, port	die **Weser**	Weser river
die **Hafenstadt**	port city	die **Elbe**	Elbe river
bayrisch	Bavarian	die **Oder**	Oder river
die **Hauptstadt**	capital city	die **Donau**	Danube river
München	Munich	**fließen**	
die **Entfernung, -en**	distance	**(fließt), floß,**	
von . . . nach	from . . . to	**ist geflossen**	to flow
gliedern	to divide, classify, arrange	der **Süden**	the South
		der **Norden**	the North
tief	deep, low	die **Nordsee**	North Sea
die **Ebene, -n**	plain, plane, flat	**münden**	to empty into, flow into
die **Tiefebene**	lowlands, plain	die **Ostsee**	Baltic Sea
mittel-	medium, mid-, middle	der **Westen**	the West
das **Gebirge, -**	mountain range, mountains	der **Osten**	the East
		Ungarn	Hungary
das **Mittelgebirge**	sub-alpine mountains	der **Balkan**	the Balkans, Balkan
die **Alpen**	Alps, Alpine mountains	das **Schwarze Meer**	the Black Sea
das **Vorland**	foothills, foreland	das **Meer, -e**	sea, ocean

STRUCTURAL EXERCISE

Underline all the subjects in the above reading.

VOCABULARY EXERCISE

Give the English equivalents of the italicized words:

1. *Es gibt* heute zwei deutsche Staaten.
2. *Die Entfernung* ist 800 Kilometer.
3. Die Bundesrepublik hat *ungefähr* 62 Millionen Einwohner.
4. München ist die *drittgrößte* Stadt.
5. Man spricht *einfach* von Westdeutschland und Ostdeutschland.
6. Deutschland ist heute ein historischer, kultureller und geographischer *Begriff.*
7. Auf dem *Gebiet* des früheren Deutschen Reiches gibt es heute zwei deutsche Staaten.

Lesson **20**

STRUCTURE

1. Future Tense

a. The future tense consists of a form of **werden** plus the infinitive of the main verb:

Er **wird** morgen nach Berlin **fliegen.** *(He will fly to Berlin tomorrow.)*
Sie **werden** heute **ankommen.** *(They will arrive today.)*

b. Review of **werden:**

er		*he*		**sie**	*they*	
sie		*she*		**die Menschen** } **werden**	*people* } *will*	
es } **wird**	*it* } *will*					
man		*one*				
das Kind		*the child*				

c. In the future tense, the main verb (= infinitive) remains the constant factor. It is the last element in a main clause:

Er **wird** morgen nach Berlin **fliegen.**

d. In subordinate clauses, the conjugated form of **werden** follows the infinitive of the main verb:

Er sagt, daß er morgen nach Berlin **fliegen wird.**
He says that he will fly to Berlin tomorrow.

e. In conversational German, the future tense is often replaced by the present tense, especially when an adverbial expression indicating future time is used:

Er **fliegt morgen** nach Berlin. *(He will fly / He flies to Berlin tomorrow.)*

f. The future tense is often used with the adverb **wohl** to express probability, expectancy, or supposition at the present time:

Sie **wird wohl** im Theater **sein.** *(She is probably at the theater.)*

SELF-PREPARATORY EXERCISE

*Change the following sentences to future tense:**

Sie geht in die Stadt.	
Der Student liest das Buch.	Sie wird in die Stadt gehen.
Studiert er an dieser Universität?	Der Student wird das Buch lesen.
Wann haben sie Zeit?	Wird er an dieser Universität studieren?
Man analysiert das Ergebnis.	Wann werden sie Zeit haben?
	Man wird das Ergebnis analysieren.

EXERCISES

A. *Supply the correct form of* **werden:**

1. Der Professor _____ den Begriff erklären.
2. Wann _____ die Kinder in die Schule gehen?
3. Man _____ es wohl morgen einsehen.
4. Wo _____ die Menschen im Jahr 2000 leben?
5. Die Schüler _____ den Film sehen.

B. *Form sentences in the future tense with the elements given:**

1. Man / benutzen / das Buch
2. Er / es / wohl / wissen
3. Wann / untersuchen / die Ökologen / das Ökosystem?
4. Die Tochter / arbeiten / wohl /
5. Sie (= they) / es / glauben / nicht

2. Past, Present Perfect, and Past Perfect

a. German and English use three tenses to express situations or events in the past:

past tense,
present perfect tense,
past perfect tense.

ZWEIHUNDERTZEHN

b. For practical purposes, the past and present perfect tenses in German are identical in meaning:

Er ging = Er ist gegangen. *(He went.)*

c. In English, the past tense generally describes an action fully completed in the past: *Abraham Lincoln was always honest.*

d. In English, actions starting in the past but not yet completed generally use the present perfect tense: *He has always been honest.* (= *and still is.*)

e. English and German use the past perfect tense to describe events or situations which precede still other events or situations in the past:

After he had finished his homework, he went to his friend.

PAST PERFECT: *he had finished*
PAST TENSE: *he went*

The example establishes the following time sequence:

Event 1: He had finished his homework.
Event 2: He went to his friend.

Event 1 precedes event 2; therefore event 1 is expressed in the past perfect tense.

f. In German, the past perfect tense consists of the past tense form of **haben** or **sein** and the past participle of the main verb:

Er hatte das Buch **gelesen.** *(He has read the book).*
Er war in die Stadt **gefahren.** *(He had gone to the city.)*

g. The past participle is in last place in statements and in questions with or without question words:

STATEMENT:	Sie **hatte** die Karte noch nicht **ge-schrieben.** *She had not written the card yet.*
QUESTION WITH QUESTION WORD:	Wann **hatte** man den Versuch **unternommen?** *When had they carried out the experiment?*
QUESTION WITHOUT QUESTION WORD:	**Hatten** die Kinder den Film **gesehen?** *Had the children seen the movie?*

h. In subordinate clauses, the past participle precedes the auxiliary verb (past tense form of **haben** or **sein**) at the end of the clause:

Man wartete, bis er den Versuch **beendet hatte.**
One waited until he had finished the experiment.

i. Subordinate clauses in the past perfect tense are often introduced by the following subordinating conjunctions:

bevor	*before*	**seitdem**	*since (then)*
bis	*until*	**nachdem**	*after (that)*
ehe	*before*		

SELF-PREPARATORY EXERCISES

*Change the following sentences to past perfect:**

Er hat den Mann gefragt.	
Sie sind ins Theater gegangen.	Er hatte den Mann gefragt.
Es ist kalt geworden.	Sie waren ins Theater gegangen.
Man hat es schon gemacht.	Es war kalt geworden.
Er ist nach Berlin gefahren.	Man hatte es schon gemacht.
	Er war nach Berlin gefahren.

EXERCISES

A. *Change the following sentences to past perfect:**

1. Dürer hat eine Reise nach Italien unternommen.
2. Die Rotation der Flüssigkeit hat den Magnetismus erzeugt.
3. Was für eine Ansicht hat Lincoln in der Sklavenfrage vertreten?
4. Was hat die Freundin angedeutet?
5. Ist das Klima im Winter kalt gewesen?

B. *Supply the German subordinating conjunction equivalent to the conjunction in parentheses:*

1. Der Wissenschaftler erklärte das Ergebnis, _____ er den Versuch beendet hatte. (after)
2. Der Schüler lernte, _____ er die Reifeprüfung gemacht hatte. (until)
3. _____ Gutenberg den Buchdruck vereinfacht hatte, hatte man nicht viele Bücher. (before)
4. _____ sie das Haus gekauft hatten, waren sie arm. (after)
5. _____ Dürer eine Reise nach Italien unternommen hatte, schuf er zahlreiche Gemälde. (after)

ZWEIHUNDERTZWÖLF

C. *Form sentences in the past perfect tense with the following elements:* *

1. Die Studentin / studieren / Anatomie
2. Die Schülerin / geben / dem Lehrer / das Buch
3. Man / bringen / ihnen / die Bilder
4. Wann / der Sohn / in Berlin / sein
5. Sie wußte, wann / er / das Buch / schreiben

D. *Give the German equivalents:*

1. She had read the translation.
2. He knew that she had been in Germany.
3. Had it been difficult?
4. They had seen it.
5. He had studied at the university.

READING

Antisemitismus

Antisemitismus bedeutet die feindliche Einstellung gegen Juden. Der Antisemit steht
den Juden aus rassischen, politischen oder religiösen Gründen feindselig gegenüber.
Diese unsinnige Einstellung hält einer kritischen Überprüfung nicht stand. Der
Antisemitismus geht zurück auf das Mittelalter, als man die Juden während der Zeit
der Kreuzzüge aus religiösen Gründen verfolgte und sie um ihr Hab und Gut   5
beraubte. Im Laufe der Geschichte hat man sie seither immer wieder verfolgt. Die
schlimmsten Judenverfolgungen gab es während der Inquisition in Spanien, im
zaristischen Rußland und im Dritten Reich in Deutschland. Unter der Herrschaft der
Nazis[1] hat man zwischen fünf und sechs Millionen europäische Juden ermordet. Der
Antisemitismus ist leider auch heute noch lebendig.   10

VOCABULARY

der **Antisemitismus**	anti-Semitism	**aus**	*here:* for
feindlich	hostile, ini-	**rassisch**	racial
	mical, un-	**religiös**	religious
	friendly	der **Grund, ̈e**	reason, motive,
die **Einstellung**	attitude		cause
der **Jude, -n**	Jew	**feindselig**	hostile, ini-
der **Antisemit, -en**	anti-Semite		mical, un-
gegenüber-stehen	to oppose, stand		friendly
(**steht gegenüber**),	opposite	**unsinnig**	senseless, ab-
stand gegenüber,			surd, non-
gegenübergestanden			sensical

1. **der Nazi** (plural: **die Nazis**): member of the National Socialist German Workers Party (**Na-
tionalsozialistische Deutsche Arbeiterpartei**).

ZWEIHUNDERTDREIZEHN

	stand-halten (hält stand), hielt stand, standgehalten	to withstand, to resist	
	kritisch	critical	
die	**Überprüfung**	examination, scrutiny	
	zurück-gehen ... auf (geht zurück), ging zurück, ist zurückgegangen	to originate from	
das	**Mittelalter**	Middle Ages	
	als	when	
	während (genitive preposition)	during	
der	**Kreuzzug, ⁻e**	crusade	
das	**Kreuz, -e**	cross	
	verfolgen ... aus	to persecute for	
das	**Hab und Gut**	goods and chattel, all one's possessions, property	

	berauben ... um	to rob of, deprive of
	im Laufe	in the course, in the process
die	**Geschichte**	history
die	**Geschichte, -n**	story
	seither	since then
	wieder	again
	immer wieder	again and again
	schlimm	bad
	schlimmst-	worst
die	**Verfolgung, -en**	persecution, pogrom
die	**Inquisition**	inquisition
	Spanien	Spain
	zaristisch	csarist
	Rußland	Russia
das	**Dritte Reich**	Third Reich, Nazi regime
die	**Herrschaft**	rule, dominion, command
	leider	unfortunately
	lebendig	alive, active, living

STRUCTURAL EXERCISES

A. *Underline all definite articles in the genitive case in the above reading.*

B. *Give the English equivalents of the following German verbs with prepositions:*

1. zurückgehen . . . auf
2. verfolgen . . . aus
3. berauben . . . um

4. entstehen . . . durch
5. erkennen . . . an

VOCABULARY EXERCISE

Give the English equivalents of the italicized words:

1. *Im Laufe* der Geschichte hat man sie seither immer wieder verfolgt.
2. Diese unsinnige Einstellung *hält* einer kritischen Überprüfung nicht *stand.*
3. Man hat sie *immer wieder* verfolgt.
4. Man verfolgte sie aus religiösen *Gründen.*
5. Sie hält einer kritischen *Überprüfung* nicht stand.
6. Man verfolgte sie *während* der Zeit der Kreuzzüge.
7. Man hat sie *seither* immer wieder verfolgt.

STRUCTURE

3. Modal Verbs

a. Modal verbs occur in both English and German. They provide additional information beyond the main verb: *You can see the man.*

The modal *can* expresses the ability to perform, while the simple statement, "You see the man," lacks the aspect of the modal (ability) and gives only the information of the main verb.

b. Modal verbs express a relationship between the subject and the main verb; they describe the attitude with which the subject relates to the main verb:

$$\text{The subject} \begin{Bmatrix} \text{has the ability} \\ \text{has the permission} \\ \text{is under compulsion} \\ \text{has the obligation} \\ \text{has the desire or intention} \\ \text{likes} \end{Bmatrix} \text{to do something.}$$

c. German expresses the relationship between the subject and the main verb by means of a modal verb:

SUBJECT	MODAL VERB	ADVERB	INFINITIVE OF MAIN VERB
Die Männer	**können**	heute	**arbeiten.**

d. German uses the following modals to express:

ability	**können**	*can, may, able to*
permission	**dürfen**	*may, is permissible*
compulsion	**müssen**	*must, have to*
obligation	**sollen**	*is supposed to, is to*
desire or intention	**wollen**	*intend, want to*
liking	**mögen**	*may, like to*

SELF-PREPARATORY EXERCISE

Give the English equivalents of the German sentences:

Die Männer wollen heute arbeiten.	
Die Kinder dürfen ihnen helfen.	The men want to work today.
Die Frauen sollen nicht in die Kirche gehen.	The children are permitted (may) help them.
Sie mögen heute nicht viel essen.	The women (wives) aren't supposed to go to church.
Die Lehrer müssen heute die Studenten fragen.	They don't like to eat a lot today.
	The teachers have to ask the students today.

EXERCISE

Give the English equivalents of the German sentences:

1. Die Bauern können keine Mineraldünger verwenden.
2. Die Abgeordneten müssen die Politik formulieren.
3. Die Ökologen sollen für die Erhaltung der urwüchsigen Landschaft plädieren.
4. Die Entwicklungsländer wollen ein höheres industrielles Niveau haben.
5. Die Schüler dürfen die Reifeprüfung machen.

4. Modal Stems

a.   In the present tense, modals have two verb stems, with the exception of **sollen.**

b.   The infinitive and plural stems of the modal are identical:

INFINITIVE STEM:	**können**	*can, to be able to, may*
PLURAL STEM:	**sie können**	*they can*

c.   The singular forms use a stem that is different from the plural stems, with the exception of **sollen:**

INFINITIVE	SINGULAR STEM
können	**kann**
dürfen	**darf**
müssen	**muß**
wollen	**will**
mögen	**mag**
sollen	**soll**

d.   In the third person singular present tense, the modal does not add any endings to the singular stem:

SINGULAR STEM: **kann**

	er kann	*he can*
THIRD PERSON	**sie kann**	*she can*
SINGULAR	**es kann**	*it can*
PRESENT TENSE	**man kann**	*one can*
	das Kind kann	*the child can*

e.   Modals in independent clauses and in questions with question words are in second position, and the dependent infinitive (the infinitive of the main verb) is at the end of the main clause:

Der Student **kann** heute nicht **studieren.** *(The student cannot study today.)*

ZWEIHUNDERTSECHZEHN

f. In subordinate clauses, the modal verb follows the dependent infinitive at the end of the clause:

Er weiß, daß er viel **lernen muß.** (*He knows that he must learn a lot.*)

SELF-PREPARATORY EXERCISE

Cover the right-hand column with a sheet of paper. Using the correct form of **können,** *express the entire sentence:*

Er _____ helfen.	
Er _____ arbeiten.	Er kann helfen.
Sie *(she)* _____ nicht laufen.	Er kann arbeiten.
Man _____ das machen.	Sie kann nicht laufen.
Sie *(pl.)* _____ ihn sehen.	Man kann das machen.
	Sie können ihn sehen.

EXERCISES

A. *Change the following sentences by adding the modals:*

1. Sie hilft ihm. (können)
2. Die Professoren arbeiten in dem Labor. (können)
3. Er liest das Buch. (können)

B. *Form sentences in the present tense, using the elements given below:*

1. das Kind / können / sehen / den Vater
2. Man / können / das Lied / singen
3. Der Erwachsene / können / gehen / auf die Volkshochschule

SELF-PREPARATORY EXERCISE

Using the correct form of **dürfen,** *express the entire sentence:*

Man _____ sie sehen.	
Sie *(pl.)* _____ das Wasser trinken.	Man darf sie sehen.
Das Kind _____ heute nicht spielen.	Sie dürfen das Wasser trinken.
Er _____ nach Berlin fliegen.	Das Kind darf heute nicht spielen.
Die Männer _____ den Film sehen.	Er darf nach Berlin fliegen.
	Die Männer dürfen den Film sehen.

EXERCISES

A. *Change the following sentences by adding the modals:**

    1. Er arbeitet hier. (dürfen)
    2. Sie untersuchen den photoelektrischen Effekt. (dürfen)
    3. Man ermittelt das Ergebnis in wenigen Stunden. (dürfen)

B. *Form sentences in the present tense, using the elements given below:*

    1. Die Tochter / dürfen / gehen / in die Stadt
    2. Der Physiker / dürfen / das Verfahren / benutzen
    3. Wann / dürfen / die Kinder / den Film / sehen?

SELF-PREPARATORY EXERCISE

Using the correct form of the modal **müssen,** *express the entire sentence:*

Die Filme _____ hier sein.	
Das Mädchen _____ in die Schule gehen.	Die Filme müssen hier sein.
Man _____ jetzt arbeiten.	Das Mädchen muß in die Schule gehen.
Sie (*pl.*) _____ das Haus kaufen.	Man muß jetzt arbeiten.
Das Buch _____ auf dem Tisch liegen.	Sie müssen das Haus kaufen.
	Das Buch muß auf dem Tisch liegen.

EXERCISES

A. *Change the following sentences by adding the modals:**

    1. Man unterscheidet zwei Grundformen. (müssen)
    2. Sie weiß, daß sie die Sprache lernt. (müssen)
    3. Sie antworten ihm. (müssen)

B. *Form sentences in the present tense, using the elements below:*

    1. Der Karpfen / vermeiden / müssen / schnelle Gewässer
    2. Das Forschungsinstitut / müssen / erproben / eine neue Roggenart
    3. Die Wissenschaftler / müssen / die Proteinstrukturen / analysieren

ZWEIHUNDERTACHTZEHN

SELF-PREPARATORY EXERCISE

Using the correct form of the modal **wollen,** express the entire sentence:

Sie (pl.) _____ Deutsch lernen.	
Er _____ das nicht berechnen.	Sie wollen Deutsch lernen.
Die Kinder _____ es nicht machen.	Er will das nicht berechnen.
Man _____ den Professor fragen.	Die Kinder wollen es nicht machen.
Sie (pl.) _____ ihn nicht sehen.	Man will den Professor fragen.
	Sie wollen ihn nicht sehen.

EXERCISES

A. Change the following sentences by adding the modals:*

1. Sie studiert Biologie. (wollen)
2. Wo kauft er den Wagen? (wollen)
3. Die Studenten beenden die Dissertationen. (wollen)

B. Form sentences in the present tense, using the elements given below:

1. Er / wollen / vereinfachen / den Buchdruck
2. Sie fragt ihn, / wann / er / wollen / kommen
3. Die Töchter / wollen / fliegen / nach Deutschland

SELF-PREPARATORY EXERCISE

Using the correct form of the modal **mögen,** express the entire sentence:

Er _____ das Bier nicht trinken.	
Das Kind _____ das Bild nicht sehen.	Er mag das Bier nicht trinken.
Sie (sing.) _____ die Zigaretten nicht rauchen.	Das Kind mag das Bild nicht sehen.
	Sie mag die Zigaretten nicht rauchen.

EXERCISES

A. Change the following sentences by adding the modals:*

1. Die Menschen sehen den Film nicht. (mögen)
2. Man hört den Chef nicht. (mögen)
3. Sie liest das Buch nicht. (mögen)

Köln: Panorama

ZWEIHUNDERTZWANZIG

B. *Form sentences in the present tense, using the elements given below:*

1. Er / mögen / arbeiten / nicht
2. Die Frau / mögen / helfen / ihm / nicht
3. Der Karpfen / mögen / das / fressen / nicht

SELF-PREPARATORY EXERCISE

Using the correct form of the modal **sollen,** *express the entire sentence:*

Er _____ ihr helfen.	
Man _____ nicht rauchen.	Er soll ihr helfen.
Die Kinder _____ mehr lernen.	Man soll nicht rauchen.
	Die Kinder sollen mehr lernen.

EXERCISES

A. *Change the following sentences by adding the modals:* *

1. Sie unternimmt die Reise. (sollen)
2. Man erzeugt das Magnetfeld. (sollen)
3. Sie fragen immer. (sollen)

B. *Form sentences in the present tense, using the elements given below:*

1. Der Bauer / sollen / keine Mineraldünger / verwenden
2. Man / sollen / vereinfachen / die Methode
3. Das Herz / sollen / befördern / das Blut

READING

Deutschland — der Rhein und die Berge

Der Rhein ist ein europäischer Fluß. Er kommt aus der Schweiz, fließt zunächst entlang der deutsch-französischen Grenze und dann vorbei an den alten Städten Mainz, Koblenz, Bonn und Köln. In den Niederlanden mündet er schließlich in die Nordsee. An den Ufern des Rheins stehen viele Burgruinen. Manche Touristen halten ihn deshalb für einen romantischen Fluß. Sein Wasser aber ist heute von der   5 Industrie verschmutzt.

   Die Bayerischen Alpen sind das größte Gebirge in Deutschland. Der höchste Berg ist die Zugspitze mit 2 963 Metern. Bekannte Mittelgebirge sind der Harz, südöstlich von Hannover, die Eifel, südwestlich von Köln, der Schwarzwald im Südwesten und der Bayerische Wald an der tschechoslowakischen Grenze. Alle diese Gebirge sind   10 beliebte Feriengebiete.

ZWEIHUNDERTEINUNDZWANZIG

VOCABULARY

der	**Berg, -e**	mountain	die	**Burg, -en**	castle, fortress
	kommen		die	**Ruine, -n**	ruins
	(kommt), kam			**manch**	some, many a
	ist gekommen	to come	der	**Tourist, -en**	tourist
	kommen . . . aus	come from,		**halten (hält),**	
		proceed from,		**hielt, gehalten**	to hold
		arise from		**halten . . . für**	to consider, look
die	**Schweiz**	Switzerland			upon
	fließen			**romantisch**	romantic
	(fließt), floß,		die	**Industrie, -n**	industry
	ist geflossen	to flow		**verschmutzen**	to pollute
	zunächst	at first		**verschmutzt sein**	to be polluted
	entlang	along		**höchst**	highest
die	**Grenze, -n**	border, boundary		**südöstlich**	southeasterly
	dann	then	der	**Schwarzwald**	Black Forest
	vorbei	past, by		**tschechoslowakisch**	Czech
	Köln	Cologne		**beliebt**	favorite, loved
	schließlich	finally	die	**Ferien** (*pl.*)	vacation, holiday
das	**Ufer, -**	bank, shore			

STRUCTURAL EXERCISE

Underline all verbs which are strong or irregular in the above reading.

VOCABULARY EXERCISE

Give the English equivalents of the italicized words:

1. *Zunächst* fließt der Rhein durch die Schweiz.
2. Er fließt *entlang* der deutsch-französischen Grenze.
3. Er mündet *schließlich* in die Nordsee.
4. Viele Burgruinen stehen an den *Ufern* des Rheins.
5. Diese Gebirge sind *beliebte* Feriengebiete.
6. Man hat sie *seither* immer wieder verfolgt.
7. Sie *halten* ihn *für* einen romantischen Fluß.

Kann die Wohnung den Menschen krank machen?

Lesson 21

STRUCTURE

1. Adjective Endings

a. Adjectives describe:

persons,
objects or ideas,
conditions.

b. Adjectives may be used before a noun as attributive (= descriptive) adjectives or as predicate adjectives after certain verbs:

ATTRIBUTIVE ADJECTIVE: They own a *beautiful* house.
PREDICATE ADJECTIVE: Today it is *warm*.

c. Predicate adjectives often follow these verbs in German:

sein	**bleiben**	**scheinen** *(to seem, appear)*
werden	**heißen**	

Example:

Heute **ist es kalt.** *(Today it is cold.)*

d. Attributive adjectives use declensional endings in German (English does not have declensional endings on adjectives)

ZWEIHUNDERTDREIUNDZWANZIG

e. There are three basic situations which determine the declensional ending of the attributive adjective:

1. Adjectives following a definite article and **der**-words:

Das **alte** Haus ist dort. *(There is the old house.)*

2. Adjectives following an indefinite article and **ein**-words:

Das ist ein **altes** Haus. *(That is an old house.)*

3. Adjectives preceding a noun without any articles at all:

Alte Häuser sind gut. *(Old houses are good.)*

f. Adjectives following a definite article take the endings **-e** or **-en**, depending on case, number, and gender as shown by the definite article:

	MASC.	FEM.	NEUT.	PLURAL
NOM.	-e	-e	-e	-en
GEN.	-en	-en	-en	-en
DAT.	-en	-en	-en	-en
ACC.	-en	-e	-e	-en

g. The same endings are used for adjectives following **der**-words:

dies-	*this*	**jen-**	*that*
welch-	*which*	**jed-**	*every*
solch	*such*	**manch-**	*some*

Examples:

Er kennt **das schöne Mädchen.** *(He knows the beautiful girl.)*

ANALYSIS: **-e** because the adjective:

follows a definite article;
precedes a neuter noun in the accusative singular.

Der Chef kauft **diesen neuen Wagen.** *(The boss buys this new car.)*

ANALYSIS: **-en** because the adjective:

follows a **der**-word;
precedes a masculine noun in the accusative singular.

EXERCISES

A. *Supply the correct nominative endings:*

1. Das ist der neu_____ Chef.
2. Wer wird der nächst_____ Präsident?

ZWEIHUNDERTVIERUNDZWANZIG

   3.   Hier steht die dick_____ Wand.
   4.   Wie heißt das klein_____ Kind?

B.   *Supply the correct genitive endings:*

   1.   Wegen der niedrig _____ Ernte hat er höhere Preise.
   2.   Sie kennt den Vater des gut_____ Freundes.
   3.   Jenseits dieser lang_____ Grenze liegt Ostdeutschland.
   4.   Er arbeitet in dem Labor der groß_____ Universität.

C.   *Supply the correct dative endings:*

   1.   Er studiert an der neu_____ Universität.
   2.   Sie hilft der klein_____ Schwester.
   3.   Er spricht mit jenem gewandt_____ Redner.
   4.   Mit welcher neu_____ Methode arbeitet er?

D.   *Supply the correct accusative endings:*

   1.   Sie kennen die englisch_____ Architektur.
   2.   Man findet dieses bekannt_____ Gemälde in London.
   3.   Er spricht über diesen historisch_____ Begriff.
   4.   Sie ist in das schön_____ Gebirge gefahren.

E.   *Supply the correct plural endings:*

   1.   Man kennt die zahlreich_____ Bodenschätze Afrikas.
   2.   Die beweglich_____ Lettern vereinfachten den Buchdruck.
   3.   Er fliegt in die Vereinigt_____ Staaten.
   4.   Der Wissenschaftler erklärte die technisch_____ Begriffe.

F.   *Supply the correct adjective endings:*

   1.   Die neu_____ Lehrerin heißt Müller.
   2.   Er hat einen gebündelt_____ Röntgenstrahl auf das Material gerichtet.
   3.   Man nennt Archäologie in der deutsch_____ Sprache auch Altertumskunde.
   4.   Die Arithmetik bezeichnet die Gesetze der verschieden_____ Rechenarten.
   5.   Diese Methode benutzt als Grundlage die mathematisch_____ Relationen unter den Faktoren der Kristallstruktur.

G.   *Substitute the pronoun in parentheses for the subject in the original sentence. Make all necessary changes in the verbs:* *

   1.   Sie wollen französische Architektur studieren.   (er)
   2.   Die Chemiker müssen ein neues Verfahren entwickeln.   (man)
   3.   Die Präsidenten dürfen nichts erklären.   (er)
   4.   Sie dürfen nicht rauchen.   (sie [*she*])
   5.   Die Kinder müssen in dem Garten spielen.   (es)

H. *Form sentences in the present tense using the elements below:*

1. Er weiß, daß / er / müssen / studieren / Chemie
2. Die Professoren / sollen / ermitteln / die Resultate
3. Warum / er / wollen / schneller / arbeiten?
4. Der Student / können / die Bücher / lesen / nicht
5. Die Rotation / müssen / erzeugen / den Magnetismus

I. *Give the German equivalents of the English sentences:*

1. She cannot hear the speaker.
2. He wants to help him.
3. When is the child allowed to play?
4. He knows that he should not smoke.
5. When does she intend to come?

READING

Atlantis

Atlantis war eine sagenhafte Insel mitten im Atlantischen Ozean. Plato hat Atlantis als ein mächtiges Reich mit hoher Kultur beschrieben, das 9 000 Jahre vor seiner Zeit durch eine Naturkatastrophe im Meer versunken ist.

VOCABULARY

	sagenhaft	legendary, mythical		**beschreiben**	to describe
die	**Insel, -n**	island		**schreiben (schreibt), schrieb, geschrieben**	to write
	atlantisch	atlantic	die	**Natur**	nature
der	**Ozean, -e**	ocean, sea	die	**Katastrophe, -n**	catastrophe
	Plato	Greek philosopher (427–347 B.C.)		**versinken**	to sink; to be swallowed up
	mächtig	powerful		**sinken (sinkt), sank, ist gesunken**	to sink

VOCABULARY EXERCISE

Give the English equivalents of the italicized words:

1. Atlantis war eine sagenhafte *Insel*.
2. Atlantis war ein *mächtiges* Reich.
3. Atlantis *hatte* eine hohe Kultur.
4. Plato *hat* Atlantis *beschrieben*.
5. Atlantis ist 9 000 Jahre *vor seiner Zeit* versunken.
6. Manche Touristen halten den Rhein *deshalb* für einen romantischen Fluß.
7. In den Niederlanden mündet er *schließlich* in die Nordsee.

ZWEIHUNDERTSECHSUNDZWANZIG

STRUCTURE

2. Modals: Past Tense

a. In the present tense, German modals differentiate between a singular and a plural stem with the exception of **sollen:**

INFINITIVE	PLURAL STEM	SINGULAR STEM	MEANING
können	**könn-**	**kann-**	*can, able*
müssen	**müss-**	**muß-**	*must, have to*
dürfen	**dürf-**	**darf-**	*may, permission*
mögen	**mög-**	**mag-**	*may, like*
wollen	**woll-**	**will-**	*want*

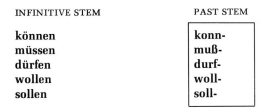

Only **sollen** does not differentiate between a singular and a plural stem:

sollen	**soll-**	**soll-**	*should, supposed to*

b. The past tense of these modal verbs has only one stem. The past-tense stem is identical to the infinitive stem but does not have an umlaut:

INFINITIVE STEM	PAST STEM
können	**konn-**
müssen	**muß-**
dürfen	**durf-**
wollen	**woll-**
sollen	**soll-**

c. The modal **verb mögen** follows the same pattern, leaving off the umlaut but changing the stem to **moch-:**

mögen	**moch-**

d. All modals add the following endings to the past stem to form the past tense:

er
sie
es   PAST STEM + **-te**
man
das Kind

sie
die Kinder   PAST STEM + **-ten**

Examples:

Er **konnte** nicht laufen.	*(He could not walk.)*
Sie **mußte** in die Schule gehen.	*(She had to go to school.)*
Sie **konnten** ihm nicht helfen.	*(They could not help him.)*

SELF-PREPARATORY EXERCISE

Give the English equivalents of the German sentences:

Er durfte nicht spielen.	
Man wollte es machen.	He wasn't allowed to play
Sie wollte es versuchen.	One (they) wanted to do it.
Der Student wollte Biologie studieren.	She wanted to try it.
Sie konnten ihm nicht helfen.	The student wanted to study biology.
	They could not help him.

EXERCISES

A. *Complete the sentences with the past tense forms of the modals in the parentheses:*

1. Der Physiker _____ in dem Labor arbeiten. (müssen)
2. Die Touristen _____ die Burgruinen sehen. (wollen)
3. Man _____ ihm nicht helfen. (können)
4. Das Mädchen _____ nicht Tennis spielen. (sollen)
5. Die Industrie _____ das Wasser nicht verschmutzen. (dürfen)

B. *Form sentences in the past tense with the elements given below:*

1. Er / müssen / gehen / in die Schule
2. Die Tochter / wollen / eine Reise / unternehmen
3. Der Papst / wollen / hören / die Thesen von Luther / nicht
4. Man / können / die gotische Baukunst / erkennen / an dem Spitzbogen
5. Die Partei / sollen / nominieren / ihn / nicht / zum Präsidentschaftskandidaten

SELF-PREPARATORY EXERCISE

Tell whether the sentence is in the present or past tense:

Er darf nicht reisen.	
Man sollte es machen.	present
Sie sollen jetzt arbeiten.	past
Das Kind konnte schnell laufen.	present
Der Wissenschaftler wollte ein Verfahren entwickeln.	past
Man muß ihr helfen.	past
	present

ZWEIHUNDERTACHTUNDZWANZIG

EXERCISES

A. *Change the following sentences to past tense:* *

1. Sie kann den Redner nicht hören.
2. Der Fanatiker will den Gegner ermorden.
3. Die Familie muß dem Sohn helfen.
4. Der Ökologe soll für die Erhaltung des Ökosystems plädieren.
5. Man will seine Wiederwahl verhindern.

B. *Give the German equivalents of the English sentences:*

1. She wanted to see her daughter.
2. He said that he wanted to simplify the method.
3. Why should they see this new university?
4. She could not explain the theory.
5. They were not permitted to smoke.

READING

Nicht nur DDT?

Wie das DDT, das bei Vögeln zu einer Verdünnung der Eierschale geführt hat, so wird auch eine schon lange vermutete Wirkung bei dem Pflanzenschutzmittel Toxaphen offenkundig. Es ruft, wenn es ins Wasser gelangt, bei Fischen eine Degeneration der Knochen hervor und führt zu Brüchen der Wirbelsäule. Vermutlich tritt als Folge der Toxaphen-Aufnahme ein Mangel an Vitamin C ein, der eine Verringerung des Knochenproteins Collagen bewirkt.   5

VOCABULARY

nur	only	der **Knochen, -**	bone
wie	like, just like	der **Bruch, ⁓e**	fracture, break
der **Vogel, ⁓**	bird	die **Wirbelsäule**	spinal column, spine
bei Vögeln	in birds	**vermutlich**	presumably, probably
die **Verdünnung**	thinning, attenuation	**ein-treten**	to occur; to happen; to enter
die **Schale, -n**	shell, peel, rind, bark	**treten (tritt),**	
führen (zu)	to lead (to)	**trat, getreten**	to step
schon lange	long ago	die **Folge, -n**	consequence, result
vermutet	suspected	**als Folge**	as a consequence (of)
die **Wirkung**	effect	die **Aufnahme, -n**	absorption, take-up
offenkundig	evident, obvious	der **Mangel, ⁓ (an)**	lack, deficiency (of)
hervor-rufen	to cause, evoke, bring about	das **Vitamin, -e**	vitamin
rufen (ruft),		die **Verringerung**	decrease, reduction, lessening
rief, gerufen	to call		
wenn	when, if	das **Protein, -e**	protein
gelangen	to reach, to get (into)	das **Collagen**	collagen
der **Fisch, -e**	fish	**bewirken**	to cause, to produce, to effect
die **Degeneration**	degeneration		

STRUCTURAL EXERCISE

Underline all verbs with separable prefixes in the above reading.

VOCABULARY EXERCISE

Give the English equivalents of the italicized words:

1. Es führt zu Brüchen der *Wirbelsäule.*
2. *Vermutlich* tritt ein Mangel an Vitamin C ein.
3. *Als Folge der* Toxaphen-Aufnahme tritt ein Mangel an Vitamin C ein.
4. Der Mangel an Vitamin C *bewirkt* eine Verringerung des Knochenproteins.
5. Es ruft eine Degeneration der *Knochen* hervor.
6. Eine *schon lange* vermutete Wirkung wird offenkundig.
7. Das Pflanzenschutzmittel darf nicht ins Wasser *gelangen.*

STRUCTURE

3.   Adjective Endings after Ein-Words

a.   Review: the adjective endings after definite articles and **der**-words are either **-e** or **-en:**

	MASC.	FEM.	NEUT.	PLURAL
NOM.	-e	-e	-e	-en
GEN.	-en	-en	-en	-en
DAT.	-en	-en	-en	-en
ACC.	-en	-e	-e	-en

b.   Attributive adjectives following the indefinite articles or **ein**-words use the ending **-en.** There are exceptions:

in the nominative masculine singular, the ending is **-er;**
in the nominative and accusative feminine singular, the ending is **-e;**
in the nominative and accusative neuter singular, the ending is **-es:**

	MASC.	FEM.	NEUT.	PLURAL
NOM.	-er	-e	-es	-en
GEN.	-en	-en	-en	-en
DAT.	-en	-en	-en	-en
ACC.	-en	-e	-es	-en

ZWEIHUNDERTDREISSIG

Examples:

Er kennt **ein schönes Land.** *(He knows a beautiful country.)*

ANALYSIS: The attributive adjective follows an indefinite article; the noun is in the accusative case and is neuter singular; the ending is **-es.**

Sie zeigt ihm **ihr altes Haus.** *(She is showing him her old house.)*
Sie finden **keine neuen Bücher.** *(They aren't finding any new books.)*

c. Attributive adjectives in a series have the same endings:

Das **schöne alte** Haus ist bekannt. *(The beautiful old house is well known.)*

EXERCISES

A. *Supply the correct adjective endings:*

1. Er kennt einen alt_____ Mann.
2. Der Sohn arbeitet in einer neu_____ Brauerei.
3. Atlantis war eine sagenhaft_____ Insel.
4. Plato beschreibt Atlantis als ein mächtig_____ Reich.
5. Der Schwarzwald ist ein beliebt_____ Feriengebiet.

B. *Supply the correct adjective endings:*

1. Sie hilft ihrer krank_____ Mutter.
2. Seine feindlich_____ Einstellung ist bekannt.
3. Der Maler zeigt ihnen seine zahlreich_____ Gemälde.
4. Der Anschlag der Thesen führte zu seiner lang_____ Gefangenschaft.
5. Der Freund hat seine deutsch_____ Übersetzung gelesen.

C. *Supply the correct adjective endings:*

1. Viele Menschen hatten kein groß_____ Interesse an der Baukunst.
2. Man soll keine chemisch_____ Mittel verwenden.
3. Es gab keine ander_____ Möglichkeit.
4. Diese Kirche hat keine stufenförmig_____ Konstruktion.
5. Abraham Lincoln stammte aus keiner reich_____ Familie.

D. *Supply the correct adjective endings:*

1. Die alt_____ deutsch_____ Bauernhäuser haben verschiedene Bauformen.
2. Die Gebäude stehen um einen viereckig_____ geschlossen_____ Hof.
3. Man richtet einen gebündelt_____ Röntgenstrahl auf ein Material.
4. Dieses Muster dient als Grundlage für die genau_____ Berechnung der Atomanordnung.
5. Mathematik ist ein griechisch_____ Wort.

E. *Change the following sentences to future:**

1. Sie hilft ihm.
2. Er kauft einen neuen Wagen.

Sigmund Freund

ZWEIHUNDERTZWEIUNDDREISSIG

    3. Der Wissenschaftler arbeitet an dem Institut.
    4. Immer mehr Bürger gehen in die Volkshochschule.
    5. Er entwickelt ein neues Druckverfahren.

F. *Change the following sentences to past perfect:**

    1. Sie gingen in die Volkshochschule.
    2. Ökologen plädierten für die Erhaltung der urwüchsigen Landschaft.
    3. Man nominierte ihn als Präsidentschaftskandidat.
    4. Die Forschung suchte seit Jahrzehnten nach einem geeigneten Bekämpfungsmittel.
    5. Man erkannte das Problem.

READING

Sigmund Freud (1856–1939)

Freud studierte Pathologie und Physiologie. Er war Nervenarzt und Wegbereiter der Psychoanalyse und Professor für Psychotherapie in Wien von 1902 bis 1938. Im Jahre 1938 emigrierte Freud wegen seiner jüdischen Abstammung nach London.

Freud betrieb zuerst hirnanatomische Forschungen. Unter anderem entdeckte er die schmerzbetäubende Wirkung des Cocains. Er untersuchte seelische Er-   5 krankungen ohne organischen Befund (Hysterien) und versuchte die Behandlung von Hysterien durch Suggestion and Hypnose. Freud entwickelte die kathartische Methode der Abreaktion von verdrängten traumatischen Erfahrungen. Zunächst behauptete Freud, daß der Hauptantrieb des menschlichen Verhaltens die Libido ist. Später stellte er der Libido den Gegentrieb gegenüber, den er im Todes- oder Destruk-   10 tionstrieb sah. Diese Antriebe stammen aus dem Unbewußten. Die Einbeziehung des Unbewußten in die Forschung ergänzte die vorangegangene Psychologie.

VOCABULARY

die **Pathologie**	pathology	
die **Physiologie**	physiology	
der **Nerv, -en**	nerve	
der **Arzt, ⁻e**	physician, doctor	
der **Nervenarzt, ⁻e**	psychiatrist	
der **Weg, -e**	way, path	
bereiten	to prepare	
der **Wegbereiter, -**	pioneer, forerunner	
die **Psychoanalyse**	psychoanalysis	
die **Psychotherapie**	psychotherapy	
Wien	Vienna	
emigrieren (nach)	to emigrate (to)	
wegen	because of, on account of	
jüdisch	Jewish	

die **Abstammung**	descent, extraction
betreiben	to pursue, carry on
treiben (treibt), trieb, getrieben	to drive, push
zuerst	at first
hirnanatomisch	cerebral, cephalic
unter anderem	among other things
entdecken	to discover
der **Schmerz, -en**	pain, ache
betäubend	anaesthetic, deadening
schmerzbetäubend	pain-killing, analgesic
das **Cocain**	cocaine

	seelisch	emotional, psychic, mental	
die	**Erkrankung, -en**	illness, disease	
	ohne	without	
	organisch	organic	
der	**Befund, -e**	finding, condition	
die	**Hysterie, -n**	hysteria	
	versuchen	to attempt, try	
die	**Behandlung**	treatment	
die	**Suggestion**	suggestion	
die	**Hypnose, -n**	hypnosis	
	kathartisch	cathartic	
die	**Abreaktion**	relief, emotional discharge	
	verdrängt	repressed	
	traumatisch	traumatic	
die	**Erfahrung, -en**	experience	
	behaupten	to assert, maintain	
der	**Hauptantrieb, -e**	main impulse, principle drive	

der	**Antrieb, -e**	drive, impulse
das	**Verhalten**	behavior, conduct
die	**Libido**	libido
	gegenüber-stellen	to contrast with, oppose to, put opposite from
der	**Gegentrieb, -e**	opposing drive, opposing force
der	**Trieb, -e**	drive, force
der	**Tod**	death
die	**Destruktion**	destruction
das	**Unbewußte**	unconscious, instinct
die	**Einbeziehung**	inclusion
	ergänzen	to supplement, to add to
	vorangegangen	former, preceding
die	**Psychologie**	psychology

STRUCTURAL EXERCISES

A. *Underline all direct objects in the above reading.*

B. *Give the English equivalents of the following compound words:*

1. der Nervenarzt
2. der Wegbereiter
3. schmerzbetäubend
4. der Hauptantrieb
5. hirnanatomisch

VOCABULARY EXERCISE

Give the English equivalents of the italicized words:

1. Er *betrieb* zuerst hirnanatomische Forschungen.
2. Er versuchte die *Behandlung* von Hysterien durch Suggestion.
3. Diese Antriebe stammen aus dem *Unbewußten.*
4. Sie *ergänzte* die vorangegangene Forschung.
5. Freud *untersuchte* seelische Erkrankungen.
6. *Unter anderem* entdeckte er die schmerzbetäubende Wirkung des Cocains.
7. Er untersuchte *seelische* Erkrankungen.

Soll der Arzt dem Patienten immer die Wahrheit sagen?

esson 22

STRUCTURE

1. Unpreceded Adjectives

a. Unpreceded adjectives have no definite or indefinite articles, **der-** or **ein-**words preceding them:

kaltes Bier   *(cold beer)*
alte Autos   *(old cars)*

b. Unpreceded adjectives have the following endings:

	MASC.	FEM.	NEUTER	PLURAL
NOM.	**-er**	**-e**	**-es**	**-e**
GEN.	**-en**	**-er**	**-en**	**-er**
DAT.	**-em**	**-er**	**-em**	**-en**
ACC.	**-en**	**-e**	**-es**	**-e**

c. These endings are almost identical to those of the definite articles and **der-**words (exceptions are the genitive masculine and neuter, in the singular).

d. **Viele, wenige, andere, einige, mehrere** are numerical adjectives. Since they are all plural expressions and are not preceded by a definite or indefinite article, they use the same endings as unpreceded adjectives in the plural:

viele	*many, a lot of*	**einige**	*some*
wenige	*few*	**mehrere**	*several*
andere	*other*		

Examples:

Er liest **viele gute Bücher.** (accusative plural)
He reads a lot of good books.
Sie hat an **mehreren großen Universitäten** studiert. (dative plural)
She has studied at several large universities.

EXERCISES

A. *Change the expressions to plural, add the word in parentheses, and make the necessary changes:**

EXAMPLE: guter Mann (viele)
            viele gute Männer

1. schönes Mädchen (viele)   4. heißer Tag (viele)
2. schlechter Chef (andere)   5. kluger Student (wenige)
3. dickes Buch (mehrere)

B. *Supply the correct adjective endings:*

1. Seelisch_____ Erkrankungen müssen behandelt werden.
2. Kalt_____ Bier ist immer gut.
3. Viel_____ bekannt_____ Maler hatten damals mehr Interesse für das weltliche Leben.
4. Ander_____ genetisch_____ Kontrollmöglichkeiten sind noch nicht bekannt.
5. Malaria bedroht immer noch viele Menschen in tropisch_____ Regionen.

C. *Supply the correct relative pronouns or adverbs:*

1. Dort ist das Kind, _____ er es gegeben hat.   (to whom)
2. Heidelberg ist die Stadt, in _____ er wohnen will.   (which)
3. Das ist alles, _____ sie sagen konnte.   (that)
4. Das sind ihre Kinder, mit _____ sie nach Köln fährt.   (whom)
5. Sie wußten nicht, _____ er gearbeitet hat.   (where)

D. *Change the following sentences to present perfect:**

1. Freud untersuchte seelische Erkrankungen.
2. Er stellte der Libido den Destruktionstrieb gegenüber.
3. Die Einbeziehung des Unbewußten ergänzte die vorangegangene Psychologie.
4. Er entdeckte die schmerzbetäubende Wirkung des Cocains.
5. Es ruft eine Degeneration der Knochen hervor.

ZWEIHUNDERTSECHSUNDDREISSIG

READING

Aktuell

Aktuell nennt man etwas, was im Augenblick wichtig oder interessant ist. Tageszeitungen müssen aktuell sein, d.h. sie müssen stets das Neueste bringen.

VOCABULARY

aktuẹll	topical, current, up to date	das **Neueste**	the newest (information), the latest news
interessạnt	interesting		
die **Zeitung, -en**	newspaper	**bringen (bringt),**	
die **Tageszeitung, -en**	daily newspaper	**brachte,**	to bring, convey,
stets	always, regularly	**gebracht**	carry

VOCABULARY EXERCISE

Give the English equivalents of the italicized words:

1. Das Neueste ist nicht immer *interessant*.
2. Sie müssen *stets* das Neueste bringen.
3. Aktuell nennt man etwas, *was* im Augenblick wichtig ist.
4. *Später* stellte er der Libido den Gegentrieb gegenüber.
5. *Zunächst* behauptete Freud, daß die Libido der Hauptantrieb ist.
6. Das ist *im Augenblick* wichtig.
7. *Tageszeitungen* müssen aktuell sein.

STRUCTURE

2. Adjectival Nouns

a.   Attributive adjectives modify nouns by limiting or specifying them:

There is the rich man . . .

The adjective *rich* expands our knowledge about *the man*.

b.   When the adjective + noun construction is reduced to merely the adjective, but the noun is still implied, we refer to the shortened form as an adjectival noun.

c.   In German, the attributive adjectives assume endings according to the gender, number, and case of the noun they modify. These endings also vary depending on whether they follow a **der-** or **ein-**word or are unpreceded:

Dort ist **der Reiche** . . .   *(There is the rich [man])*
Dort ist **ein Reicher** . . .   *(There is a rich [man])*
Reiche gibt es hier nicht.   *(There are no rich [people] here.)*

ZWEIHUNDERTSIEBENUNDDREISSIG

d.   As the term adjectival noun indicates, this construction retains the properties of an adjective (endings) and it acquires those of a noun (capitalization):

Der Dicke im Fernsehen ist ein Detektiv.
The fat (guy, man) on TV is a detective.
Ein Dicker spielt die Rolle des Detektivs.
A fat (guy, man) plays the role of the detective.
Die Studenten kennen **einen Deutschen.**
The students know a German (person, man).
Deutsche gibt es in Wisconsin und Texas.
There are Germans in Wisconsin and Texas.

e.   Adjectival nouns have the same endings as attributive adjectives:

1.   After **der**-words

	MASC.	FEM.	NEUT.	PLURAL
NOM.	der Reiche	die Schöne	das Gute	die Reichen
GEN.	des Reichen	der Schönen	des Guten	der Reichen
DAT.	dem Reichen	der Schönen	dem Guten	den Reichen
ACC.	den Reichen	die Schöne	das Gute	die Reichen

2.   After **ein**-words

	MASC.	FEM.	NEUT.	PLURAL
NOM.	ein Reicher	eine Schöne	ein Gutes	keine Reichen
GEN.	eines Reichen	einer Schönen	eines Guten	keiner Reichen
DAT.	einem Reichen	einer Schönen	einem Guten	keinen Reichen
ACC.	einen Reichen	eine Schöne	ein Gutes	keine Reichen

f.   After **viele, wenige, mehrere, einige, andere:**

NOM.	viele Reiche
GEN.	vieler Reicher
DAT.	vielen Reichen
ACC.	viele Reiche

g.   Unpreceded adjectival nouns take the following endings:

	MASC.	FEM.	NEUT.	PLURAL
NOM.	-er	-e	-es	-e
GEN.	-en	-er	-en	-er
DAT.	-em	-er	-em	-en
ACC.	-en	-e	-es	-e

ZWEIHUNDERTACHTUNDDREISSIG

Examples:

Er ist **Amerikaner.**	Sie ist **Deutsche.**	Sie sind **Fremde.**
He is an American.	*She is a German.*	*They are strangers.*

h. Many adjectives are used to form adjectival nouns with special meanings:

der Bekannte	*acquaintance, friend*
der Gefangene	*captured person, prisoner*
die Moderne	*modern art, modern times*
die Gerade	*the straight line*
die Senkrechte	*the vertical line*
die Horizontale	*the horizontal line*
das Deutsche	*(the) German (language)*
das Italienische	*(the) Italian (language)*
das Beste	*the best (thing)*
das Schönste	*the most beautiful (thing)*
das Gute	*the good (thing, part)*
das Grüne	*the green color*
das Graue	*the gray color*
etwas Großes	*something big*
viel Schlechtes	*a lot of bad (things)*

SELF-PREPARATORY EXERCISE

Form adjectival nouns from the following:

der reiche Mann	
eine schöne Frau	der Reiche
viele bekannte Menschen	eine Schöne
das beste Ding	viele Bekannte
ein deutscher Mann	das Beste
	ein Deutscher

das Ding = *thing, affair*

EXERCISE

Form adjectival nouns from the following:

1. Er ist der größte Boxer. Er ist der _____.
2. Weiß er das neueste Ding? Weiß er das _____?
3. Man sprach damals immer über das weltliche Interesse. Man sprach damals immer über das _____.
4. In der Politik spricht man von den unabhängigen Ländern. In der Politik spricht man von den _____.
5. Er erklärte das wesentliche Merkmal an der Konstruktion. Er erklärte das _____ an der Konstruktion.

ZWEIHUNDERTNEUNUNDDREISSIG

SELF-PREPARATORY EXERCISE

Give the German equivalents of the English nouns:

the prisoner	
modern art	der Gefangene
(the) German (language)	die Moderne
many rich (people)	das Deutsche
something big	viele Reiche
the best (thing)	etwas Großes
	das Beste

EXERCISE

Give the German equivalents of the English nouns:

1. the most beautiful (thing)
2. the vertical (line)
3. something new

4. the Italian (language)
5. the straight (line)

READING

Neue Quellen der Energie

Die Bundesrepublik Deutschland ist das erste Land auf der Erde, für das man einen ,,Wärmeatlas'' erstellen will. Dieser Atlas soll angeben, wo und zu welchen Zeiten im Lande man Energie verbraucht. Außerdem teilt er mit, wo im Jahre 2 000 ein Fernwärmenetz bestehen soll. Auf diese Weise kann man langfristig die Energieversorgung auf Kernenergie und andere Arten von Energie umstellen.   5

VOCABULARY

die **Quelle, -n**	source, spring, fountain	**außerdem**	besides, aside from that
die **Energie**	energy	**mit-teilen**	to tell, inform, state
die **Wärme**	heat, warmth	**fern**	distant, far away
der **Atlas, -se**	atlas, map	das **Netz, -e**	network, net, mesh
der **Wärmeatlas**	heat atlas, heat map	das **Fernwärmenetz**	comprehensive heating network
erstellen	to prepare, produce		
an-geben (gibt an), gab an, angegeben	to indicate, state	**langfristig**	over a long period of time
wo	where	die **Versorgung**	supply
welch-	which	der **Kern, -**	nucleus, kernel, pit
die **Zeit, -en**	time	die **Kernenergie**	nuclear energy
verbrauchen	to use (up), to consume	**um-stellen (auf)**	to convert (to), change over (to)

ZWEIHUNDERTVIERZIG

STRUCTURAL EXERCISE

Underline all modals and their dependent infinitives in the above reading.

VOCABULARY EXERCISE

Give the English equivalents of the italicized words:

1. Man will einen „Wärmeatlas" *erstellen.*
2. Der Atlas soll *angeben,* wo man Energie verbraucht.
3. Das Land *verbraucht* viel Energie.
4. *Außerdem* teilt der Atlas mit, wo das Fernwärmenetz bestehen soll.
5. Man will die Versorgung auf *Kernenergie* umstellen.
6. Hat er ihr das Neueste *mitgeteilt?*
7. Man will die Versorgung auf andere Arten von Energie *umstellen.*

STRUCTURE

3.   Modals — Present Perfect Tense

a.   Modals rarely occur alone in a sentence. They are almost always accompanied by a dependent infinitive.

b.   Only the modal is conjugated. The dependent verb is never conjugated.

c.   The present perfect tense of the modals consists of two different constructions:

    1.   Regular construction when the modal occurs alone:

> **haben** + past participle of the modal

    Example:

    Er **hat** es so **gewollt.** *(He wanted it that way.)*

    2.   The regular construction is used only when the modal verb is not accompanied by another verb.

    3.   Double infinitive construction

> **haben** + infinitive of verb + infinitive of modal

    Example:

    Er **hat** zehn Stunden **arbeiten müssen.** *(He had to work for ten hours.)*

    4.   The double infinitive construction is used in the perfect tenses when the modal is linked with another verb (the dependent infinitive).

d.   Double infinitive constructions have the following word order:

1. Statements and questions with question words:

The auxiliary verb **haben** is in second position; the dependent infinitive precedes the infinitive of the modal at the end of the sentence or question:

Er **hat** in die Schule ⌐ **gehen müssen.** ¬   *(He has had to go to school.)*

Wann **hat** sie im Büro ⌐ **sein sollen?** ¬   *(When was she supposed to be in the office?)*

2. Subordinate clauses:

The conjugated form of the auxiliary verb **haben** precedes the double infinitive construction at the end of the clause:

Er wußte nicht, bis wann er das Buch ⌐ **hat** ¬ **behalten dürfen.**
He did not know how long (until when) he was allowed to keep the book.

SELF-PREPARATORY EXERCISE

*Using the modal, express each sentence in the present perfect tense and make necessary changes in the sentence:**

Er hat gestern gearbeitet. (müssen)	
Die Kinder haben gespielt. (wollen)	Er hat gestern arbeiten müssen.
Sie ist nach Berlin gefahren. (dürfen)	Die Kinder haben spielen wollen.
Die Tochter hat viel studiert. (sollen)	Sie hat nach Berlin fahren dürfen.
Die Frauen haben den Film gesehen. (können)	Die Tochter hat viel studieren sollen.
	Die Frauen haben den Film sehen können.

EXERCISES

A.   *Change the following sentences to present perfect:**

1. Sie soll um zehn Uhr arbeiten.
2. Der Chef will nach Berlin fliegen.
3. Die Wissenschaftler können ein neues Verfahren entwickeln.
4. Man soll hier nicht rauchen.
5. Die Kinder wollen im Garten spielen.

ZWEIHUNDERTZWEIUNDVIERZIG

B. *Add the modal and change the following sentences to present perfect:**

    1. Sie definierte die Verteilung der Materie. (können)
    2. Man benutzte diese Methode als Grundlage. (wollen)
    3. Sie untersuchten den photoelektrischen Effekt. (müssen)
    4. Die Erwachsenen gingen auf die Volkshochschule. (wollen)
    5. Der Schüler machte die Prüfung. (müssen)

C. *Give the English equivalents:*

    1. Sie hat viel lernen müssen.
    2. Er hat den Film sehen wollen.
    3. Man hat diese Methode benutzen können.
    4. Sie wußte, daß der Vater nicht hat kommen können.
    5. Es war bekannt, daß er kein Bier hat trinken können.

4. Ordinal Numbers

a. Ordinal numbers determine the position of something in an enumeration or succession.

Examples:

Henry *VIII.*
He is the *second* best in his class.
She is the *fifth* student who complained.

b. In German, ordinal numbers are based on cardinal numbers, with the exception of "first" **(erst-)** and "third" **(dritt-).**

c. Ordinal numbers add:

    1. the ending **-t** to the cardinal numbers from 2 to 19:

        der **zweite** Wagen   die **fünfte** Kolonne

    2. the ending **-st** to the cardinal numbers from 20 onward:

        der **zwanzigste** Fall   die **dreiundvierzigste** Stelle

d. Ordinal numbers add endings after the **-t** or **-st** since they modify a noun. They behave like attributive adjectives:

Karl der Große war der **erste** Kaiser.
Charles the Great was the first emperor.
Dann trank er sein **drittes** Bier.
Then he drank his third beer.
Jeder **dritte** Bürger starb in der Katastrophe.
One of every three citizens (Every third citizen) died in the catastrophe.

e. In compound numbers, only the last number adds the ending:

Das war der **zweihundert(und)dreißigste** Besucher.
That was the 230th visitor.

f. When the ordinal numbers are written as numerals, a period is added to the cardinal number:

Heute ist der **12.** Oktober. (. . . der zwölfte Oktober)
Today is the 12th of October.
Wilhelm **II.** regierte bis 1918. (Wilhelm der Zweite . . .)
Wilhelm II ruled until 1918.

g. The ordinal number for "one" is **erst-:**

Der **Erste** Weltkrieg dauerte von 1914 bis 1918.
The First World War lasted from 1914 to 1918.
Damals regierte Friedrich der **Erste** in Deutschland.
At that time Frederic I ruled in Germany.

h. Examples of ordinal numbers:

erst-	*first*
zweit-	*second*
dritt-	*third*
viert-	*fourth*
fünft-	*fifth*
sechst-	*sixth*
siebt-	*seventh*
acht-	*eighth*
neunt-	*ninth*
zehnt-	*tenth*
zwölft-	*twelfth*
neunzehnt-	*nineteenth*
fünfundzwanzigst-	*twenty-fifth*
dreihundertvierundvierzigst-	*three hundred forty-fourth*

EXERCISES

A. *Write out the following ordinal numbers:*

1. Heute ist der 4. Juli.
2. Er sprach über Richard II.
3. Sie fuhr im 3. Wagen.
4. Sie haben ihr 5. Haus gekauft.
5. Heinrich VIII. hatte viele Frauen.

ZWEIHUNDERTVIERUNDVIERZIG

B. *Supply the correct adjective endings:*

1. Das Dritt_____ Reich dauerte von 1933 bis 1945.
2. Der Fanatiker ermordete den dreiunddreißigst_____ Präsidenten.
3. Als erst_____ Physiker hat Einstein den photoelektrischen Effekt untersucht.
4. Willi las sein dritt_____ Buch.
5. Es war Papst Johannes der dreiundzwanzigst_____.

READING

Renaissance — Humanismus — Reformation

Die Renaissance ist die große europäische Kulturepoche, die die Wende vom Mittelalter zur Neuzeit umfaßt. Sie überwindet das mittelalterliche Welt- und Menschenbild und die überkommene Staats- und Gesellschaftsordnung. An die Stelle des Autoritätsglaubens tritt der Geist kritischer Forschung; der Mensch wird zum Maß aller Dinge; die Staatsraison zum Prinzip der Politik. Die italienischen Fürstenhöfe 5 — besonders das Florenz der Medici — sind beispielhaft für Europa. Byzantinische Gelehrte, die nach der Eroberung von Byzanz und Griechenland durch die Türken nach Italien geflüchtet waren, haben das Studium der antiken Literatur angeregt. Die Kunst- und Lebensauffassung der Antike gelten den Humanisten als Vorbild. Die Reformation zerstört die Einheit des Glaubens. Neben der lateinischen Dichtung der 10 Humanisten entsteht in Deutschland ein reiches literarisches Leben. Durch den Buchdruck werden die literarischen Erzeugnisse rasch zum Gemeingut aller Gebildeten.

Vertreter der Renaissance, des Humanismus und der Reformation waren:

Johannes Reuchlin, 1455–1522	Martin Luther, 1483–1546
Erasmus von Rotterdam, 1469–1536	Ulrich von Hutten, 1488–1523

VOCABULARY

die **Renaissance**	Renaissance	das **Bild, -er**	picture
der **Humanismus**	Humanism	das **Weltbild**	world view
die **Reformation**	Reformation	das **Menschenbild**	view of man
die **Epoche, -n**	epoch, era, age	**überkommen**	traditional, handed-down
die **Wende**	change, turning point		
		der **Staat, -en**	state
die **Neuzeit**	modern times	die **Ordnung**	order
umfassen	to include, comprise, embrace	die **Staatsordnung**	political system
		die **Gesellschaft, -en**	society, company
überwinden		die **Gesellschafts-**	
(**überwindet**),		**ordnung**	social system
überwand,		die **Stelle, -n**	place
überwunden	to overcome	**an die Stelle**	in place (of)
mittelalterlich	medieval	die **Autorität, -en**	authority

Ulrich von Hutten

ZWEIHUNDERTSECHSUNDVIERZIG

der	**Glauben**	belief, faith, trust		**Griechenland**	Greece
der	**Autoritätsglauben**	faith in the authority	der	**Türke, -n**	Turk
	treten (tritt), trat			**flüchten (nach)**	to flee (to), escape (to)
	ist getreten	to step; to appear		**antik**	classical, antique
	an die Stelle		die	**Literatur**	literature
	treten	to take the place of		**an-regen**	to stimulate
der	**Geist**	spirit, mind, intellect	die	**Antike**	(classical) antiquity
das	**Maß, -e**	measure, standard, criterion		**gelten (gilt), galt gegolten**	to be valid; to be considered
das	**Ding, -e**	thing, matter, object		**gelten den Humanisten**	are considered by the humanists
die	**Raison**	reason	das	**Vorbild, -er**	model, example, idol
die	**Staatsraison**	reason of state, ability to rule a country prudently		**zerstören**	to destroy
der	**Fürst, -en**	prince, sovereign	die	**Einheit**	unity
der	**Hof, -̈e**	court		**neben**	in addition to, besides, next to
	besonders	especially		**lateinisch**	Latin (adjective)
	Florenz	Florence (Italy)	die	**Dichtung**	poetry, literary work
die	**Medici**	name of a rich powerful family of Florence, celebrated as bankers, rulers and patrons of art and literature		**entstehen (entsteht) entstand, entstanden**	to come about, arise; to develop
	beispielhaft	exemplary, typical		**literarisch**	literary
	byzantisch	Byzantine	das	**Erzeugnis, -se**	product,
der	**Gelehrte, -n**	scholar		**rasch**	quickly, fast
die	**Eroberung, -en**	conquest		**werden zu**	become
	Byzanz	Byzantium; today: Istanbul	das	**Gemeingut**	common or public property
			der	**Gebildete, -n**	educated, sophisticated person
			der	**Vertreter, -**	representative

STRUCTURAL EXERCISE

A. *Underline all attributive adjectives in the above reading.*

B. *Give the English equivalents of the compound nouns:*

1. die Kulturepoche
2. die Neuzeit
3. die Gesellschaftsordnung
4. der Autoritätsglauben
5. die Lebensauffassung

VOCABULARY EXERCISE

Give the English equivalents of the italicized words:

1. Die Renaissance *umfaßt* die Wende vom Mittelalter zur Neuzeit.
2. Die italienischen Fürstenhöfe sind *beispielhaft* für Europa.
3. *An die Stelle* des Autoritätsglaubens tritt der Geist der kritischen Forschung.
4. Byzantinische Gelehrte *waren* nach Italien *geflüchtet*.
5. Die Reformation *zerstört* die Einheit des Glaubens.
6. Den Humanisten gilt die Antike als *Vorbild*.
7. Die byzantinischen Gelehrten *haben* das Studium der antiken Literatur *angeregt*.

Lesson **23**

STRUCTURE

1. Infinitive Constructions

a. There are two types of infinitive constructions in German:

without **zu** *(to)*;
with **zu.**

b. Modal verbs are linked with a dependent infinitive without **zu:**

Er **soll studieren.**   Sie **können lesen.**
He should study.   *They can read.*

c. The infinitive of the verb is listed in dictionaries without **zu: arbeiten** = *to work*

d. Other infinitive constructions use **zu:**

   1.   After certain verbs:

   scheinen *seem*   **brauchen** *need*   **haben** *have*

   Examples:

   Sie **scheint zu schlafen.** *(She seems to be asleep.)*
   Er **braucht** heute nicht **zu studieren.** *(He does not need to study today.)*
   Die Leute **haben** nichts **zu tun.** *(The people have nothing to do.)*

   2.   With the following prepositional constructions:

um . . . zu	*in order to*
(an) statt . . . zu	*instead of*
ohne . . . zu	*without . . . -ing*

Examples:

Er flog nach Amerika, **um** seine Verwandten **zu besuchen.**
He flew to America (in order) to visit his relatives.
Er ging ins Kino, **anstatt zu arbeiten.**
He went to the movies instead of working.
Er verließ das Haus, **ohne** etwas **zu sagen.**
He left the house without saying anything.

In infinitive sentences with these prepositional constructions, the infinitive occupies the last position in the sentence.

e.   Modals may also be used in sentences containing a prepositional construction. The order of the final three elements is:

> dependent infinitive + **zu** + modal

Example:

Er stand da, **ohne** etwas **sagen zu können.**
He stood there without being able to say anything.

f.   Verbs with separable prefixes insert **zu** between the prefix and the main verb:

Er ging in die Schule, **ohne** seine Bücher **mitzunehmen.**
He went to school without taking his books along.

g.   Verbs with inseparable prefixes follow **zu** at the end of the clause.

Der Bauer erzielte eine gute Ernte, **ohne** Pflanzenschutzmittel **zu benutzen.**
The farmer obtained a good harvest without using pesticides.

EXERCISES

A.   *Give the German equivalents of the infinitive constructions:*

1.   Er studiert an der Universität, _____ (in order to learn something).
2.   Man muß viel arbeiten, _____ (in order to become rich).
3.   Er schläft, _____ (instead of studying).
4.   Sie nahm sein Buch, _____ (without asking him).
5.   Sie gingen in die Stadt, _____ (in order to buy a car).

B.   *Give the German equivalents of the infinitive constructions:*

1.   They don't need to work.
2.   She doesn't have anything to do.
3.   It seems to be cold.

ZWEIHUNDERTNEUNUNDVIERZIG

C. *Give the English equivalents of the following sentences:*

1. Der Abgeordnete scheint auf den Widerstand der Partei zu stoßen.
2. Man erstellt einen „Wärmeatlas", um die Energieversorgung langfristig auf Kernenergie umstellen zu können.
3. Er wurde Präsident der Vereinigten Staaten, ohne ein guter Redner zu sein.
4. Der meiste Schnee scheint im Gebirge zu fallen.
5. Der Wissenschaftler untersuchte den Fisch, um den Einfluß des Pflanzenschutzmittels auf die Knochen bestimmen zu können.

READING

Heinrich Schliemann

Man wird wohl für immer den Namen Heinrich Schliemanns mit der Ausgrabung der Stadt Troja verbinden.

Heinrich Schliemann (1822–1890) ist ein bedeutender deutscher Archäologe, der an den Ausgrabungen mehrerer antiker Städte teilnahm. Außer Troja wirkte er mit an den Ausgrabungen von Mykena, Orchomenos, Tiryns und Ithaka. Die Ausgrabung   5
von Troja dauerte 24 Jahre. Troja war eine antike Stadt in Kleinasien. Nach Homer war sie der Schauplatz des trojanischen Krieges. Die Sage beschreibt den Kampf der Griechen um Troja zur Befreiung von Helena. Der trojanische Sagenheld Paris hatte den Krieg verursacht, weil er Helena geraubt hatte.

Bei der Ausgrabung der Stadt Troja hat Schliemann einige wichtige Gebäude   10
zerstört, weil er durch die Mitte der Ansiedlung einen Suchgraben legte. Die Forschung hatte damals noch wenig Erfahrung auf dem Gebiet der Ausgrabungen. Viele Forscher waren zu dieser Zeit entweder Laien, Autodidakten oder Liebhaber, die die Fachgebiete langsam erarbeiteten. Schliemann hat bei den Ausgrabungen genaue Tagebücher geführt, die noch heute zur Rekonstruktion wichtiger Ein-   15
zelheiten dienen.

VOCABULARY

wohl	probably	**teil-nehmen (an)**	to participate (in), take part (in)
die **Ausgrabung, -en**	excavation		
Troja	Troy	**außer**	besides, in addition to
bedeutend	important, significant		
		mit-wirken (an)	to take part (in); to cooperate (in)
der **Archäologe, -n**	archaeologist		
mehrer-	several	**Mykena**	Mycenae (Greece)
teil-nehmen (nimmt teil), nahm teil, teilgenommen	to participate, take part	**Orchomenos**	Orchomenos (Greece)
		Tiryns	Tiryns (Greece)
		Ithaka	Ithaca (Greece)
		dauern	to last; to take (time)

ZWEIHUNDERTFÜNFZIG

	Kleinasien	Asia Minor	der	Suchgraben	exploratory ditch
der	Schauplatz, ̈e	arena, theater, stage, theater of war, battle field		noch wenig	very little
			die	Erfahrung	experience
			der	Forscher, -	researcher
	trojanisch	Trojan		entweder . . . oder	either . . . or
die	Sage, -n	legend, saga, myth	der	Laie, -n	layman, amateur
der	Kampf, ̈e (um)	battle (for)	der	Autodidakt, -en	self-taught person
die	Befreiung	liberation, freeing	der	Liebhaber, -	amateur, dilettante
	zur Befreiung von Helena	for the liberation of Helen (of Troy)	das	Fach, ̈er	subject, speciality (area)
der	Held, -en	hero	das	Fachgebiet, -e	subject area, specialty area
	verursachen	to cause, bring about		erarbeiten	to earn by work, achieve by work
	weil	because			
	rauben	to steal	das	Tagebuch, ̈er	diary, log, journal
	einig	a few		noch heute	even today, still to-day
das	Gebäude, -	building			
die	Mitte	middle	die	Rekonstruktion	reconstruction
die	Ansiedlung, -en	settlement, colony	die	Einzelheiten (pl.)	details, particulars
der	Graben	ditch, excavation		dienen	to serve, assist, be useful to
	einen Graben legen	to dig a ditch			

STRUCTURAL EXERCISES

A. *Underline all definite articles used in the genitive case in the above reading.*

B. *Give the English equivalents of the following compound nouns:*

1. der Schauplatz   3. der Suchgraben   5. das Fachgebiet
2. das Tagebuch   4. der Liebhaber

VOCABULARY EXERCISE

Give the English equivalents of the italicized words:

1. Die Sage *beschreibt* den Kampf der Griechen um Troja.
2. Er *nahm* an der Ausgrabung antiker Städte *teil.*
3. Er *wirkte* an der Ausgrabung von Mykena *mit.*
4. Viele Forscher waren *entweder* Laien *oder* Liebhaber.
5. Paris *hatte* den Krieg *verursacht.*
6. Die Tagebücher *dienen zur* Rekonstruktion wichtiger Einzelheiten.
7. Bei der Ausgrabung hat er einige *wichtige* Gebäude zerstört.

STRUCTURE

2. Subjective Use of Modals

a. Modals are auxiliary verbs that express the speaker's attitude toward the action of the main verb. This attitude may be treated in two different ways: (1) objectively; (2) subjectively.

b. In the objective use of the modal, the speaker states the event or situation factually and objectively.

Das Kind **muß** in die Schule **gehen.** *(The child must [has to] go to school.)*

The example expresses a situation in which the child is compelled to go to school. The speaker states this compelling aspect through the objective use of the modal.

c. The subjective use of the modal in German indicates a conclusion at which the speaker has arrived after some deliberation:

Er fährt so einen großen Wagen. **Er muß reich sein.**
He drives such a big car. He must be rich.
Der Student hat eine gute Note bekommen. **Er muß viel studiert haben.**
The student got a good grade. He must have studied a lot.

In these examples, the speaker has drawn his own conclusions. His judgement may be right or wrong. He is merely expressing an opinion. In this situation, the modal is used subjectively.

d. In the present tense of the modal, the objective or subjective use may be inferred only from the context and not from the verbal structure. That is, the sentences, when isolated, would not indicate whether an objective or subjective use was intended.

e. The English equivalents of the modals used subjectively are:

können	*may, might*
sollen	*to be said to, be supposed to*
dürfen	*must, should, ought to be*
müssen	*must, has to*
wollen	*to claim to, pretend to*
mögen	*may*

Examples:

Morgen **kann** das ganz anders aussehen.
That may look totally different tomorrow.
Er **soll** Präsident der Universität sein.
He is said to be president of the university.
Er **dürfte** jetzt in Berlin sein.   (subjunctive form of **dürfen**)
He should (ought to) be in Berlin now.
Wer so viel arbeitet, **muß** reich werden.
Whoever works so much, must (has to) become rich.
Sie **will** ein intelligentes Mädchen sein!
She pretends to be an intelligent girl.
Mag sein!
That may be.

ZWEIHUNDERTZWEIUNDFÜNFZIG

EXERCISE

Give the English equivalents of the German sentences:

1. Er soll aus Deutschland sein.
2. Die Frau will Chefin sein.
3. Morgen kann das Wetter besser werden.
4. Sie mag jetzt in Berlin sein.
5. Der Mann muß sehr reich sein.

3.　Wenn — wann — als

a.　The three conjunctions **wenn, wann, als** introduce subordinate clauses and are equivalent to English *when.*

b.　**Wenn** introduces both conditional and time clauses. In conditional clauses, **wenn** means *if,* but in customary or habitual actions **wenn** means *when* or *whenever:*

Er kauft es nicht, **wenn es zu teuer ist.**
He will not buy it if it is too expensive.

c.　In time clauses, **wenn** means *when* or *whenever:*

Man holt ihn ab, **wenn er ankommt.**
One / people will pick him up when (= at the time) he arrives.
Er mußte jedesmal lachen, **wenn er sie sah.**
He had to laugh every time when (= whenever) he saw her.

d.　**Wann** is used to introduce questions:

Wann kommt sie nach Deutschland? *(When is she coming to Germany?)*

e.　**Wann** is used as an interrogative conjunction to introduce a subordinate clause:

Er fragte, **wann sie nach Deutschland kommt.**
He asked when she was coming to Germany.

f.　**Als** as a conjunction means *when* and introduces a subordinate clause referring to a single event or situation in the past:

Als er im Jahre 1945 in Deutschland war, waren viele Städte zerstört.
When he was in Germany in 1945, many cities were destroyed.

EXERCISES

A.　*Give the German equivalent of "when":*

　　1.　_____ Lincoln Präsident war, gab es einen Bürgerkrieg in Amerika.
　　2.　Der Tourist sieht viele Burgruinen, _____ er nach Deutschland kommt.

ZWEIHUNDERTDREIUNDFÜNFZIG

3. _____ sie damals Ferien hatten, fuhren sie in die Schweiz.
4. Er wird zu seiner Freundin gehen, _____ er Zeit hat.
5. _____ das Pflanzenschutzmittel ins Wasser gelangt, ruft es eine Degeneration der Knochen hervor.

B. *Give the English equivalents of the German sentences:*

1. Er weiß nicht, wann er die Tageszeitung lesen kann.
2. Wenn man einen „Wärmeatlas" erstellt hat, kann man angeben, wo und wann man im Lande Energie verbraucht.
3. Als Schliemann einen Suchgraben anlegte, zerstörte er einige wichtige Gebäude.
4. Man weiß nicht, wann Paris Helena geraubt hat.
5. Als byzantinische Gelehrte nach Italien geflüchtet waren, haben sie das Studium der antiken Literatur angeregt.

C. *Complete the subordinate clauses in the tenses indicated:*

1. Er will das Museum sehen, wenn / er / kommen / nach Berlin.   (present)
2. Sie will wissen, wann / der Freund / ankommen.   (future)
3. Lincoln hatte viele Gegner, als / er / sein / Präsident.   (past)
4. Man kann die Alpen sehen, wenn / man / sein / in Bayern.   (present)
5. Einstein formulierte die Relativitätstheorie, als / er / arbeiten / in Zürich. (past)

SELF-PREPARATORY EXERCISE

Express in German the following ordinal numbers:

the 21st house	
the second step	das einundzwanzigste Haus
the first decade	die zweite Stufe
the 25th line	das erste Jahrzehnt
the 36th student	die fünfundzwanzigste Zeile
the 51st university	der sechsunddreißigste Student
	die einundfünfzigste Universität

EXERCISES

A. *Write out the German equivalents of the ordinal number and noun:*

1. the second generation
2. the sixth century
3. the first continent
4. the forty-sixth speaker
5. the hundred and fiftieth painting

ZWEIHUNDERTVIERUNDFÜNFZIG

B. *Supply the correct adjective endings:*

1. Die Wissenschaftlerin arbeitet in dem Labor einer groß_____ Universität.
2. Einstein war Direktor für theoretisch_____ Physik am Kaiser Wilhelm Institut in Berlin.
3. Das heutig_____ technisch_____ Zeitalter ist ohne die mathematisch_____ Grundlagen nicht denkbar.
4. Das Abitur ist die Reifeprüfung an höher_____ Schulen.
5. Deutschland hat ein kühl_____, gemäßigt_____ Klima.

C. *Change the following sentences to present perfect:* *

1. Der meiste Schnee fällt in den Gebirgen.
2. Atlantis war eine sagenhafte Insel.
3. Der Mangel an Vitamin C bewirkte eine Verringerung des Knochenproteins.
4. Freud betrieb zuerst hirnanatomische Forschungen.
5. Sie regten das Studium der antiken Literatur an.

D. *Supply the correct form of the modal in the present tense:*

1. Er _____ den Film nicht sehen. (to like to)
2. Die Tageszeitung _____ aktuell sein. (to have to)
3. Auf diese Weise _____ man die Energieversorgung umstellen. (to be able to)
4. Sie weiß noch nicht, wann sie *(singular)* kommen _____. (to be supposed to)
5. Der Chef _____ wissen, wo die Tagebücher sind. (to want to)

E. *Supply the relative pronouns:*

1. Wer ist der Mann, _____ er es gegeben hat? (to whom)
2. Aktuell nennt man etwas, _____ im Augenblick wichtig oder interessant ist. (that)
3. Es ist das erste Land, für _____ man einen „Wärmeatlas" erstellt. (which)
4. Die Renaissance ist die große europäische Kulturepoche, _____ die Wende vom Mittelalter zur Neuzeit umfaßt. (which)
5. Er ist ein bedeutender Archäologe, _____ an den Ausgrabungen mehrerer antiker Städte teilnahm. (who)

READING

Lebenskeime im Weltall

Wissenschaftler haben das erste organische Molekül im Weltall, im Zentrum der Milchstraße, gefunden. Entdeckt hat es ein deutscher Physiker vom Max-Planck-Institut für Radioastronomie gemeinsam mit einem australischen Kollegen. Das Molekül ist ein Vinylcyanid. Dieses Vinylcyanid kann eine Verbindung mit größeren Molekülverbänden eingehen. Damit hat man eine wichtige Voraussetzung für die Entstehung von noch komplizierteren Molekülen im Weltraum entdeckt. Man ist bei der Suche nach Bio-Molekülen im interstellaren Raum einen bedeutenden,

5

ZWEIHUNDERTFÜNFUNDFÜNFZIG

möglicherweise sogar entscheidenden Schritt vorangekommen. Das bestätigt die Wissenschaftler in der Hoffnung, auch künftig einfache Aminosäuren zu finden. Aminosäuren bilden die Grundbausteine der Eiweißstoffe (Proteine), die eine we-   10 sentliche Voraussetzung für die Entstehung von Leben darstellen.

VOCABULARY

der **Keim, -e**	organism, germ	
der **Lebenskeim, -e**	living organism, germ of life	
der **Raum, ̈e**	space, room	
der **Weltraum**	outer space, universe	
das **Weltall**	outer space, universe	
das **Zentrum, Zentren**	center	
die **Straße, -n**	street, road	
die **Milch**	milk	
die **Milchstraße**	Milky Way	
finden (findet), fand, gefunden	to find	
entdecken	to discover	
die **Astronomie**	astronomy	
das **Radio**	radio	
die **Radioastronomie**	radio astronomy	
gemeinsam (mit)	together (with)	
australisch	Australian	
der **Kollege, -n**	colleague	
das **Vinylcyanid**	vinyl cyanide	
die **Verbindung, -en**	compound, bond, combination	
größer	greater, larger	
der **Verband, ̈e**	combination, unit, union, binding	
ein-gehen (geht ein), ging ein, ist eingegangen	to enter into, join	
damit	thereby, with that (discovery)	

die **Voraussetzung, -en**	prerequisite	
die **Entstehung**	development, origin, beginning	
noch komplizierteren	even more complicated	
bei der Suche nach	in the search for	
die **Suche**	search	
interstellar	interstellar, among the stars	
möglicherweise	possibly	
sogar	even	
entscheidend	decisive, critical	
der **Schritt, -e**	step	
voran-kommen (kommt voran), kam voran, ist vorangekommen	to advance, to progress	
bestätigen	to confirm	
die **Hoffnung**	hope, aspiration	
auch	also	
künftig	in the future	
einfach	simple	
die **Säure, -n**	acid	
die **Aminosäure, -n**	amino acid	
der **Grund**	basis, foundation	
der **Baustein, -e**	building block	
die **Grundbausteine**	basic building blocks	
das **Eiweiß**	protein, albumen	
dar-stellen	to represent	

STRUCTURAL EXERCISES

A. *Underline all past participles in the above reading.*

B. *Give the English equivalents of the compound nouns:*

1. der Molekülverband
2. die Eiweißstoffe
3. der Weltraum
4. die Milchstraße
5. die Grundbausteine

ZWEIHUNDERTSECHSUNDFÜNFZIG

VOCABULARY EXERCISE

Give the English equivalents of the italicized words:

1. Aminosäuren *bilden* die Grundbausteine der Eiweißstoffe.
2. Er hat es *gemeinsam mit* einem Kollegen entdeckt.
3. Es kann eine Verbindung mit größeren Molekülverbänden *eingehen*.
4. Man hofft, künftig andere *einfache* Aminosäuren zu finden.
5. Man ist einen *entscheidenden* Schritt vorangekommen.
6. Damit hat man eine wichtige *Voraussetzung* entdeckt.
7. Proteine *stellen* eine wesentliche Voraussetzung für die Entstehung von Leben *dar*.

esson 24

STRUCTURE

1. Reflexive Verbs

a. Observe the following sentence:

The man	cuts	the bread.

In this example, the subject *(man)* relates to the object *(bread)* in some way (the act of cutting). Subject and object are two separate entities:

The man	$\neq$	bread
SUBJECT	$\neq$	OBJECT

$S \neq O$

b. The object may be replaced by a pronoun, but the relationship does not change:

The man	cuts	it.

The man	$\neq$	it.
SUBJECT	$\neq$	OBJECT

$S \neq O$

c. Assume that the man does not cut the bread but his finger or his hand:

The man	cuts	himself.

$S = O$

This sentence expresses the fact that the subject (man) and the object (himself) refer to the same person:

The man	=	himself
SUBJECT		OBJECT

$S = O$

d. Whenever subject and object refer to the same entity, the verb in the sentence is called a *reflexive verb* (that is, it refers back), and the pronoun object accompanying it is called the *reflexive pronoun.*

e. In German, the same relationship exists:

Or with the pronoun replacement:

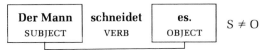

BUT:

Der Mann and **sich** describe the same entity; **sich** is a reflexive pronoun and the verb is now used in a reflexive form.

f. As you can see from this example, some verbs are used either reflexively or nonreflexively:

NONREFLEXIVELY   **schneiden** *(to cut)*
REFLEXIVELY   **sich schneiden** *(to cut oneself)*

g. Other verbs are only used reflexively:

sich freuen: Er freut sich *(He is happy.)*

h. The infinitive form of the reflexive verb consists of

| **sich** + infinitive of verb | **sich freuen** = *to be happy* |

i. The reflexive pronoun **sich** is used with the reflexive verb in the following forms:

INFINITIVE: **sich freuen**   *to be happy*

THIRD PERSON SINGULAR:
- **er freut sich** — *he is happy*
- **sie freut sich** — *she is happy*
- **man freut sich** — *people are happy*

THIRD PERSON PLURAL: **sie freuen sich**   *they are happy*

j. The reflexive pronoun **sich** is retained in all tenses:

Er hat sich gefreut. (present perfect)
He has been happy; he was happy.

k.   The reflexive pronoun is a grammatical necessity in German with reflexive verbs and may not be omitted even if the English equivalent is not reflexive:

Er freut sich. *(He is happy.)*

SELF-PREPARATORY EXERCISE

Give the English equivalents of the German sentences. (Both reflexive and non-reflexive verbs appear here):

Der Mann schneidet das Brot.	
Der Mann schneidet sich.	The man cuts the bread.
Die Studenten freuen sich.	The man cuts himself.
Er schneidet es.	The students are happy.
Er hat sich gefreut.	He cuts it.
	He was happy.

2.   Reflexive Verbs (continued)

a.   Partial list of verbs used reflexively or nonreflexively:

NONREFLEXIVE:		REFLEXIVE	
waschen	*to wash*	**sich waschen**	*to wash oneself*
rasieren	*to shave*	**sich rasieren**	*to shave oneself*
setzen	*to set*	**sich setzen**	*to sit (down)*
stellen	*to put, place*	**sich stellen**	*to place oneself*
legen	*to lay*	**sich legen**	*to lie (down)*
öffnen	*to open*	**sich öffnen**	*to open*
schließen	*to close*	**sich schließen**	*to close*
wundern	*to amaze, surprise*	**sich wundern (über)** + *acc.*	*to be surprised (about)*
interessieren	*to interest*	**sich interessieren (für)** + *acc.*	*to be interested (in)*
erinnern	*to remind*	**sich erinnern (an)** + *acc.*	*to remember remind oneself (of)*
vorbereiten	*to prepare*	**sich vorbereiten (auf)** + *acc.*	*to prepare oneself (for)*

b.   Partial list of totally reflexive verbs:

sich beeilen	*to hurry*
sich bemühen (um)	*to strive (for), endeavor*
sich entschließen	*to decide*
sich erkälten	*to catch cold*
sich freuen (auf) + *acc.*	*to look forward to*
sich freuen (über) + *acc.*	*to be happy about*
sich sehnen (nach)	*to long for*
sich irren	*to make a mistake*
sich schämen (vor)	*to be ashamed (of)*
sich genieren (vor)	*to be ashamed (of); to be embarrassed (about)*

SELF-PREPARATORY EXERCISE

Give the English equivalents of the German sentences. Note that the verbs occurring here are from the reflexive/nonreflexive category:

Das Kind schneidet den Fisch.	
Es schneidet sich.	The child cuts the fish.
Der Student legt das Buch auf den Tisch.	It cuts itself.
Er legte sich in den Schnee.	The student lays the book on the table.
Die Mutter hat die Tür geöffnet.	He lay down in the snow.
Die Tür hat sich geöffnet.	The mother opened the door.
Sie setzt es auf den Stein.	The door opened.
Er setzt sich auf den Stein.	She places it on the stone.
	He is sitting down on the stone.

EXERCISE

Give the English equivalents of the German sentences:

1. Sie öffnete das Fenster.
2. Das Fenster öffnete sich.
3. Der Schüler bereitete sich auf die Prüfung vor.
4. Der Lehrer bereitete eine Prüfung vor.
5. Sie schlossen die Tür.
6. Die Tür schloß sich.
7. Viele Erwachsene interessieren sich für die Volkshochschule.
8. Das Gemälde von Dürer interessiert ihn.

SELF-PREPARATORY EXERCISE

Give the English equivalents of the German sentences. The verbs used in this exercise are derived from the category of totally reflexive verbs:

Die Studentin freut sich auf die Ferien.	
Man gewöhnt sich an das Klima.	The student is looking forward to vacation.
Im Winter kann man sich leicht erkälten.	One gets used to the climate.
Sie entschloß sich, nach Köln zu fahren.	One can catch cold easily in the winter.
Das Kind freut sich über das Rätsel.	She decided to go to Cologne.
	The child is happy about the puzzle.

EXERCISE

Give the English equivalents of the German sentences:

1. Sie beeilt sich, um den Film sehen zu können.
2. Der Professor freut sich über die Dissertation.
3. Viele Studenten freuen sich nicht auf den Semesterbeginn.
4. Der Sklave sehnt sich nach Freiheit.
5. Sie haben sich entschlossen, eine Reise durch Europa zu unternehmen.
6. Er gibt zu, daß er sich geirrt hat.
7. Wann hat sie sich erkältet?
8. Er schämt sich, weil er ihr nicht geholfen hat.
9. Wer sich bemüht, erreicht auch etwas.
10. Der Wissenschaftler bemüht sich um die Erhaltung des Ökosystems.

READING

Barock

Die Kunstepoche des Barocks löste die der Renaissance ab. Das Zeitalter des Barocks gliedert man gewöhnlich in Frühbarock (1550 bis 1600), Hochbarock (1600 bis 1700) und Spätbarock (1700 bis 1800).

   Die Ursprünge der europäischen Barockbaukunst findet man in Italien. Die barocke Architektur verwendet viele Formen der Renaissance. Das Schönheitsideal   5
drückt man in einer majestätischen Größe, im Prunk und Pathos aus. Die vertikalen Linien bestimmen den Bau und durchbrechen die Dachlinie. Wandflächen haben Vor- oder Rücksprünge. Doppelte Stützen und ornamentale Motive geben den Eindruck reicher Fülle. In der Raumgestaltung erreicht das Barock eine Großzügigkeit und Mannigfaltigkeit, die vorher noch kein Stil besessen hat.   10

ZWEIHUNDERTZWEIUNDSECHZIG

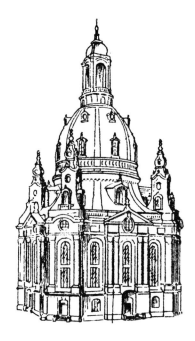

Barockkirche

VOCABULARY

das **Barock**	Baroque	der **Vorsprung, ⁻e**	here: projection, protrusion
ab-lösen	to succeed; to end; to relieve	der **Rücksprung, ⁻e**	recession, indentation
die der Renaissance	that of the Renaissance	**doppelt**	double(d)
gewöhnlich	usually	die **Stütze, -n**	pillar, column, support
der **Ursprung, ⁻e**	origin, source, beginning	**ornamental**	ornamental
die **Schönheit**	beauty	das **Motiv, -e**	motif, feature, design, main theme, repeated figure in design
das **Ideal, -e**	ideal		
aus-drücken	to express		
majestätisch	majestic		
die **Größe**	size; here: dimension, greatness	der **Eindruck, ⁻e**	impression
		die **Fülle**	abundance, wealth
der **Prunk**	pomp, splendor		
das **Pathos**	pathos, fervor, exuberance	die **Großzügigkeit**	generosity, grandiose quality
vertikal	vertical	die **Mannigfaltigkeit**	variety, diversity, multiplicity
die **Linie, -n**	line		
durchbrechen (durchbricht), durchbrach, durchbrochen	to break through, to interrupt	**vorher**	before, previously
die **Fläche, -n**	plain surface, expanse, plain	der **Stil, -e**	style
		besitzen (besitzt), besaß, besessen	to possess

ZWEIHUNDERTDREIUNDSECHZIG

STRUCTURAL EXERCISES

A. *Underline all verbs with inseparable prefixes in the above reading.*

B. *Give the English equivalents of the compound words:*

1. die Barockbaukunst   3. die Wandfläche   5. die Raumgestaltung
2. das Schönheitsideal   4. das Zeitalter

VOCABULARY EXERCISE

Give the English equivalents of the italicized words:

1. Die barocke Architektur *verwendet* viele Formen der Renaissance.
2. Die vertikalen Linien *durchbrechen* die Dachlinie.
3. Das Schönheitsideal *drückt* man in einer majestätischen Größe *aus.*
4. Die Großzügigkeit des Barocks hat *vorher* noch kein Stil besessen.
5. Die *Ursprünge* des Barocks findet man in Italien.
6. Der Barock *löste* die Renaissance *ab.*
7. Man gliedert das Zeitalter des Barocks *gewöhnlich* in Frühbarock, Hochbarock und Spätbarock.

EXERCISES

A. *Form sentences with the elements given below in the tense indicated (remember, the reflexive pronoun generally follows the subject-verb or verb-subject unit):**

1. Die Tür / sich öffnen / langsam (present perfect)
2. Man / können / sich gewöhnen / an das Klima (present)
3. Die Chefin / müssen / sich entschließen / jetzt (present)
4. Er / sich freuen / über / das gute Ergebnis (past)
5. Der Mathematiker / sich irren / in der Zahl (present perfect)

B. *Give the English equivalents of the German sentences:*

1. Der Student hat sich über die gute Prüfung gefreut.
2. Sie haben sich über das Forschungsergebnis gewundert.
3. Viele Physiker interessieren sich für Bio-Moleküle im interstellaren Raum.
4. Der Mann will sich nicht rasieren.
5. Sie will sich bemühen, ihre Arbeit schnell zu beenden.

STRUCTURE

4.   Verbs with Dative Reflexive Pronoun

a.   There are a few German reflexive verbs which take both a dative reflexive pronoun and a direct object:

Er sieht sich den Film an. *(He looks at the movie.)*

ZWEIHUNDERTVIERUNDSECHZIG

In this example, the direct object (**den Film**) and the subject are not identical. Since a verb can have only one direct object, the reflexive pronoun must be an indirect object.

b. The reflexive pronoun in the dative case (indirect object) is **sich** in the infinitive, the third person singular, and the plural.

c. Partial list of verbs with a dative reflexive pronoun (Note that the word **etwas** is added in the listing to indicate that the verb uses a direct object and a dative reflexive pronoun):

sich etwas kaufen	*to buy something (for oneself)*
sich etwas ansehen	*to look at, view something (oneself)*
sich etwas anhören	*to listen to something (oneself)*
sich etwas holen	*to fetch something (for oneself)*
sich etwas vorstellen	*to imagine something (oneself)*
sich etwas bestellen	*to order something (for oneself)*
sich etwas suchen	*to look for something (for oneself)*

d. The reflexive pronoun is also used in the dative case whenever the reflexive verb refers to parts of the body. English uses a possessive pronoun instead:

Sie wäscht sich die Hände. *(She washes her hands.)*

Dative reflexive verbs expressing an action which affects the subject's body are limited in number:

Er **kämmt sich** die Haare.	*(He combs his hair.)*
Er **wäscht sich** die Hände.	*(He washes his hands.)*
Sie **hat sich** den Finger **gebrochen.**	*(She broke her finger.)*
Sie **putzt sich** die Zähne.	*(She is brushing her teeth.)*

EXERCISE

Give the English equivalents of the German sentences:

1. Der reiche Mann hat sich einen neuen Wagen bestellt.
2. Das Kind holt sich ein anderes Buch.
3. Die Studentin hat sich den Arm gebrochen.
4. Er kann sich die Situation nicht vorstellen.
5. Sie wollen sich das Gemälde ansehen.
6. Die Mutter wäscht sich die Haare.
7. Sie haben sich ein größeres Haus gesucht.
8. Sie soll sich die Rede des Präsidenten anhören.
9. Er kann sich eine interessante Tageszeitung kaufen.
10. Die Touristen wollen sich die Ausgrabungen von Troja ansehen.

READING

Das Schulsystem der Bundesrepublik Deutschland (1)

Das Schulsystem der Bundesrepublik ist staatlich geregelt, aber nicht einheitlich. Der Schulaufbau ist in den Bundesländern verschieden, aber im wesentlichen sieht es so aus: alle Kinder müssen ab sechs Jahren in die Schule gehen, und zwar mindestens neun Jahre lang (an ihrem ersten Schultag bekommen viele Kinder eine große Tüte mit Süßigkeiten und Obst). Vier Jahre lange gehen alle in die Volks- 5 schule. Im Alter von zehn Jahren können sie auf eine weiterführende Schule gehen. Durchschnittlich besuchen 50% die Hauptschule (Volksschuloberstufe), die fünf bis sechs Jahre dauert, 22% die Realschule (Mittelschule), die sechs Jahre dauert, 28% das Gymnasium (die höhere Schule, Oberschule) von neun Jahren Dauer.

Nach Abschluß der Hauptschule können die Schüler mit einer Berufsaufbildung 10 anfangen, zum Beispiel mit einer dreijährigen Lehre als Facharbeiter oder Handwerker oder einer kaufmännischen Lehre. Nach dem Realschulabschluß, der „mittleren Reife", kann man zum Beispiel in kaufmännische Berufe, zur Bank oder in die Verwaltung gehen. Wer studieren will, muß normalerweise das Gymnasium mit der Reifeprüfung, dem Abitur, beenden. Während der neunjährigen Schulzeit 15 darf man nur zweimal „sitzenbleiben", d.h. eine Klasse wiederholen.

VOCABULARY

das **System, -e**	system	
staatlich	state, by the state, public, civic	
regeln	to control, to regulate	
einheitlich	uniform, centralized	
der **Aufbau**	structure	
im wesentlichen	essentially, in essence	
aus-sehen (sieht aus), sah aus, ausgesehen	to look like	
das **Kind, -er**	child	
ab	from, beginning with	
in die Schule gehen	to go to school	
zwar	namely, to be sure	
mindestens	at least	
bekommen (bekommt), bekam, bekommen	to get, receive, obtain	
die **Tüte, -n**	paper bag	

die **Süßigkeit, -en**	sweet(s), candy	
das **Obst**	fruit	
die **Volksschule, -n**	basic (elementary) school	
im Alter von	at the age of	
das **Alter**	age	
weiterführend	continuing	
besuchen	to visit; here: to attend	
die **Hauptschule, -n**	upper level of elementary school	
die **Oberstufe**	upper level, higher grades	
die **Dauer**	length, duration	
der **Abschluß**	conclusion	
der **Beruf, -e**	job, profession	
die **Ausbildung**	education, training	
die **Berufsausbildung**	career education, vocational training	
an-fangen (fängt an), fing an, angefangen	to begin, start	
zum Beispiel	for example	
das **Beispiel**	example	

	dreijährig	three year	die	**Bank, -en**	bank
	-jährig	*suffix meaning year*	die	**Verwaltung, -en**	administration, government
die	**Lehre**	*here:* apprentice-ship		**normalerweise**	normally
	als	as		**neunjährig**	nine year
der	**Facharbeiter, -**	skilled worker, specialist	die	**Schulzeit**	time in school, education
das	**Fach, ¨er**	subject, specialty, line		**sitzen-bleiben (bleibt sitzen), blieb sitzen, ist sitzen-geblieben**	to fail, remain in the same grade
der	**Arbeiter, -**	worker			
der	**Handwerker**	craftsman, artisan			
	kaufmännisch	commercial, business, merchant	die	**Klasse, -n**	class, grade
die	**Realschule, -n**	modern secondary school		**wiederholen**	to repeat
die	**mittlere Reife**	intermediate "maturity" *(degree at the end of the modern secondary school)*			

STRUCTURAL EXERCISES

A. *Underline all modals and their dependent infinitives in the above reading.*

B. *Give the English equivalents of the compound nouns:*

1. der Schulaufbau   3. der Facharbeiter   5. die Reifeprüfung
2. die Berufsausbildung   4. der Handwerker

VOCABULARY EXERCISE

Give the English equivalents of the italicized words:

1. Die Kinder müssen *mindestens* neun Jahre lang in die Schule gehen.
2. Das Schulsystem ist nicht *einheitlich.*
3. *Vier Jahre lang* gehen alle Kinder in die Volksschule.
4. Mit der „mittleren Reife" kann man *zum Beispiel* in kaufmännische Berufe gehen.
5. Wer *studieren will,* muß das Abitur haben.
6. Man darf eine Klasse nur zweimal *wiederholen.*
7. Nach Abschluß der Hauptschule *können* die Schüler mit einer Berufsausbildung *anfangen.*

Da freut sich der müde Kreislauf

esson **25**

STRUCTURE

1. Impersonal Reflexive Verbs

a. Some reflexive verbs frequently use **es** as an impersonal subject.

b. Partial list of impersonal reflexive verbs:

sich zeigen	*to become apparent*
sich erweisen	*to prove to be, turn out to be*
sich ergeben (aus)	*to result (from), follow (from)*
sich lassen	*to be able to, can*
sich handeln (um)	*to be a matter (of), deal (with)*
sich heraus-stellen	*to turn out, come out*

Examples:

Es zeigte sich, daß der Student das Buch nicht gelesen hatte.
It became apparent that the student had not read the book.
Es muß sich um ein neues Verfahren **handeln.**
It must deal with a new process.
Es stellte sich heraus, daß sie nicht in New York gewesen war.
It turned out that she had not been in New York.
Es läßt sich nicht leugnen, daß er zu schnell gefahren ist.
It cannot be denied that he drove too fast.

ZWEIHUNDERTACHTUNDSECHZIG

EXERCISES

A. *Give the English equivalents of the German sentences:*

1. Es ergab sich aus der Analyse, daß man eine andere Methode versuchen mußte.
2. Es stellte sich heraus, daß seine Einstellung einer kritischen Überprüfung nicht standhielt.
3. Es handelt sich um einen politischen Begriff, den man jetzt neu definieren muß.
4. Es läßt sich leicht angeben, wo und zu welchen Zeiten man Energie verbraucht.
5. Es wird sich wohl zeigen, was man durch die Ausgrabung zerstört hat.

B. *Give the English equivalents of the German sentences:*

1. Die Gelehrten entschlossen sich, das Studium der antiken Literatur anzuregen.
2. Sie will sich eine Zeitung kaufen.
3. Man bemühte sich, den Einfluß des Unbewußten auf das Verhalten zu bestimmen.
4. Man freute sich, daß man einen entscheidenden Schritt vorangekommen war.
5. Sie wäscht sich die Hände.

2. The Preposition <u>bei</u>

a. The preposition **bei** is followed by the dative case and usually means *by, near,* or *at.*

b. With expressions of temperature and pressure, the preposition **bei** means *at:*

Bei einer Temperatur von 600 Grad. . . *(At a temperature of 600 degrees. . .)*

c. With expressions of action, **bei** means *on, in, in the process of,* or *during.*

Bei der Suche nach Bio-Molekülen im interstellaren Raum. . .
In the search for biomolecules in interstellar space. . .

d. With names of metals and chemical compounds **bei** means *in* or *in the case of:*

Bei Vinylcyanid. . . (In [the case of] vinyl cyanide. . .)

e. When referring to people, **bei** also means *with:*

Sie wohnt **bei ihrer Freundin.** *(She lives with her girl friend.)*

ZWEIHUNDERTNEUNUNDSECHZIG

EXERCISE

Give the English equivalents of the German sentences:

1. Bei der Ausgrabung von Troja hat man einige wichtige Gebäude zerstört.
2. Sie wohnt bei ihm.
3. Bei Aminosäuren handelt es sich um die Grundbausteine der Eiweißstoffe, die eine wesentliche Voraussetzung für die Entstehung von Leben darstellen.
4. Bei einer Wärme von 5 000 Grad verbraucht man viel Energie.
5. Bei den ornamentalen Motiven des Barocks hat man den Eindruck reicher Fülle.

3. Personal Pronouns (continued)

a. From previous lessons we are familiar with the following personal pronouns:

THIRD PERSON SINGULAR: **er**   *he*
                         sie *she*
                         es   *it*

THIRD PERSON PLURAL: **sie** *they*

b. For the pronouns **er, sie, es,** the stem of most verbs adds **-t.** Exceptions are modals, which add no ending, and irregular verbs like **sein, haben, werden:**

Sie geht in die Schule. *(She is going to school.)*

But:

Sie kann in die Schule gehen. *(She can go to school.)*

c. In the present tense, the plural pronoun **sie** *(they)* uses the infinitive form of the verb:

INFINITIVE: **geben**
THIRD PERSON PLURAL: **sie geben**

d. For the pronoun **ich,** the verb stem adds **-e** in the present-tense form of most verbs. There are no stem-vowel changes in the first person singular, present tense:

Ich gebe ihr das Buch. *(I am giving her the book.)*
Er gibt ihr das Buch. *(He is giving her the book.)*

e. With modals, there is no ending in the present tense for **ich.** Modals simply use the singular stem:

Ich kann dem Vater helfen. *(I can help father.)*

ZWEIHUNDERTSIEBZIG

f.   Following are the first-person singular forms of the irregular verbs **sein, haben, werden, wissen** in the present tense:

sein	**ich bin**	*(I am)*	**werden**	**ich werde**	*(I will)*
haben	**ich habe**	*(I have)*	**wissen**	**ich weiß**	*(I know)*

g.   The personal pronoun **wir** uses the infinitive form of the verb (with the exception of **sein**) to form the present tense:

Wir kaufen ein neues Haus.	*(We are buying a new house.)*
Wir haben jetzt keine Zeit.	*(We don't have any time now.)*
Wir werden den Film sehen.	*(We will see the film.)*
Wir wissen nicht, wann er ankommt.	*(We don't know when he arrives.)*

h.   In the first person plural, the form of **sein** is: **wir sind.**

EXERCISES

A.   *Supply the correct endings to the verbs:*

1. Ich fahr_____ nach Deutschland.
2. Wir seh_____ die Bücher.
3. Wir woll_____ in das Labor gehen.
4. Ich kenn_____ seine Schwester.
5. Ich zeig_____ ihr das Gemälde.

B.   *Supply the correct form of the verb in the present tense:*

1. Ich _____ den Lehrer.   (fragen)
2. Wir _____ eine Fremdsprache.   (lernen)
3. Ich _____ in dem Labor.   (arbeiten)
4. Wir _____ an einer Universität.   (studieren)
5. Ich _____ die Tageszeitung.   (lesen)

C.   *Supply the correct form of the verb in the present tense:*

1. Ich _____, daß er keine Zeit hat.   (wissen)
2. Wir _____ keine Zeit.   (haben)
3. Ich _____ in das Büro gehen.   (werden)
4. Wir _____ jetzt in Berlin.   (sein)
5. Ich _____ ihn nicht sehen.   (dürfen)

D.   *Give the German equivalents of the following sentences:*

1. I have the book.
2. We are in the United States.
3. I am coming.
4. I can see it.
5. I will read the book.

Zürich in der Deutsch sprechenden Schweiz

In Genf sprechen die meisten Schweizer Französich

ZWEIHUNDERTZWEIUNDSIEBZIG

READING

Die Schweiz

Die Schweiz liegt mitten in Europa. Ihre Nachbarn sind: Frankreich, Italien, Österreich, Liechtenstein und Deutschland. Die Schweiz ist eine Bundesrepublik mit
41 288 km² (Quadratkilometer) Fläche und 6 Millionen Einwohnern. 74,4% der
Schweizer Bürger sprechen Deutsch, 20,2% Französisch, 4,1% Italienisch und 1%
Rätoromanisch. Neben den Amtssprachen Deutsch, Französich, Italienisch erkennt   5
man auch seit 1938 Rätoromanisch als Landessprache an. Die Schweiz ist ein
Bundesstaat mit 22 souveränen Kantonen. Die landwirtschaftliche Nutzung besteht
aus Getreide-, Wein- und Obstbau. Die Schweiz hat sehr geringe Bodenschätze
und exportiert einen großen Teil ihrer Industriegüter, besonders Maschinen, Uhren,
chemische Erzeugnisse, Textil- und Nahrungsmittel. Die Handelsbilanz ist auf   10
Grund der hohen Einfuhren von Nahrungs- und Genußmitteln, von Spezialmaschinen, Autos und Instrumenten stark passiv. Das Land gleicht sie jedoch durch
Kapitalerträge, Gütertransit und Fremdenverkehr aus.

Die heutige Schweiz mit ihren 22 Kantonen ist das Resultat der Bundesverfassung
von 1814, die der Wiener Kongreß bestätigte. Zugleich erkannte der Kongreß die   15
Neutralität der Schweiz und die Unverletzbarkeit ihres Gebietes an. Die Verfassung
von 1814 machte die Schweiz zu einem losen Staatenbund. Dann folgten politische
Auseinandersetzungen, bis schließlich 1847 die liberalen Sieger den Staatenbund in
einen Bundesstaat umwandelten, der noch heute besteht.

VOCABULARY

die	**Schweiz**	Switzerland	die	**Nutzung**	use, utiliza-tion, pro-duce
	liegen (liegt),	to lie, be			
	lag, gelegen	located			
der	**Nachbar, -n**	neighbor	der	**Wein, -e**	wine
die	**Bundesrepublik**	Federal Re-public	der	**Anbau**	growing, culti-vation
	Rätoromanisch	Raeto-Romanic		**exportieren**	to export
das	**Amt, ⁻er**	office, official position	der	**Teil, -e**	part, portion
			die	**Industrie, -n**	industry
die	**Amtssprache, -n**	official lan-guage	das	**Gut, ⁻er**	commodity, good
	an-erkennen	to recognize,		**besonders**	particularly, especially
	(erkennt an),	acknowledge			
	erkannte an,		die	**Maschine, -n**	machine
	anerkannt		die	**Uhr, -en**	clock
die	**Landessprache, -n**	language of the country, vernacular	das	**Erzeugnis, -se**	product
			die	**Handelsbilanz**	balance of trade
der	**Bundesstaat, -en**	federal state		**auf Grund** (+ *genitive*)	by virtue of, on account of
	souverän	sovereign			
der	**Kanton -e**	district, Swiss canton		**hoh**	high

ZWEIHUNDERTDREIUNDSIEBZIG

die	**Einfuhr, -en**	import	die	**Verfassung**	constitution
der	**Genuß**	enjoyment, pleasure	der	**Wiener Kongreß**	Congress of Vienna (1814–1815)
die	**Genußmittel** *(pl.)*	luxury items		**bestätigen**	to confirm, make valid, validate
	spezial	special			
das	**Auto, -s**	car	die	**Neutralität**	neutrality
das	**Instrument, -e**	instrument	die	**Unverletzbarkeit**	inviolability, sovereignty
	stark	strong(ly)			
	passiv	passive		**los**	loose
	stark passiv	very unfavorable	der	**Staatenbund**	confederation, federal union
	aus-gleichen (gleicht aus), glich aus, ausgeglichen	to equalize, compensate		**dann**	then, thereafter
	jedoch	however		**folgen**	to follow
der	**Kapitalertrag, -̈e**	capital gain	die	**Auseinandersetzung, -en**	dispute, fight, argument
das	**Kapital**	capital		**bis**	until
der	**Ertrag, -̈e**	proceeds, revenue, gain		**schließlich**	finally
				liberal	liberal
der	**Gütertransit**	transit trade, through traffic	der	**Sieger, -**	victor, winner
				um-wandeln	to transform, to convert, to change
der	**Verkehr**	traffic			
der	**Fremde, die Fremde, -n**	foreigner, stranger, tourist		**bestehen**	to exist
der	**Fremdenverkehr**	tourist traffic, tourism			

STRUCTURAL EXERCISES

A. *Underline all verbs with separable prefixes in the above reading.*

B. *Give the English equivalents of the compound nouns:*

1. die Handelsbilanz   3. der Bundesstaat   5. die Industriegüter
2. der Staatenbund   4. der Fremdenverkehr

VOCABULARY EXERCISE

Give the English equivalents of the italicized words:

1. Die *landwirtschaftliche* Nutzung besteht aus Getreide-, Obst- und Weinanbau.
2. Der Kongreß *erkannte* die Neutralität der Schweiz *an.*
3. Der Bundesstaat *besteht* heute noch.
4. Die Handelsbilanz ist *auf Grund der* hohen Einfuhren stark passiv.
5. Die Schweiz exportiert *besonders* Uhren.
6. Die Schweiz *gleicht* die Handelsbilanz durch Fremdenverkehr *aus.*
7. *Schließlich* haben die liberalen Sieger den Staatenbund in einen Bundesstaat umgewandelt.

ZWEIHUNDERTVIERUNDSIEBZIG

STRUCTURE

4.   Personal Pronouns (continued)

a.   German has three personal pronouns equivalent to the English pronoun *you:*

du   (singular)
ihr   (plural)
Sie   (singular and plural, always capitalized)

b.   The pronouns **du** and **ihr** are used to address close friends, members of the family, and young children; **Sie** is used to address superiors, strangers, and people who are also greeted with titles:

Hast du viel Zeit, Hans? *(Do you have a lot of time, John?)*
Haben Sie viel Zeit, Herr Müller? *(Do you have a lot of time, Mr. Müller?)*

c.   Verbs generally add **-st** to the verb stem to form the present tense when used with **du:**

Du gehst jetzt nicht in die Schule, Hans? *(Aren't you going to school now, John?)*

d.   Verbs whose stem end in an / s /-sound **(-s, -ss, -ß, -tz, -z)**, only add **-t** in the **du**-form of the verb in the present tense:

Du liest zu viel, Barbara. *(You are reading too much, Barbara.)*

e.   Verbs with stem-vowel change in the present tense retain the stem vowel change in the **du**-form.

Fährst du in die Stadt oder **läufst du?**
Are you driving into the city or are you walking?

f.   Modal verbs add **-st** to their singular stem in the **du**-form:

Willst du ihm helfen, Paula? *(Do you want to help him, Paula?)*

g.   The verbs **sein, haben, werden,** and **wissen** have the following forms in the second person singular:

sein	**du bist**	*(you are)*
haben	**du hast**	*(you have)*
werden	**du wirst**	*(you will, you become)*
wissen	**du weißt**	*(you know)*

EXERCISES

A. *Supply the correct form of the verb:*

    1. Du _____ in die Schweiz. (fahren)
    2. Wann _____ du in das Labor? (kommen)
    3. _____ du den Professor? (kennen)
    4. Warum _____ du immer? (schlafen)
    5. _____ du das Haus? (sehen)

B. *Supply the correct form of the verb:*

    1. Wann _____ du Zeit? (haben)
    2. Du _____ jetzt in Deutschland. (sein)
    3. Was _____ du über die Schweiz? (wissen)
    4. _____ du Professor oder Wissenschaftler? (werden)
    5. Du _____ viele Bücher. (lesen)

C. *Give the German equivalents (you = **du**):*

    1. You work a lot, Robert.
    2. Are you here, mother?
    3. Do you know that, Elisabeth?
    4. You can wait in this room, Rudolf.
    5. You must ask the teacher, Julie.

5. Personal Pronouns (continued)

a. The verb ending in the second person plural, present tense (after **ihr**), is **-t**:

    Geht ihr in die Schule, Kinder? *(Are you going to school, children?)*

b. Verbs whose stems end in **-d** or **-t** add **-e** between the stem ending and the **-st** personal ending for **du** and the **-t** personal ending for **ihr**:

    Arbeitest du in der Brauerei, Karl?
    Are you working in the brewery, Karl?
    Arbeitet ihr noch im Garten, Hans und Paul?
    Are you still working in the garden, John and Paul?

c. Modals add **-t** to their infinitive stem in the present tense after **ihr**:

    Ihr dürft jetzt nicht spielen, Kinder.
    You are not allowed to play now, children.

ZWEIHUNDERTSECHSUNDSIEBZIG

d. The verbs **sein, haben, werden,** and **wissen** have the following forms after **ihr** in the present tense:

sein	**ihr seid**	*(you are)*
haben	**ihr habt**	*(you have)*
werden	**ihr werdet**	*(you will, you become)*
wissen	**ihr wißt**	*(you know)*

e. Whether referring to one person or several persons, **Sie,** the common equivalent for "you," uses the infinitive form for the present tense:

Gehen Sie jetzt ins Büro, Fräulein Schmidt?
Are you going to the office now, Miss Schmidt?
Arbeiten Sie immer noch im Labor, Fräulein Kraft und Herr Heinz?
Are you still working in the laboratory, Miss Kraft and Mr. Heinz?

SELF-PREPARATORY EXERCISE

Supply the German pronoun corresponding to the context of the English sentences:

What are you doing, Fritz?	
When are you leaving, Mr. Schmidt?	du
You don't understand, Mother.	Sie
You can go now, Inge.	du
What are you doing, children?	du
	ihr

EXERCISES

A. *Supply the correct verb endings:*

1. Du lies_____ die Zeitung.
2. Ihr wart_____ in dem Hotel. *(to wait)*
3. Kauf_____ Sie das Obst, Herr Klein?
4. Fähr_____ du nach Italien?
5. Wo arbeit_____ ihr?

B. *Supply the correct form of the verb:*

1. Ihr _____ ihm die Uhr. (geben)
2. Wann _____ Sie die neue Maschine, Herr Wagner? (kaufen)
3. Du _____ den Professor. (kennen)
4. Wie _____ du? (heißen)
5. Wie _____ ihr die Energie? (verbrauchen)

C.   *Supply the correct form of the verb:*

1. Du _____ immer noch in dem Hotel.   (sein)
2. Ihr _____ ihn nicht sehen.   (werden)
3. _____ du, wie man das Gemälde raubt?   (wissen)
4. Du _____ die Reise nicht unternehmen.   (können)
5. _____ Sie die Einleitung lesen, Herr Professor?   (wollen)

D.   *Give the German equivalents of the English sentences:*

1. Are you waiting, Rudolf?
2. Can you help them, children?
3. Are you here, Miss Schneider?
4. Where will you be, Willi?
5. Do you know where she is, Robert?

READING

Der Optimist   (von Sigismund von Radecki)

Diese Geschichte ist ein Märchen und daher besonders zur Veröffentlichung geeignet.

Es waren einmal zwei Frösche, die einen Kuhstall besuchten. Der eine Frosch war seiner seelischen Einstellung nach Optimist. Der andere Frosch war aus Natur pessimistisch.   5

Mit einem riesigen Sprung sprangen beide in einen Metalleimer und plumpsten in die Milch. Der Pessimist starrte entsetzt auf die spiegelglatten, unbekletterbaren Metallwände, schwamm ein paar Minuten, gab endlich den hoffnungslosen Kampf auf, sank auf den Grund und ertrank.

Der optimistische Frosch starrte ebenfalls auf die spiegelglatten Metallwände.   10
Dann aber faßte er sich ein Herz und ist die ganze Nacht hindurch so unverdrossen geschwommen, rückgeschwommen, hat gekrault und gestrampelt — daß er beim Morgengrauen hoch oben auf einem Berg von Butter saß!

VOCABULARY

der **Optimist**	optimist	der **Frosch, ⁻e**	frog
von	by	der **Kuhstall, ⁻e**	cow stall
das **Märchen**	tale, fairy tale	**besuchen**	to visit
dah<u>e</u>r	therefore	**der eine Frosch**	one of the frogs
die **Veröffentlichung,**		**nach**	according to
-en	publication	**seiner Einstellung**	to judge by his at-
geeignet (zu)	suited (for), ap-	**nach**	titude
	propriate (for)	die **Einstellung**	attitude
es war einmal	a long time ago	**aus Natur**	by nature
	there was, once	**pessimistisch**	pessimistic
	upon a time	**riesig**	huge, giant

ZWEIHUNDERTACHTUNDSIEBZIG

der **Sprung, ⸚e** — jump, leap
    springen (springt),
      sprang,
      ist gesprungen — to jump; to leap
    beide — both (of them)
das **Metall, -e** — metal
der **Eimer, -** — bucket, pail
    plumpsen — to fall with a thud
    starren — to stare, look fixedly
    entsetzt — horrified
der **Spiegel, -** — mirror
    glatt — smooth, slippery
    spiegelglatt — slippery, shiny, smoothly polished
    unbekletterbar — unsurmountable, insuperable
    schwimmen (schwimmt),
      schwamm,
      ist geschwommen — to swim
die **Minute, -n** — minute
    ein paar Minuten — a few minutes
    auf-geben (gibt auf),
      gab auf,
      aufgegeben — to give up, quit, surrender
    endlich — finally
    hoffnungslos — hopeless
    sinken (sinkt), sank,
      ist gesunken — to sink

der **Grund** — *here:* bottom
    ertrinken (ertrinkt),
      ertrank
      ist ertrunken — to drown
    optimistisch — optimistic
    ebenfalls — also, likewise
    sich fassen — to collect oneself, pull oneself together
    sich ein Herz fassen — to take courage, take heart
    ganz — entire, all, whole
die **Nacht, ⸚e** — night
    die ganze Nacht hindurch — all night long, the whole night through
    unverdrossen — indefatigably, untiringly
    rück-schwimmen — to swim on one's back
    kraulen — to swim the crawl
    strampeln — to kick
das **Morgengrauen** — dawn, break of day
    beim Morgengrauen — at dawn, at the break of day
    hoch oben — high up
die **Butter** — butter
    sitzen (sitzt),
      saß, gesessen — to sit

STRUCTURAL EXERCISES

A. *Underline all past forms of strong verbs in the above reading.*

B. *Give the English equivalents of the compound nouns:*

   1. die Metallwand   3. die Tageszeitung   5. das Tagebuch
   2. das Morgengrauen   4. die Kernenergie

VOCABULARY EXERCISE

Give the English equivalents of the italicized words:

1. Diese Geschichte ist zur Veröffentlichung *geeignet.*
2. Der Frosch gab den *hoffnungslosen* Kampf auf.
3. Der Pessimist schwamm ein *paar* Minuten.
4. *Es waren einmal* zwei Frösche.
5. Der andere Frosch war *aus Natur* pessimistisch.
6. *Endlich* gab er den hoffnungslosen Kampf auf.
7. Der Frosch sank *auf den Grund.*

esson 26

STRUCTURE

1. Past-Tense Forms of Weak Verbs

a. With the personal pronouns **er, sie,** and **es,** weak verbs add **-te** to the stem to form the past tense:

Er **fragte** den Lehrer. *(He asked the teacher.)*

b. In addition to **-te,** some personal pronouns also require personal verb endings:

SINGULAR	STEM	+	**-te**	+	ENDING		
ich	frag		-te		—	=	ich fragte
du	frag		-te		st	=	du fragtest
er	frag		-te		—	=	er fragte
sie	frag		-te		—	=	sie fragte
es	frag		-te		—	=	es fragte
PLURAL							
wir	frag		-te		n	=	wir fragten
ihr	frag		-te		t	=	ihr fragtet
sie	frag		-te		n	=	sie fragten
Sie	frag		-te		n	=	Sie fragten

c.   Weak verbs with stems ending in **-t** add an **-e** between stem and **-te** plus ending:

PERSON

1	**ich wart -e -te**	=	**ich wartete**	*(I waited)*
2	**du wart -e -test**	=	**du wartetest**	
3	**er wart -e -te**	=	**er wartete**	
	sie wart -e -te	=	**sie wartete**	
	es wart -e -te	=	**es wartete**	

— —

1	**wir wart -e -ten**	=	**wir warteten**	
2	**ihr wart -e -tet**	=	**ihr wartetet**	
3	**sie wart -e -ten**	=	**sie warteten**	
	Sie wart -e -ten	=	**Sie warteten**	

EXERCISES

A.   *Supply the correct personal verb endings in the past tense:*

    1.   Ich sagt_____ ihm das Resultat.
    2.   Wir macht_____ die Reifeprüfung.
    3.   Wann fragt_____ Sie den Arzt, Fräulein Weiß?
    4.   Du hört_____ das Radio.
    5.   Ihr besucht_____ das Labor.

B.   *Supply the correct form of the verb in the past tense:*

    1.   Er _____ eine neue Methode.   (entdecken)
    2.   Warum _____ die Kinder nicht?   (antworten)
    3.   Der Frosch _____ die ganze Nacht.   (strampeln)
    4.   Der Wiener Kongreß _____ die Neutralität.   (bestätigen)
    5.   Das Land _____ viele Maschinen.   (exportieren)

C.   *Give the German equivalents of the English sentences in the past tense:*

    1.   We asked him.
    2.   She said it.
    3.   You answered him, Fritz.
    4.   Did you buy it, Mr. Weinberg?
    5.   Did you smoke, children?

READING

Macht

„Wenn wir einmal die Macht bekommen, dann werden wir sie, so wahr uns Gott helfe, behalten. Wegnehmen lassen wir sie uns dann nicht mehr." (Adolf Hitler, 1932).

VOCABULARY

die **Macht, ̈e**	power, force	**behalten (behält),**	to retain,
einmal	once, someday	**behielt,**	to keep
bekommen (bekommt),	to get,	**behalten**	
bekam,	receive,	**weg-nehmen**	to take
bekommen	obtain	**(nimmt weg),**	away
die Macht bekommen	to assume	**nahm weg,**	
	power	**weggenommen**	
so wahr uns Gott	so help us	**(sich) lassen (läßt), ließ,**	to let,
helfe	God	**gelassen**	allow
helfen (hilft), half,	to help, as-	**nicht mehr**	not any more,
geholfen	sist		not again

VOCABULARY EXERCISE

Give the English equivalents of the italicized words:

1. Er will die Macht *behalten.*
2. Sie *haben* die Macht *bekommen.*
3. Die Frösche *sprangen* in die Milch.
4. Er ist *die ganze Nacht hindurch* geschwommen.
5. Die Schweiz hat sehr *geringe* Bodenschätze.
6. Mit der ,,mittleren Reife'' kann man in *die Verwaltung* gehen.
7. Das Schönheitsideal *drückt sich* im Prunk *aus.*

STRUCTURE

2. Past-Tense Forms of Strong Verbs

a. Strong verbs, instead of using **-te** to form the past tense, change the stem vowel:

PRESENT: Er **sieht** das Haus.   PAST: Er **sah** das Haus.
          He sees the house.   *He saw the house.*

b. Strong verbs retain the past-tense stem with all personal pronouns, singular and plural. The personal endings are the same as those for weak verbs:

INFINITIVE: **gehen**
PAST TENSE STEM: **ging**

PERSON			PERSON	
1	**ich ging**	(*I went*)	1	**wir gingen**
2	**du gingst**		2	**ihr gingt**
3	**er ging**		3	**sie gingen**
	sie ging			**Sie gingen**
	es ging			

EXERCISES

A. *Supply the correct personal endings:*

1. Wir fuhr_____ in die Stadt.
2. Ich lief_____ durch das Labor.
3. Der Frosch schwamm_____ in der Milch.
4. Ihr kam_____ zu früh.
5. Warum ging_____ Sie so langsam, Fräulein Lenz?

B. *Supply the correct past-tense form of the verb:*

1. Ich _____ dem Freund.   (helfen)
2. Der Frosch _____ auf den Grund des Eimers.   (sinken)
3. Warum _____ ihr ins Wasser, Kinder?   (springen)
4. Am ersten Schultag _____ sie *(pl.)* eine Tüte mit Süßigkeiten.   (bekommen)
5. Die Ursprünge _____ man in Italien.   (finden)

C. *Give the German equivalents of the English sentences in the past tense:*

1. She drove the car.
2. We went to school.
3. Did you see the newspaper, Karl?
4. Did you give it to him, children?
5. They read the book.

3. Past-Tense Forms of <u>haben</u> and <u>sein</u>

1	**ich hatte**	*(I had)*		1	**ich war**	*(I was)*
2	**du hattest**			2	**du warst**	
3	**er hatte** **sie hatte** **es hatte**			3	**er war** **sie war** **es war**	
1	**wir hatten**			1	**wir waren**	
2	**ihr hattet**			2	**ihr wart**	
3	**sie hatten** **Sie hatten**			3	**sie waren** **Sie waren**	

EXERCISES

A. *Supply the correct endings:*

1. Du war_____ in dem Schloß.
2. Ich hatt_____ keine Zeit.
3. Wir war_____ nicht in der Schweiz.
4. Ihr hatt_____ eine stark passive Handelsbilanz.
5. Ihr war_____ in der Bank.

B.   *Supply the correct form of* **haben** *and* **sein** *in the past tense:*

1. Es _____ eine seelische Erkrankung.   (sein)
2. Ich _____ einen Bruch der Wirbelsäule.   (haben)
3. Du _____ an der deutschen Grenze.   (sein)
4. Ihr _____ immer noch Ferien.   (haben)
5. Du _____ die Gesamtausgabe.   (haben)

C.   *Give the German equivalents in the past tense:*

1. You were an optimist, Rudolf.
2. She had the butter.
3. I was in Troy.
4. They were in Greece.
5. Did you have the book, Miss Kleinschmidt?

4.   Personal Pronouns in the Nominative, Dative, and Accusative

a.   Pronouns may be substituted for nouns. Pronouns require the same case, gender, and number as the nouns they replace:

NOMINATIVE	DATIVE	ACCUSATIVE	
ich *(I)*	**mir** *([to] me)*	**mich** *(me)*	
du *(you)*	**dir** *([to] you)*	**dich** *(you)*	
er *(he)*	**ihm** *([to] him, it)*	**ihn** *(him, it)*	SINGULAR
sie *(she)*	**ihr** *([to] her, it)*	**sie** *(her, it)*	
es *(it)*	**ihm** *([to] it)*	**es** *(it)*	
wir *(we)*	**uns** *([to] us)*	**uns** *(us)*	
ihr *(you)*	**euch** *([to] you)*	**euch** *(you)*	
sie *(they)*	**ihnen** *([to] them)*	**sie** *(them)*	PLURAL
Sie *(you)*	**Ihnen** *([to] you)*	**Sie** *(you)*	

EXERCISES

A.   *Substitute a personal pronoun for the noun in the nominative:**

1. Das Kind spielt im Garten.
   _____ spielt im Garten.
2. Der Wissenschaftler arbeitet im Labor.
   _____ arbeitet im Labor.
3. Die Mutter liest die Zeitung.
   _____ liest die Zeitung.

ZWEIHUNDERTVIERUNDACHTZIG

4. Die Aminosäuren sind die Grundbausteine der Eiweißstoffe.
   _____ sind die Grundbausteine der Eiweißstoffe.
5. Das Barock dauerte von 1500 bis 1800.
   _____ dauerte von 1500 bis 1800.

B. *Replace the noun in the dative by a personal pronoun:**

1. Ich helfe dem Arzt.
   Ich helfe _____.
2. Ich gab der Mutter das Obst.
   Ich gab _____ das Obst.
3. Du sollst den Gelehrten glauben.
   Du sollst _____ glauben.
4. Sie schickte dem Vater die Karte.
   Sie schickte _____ die Karte.
5. Sie zeigt den Kindern das Bild.
   Sie zeigt _____ das Bild.

C. *Replace the noun in the accusative by a personal pronoun:**

1. Ich kenne das Tagebuch.
   Ich kenne _____
2. Man hat die Aminosäuren entdeckt.
   Man hat _____ entdeckt.
3. Luther hat gegen den Papst geschrieben.
   Luther hat gegen _____ geschrieben.
4. Ihr findet den Atlas.
   Ihr findet _____
5. Ich gab der Lehrerin die Prüfung.
   Ich gab _____ der Lehrerin.

D. *Supply the correct personal pronoun:*

1. Er zeigte es _____. (to me)
2. Ich wollte _____ helfen, Marion. (you)
3. Wir wollen _____ die Bilder zeigen, Kinder. (you)
4. Er kennt _____, Heinz. (you)
5. Wann kann ich _____ sehen, Herr Kaiser? (you)

E. *Give the German equivalents in the tenses indicated:*

1. I answered you, Heidi. (past)
2. She gave it to us. (past)
3. We did not see him. (present perfect)
4. They will ask her. (future)
5. Why don't you want to show it to them, Herbert? (present)

ZWEIHUNDERTFÜNFUNDACHTZIG

READING

Der Blutkreislauf

Der Kreislauf gewährleistet die Versorgung der einzelnen Organe mit Nährstoffen und Sauerstoff und transportiert Abfallstoffe zur Lunge (Kohlendioxid), Leber und Niere. Der Anteil an der Gesamtblutmenge (5 bis 7 Liter) der einzelnen Organe entspricht in Ruhelage folgenden Werten: Herzgefäße 5%, Gehirn 15%, Muskeln 15%, Eingeweide 35%, Niere 20%, Haut und Skelett 10%. Das Herz pumpt in der Minute ca. 5 Liter Blut in den Körper. Von der linken Herzkammer gelangt das sauerstoffreiche Blut in die Körperschlagader (Aorta) und über die Arterien in die Haargefäße der Organe und Gewebe. Hier erfolgt die Abgabe von Sauerstoff und Nährstoffen und die Aufnahme von Kohlendioxid und Abfallstoffen. Das sauerstoffarme Blut fließt durch die Venen über die große Hohlvene zurück in den rechten Vorhof (großer Kreislauf), die rechte Kammer pumpt es über die Lungenarterie in die Lungenkapillaren, und es gibt Kohlendioxid (CO_2) ab und nimmt Sauerstoff (O_2) auf. Die Lungenvene, die in die linke Vorkammer führt, schließt den Kreislauf.

5

10

VOCABULARY

	gewährleisten	to guarantee
die	**Versorgung**	supply
das	**Organ, -e**	organ
der	**Nährstoff, -e**	nutrient
der	**Sauerstoff**	oxygen
	transportieren	to transport
der	**Abfall, -̈e**	waste, refuse
der	**Abfallstoff, -e**	by-product, waste product
die	**Lunge, -n**	lung
das	**Kohlendioxyd** or **Kohlendioxid**	carbon dioxide
die	**Leber**	liver
die	**Niere, -n**	kidney
der	**Anteil, -e**	share, portion
die	**Gesamtblutmenge**	total amount of blood, total blood volume
die	**Ruhelage**	at rest, resting, in rest position
	folgend	following
der	**Wert, -e**	value, worth
die	**Herzgefäße** (pl.)	cardiovascular system
das	**Gehirn**	brain
die	**Eingeweide** (pl.)	intestines
die	**Haut**	skin

das	**Skelett, -e**	skeleton
	pumpen	to pump
	in der Minute	per minute
	ca. (cirka)	approximately, about
	link-	left
die	**Kammer, -n**	chamber
die	**Herzkammer**	ventricle of the heart
	sauerstoffreich	oxygen containing
die	**Körperschlagader**	aorta
die	**Aorta**	aorta
die	**Arterie, -n**	artery
die	**Haargefäße** (pl.)	capillary vessels
das	**Gewebe**	tissue
die	**Abgabe**	here: exchange, emission, discharge
die	**Aufnahme**	absorption
	sauerstoffarm	deficient in oxygen
	fließen (fließt), floß, ist geflossen	to flow
die	**Vene, -n**	vein
	recht-	right
der	**Vorhof**	auricle
der	**Kreislauf**	circulation

ZWEIHUNDERTSECHSUNDACHTZIG

über	by way of, through	**auf-nehmen (nimmt auf),**	to take up, absorb
die **Kapillare, -n**	capillary	**nahm auf,**	
ab-geben	to give off,	**aufgenommen**	
(gibt ab),	emit; to de-	die **Vorkammer, -n**	auricle
gab ab,	liver	**schließen (schließt),**	
abgegeben		**schloß, geschlossen**	to close

STRUCTURAL EXERCISES

A. *Underline the following items in the reading above:*

All dative prepositions (straight line)
All two-way prepositions (dotted line)

B. *Give the English equivalents of the compound nouns:*

1. der Sauerstoff   3. die Abfallstoffe   5. die Gesamtblutmenge
2. der Nährstoff   4. der Kreislauf

VOCABULARY EXERCISE

Give the English equivalents of the italicized words:

1. Von der linken Herzkammer *gelangt* das sauerstoffreiche Blut in die Körperschlagader.
2. Der Kreislauf gewährleistet die Versorgung der *einzelnen* Organe.
3. Die Lungenvene *schließt* den Kreislauf.
4. Das sauerstoffarme Blut *gibt* Kohlendioxid *ab.*
5. Das sauerstoffarme Blut *nimmt* Sauerstoff *auf.*
6. Nach *Abschluß* der Hauptschule können die Schüler mit einer Berufsausbildung anfangen.
7. Aminosäuren sind eine wichtige Voraussetzung für die *Entstehung* von Leben.

STRUCTURE

5. Present Perfect Tense

a. Two verb elements are necessary for the present perfect tense when no modal is present:

haben		
or	+	PAST PARTICIPLE
sein		

b.   Almost all weak verbs take these forms:

> a form of
>
> **haben**
>
>   or   +   ge + VERB STEM + **t**
>
> **sein**

c.   Strong verbs have the following forms:

> a form of
>
> **haben**
>
>   or   +   ge + VERB STEM + **en**
>
> **sein**

d.   The past participle is the last element in a main clause:

Er **ist** gestern nach Hause **gegangen.** *(He went home yesterday.)*

e.   **Sein** is used as a helper verb with strong verbs when:

1.   The verb is intransitive (means no direct object = no accusative).
2.   The verb expresses motion or a change of condition.

f.   The verb **reisen** *(to travel)* is a weak verb but uses **sein** in the present and past perfect:

Er **ist** nach Hamburg **gereist.**
He traveled to Hamburg. He has traveled to Hamburg.

g.   The present perfect tense for the third person singular **(er, sie, es)** is formed with either **hat** or **ist** plus past participle:

Er **ist** nach Berlin **gefahren.** *(He went to Berlin.)*
Sie **hat** den Mann **gesehen.** *(She saw the man.)*

h.   The present perfect tense for the third person plural **(sie)** is formed with either **haben** or **sind** plus past participle:

Sie **sind** nach Berlin **gefahren.** *(They went to Berlin.)*
Sie **haben** den Mann **gesehen.** *(They saw the man.)*

i.   The present perfect tense for the first person **(ich, wir)** and second person **(du, ihr, Sie)** is also formed with **haben** or **sein** plus past participle:

Ich **bin** nach Washington **gefahren.** *(I went to Washington.)*

ZWEIHUNDERTACHTUNDACHTZIG

Ich **habe** die Milch **getrunken.** *(I drank the milk.)*
Du **bist** zu spät **gekommen.** *(You came too late.)*
Du **hast** zu lange **gewartet.** *(You waited too long.)*
Wir **sind** in Deutschland **gewesen.** *(We were in Germany.)*
Wir **haben** einen neuen Wagen **gekauft.** *(We bought a new car.)*

EXERCISES

A. *Supply the correct form of* **haben** *or* **sein:**

1. Er _____ ins Büro gegangen.
2. Wir _____ den Wagen in die Scheune gefahren.
3. Ihr _____ den armen Lehrer gefragt.
4. Sie _____ die Karte geschrieben.   (sie = she)
5. Ihr _____ in Europa gewesen.

B. *Supply the past participle:*

1. Sie hat die ganze Nacht hindurch _____.   (studieren)
2. Ich habe es ihm _____.   (geben)
3. Habt ihr Zeit _____?   (haben)
4. Du hast nur Deutsch _____.   (lernen)
5. Ihr seid im Fluß _____.   (schwimmen)

C. *Change the following sentences to present perfect:**

1. Ich schließe die Tür.
2. Du hilfst der Mutter.
3. Er behält die Macht.
4. Wir geben die Hoffnung auf.
5. Er ertrinkt in der Milch.

D. *Give the German equivalents in the present perfect tense:*

1. They sat in a bucket.
2. I attended the school.
3. Why did you drive the car, Richard?
4. She analyzed the acid.
5. Did you find the butter, children?

E. *Give the English equivalents of the German sentences:*

1. Den Prunk des Barocks hat vorher noch kein Stil besessen.
2. Alle Schüler haben am ersten Schultag eine Tüte mit Obst und Süßigkeiten bekommen.
3. Sie ist in eine kaufmännische Lehre gegangen.
4. Drei Schüler haben die Klasse wiederholt, d.h., sie sind sitzengeblieben.
5. Das Land hat die Handelsbilanz ausgeglichen.

ZWEIHUNDERTNEUNUNDACHTZIG

READING

Bauhaus

Mit dem Begriff „Bauhaus" verbindet man eine deutsche Hochschule mit Werkstätten für Handwerk, Architektur und bildende Kunst, die Walter Gropius im Jahre 1919
in Weimar unter dem Namen „Hochschule für Bau und Gestaltung" gegründet hat.
Das Bauhaus erstrebte „die Wiedervereinigung aller werkkünstlerischen Disziplinen
zu einer neuen Baukunst". Man gab Unterricht auf allen Gebieten des gestaltenden   5
Handwerks, der bildenden Künste und der Architektur. Neben den Architekten wie
Gropius und Mies van der Rohe arbeiteten viele berühmte Maler an der Bauhausschule, unter anderem Kandinsky, Feininger und Klee.

Im Jahre 1925 verlegte man das Bauhaus nach Dessau, wo man Lehr- und Werk-
stättengebäude mit Studentenheimen hatte. Die Nationalsozialisten lösten 1934 das   10
Bauhaus auf. 1937 errichtete man ein „New Bauhaus" in Chicago und 1946 gründete
man ein neues Bauhaus in Berlin.

Die Hauptaufgaben des Bauhauses sah man im Entwurf eines klaren, sachlichen
Stils und in einer zweckentsprechenden Anwendung des Baumaterials. Das
sachliche Konzept des Bauhauses beeinflußt noch heute die Entwürfe von Archi-   15
tektur und Handwerk, Kunst und Design. Die leicht erkennbaren Merkmale des
Bauhausstils sind: klare Gliederung der horizontalen und vertikalen Baukörper, gute
proportionale Abstimmung von Wandflächen und Öffnungen, helle glatte Flächen
neben zusammengefaßten Fenster- und Türreihen und flache Dächer.

VOCABULARY

das **Bauhaus**	architectural school founded in Germany in 1919	**gestaltend** **berühmt**	formative, creative famous, well-known, re-nowned
bauen	to build	**unter anderem**	among others,
der **Begriff, -e**	concept, idea, no-tion	**verlegen (nach)**	especially to transfer (to),
die **Werkstatt, ̈-en**	workshop, place to work	das **Studentenheim, -e**	relocate (to) dormitory
Weimar	city in East Germany	**auf·lösen**	to dissolve, to break up
gründen	to found, establish	**errichten**	to establish, erect
erstreben	to strive for, aspire to	die **Aufgabe, -n** die **Hauptaufgabe**	task, assignment main task, main as-signment, main
die **Wiedervereinigung** **werkkünstlerisch**	reunification pragmatic and artistic		idea
die **Disziplin, -en**	discipline	der **Entwurf, ̈-e**	outline, design, plan
der **Unterricht**	instruction, teach-ing	**klar** **sachlich**	clear objective, factual,
Unterricht geben	to teach, give instruction		functional

	zweckentsprechend	expedient, purposeful, functional	
die	**Anwendung**	application, utilization, use	
das	**Baumaterial**	building material	
das	**Konzept, -e**	concept, plan, idea	
	beeinflussen	to influence	
	noch heute	even today	
	leicht	easily	
	erkennbar	recognizable, discernable	
die	**Abstimmung**	balance, harmony, agreement	
die	**Öffnung, -en**	opening	
	hell	light, bright	
	zusammengefaßt	cohesive, united	
die	**Reihe, -n**	row, series, line	
	flach	flat, level, plain	

STRUCTURAL EXERCISES

A. *Underline all definite articles used in the genitive case in the above reading.*

B. *Give the English equivalents of the compound words:*

1. das Studentenheim
2. die Wiedervereinigung
3. die Hochschule
4. die Werkstatt
5. die Hauptaufgabe

VOCABULARY EXERCISE

Give the English equivalents of the italicized words:

1. Das sachliche Konzept *beeinflußt* noch heute die Architektur.
2. Man *verlegte* das Bauhaus nach Dessau.
3. Viele *berühmte* Maler arbeiteten an der Bauhausschule.
4. 1946 *gründete* man ein neues Bauhaus in Berlin.
5. Die Nationalsozialisten *lösten* das Bauhaus *auf.*
6. Der Bauhausstil hat *leicht* erkennbare Merkmale.
7. Man *erstrebte* die Wiedervereinigung aller werkkünstlerischen Disziplinen.

esson 27

STRUCTURE

1. Prepositions with Pronouns and in Da-Compounds

a. Pronouns may replace nouns to which reference has already been made:

Da ist **der Chef.**   Ich kenne **ihn.**
There is the boss.   *I know him.*

b. The pronoun must correspond in case and number to the noun it replaces: **ihn = den Chef.**

c. Prepositions may be used with nouns and pronouns:

Er spricht **mit dem Chef.**   Er spricht **mit ihm.**
He is speaking with the boss.   *He is speaking with him.*

d. When the object of a preposition is a person, the object may be either a noun **(dem Chef)** or a pronoun **(ihm).**

e. When the object of a preposition is a thing, the object may be either:

1. a noun or

2. a compound composed of $\boxed{\textbf{da} + \text{preposition}}$

   Examples: Ich bin fertig **mit der Arbeit.**   (noun)
   Ich bin fertig **damit.**   (da-compound)

   da is used when the preposition begins with a consonant:

   damit   **danach**   **dabei**

dar is used when the preposition begins with a vowel:

darüber   **darunter**   **daraus**

f.   A **da**-compound is best rendered into English by the preposition plus *it*:

Sie wartete fünf Minuten **auf den Bus.**
Sie wartete fünf Minuten **darauf.**
She waited five minutes for it.

g.   **Da**-compounds are formed from prepositions following verbs, adjectives, and nouns:

Sie **wartete** fünf Minuten **auf den Bus.**
Sie **wartete** fünf Minuten **darauf.**
She waited five minutes for it.

Sie waren **fertig mit der Arbeit.**
Sie waren **fertig damit.**
They were finished with it.

Sie hatten kein **Interesse an der Politik.**
Sie hatten kein **Interesse daran.**
They had no interest in it.

EXERCISES

A.   *Replace the objects of the prepositions with a personal pronoun or a **da**-compound:* *

1.   Er dachte an seinen Vater.
2.   Sie wartet auf ihren Freund.
3.   Er plädiert für das Ökosystem.
4.   Man fragte nach der Mutter.
5.   Die Forscher suchten nach einem Bekämpfungsmittel.

B.   *Give the English equivalents of the following sentences:*

1.   Schliemann hat an den Ausgrabungen teilgenommen. Schliemann hat daran teilgenommen.
2.   Man erkennt die Gotik an dem Spitzbogen. Man erkennt die Gotik daran.
3.   Die Forschung sucht nach einem geeigneten Bekämpfungsmittel. Die Forschung sucht danach.
4.   Man richtet einen Röntgenstrahl auf die Materie. Man richtet einen Röntgenstrahl darauf.
5.   Der Christ glaubt an die Existenz Gottes. Der Christ glaubt daran.

ZWEIHUNDERTDREIUNDNEUNZIG

Bertolt Brecht

ZWEIHUNDERTVIERUNDNEUNZIG

READING

Bertolt Brecht (1898–1956)

Die Dreigroschenoper *(Die Moritat von Mackie Messer)*

Und der Haifisch, der hat Zähne
Und die trägt er im Gesicht
Und Macheath, der hat ein Messer.
Doch das Messer sieht man nicht.

Ach, es sind des Haifischs Flossen   5
Rot, wenn dieser Blut vergießt!
Mackie Messer trägt 'nen Handschuh
Drauf man keine Untat liest.

An 'nem schönen blauen Sonntag
Liegt ein toter Mann am Strand   10
Und ein Mensch geht um die Ecke
Den man Mackie Messer nennt.

Und das große Feuer in Soho
Sieben Kinder und ein Greis
In der Menge Mackie Messer, den   15
Man nichts fragt und der nichts weiß.

Und er kann sich nicht erinnern
Und man kann nicht an ihn ran:
Denn ein Haifisch ist kein Haifisch
Wenn man's nicht beweisen kann.   20

VOCABULARY

Bertolt Brecht	German dramatist	**sehen (sieht), sah, gesehen**	to see
die **Dreigroschenoper**	Three Penny Opera	**ach!**	oh! alas!
die **Moritat**	street song about violence	**es sind des Haifischs Flossen . . .**	the shark's fins are
Mackie Messer	Mack the Knife	die **Flosse, -n**	fin
das **Messer**	knife	**rot**	red
der **Haifisch, -e**	shark	**vergießen (vergießt), vergoß, vergossen**	to spill
der **Zahn, ̈e**	tooth	**'nen = einen**	a, an
das **Gesicht**	face	der **Handschuh, -e**	glove
Macheath	MacHeath *(Mack the Knife)*	**drauf = darauf**	on which
		die **Untat, -en**	crime
doch	however	**'nem = einem**	a, an

schön	beautiful		**Soho**	district in London
blau	blue	der	**Greis, -e**	old man
der **Sonntag**	Sunday	die	**Menge**	crowd
tot	dead		**nichts**	nothing
Strand	street in London		**sich erinnern (an)**	to remember
die **Ecke**	corner		**ran = heran**	to get close to
das **Feuer**	fire			

STRUCTURE

2. Anticipatory <u>Da</u>-Compounds

a. **Da**-compounds are often used in combination with other elements, such as **daß**, to anticipate an action or an event described in a following clause:

Der Magnetismus entsteht **dadurch, daß der Planet rotiert.**
The magnetism comes about through the fact that the planet rotates.

In this example, **dadurch** anticipates the subordinate clause **daß der Planet rotiert.**

b. To infer the meaning of an anticipatory **da**-compound, we distinguish two main types of subordinate elements preceded by **da**-compounds:

infinitive phrases with **zu;**
subordinate clauses with **daß.**

c. To render a **da**-compound + infinitive with **zu,** follow these steps:

1. Spot the **da**-compound used as an anticipatory element:

Das Abitur berechtigt ihn **dazu,** auf die Universität zu gehen.

2. Render the main clause:

The Abitur entitles him.

3. Spot the verb in the infinitive phrase with **zu:**

Das Abitur berechtigt ihn dazu, auf die Universität **zu gehen.**

4. Disregard the **da**-compound and continue with the infinitive phrase:

The Abitur entitles him . . . to go to the university.

d. To render a **da**-compound + **daß**-clause, follow these steps:

1. The prepositional compound, **dadurch, daß,** may generally be rendered as follows:

by + ing-form of the verb in the **daß**-clause

Die schnellere Produktion erreicht man **dadurch, daß man die Methode vereinfacht.**

One achieves faster production by simplifying the method.

2. The prepositional compound **dadurch, daß** may also be equivalent to *through the fact that*:

Der Magnetismus entsteht **dadurch, daß der Planet rotiert.**

The magnetism comes about through the fact that the planet rotates.

3. Render these **da**-compounds in the following way:

daran, daß	*that, through the fact that*
darin, daß	*in that*
darauf, daß	*on the fact that, about the fact that, of the fact that*
davon, daß	*from the fact that*

Examples:

Man muß **daran** denken, **daß** es immer weniger Energie geben wird.
One has to remember that there will be less and less energy.
Er sah ein Problem **darin, daß** er keine Zeit hatte.
He saw a problem in that he did not have time (. . . of not having time).
Sie war stolz **darauf, daß** sie ein Auto hatte.
She was proud of the fact that she had a car (. . . of having a car).
Man muß **davon** ausgehen, **daß** es viele Arten von Mücken gibt.
One has to proceed from the fact that there are many kinds of flies.

EXERCISE

Give the English equivalents of the following sentences:

1. Gutenberg hat den Buchdruck dadurch vereinfacht, daß er bewegliche Lettern benutzte.
2. Der Fremdenverkehr dient dazu, die passive Handelsbilanz auszugleichen.
3. Man erkennt den gotischen Stil daran, daß die Fenster und Türen einen Spitzbogen haben.
4. Die genetische Kontrolle beruht darauf, daß sie auf Grund der Unvereinbarkeit von Männchen und Weibchen die Fortpflanzung verhindert.
5. Paris hat den trojanischen Krieg dadurch verursacht, daß er Helena raubte.

READING

Karl Marx (1818–1883)

Man bezeichnet Karl Marx als den Begründer des wissenschaftlichen Sozialismus. Der Vater von Karl Marx war Rechtsanwalt in Trier, einer alten Stadt an der Mosel. Auch der junge Marx sollte Jura studieren, aber seine wahren Interessen lagen in der Philosophie und Geschichte. In der Philosophie beeindruckten ihn die Schriften von

Karl Marx

Hegel, aus denen Marx das dialektische Prinzip (These-Antithese = Synthese) für   5
seine Erklärung des dialektischen Materialismus ableitete.

Marx wollte eigentlich Universitätsprofessor werden, aber statt dessen begann er
eine Karriere als Reporter und Herausgeber der Kölner *Rheinischen Zeitung*. 1843
verließ er Deutschland und ging nach Paris, wo er weiterhin als Redakteur arbeitete.
1845 mußte er Paris verlassen. Marx ging mit seiner Familie nach Brüssel, wo er das   10
„Kommunistische Manifest" schrieb. Nach seiner Rückkehr nach Köln war er Mitarbeiter an der *Neuen Rheinischen Zeitung*. 1849 verließ er Deutschland für immer
und lebte danach in London, wo er eingehend Wirtschaftsysteme untersuchte. 1867
erschien der erste Band des „Kapitals". Die beiden anderen Bände des „Kapitals"
erschienen nach dem Tode von Karl Marx.   15

VOCABULARY

der **Begründer, -**	founder	**statt dessen**	instead of that
wissenschaftlich	scientific	die **Karriere**	career
der **Sozialismus**	socialism	der **Reporter, -**	reporter
der **Rechtsanwalt, ̈e**	lawyer, attorney	der **Herausgeber, -**	publisher, editor
die **Mosel**	Moselle River	**verlassen (verläßt),**	to leave, go away
sollte	was supposed to	**verließ, verlassen**	
	(past tense of	**gehen (geht), ging,**	
	sollen)	**ist gegangen**	to go
das **Jus,** die **Jura**	law	**weiterhin**	to continue . . . ;
Jura studieren	to study law		furthermore
liegen (liegt), lag,	to lie; to be	**Brüssel**	Brussels
gelegen		**kommunistisch**	communist
die **Philosophie**	philosophy	das **Manifest**	manifest, manifesto
beeindrucken	to impress	die **Rückkehr (nach)**	return (to)
die **Schriften** *(pl.)*	writings, works	der **Mitarbeiter**	co-worker, contribu-
dialektisch	dialectic		tor, staff member
das **Prinzip, -ien**	principle	**für immer**	forever, for good
die **Erklärung, -en**	explanation	**danach**	after that
der **Materialismus**	materialism	**eingehend**	thoroughly, exhaus-
ab-leiten	to deduce, derive		tively, in detail
wollte	wanted to *(past	der **Band, ̈e**	volume
	tense of* **wollen)**	**die beiden ander-**	the other two
eigentlich	actually		

STRUCTURAL EXERCISE

Underline all past-tense forms of strong verbs in the above reading.

VOCABULARY EXERCISE

Give the English equivalents of the italicized words and phrases:

1. *Nach seiner Rückkehr nach Köln* war er Mitarbeiter an der „Neuen Rheinischen
   Zeitung".
2. *Die beiden anderen Bände des „Kapitals" erschienen* nach dem Tode von Karl
   Marx.

3. Marx ging nach Paris, *wo er weiterhin als Redakteur arbeitete.*
4. Die Schriften von Hegel, *aus denen er das dialektische Prinzip ableitete,* beeindruckten ihn.
5. Er lebte danach in London, *wo er eingehend Wirtschaftssysteme untersuchte.*

STRUCTURE

3. Past Tense — Modals

a.   The present tense of modal verbs consists of an inflected form of the modal stem with personal endings plus an infinitive at the end of the main clause:

(Singular) **kann**	
	+ PERSONAL ENDING + INFINITIVE
(Plural) **könn**	

Examples:

Er **kann** Tennis **spielen.** *(He can play tennis.)*
Die Männer **können** schnell **laufen.** *(The men can run fast.)*

b.   The past tense of modal verbs consists of the past tense stem of the modal with personal endings plus an infinitive:

konnte + PERSONAL ENDING + INFINITIVE

Examples:

Er **konnte** Tennis **spielen.** *(He was able to play tennis.)*
Die Männer **konnten** schnell **laufen.** *(The men were able to run fast.)*

c.   Personal endings for all modals in the past tense:

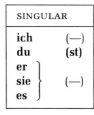

SINGULAR		PLURAL	
ich	(—)	**wir**	(n)
du	(st)	**ihr**	(t)
er		**sie**	
sie	(—)	**Sie**	(n)
es			

DREIHUNDERT

Examples:

Ich durfte nicht fahren.	**ich (—)**
I was not allowed to drive.	
Du wolltest in das Büro gehen.	**du (st)**
You wanted to go to the office.	
Wir mußten den Wagen waschen.	**wir (n)**
We had to wash the car.	
Ihr solltet nicht arbeiten.	**ihr (t)**
You should not work.	
Konnten Sie ihm helfen, Fräulein Wolf?	**Sie (n)**
Were you able to help him, Miss Wolf?	

SELF-PREPARATORY EXERCISE

Substitute the pronoun in parentheses for the subject of the sentence and make the necessary changes in the verb:*

Sie mußte den Nährstoff analysieren. (du)	
Wir wollten nicht arbeiten. (ich)	Du mußtest den Nährstoff analysieren.
Sie mußten Unterricht geben. (ihr)	Ich wollte nicht arbeiten.
Ich durfte ins Wasser springen. (du)	Ihr mußtet Unterricht geben.
	Du durftest ins Wasser springen.

EXERCISES

A. *Supply the correct form of the modal in the tense indicated:*

1. Ihr _____ nicht so viel trinken.   (sollen, *present*)
2. Du _____ die Hoffnung nicht aufgeben.   (dürfen, *present*)
3. Er _____ den Wein exportieren.   (können, *past*)
4. Ich _____ das Auto fahren.   (wollen, *past*)
5. Du _____ die Klasse wiederholen.   (müssen, *past*)

B. *Give the German equivalents:*

1. You should not go to the office, Mr. Becker.   (past)
2. I could not work.   (past)
3. They may buy the book.   (present)
4. We wanted to see the house.   (past)
5. You must come, Maria.   (present)

4.   Present Perfect and Past Perfect — Modals

a.   The present perfect tense of modal verbs consists of an inflected form of **haben** plus two infinitives at the end of the main clause:

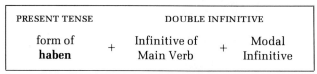

PRESENT TENSE		DOUBLE INFINITIVE	
form of **haben**	+	Infinitive of Main Verb	+ Modal Infinitive

Examples:

Er **hat** nach Berlin **fahren können.**
He was able to drive to Berlin. He has been able to drive to Berlin.
Die Frauen **haben** gestern viel **sprechen müssen.**
The women had to speak a lot yesterday.

b.   The past perfect tense of modal verbs consists of the past tense form of **haben** and two infinitives:

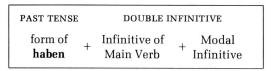

PAST TENSE		DOUBLE INFINITIVE	
form of **haben**	+	Infinitive of Main Verb	+ Modal Infinitive

Examples:

Er **hatte** zu viel **arbeiten müssen.** *(He had had to work too much.)*
Du **hattest** früh **aufstehen wollen.** *(You had wanted to get up early.)*

EXERCISES

A.   *Add the modal verbs and make necessary changes, first in the present perfect tense, then in the past perfect tense:*

1.   Die Frauen haben gestern gesprochen.   (wollen)
2.   Er ist nach Berlin gefahren.   (müssen)
3.   Du bist nicht ins Büro gegangen.   (dürfen)
4.   Ich habe nicht gearbeitet.   (können)

B.   *Form sentences in the present perfect tense:*

1.   Er / arbeiten / können / gestern   3.   Du / gehen / können / ins Büro
2.   Ihr / fahren / müssen / nach Berlin   4.   Ich / abfahren / sollen / später

C.   *Give the English equivalents:*

1.   Sie hat heute nicht arbeiten können.
2.   Ihr habt den Wagen nicht kaufen können.
3.   Du hast später abfahren müssen.
4.   Er hat nicht ins Büro gehen dürfen.

DREIHUNDERTZWEI

5. Past Infinitive

a. Verbs have two infinitive forms:

PRESENT INFINITIVE: **sagen**   *(to say)*
PAST INFINITIVE: **gesagt haben**   *(to have said)*

b. The past infinitive consists of the past participle of the verb and the auxiliary **haben** or **sein:**

gefragt haben   *(have asked)*
gefahren sein   *(have driven)*

c. The past infinitive **(gefahren sein),** refers to an event in the past, but the moment of speaking itself is in the present **(muß):**

Er muß schnell gefahren sein. *(He must have driven fast.)*

d. The past infinitive is used with modals or in infinitive phrases with **zu:**

Er muß viel **gelesen haben.** *(He must have read a lot.)*
Sie behauptet, das Buch **gelesen zu haben.** *(She claims to have read the book.)*

e. The past infinitive occurs both with the objective and subjective use of modals:

Wer auf die Universität gehen will, **muß** das Abitur **gemacht haben.**
Whoever wants to go to the university must have achieved the Abitur. (objective)

Sie **will** in Berlin **gewesen sein.**
She claims to have been in Berlin.   (subjective)

The context determines whether the modal is used subjectively or objectively.

EXERCISES

A. *Give the English equivalents:*

1. Dürer soll viele Gemälde gemalt haben.
2. Der Frosch muß sehr schnell geschwommen sein.
3. Das Zeitalter des Barocks muß sehr schön gewesen sein.
4. Sie behauptet, den Planeten gesehen zu haben.
5. Der Fanatiker soll das Land verlassen haben.

B. *Give the English equivalents:*

1. Das Brechungsmuster dient dazu, die Atomanordnung genau zu bestimmen.
2. Das Land hat den Mangel an Energie dadurch überwunden, daß es jetzt Kernenergie verwendet.

DREIHUNDERTDREI

Österreich: Im Alpengebiet

Österreich: Die Hauptstadt Wien

DREIHUNDERTVIER

3. Die Arbeit an der Dissertation führte ihn dazu, die Bewegung der Atome zu untersuchen.
4. Die Politik des Präsidenten zielte darauf, den Süden zu besiegen.
5. Er konnte sich nicht daran erinnern, daß er das Buch gelesen hatte.

READING

Österreich

Das heutige Österreich ist das Resultat eines Abkommens der Alliierten (Amerikaner, Engländer, Franzosen und Russen) aus dem Jahre 1945, das diesem Land die Grenzen von 1937 gewährleistete. Zwischen 1945 und 1955 bestand Österreich aus vier Besatzungszonen, hatte aber trotz der Besatzungsmächte eine eigene Regierung. In einem Vertrag vom April 1955 erlangte Österreich seine Souveränität wieder. Der ⁵ Vertrag verlangt, daß Österreich keine politische oder wirtschaftliche Vereinigung mit Deutschland eingeht. Die Dynastie der Habsburger regierte in Österreich von 1278 bis 1918. Unter den Habsburgern wuchs Österreich zu der sogenannten Donaumonarchie, die außer Österreich auch Teile der heute selbständigen Länder Ungarn, Jugoslawien, Tschechoslowakei und Polen verwaltete. Die Donaumonarchie ¹⁰ brach mit dem Ende des Ersten Weltkrieges zusammen. Nach 1918 war Österreich eine Republik. 1938 annektierte Hitler Österreich.

Die Landwirtschaft erzeugt vor allem Weizen, aber auch Wein und Obst. Viehwirtschaft dominiert im Alpengebiet und teilweise im Alpenvorland. An Bodenschätzen besitzt Österreich hauptsächlich Eisenerz, Blei, Zink, Graphit, ¹⁵ Magnesit und Salz. Wichtige Industriezweige sind: Textil-, Nahrungs- und Genußmittelindustrie, Maschinenbau, Eisenerzeugung und Chemikalien.

VOCABULARY

	Österreich	Austria	
das	**Abkommen**	agreement	
die	**Alliierten**	allies	
der	**Amerikaner, -**	American	
der	**Engländer, -**	Englishman	
der	**Franzose, -n**	Frenchman	
der	**Russe, -n**	Russian	
	bestehen (besteht), bestand, bestanden	to exist	
	bestehen (aus)	to consist (of)	
die	**Besatzung**	occupation	
die	**Zone, -n**	zone, district	
die	**Macht, ⁻e**	power	
	eigen	own	
die	**Regierung, -en**	government	
der	**Vertrag, ⁻e**	treaty, agreement	

	wieder-erlangen	to regain, reacquire
die	**Souveränität**	sovereignty
	verlangen	to demand
	wirtschaftlich	economic
die	**Vereinigung**	union, alliance
	ein-gehen (geht ein) ging ein, ist eingegangen	to enter, join into
die	**Dynastie, -n**	dynasty
die	**Habsburger**	Hapsburg dynasty
	regieren	to govern, to rule
	von ... bis	from ... to

	wachsen (wächst), wuchs, ist gewachsen	to grow
die	Monarchie, -n	monarchy
	selbständig	independent
	Ungarn	Hungary
	Jugoslawien	Yugoslavia
die	Tschechoslowakei	Czechoslovakia
	Polen	Poland
	verwalten	to administer
	annektieren	to annex
der	Quadratkilometer	square kilometer
die	Landwirtschaft	agriculture, farming
	erzeugen	to produce
	vor allem	above all, especially
der	Weizen	wheat
die	Viehwirtschaft	animal husbandry

	dominieren	to dominate
	teilweise	partially, in part, somewhat
	hauptsächlich	mainly
das	Eisen	iron (ore)
das	Erz, -e	ore
das	Blei	lead
das	Zink	zink
der	Graphit	graphite
der	Magnesit	magnesium
das	Salz, -e	salt
der	Zweig, -e	branch, section
der	Maschinenbau	machine production
die	Erzeugung	production
die	Chemikalien (pl.)	chemicals

STRUCTURAL EXERCISES

A. Underline all subordinating conjunctions.   (straight line)

B. Underline all relative pronouns.   (dotted line)

VOCABULARY EXERCISE

Give the English equivalents of the italicized words and phrases:

1. An Bodenschätzen *besitzt Österreich hauptsächlich* Eisenerz.
2. *Das Abkommen aus dem Jahre* 1945 *gewährleistete Österreich die Grenzen von* 1937.
3. Österreich hatte *trotz der Besatzungsmächte* eine eigene Regierung.
4. Der Vertrag verlangt, *daß Österreich* keine politische oder wirtschaftliche Vereinigung mit Deutschland *eingeht*.
5. *Die Donaumonarchie brach mit dem Ende des 1. Weltkrieges zusammen.*

 esson 28

STRUCTURE

1. Future Tense

a. The verb **werden** combined with an infinitive forms the future tense:

Sie **werden** morgen **kommen.** *(They will come tomorrow.)*

b. The auxiliary verb **werden** changes according to person and number:

Ich werde das Experiment **durchführen.** *(I will carry out the experiment.)*

c. Word order: The infinitive stands last in the clause:

Er wird das Studium der Medizin nächstes Jahr **abschließen.**
He will complete the study of medicine next year.

EXERCISE

Supply the forms of **werden** *(see page 209):*

1. Sie *(they)* _____ die Zeitung finden.
2. Man _____ ein neues Verfahren entwickeln.
3. Der Biologe _____ es ihnen erklären.
4. Wo _____ er den Widerstand messen?
5. Du _____ die Arbeit heute beenden.

2. Future Perfect Tense

a. The future perfect tense uses:

werden +	PAST PARTICIPLE +	AUXILIARY OF MAIN VERB
PRESENT TENSE	OF MAIN VERB	**(haben** or **sein)**

Examples:

Morgen **werde** ich meine Arbeit **beendet haben.**

By tomorrow I will have finished my work.

Der Chef **wird** nach Berlin **gefahren sein.**

The boss probably went to Berlin.

b. The future perfect tense expresses the expectation that something will have happened at a certain time in the future:

Morgen **werde** ich meine Arbeit **beendet haben.**
By tomorrow I will have finished my work.

c. The future perfect tense also expresses the supposition or probability that something has already ended either at the moment of speaking or at some point in the past:

Meine Eltern **werden** (wohl) gestern abend im Kino **gewesen sein.**
My parents (probably) were at the movies last night.
Er **wird** (wohl) die Karte heute **bekommen haben.**
He (probably) got the card today.

EXERCISES

A. *Give the English equivalents:*

1. Er wird das Experiment beendet haben.
2. Sie wird heute ihren Freund gesehen haben.
3. Der Chef wird nach Berlin gefahren sein.
4. Die Studentin wird das Buch gelesen haben.
5. In zehn Jahren wird man die Energie verbraucht haben.

B. *Change the following sentences to future:**

1. Ihr analysiert die Proteinstrukturen mit Hilfe des Computers.
2. Man errechnet die Molekularstrukturen nach physikalischen Prinzipien.
3. Das Herz befördert am Tag 5 760 Liter Blut.
4. Man erzeugt bald Eisen mit Hilfe von Kernenergie.
5. Das Pflanzenschutzmittel bewirkt eine Verringerung des Knochenproteins.

DREIHUNDERTACHT

C. *Express in German:*

1. The physician will examine the heart.
2. How will he explain the molecular structures?
3. They will soon produce cars.
4. The pesticide will cause a reduction of the bone protein.
5. One will calculate the resistance.

3. **Werden as Independent Verb**

a. **werden** may be used with a predicate adjective:

Der Mann **wird alt.** *(The man is getting old.)*

werden = to get, to become (used as independent verb)
alt = predicate adjective

b. **werden** used in all tenses:

PRESENT TENSE:	Der Mann **wird** alt.
	The man is getting old.
PAST TENSE:	Der Mann **wurde** alt.
	The man was getting (got) old.
PRESENT PERFECT:	Der Mann **ist** alt **geworden.**
	The man has gotten old.
PAST PERFECT:	Der Mann **war** alt **geworden.**
	The man had gotten old.
FUTURE:	Der Mann **wird** alt **werden.**
	The man will get old.
FUTURE PERFECT:	Der Mann **wird** alt **geworden sein.**
	The man will have gotten old.

EXERCISES

A. *Change the following sentences to the tenses indicated:**

1. Die Familie wurde arm.   (present perfect)
2. Im Sommer wird es warm.   (future)
3. Am Ende ist die Prüfung schwer geworden.   (past perfect)
4. Seine Arbeitsmethode wird erkennbar.   (past)
5. Ihre Rede ist sachlich geworden.   (past perfect)

B. *Give the English equivalents:*

1. Der Frosch wurde pessimistisch.
2. Ihr Werk ist beispielhaft geworden.
3. Seine Einstellung zur Sklavenfrage wurde offenkundig.
4. Die Handelsbilanz wird stark passiv werden.
5. Das Studium wird schwer werden.

READING
Arbeiter und die Wirtschaft

Wenn die Nachfrage nach Arbeitern steigt, so steigen die Arbeiter im Preis. Wenn die Nachfrage fällt, dann fällt sie so sehr, daß eine Anzahl von Arbeitern nicht verkäuflich ist, d.h. „auf Lager bleiben", so bleiben sie eben liegen, und da sie vom bloßen Liegen nicht leben können, so sterben sie Hungers. . . . (Aus dem Buch von Friedrich Engels: „Die Lage der arbeitenden Klassen in England")

VOCABULARY

der **Arbeiter, -**	worker	**liegen-bleiben (bleibt**	to be left be-
die **Wirtschaft**	economy	**liegen), blieb liegen,**	hind; to
wenn	if	**ist liegengeblieben**	remain un-
die **Nachfrage (nach)**	demand (for)		sold
steigen (steigt),	to increase,	**eben**	simply, just
stieg, ist gestiegen	climb, rise	**bloß**	mere, sole
fallen (fällt), fiel,		das **Liegen**	lying, reposing,
ist gefallen	to decrease, fall		resting
so sehr	so much	**sterben (stirbt),**	
die **Anzahl**	number	**starb, ist gestorben**	to die
verkäuflich	marketable,	der **Hunger**	hunger, famine
	saleable	**des Hungers sterben**	to die of starva-
auf Lager bleiben	to remain in		tion
	stock	die **Lage**	situation, condi-
das **Lager, -**	storehouse,		tion, lot
	storage, camp	**arbeitend**	working

STRUCTURE
4. Passive Voice

a. In the active voice, the focus of attention is on the agent / doer of an action. The subject of the sentence is actively involved in the action:

Der Mann baut das Haus. (*The man is building / builds the house.*)

b. In comparison to the active voice, the passive voice enables a speaker to express an action from another perspective:

Das Haus wird gebaut. (*The house is being built.*)

In this passive sentence, something is happening to the subject (**das Haus**). Someone (here unnamed) is doing something to the subject. Someone is building the house. This aspect of passive involvement of the subject is best expressed through the passive voice.

The change of perspective may also be seen in the grammatical shift of subject and direct object. In the active sentence **Der Mann baut das Haus**, the direct object (= accusative) is **das Haus.**

DREIHUNDERTZEHN

In the passive sentence, **das Haus** functions as the subject. Someone (unnamed) is acting upon the subject: **Das Haus wird gebaut.**

c.   The passive voice is formed with a form of **werden** plus the past participle of the main verb:

> FORM OF **werden** + PAST PARTICIPLE OF MAIN VERB

Examples:

Das Haus **wird** in München **gebaut.** *(The house is being built in Munich.)*
Die Häuser **werden** in München **gebaut.** *(The houses are being built in Munich.)*

EXERCISES

A.   *Supply the correct form of* **werden** *in the present tense:*

1.   Der Wärmeatlas _____ erstellt.
2.   Die Versorgung _____ auf Kernenergie umgestellt.
3.   Die Arbeiter _____ zu den Werkstätten befördert.
4.   Neue Chemikalien _____ entwickelt.

B.   *Supply the correct form of the past participle:*

1.   In Kanada wird viel Weizen _____.   (erzeugen)
2.   Die Versorgung der Organe mit Sauerstoff wird _____.   (gewährleisten)
3.   Die Handelsbilanz wird durch den Fremdenverkehr _____.   (ausgleichen)
4.   Das Tagebuch Schliemanns wird noch heute zur Rekonstruktion _____.   (benutzen)

5.   Word Order in the Passive Voice

a.   Main clauses:

Neue Chemikalien **werden entwickelt.**
New chemicals are (being) developed.

In den Vereinigten Staaten **werden** viele Autos **gebaut.**
A lot of cars are (being) built in the United States.

The helper verb **werden** occupies the second position in a statement. The past participle occupies the last position in a statement.

b.   Questions:

In questions with question words, the helper verb **werden** follows the question verb immediately. The past participle remains in last position:

Warum **werden** viele Autos **gebaut?**
Why are a lot of cars being built?

c. Subordinate clauses:

In subordinate clauses, the past participle precedes the conjugated form of the **werden:**

Man weiß, daß der Rhein durch die Industrie $\boxed{\text{verschmutzt}}$ wird.
It is known that the Rhine is (being) polluted by industry.

d. The complete forms of passive voice, present tense, in all persons are:

SINGULAR:		PLURAL:	
ich	**werde gefragt** *(asked)*	**wir**	**werden gefragt**
du	**wirst gefragt**	**ihr**	**werdet gefragt**
er		**sie**	
sie	**wird gefragt**	**Sie**	**werden gefragt**
es			

EXERCISES

A. *Form complete sentences in the passive voice, present tense:*

1. Der Magnetismus / erzeugen / durch die Rotation.
2. Die Menschen / bedrohen / immer noch von Malaria.
3. Das Ökosystem / zerstören / durch die Unterbrechung der Kreisläufe.
4. Der Buchdruck / vereinfachen / durch das neue Verfahren.
5. Warum / ein gebündelter Röntgenstrahl / richten / auf ein Material?

B. *Give the English equivalents:*

1. Die Molekularstrukturen werden nach physikalischen Prinzipien errechnet.
2. Das Röntgenstrahl-Brechungsmuster wird auf einem Film registriert.
3. Die Strömungsgeschwindigkeit des Blutes wird durch das Zigarettenrauchen vermindert.
4. Die deutsche Sprache wird in Deutschland, Österreich und der Schweiz als Muttersprache gesprochen.
5. Eine neue Getreidesorte wird jetzt von einem Forschungsinstitut erprobt.

READING

Säuren, Laugen und Salze

Säuren sind chemische Verbindungen, die in wäßriger Lösung Wasserstoffionen abspalten. In je größerem Umfange dies geschieht, um so stärker ist die saure Wirkung. Laugen oder Basen sind chemische Verbindungen, die in wäßriger Lösung Hydroxylionen abspalten. Säuren sind z.B. alle Wasserstoffverbindungen der Nichtmetalle (insbesondere die Halogenwasserstoffe) sowie die Verbindungen der Nichtmetalle (vor allem der Schwefel-, Stickstoff-, Chlor- und Phosphoroxide sowie des

Kohlendioxids) mit Wasser. Basen sind z.B. alle Oxide und Hydroxide der Metalle (insbesondere der Alkalimetalle), sowie das Ammoniumhydroxid. Beim Zusammentreffen von Säuren und Basen entstehen unter gleichzeitiger Bildung von Wasser die Salze, bei denen statt der Wasserstoffionen Metallionen, die von den Basen stammen,   10
an den jeweiligen Säurerest gebunden sind. An dem Namen eines Salzes kann man erkennen, aus welcher Säure und welcher Base es zustandekam.

VOCABULARY

die	**Lauge, -n**	base
das	**Salz, -e**	salt
	wäßrig	watery, aqueous
die	**Lösung, -en**	solution
der	**Wasserstoff**	hydrogen
das	**Ion, -en**	ion
	ab-spalten	to split off, separate
	je . . . um so	the . . . the
	größer	greater, larger
der	**Umfang**	extent, size, circumference
	geschehen (geschieht), geschah, ist geschehen	to happen, to occur
	stärker	stronger
	sauer, saur-	acidic
die	**Wirkung**	effect
die	**Base, -n**	base
das	**Hydroxylion**	hydroxide ion
das	**Nichtmetall, -e**	nonmetal, metalloid
	insbesondere	especially, particularly
der	**Halogenwasserstoff**	hydrogen halide
	sowie	as well as, as also
das	**Oxyd (Oxid), -e**	oxide
der	**Schwefel**	sulphur
der	**Stickstoff**	nitrogen
das	**Chlor**	chlorine
das	**Phosphor**	phosphorus

das	**Hydroxyd (Hydroxid), -e**	hydroxide
das	**Alkali, -en**	alkali
das	**Ammonium**	ammonium
das	**Zusammentreffen**	meeting
	entstehen (entsteht), entstand, ist entstanden	to arise, to come about, to form
	unter	here: with
	gleichzeitig	simultaneous, at the same time
die	**Bildung**	formation
	statt (+ genitive)	instead of
	jeweilig	respective, corresponding
der	**Rest, -e**	residue, remainder, remnant
der	**Säurerest**	acid residue
	binden (bindet), band, gebunden	to be attached, be bound; to bind
	erkennen (erkannt), erkannte, erkannt	to recognize
	erkennen (an)	to recognize (by)
	zustande-kommen (kommt zustande), kam zustande, ist zustandegekommen	to occur, happen, materialize

STRUCTURAL EXERCISE

Underline the following items in the above reading:

a. definite relative pronouns (straight line)
b. prepositions with definite relative pronouns (dotted line)

DREIHUNDERTDREIZEHN

VOCABULARY EXERCISE

Give the English equivalents of the italicized words or phrases:

1. Säuren sind chemische Verbindungen, *die in wäßriger Lösung Wasserstoffionen abspalten.*
2. *Beim Zusammentreffen von Säuren und Basen* entstehen Salze.
3. Man kann erkennen, *aus welcher Säure und welcher Base* das Salz zustandekam.
4. Säuren sind alle *Verbindungen der Nichtmetalle* mit Wasser.
5. Basen sind alle Oxide und Hydroxide der Metalle, *sowie das Ammonium-hydroxid.*

STRUCTURE

6. Passive Voice — Past Tense

The past tense of the passive voice consists of the past tense forms of **werden** plus the past participle of the main verb:

ich wurde	wir wurden	
du wurdest	ihr wurdet	
er wurde 〉 gefragt	sie wurden 〉 gefragt	
sie wurde	Sie wurden	
es wurde		

Example:

Das Haus **wurde** in Berlin **gebaut.**
The house was (being) built in Berlin.

EXERCISES

A. *Change the following sentences to past tense:* *

1. Die Versorgung der Stadt wird auf Kernenergie umgestellt.
2. Von wem wird der „Wärmeatlas" erstellt?
3. Wasserstoffionen werden in wäßriger Lösung abgespalten.
4. Verschiedene Wirtschaftssysteme werden untersucht.
5. Das sauerstoffarme Blut wird in die Lungenkapillare gepumpt.

B. *Give the English equivalents:*

1. Das Bauhaus wurde 1925 nach Dessau verlegt.
2. Die Souveränität des Gebietes wurde anerkannt.
3. Die Handelsbilanz wurde jedoch durch Kapitalerträge ausgeglichen.
4. Der Staatenbund wurde in einen Bundesstaat umgewandelt.
5. Das Schönheitsideal des Barocks wurde im Prunk und Pathos ausgedrückt.

DREIHUNDERTVIERZEHN

7. Passive Voice — Present Perfect Tense

a. The present perfect tense of the passive voice uses:

PRESENT TENSE OF **sein**	+	PAST PARTICIPLE OF MAIN VERB	+	**worden**

Example:

Das Haus **ist** im Jahre 1882 **gebaut worden.**
The house was (has been) built in 1882.

b. **worden** is an abridged form of the usual past participle of **werden (geworden).**

c. In the passive as in the active voice, the present perfect and the past tense often have the same meanings in English.

SELF-PREPARATORY EXERCISE

Change the following sentences to present perfect of the passive voice:*

Das erste organische Molekül im Weltall wurde gefunden.	
Die Hoffnung der Forscher wurde bestätigt.	Das erste organische Molekül im Weltall ist gefunden worden.
Die Befreiung von Helena wurde in der Sage beschrieben.	Die Hoffnung der Forscher ist bestätigt worden.
Genaue Tagebücher wurden bei den Ausgrabungen geführt.	Die Befreiung von Helena ist in der Sage beschrieben worden.
Helena wurde von Paris geraubt.	Genaue Tagebücher sind bei den Ausgrabungen geführt worden.
	Helena ist von Paris geraubt worden.

EXERCISES

A. *Complete. The constant factors are* **ist / sind . . . worden:**

1. Das Klima _____ durch den Golfstrom beeinflußt _____.
2. Das Bauhaus _____ 1925 nach Dessau verlegt _____.
3. Verschiedene Wirtschaftssysteme _____ untersucht _____.
4. Die Neutralität des Landes _____ bestätigt _____.
5. Wasserstoffionen _____ in wäßriger Lösung abgespalten _____.

B. *Supply the correct form of the past participle:*

1. Das Studium der antiken Literatur ist von byzantinischen Gelehrten
   _____worden. (anregen)
2. Der „Wärmeatlas" gibt an, wo im Lande viel Energie _____ worden ist.
   (verbrauchen)
3. Die kathartische Methode der Abreaktion ist von Freud _____ worden.
   (entwickeln)
4. Die Libido ist der Destruktionstrieb _____ worden. (gegenüberstellen)
5. Eine Verringerung des Knochenproteins ist durch den Mangel an Vitamin C
   _____ worden. (bewirken)

C. *Give the English equivalents:*

1. Eine Degeneration der Knochen ist hervorgerufen worden.
2. Atlantis ist als ein mächtiges Reich beschrieben worden.
3. Atlantis ist 9 000 Jahre vor Plato zerstört worden.
4. Das Wasser des Rheins ist von der Industrie verschmutzt worden.
5. Die Juden sind im Laufe der Geschichte immer wieder verfolgt worden.

8. Passive Voice — Past Perfect Tense

The past perfect tense of the passive voice uses

PAST TENSE OF **sein**	+	PAST PARTICIPLE OF MAIN VERB	+	**worden**

Examples:

Das Haus **war** damals **gebaut worden.**
The house had been built at that time.
Die Häuser **waren** damals **gebaut worden.**
The houses had been built at that time.

EXERCISES

A. *Change the following sentences to past perfect:**

1. Die Befreiung von Helena ist in der Sage beschrieben worden.
2. Genaue Tagebücher sind bei den Ausgrabungen geführt worden.
3. Die Versorgung der Stadt ist auf Kernenergie umgestellt worden.
4. Organische Moleküle sind im Weltall gefunden worden.
5. Das Bauhaus ist 1934 aufgelöst worden.

B. *Give the English equivalents of the following sentences:*

1. Das Bauhaus war 1925 nach Dessau verlegt worden.
2. Deutschland war in vier Besatzungszonen gegliedert worden.

DREIHUNDERTSECHZEHN

3. Der Wagen war gewaschen worden.
4. Helena war geraubt worden.
5. Das Magnetfeld war durch die Rotation der Flüssigkeit erzeugt worden.

READING

Das Schulsystem der BRD (2)

Es gibt verschiedene Arten von Gymnasien, darunter das altsprachliche (Hauptsprachen: Latein und Griechisch), das neusprachliche (Hauptsprachen: Englisch und Französisch) und das mathematisch-naturwissenschaftliche Gymnasium. Ein Schüler hat pro Woche etwa 30 Stunden Unterricht in 12 bis 14 Fächern. Der Unterricht beginnt meist um 8 Uhr und endet gegen 13 Uhr. Nachmittags ist nor- 5
malerweise kein Unterricht. Für die höheren Klassen finden an ein oder zwei Nachmittagen Arbeitsgemeinschaften statt. Dort soll jeder das lernen, was ihn besonders interessiert, z.B. Philosophie, Musik, Literatur, Physik oder eine zusätzliche Fremdsprache.

Die jüngeren Schüler sollen im Durchschnitt täglich ein bis zwei Stunden 10
Hausaufgaben machen, die älteren zwei bis drei Stunden. Der Stundenplan eines 16jährigen Oberschülers in einem neusprachlichen Gymnasium sieht ungefähr so aus:

	MONTAG	DIENSTAG	MITTWOCH	
1	Englisch	---	Sozialkunde	15
2	Geschichte	Latein	Englisch	
3	Kunst	Physik	Deutsch	
4	Kunst	Französisch	Mathematik	
5	Deutsch	Sport	Religion	
6	---	Musik	---	20

	DONNERSTAG	FREITAG	SAMSTAG	
1	Französisch	Physik	Chemie	
2	Latein	Deutsch	Mathematik	
3	Geschichte	Mathematik	Deutsch	
4	Englisch	Erdkunde	Englisch	25
5	Sport	Französisch	Erdkunde	
6	---	---	---	

Das Schuljahr beginnt nach den Sommerferien und endet im Juni oder Juli. Im Jahr hat ein Schüler etwa drei Monate Ferien. Die Sommerferien zwischen Juli und September sind die längsten Ferien und dauern etwa sechs Wochen. Zu Weihnachten 30
und um Ostern gibt es noch einmal kurze Ferien von zwei bis drei Wochen Dauer.

Das Schulsystem der BRD

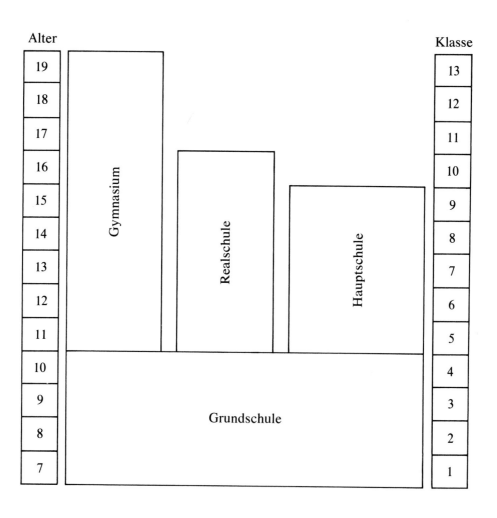

Alter

Alter		Klasse
19		13
18		12
17		11
16		10
15		9
14		8
13		7
12		6
11		5
10		4
9		3
8		2
7		1

Gymnasium

Realschule

Hauptschule

Grundschule

VOCABULARY

	darunter	among those
	altsprachlich	classical language (curriculum)
die	Hauptsprache, -n	main language
das	Latein	Latin (language)
das	Griechisch	Greek (language)
	neusprachlich	modern language (curriculum) (adj.)
	naturwissen-schaftlich	natural science (curriculum) (adj.)
	pro Woche	per week
die	Woche, -n	week
die	Stunde, -n	hour
	etwa	about, approximately
das	Fach, -er	subject, class
	meist	mostly, generally
	um	at (with time reference)
	gegen	by about, at about
	Uhr	o'clock
	nachmittags	afternoons
	normalerweise	normally
	statt-finden (findet statt), fand statt, stattgefunden	to take place, to occur
der	Nachmittag, -e	afternoon
die	Arbeitsgemein-schaft, -en	work group
	dort	there
	jeder	each person, everyone
	besonders	especially, particularly
	interessieren	to interest
	z.B. (zum Beispiel)	for instance, for example

die	Musik	music
die	Physik	physics
	zusätzlich	additional
	jünger	younger
der	Durchschnitt	average
	im Durchschnitt	on the average
	täglich	daily
die	Aufgabe, -n	task, assignment
die	Hausaufgabe, -n	homework assignment
die	Hausaufgaben machen	to do one's homework
	älter	older
der	Stundenplan, -e	class (hour) schedule
	-jährig	years old
der	Oberschüler, -	pupil in the Upper School
	aus-sehen (sieht aus), sah aus, ausgesehen	to look like
	ungefähr	about, approximately
der	Sport	sports, physical education
die	Sozialkunde	social studies
die	Religion	religion, theology
die	Erdkunde	geography, earth science
das	Schuljahr	school year, academic year
die	Sommerferien (pl.)	summer vacation
der	Monat, -e	month
	längst	longest
	Weihnachten	Christmas
	Ostern	Easter
	noch einmal	once again
	kurz	short
	von . . . bis	from . . . to

STRUCTURAL EXERCISE

Underline all two-way prepositions in the above reading.

VOCABULARY EXERCISE

Give the English equivalents of the italicized words or phrases:

1. *Es gibt verschiedene Arten von Gymnasien.*
2. *Dort soll jeder das lernen, was ihn besonders interessiert.*
3. *Die jüngeren Schüler sollen täglich ein bis zwei Stunden Hausaufgaben machen.*
4. *Nachmittags ist normalerweise kein Unterricht.*
5. *Zu Weihnachten und um Ostern gibt es noch einmal kurze Ferien.*

DREIHUNDERTNEUNZEHN

esson 29

STRUCTURE

1. Passive Voice — Future Tense

The future tense in the passive voice is formed by using:

PRESENT TENSE **werden**	+	PAST PARTICIPLE OF MAIN VERB	+	INFINITIVE **werden**

Examples:

Das Haus **wird gebaut werden.** (The house will be built.)
Die Häuser **werden gebaut werden.** (The houses will be built.)

EXERCISES

A. Supply the correct form of **werden** + past participle to complete the following sentences:

1. Hydroxylionen _____ in wäßriger Lösung _____ werden. (abspalten)
2. Das Land _____ von einer Besatzungsmacht _____ werden. (verwalten)
3. Mackie Messer _____ nicht _____ werden. (fragen)
4. Die Versorgung der Stadt mit Energie _____ durch Kernenergie _____ werden. (gewährleisten)
5. Die Architektur _____ durch den Bauhausstil _____ werden. (beeinflussen)

B. Form complete sentences in the future tense (passive voice) with the following elements:

1. Der Buchdruck / vereinfachen.
2. Die Bilanz / ausgleichen.

DREIHUNDERTZWANZIG

    3. Die Neutralität / anerkennen.
    4. Das Fachgebiet / langsam / erarbeiten.
    5. Genaue Tagebücher / führen.

C. *Give the English equivalents of the following sentences:*

    1. Er sagte, daß die heutige Gesellschaftsordnung überwunden werden wird.
    2. Wann wird das Schloß gebaut werden?
    3. Die Versorgung mit Energie wird langfristig auf Kernenergie umgestellt werden.
    4. Der Regenwald des Amazonas wird durch Eingriffe zerstört werden.
    5. Die große Leistung wird vollbracht werden.

2. Passive Voice — Future Perfect

a. The future perfect tense commonly expresses the expectation of an event to be completed in the future or the probability that an event has already occurred in the present or in the past.

b. The future perfect tense in the passive voice uses:

PRESENT TENSE **werden**	+	PAST PARTICIPLE OF MAIN VERB	+	**worden**	+	**sein**

Examples:

Das Haus **wird gebaut worden sein.**
The house will have been built.
(or: *The house probably has been built.*)

Die Häuser **werden gebaut worden sein.**
The houses will have been built.
(or: *The houses probably have been built.*)

EXERCISES

A. *Change the following sentences to future perfect of the passive voice:**

    1. Das Experiment wird beendet werden.
    2. Das Problem wird besprochen.
    3. Die Autos wurden verkauft.
    4. Die Proteinstrukturen werden mit Hilfe eines Computers analysiert.
    5. Die Zeitung wird gelesen.

B. *Translate the following sentences into English:*

    1. Diese Molekularstrukturen werden wohl nach physikalischen Prinzipien errechnet worden sein.
    2. Durch diese Methode wird die Verteilung der Materie innerhalb eines Moleküls definiert worden sein.

3. In der Brauerei wird viel Bier gebraut worden sein.
4. Helena wird wohl von Paris geraubt worden sein.
5. Vermutlich wird durch den Vitaminmangel eine Verringerung des Knochenproteins verursacht worden sein.

READING

Aphorismen

1. Enthaltsamkeit ist das Vergnügen an Sachen, die wir nicht kriegen. (Wilhelm Busch)
2. Ein Anständiger braucht keine Religion — und bei den anderen ist sie wirkungslos. (Georg Kaiser)
3. Wer fremde Sprachen nicht kennt, weiß nichts von seiner eigenen. (Goethe)   5
4. Es ist fast unmöglich, die Fackel der Wahrheit durch ein Gedränge zu tragen, ohne jemandem den Bart zu versengen. (Lichtenberg)
5. Überzeugungen sind gefährlichere Feinde der Wahrheit als Lügen. (Nietzsche)
6. Alles ist Vorübung für etwas, das wir nicht leisten werden. (Georg Kaiser)
7. Ein Aphorismus ist der letzte Ring einer langen Gedankenkette. (Marie von   10 Ebner-Eschenbach)
8. Denken und tun, das ist die Summe aller Weisheit. (Goethe)
9. Die glücklichsten Sklaven sind die erbittertesten Feinde der Freiheit. (Marie von Ebner-Eschenbach)

VOCABULARY

der **Aphorismus,**		
Aphorismen	aphorism	
die **Enthaltsamkeit**	temperance, abstention	
das **Vergnügen**	pleasure, joy	
kriegen	to get, obtain, receive	
anständig	decent	
ein Anständiger	a decent man (person)	
brauchen	to need	
wirkungslos	ineffective	
wer	whoever, he who	
kennen (kennt), kannte, gekannt	to know	
fast	almost	
unmöglich	impossible	
die **Fackel, -n**	torch, light	
die **Wahrheit**	truth	
das **Gedränge**	crowd	
der **Bart, ⸚e**	beard	
versengen	to singe	

die **Überzeugung, -en**	conviction
gefährlich	dangerous
gefährlicher	more dangerous
der **Feind, -e**	enemy, adversary
die **Lüge, -n**	lie, untruth
die **Vorübung**	preparatory exercise
leisten	to achieve; to perform, do
letzt-	last
der **Ring, -e**	ring, circle
der **Gedanke, -n**	thought, idea
die **Kette, -n**	chain
tun (tut), tat, getan	to do
die **Summe, -n**	sum
die **Weisheit, -en**	wisdom
glücklich	happy
glücklichst	happiest
erbittert	embittered, exacerbated
erbittertest	most embittered

DREIHUNDERTZWEIUNDZWANZIG

STRUCTURE

3. Passive Voice with Modals

a. Basic verb compositions for modals with verbs in the passive voice:

MODAL	+	PAST PARTICIPLE OF MAIN VERB	+	**werden**

Examples:

Das Haus **muß** heute **gebaut werden.**
The house has to be built today.
Das Experiment **soll** morgen **beendet werden.**
The experiment is supposed to be finished by tomorrow.

b. Only the modal verb is conjugated in all passive forms. The past participle and the **werden**-infinitive are constant:

PRESENT TENSE:	**muß . . . gebaut werden**	*(has to be built)*
PAST TENSE:	**mußte . . . gebaut werden**	*(had to be built)*
PRESENT PERFECT:	**hat . . . gebaut werden müssen**	*(had to be built)*
PAST PERFECT:	**hatte . . . gebaut werden müssen**	*(had had to be built)*
FUTURE TENSE:	**wird . . . gebaut werden müssen**	*(will have to be built)*

EXERCISES

A. *Add the modal to the following passive voice sentences and make all necessary changes. Retain the original tense:**

1. Der photoelektrische Effekt wird untersucht.   (müssen)
2. Das Brechungsmuster des Röntgenstrahls wird registriert.   (können)
3. Die Bewegung der Atome wird erklärt.   (sollen)
4. Die Betriebskosten werden bestimmt.   (können)
5. Die Geschwindigkeit des Autos wird ermittelt.   (sollen)

B. *Change the following sentences to the tenses indicated:**

1. Eine große Leistung muß vollbracht werden.   (past)
2. Die Strömungsgeschwindigkeit des Blutes sollte vermindert werden. (present perfect)
3. Die Blutzirkulation konnte gemessen werden.   (present)
4. Eine höhere Ernte soll erzielt werden.   (past)
5. Nur natürliche Düngemittel durften verwendet werden.   (present)

C. *Give the English equivalents:*

1. Die Bauweise soll variiert werden.
2. Schnelle Gewässer müssen vermieden werden.
3. Eine neue Getreidesorte konnte erprobt werden.
4. Das Experiment hat nicht beendet werden können.
5. Das Pflanzenschutzmittel durfte nicht verwendet werden.

4. Passive Constructions Without Subject

a. When an active construction with a direct object is transformed into a passive construction, the direct object of the active becomes the subject of the passive:

Der Mann baut das Haus.   (active voice)
DIRECT OBJECT: **das Haus**

Das Haus wird gebaut.   (passive voice)
SUBJECT: **das Haus**

b. When the verb of an active construction cannot have a direct object, the passive construction with the same verb likewise cannot have a subject in German:

Sie hilft dem Mann.   (active voice)   NO DIRECT OBJECT

Dem Mann wird geholfen.   (passive voice)   NO SUBJECT

Note that English treats **dem Mann** as a subject in the equivalent sentence:

Dem Mann wird geholfen. *(The man is being helped.)*

c. The impersonal pronoun **es** may occupy the position of grammatical subject of a passive construction without true subject:

Es wird dem Mann geholfen. *(The man is being helped.)*

As soon as another structural part (for example, an indirect object or an adverb) opens a clause, the impersonal pronoun **es** is omitted:

Es wird dem Mann geholfen.
Dem Mann wird geholfen.

d. The impersonal pronoun **es** may also occur in passive constructions involving:

VERB + PREPOSITION STRUCTURES

Example:

Es wurde über sein Buch gesprochen. *(His book was being discussed.)*

VERB + PREPOSITION STRUCTURE
sprechen +   **über** *(acc.)*

DREIHUNDERTVIERUNDZWANZIG

e. For the English equivalents of passive constructions with **es**, remember that **es** in the German construction may be filling the gap left by:

1. a missing subject; or
2. a structural element shifted to another position in the clause.

Examples:

Es wird dem Mann geholfen.
Es wurde ein Haus gebaut.

f. The English equivalent of a German passive construction with **es** may be obtained either by:

1. Spotting the structural element (for example, the indirect object or the object of the prepositional phrase) and treating it as the subject in English:

Es wurde ihr nicht geantwortet. (Indirect object: **ihr**)
She was not (being) answered. (Subject: *she*)

Es wurde nach einer Lösung gesucht. (Prepositional object: **einer Lösung**)
A solution was (being) sought. (Subject: *A solution*)

2. Using an English active construction:

Es wird auf den Bus gewartet. *(People are waiting for the bus.)*

EXERCISES

A. *Give the English equivalents:*

1. Es wurde dem Redner geglaubt.
2. Es wird der Mutter geholfen.
3. Es ist der Regierung vertraut worden.
4. Es wurde dem Lehrer geantwortet.
5. Es wurde ihm nicht geantwortet.

B. *Give the English equivalents:*

1. Es wurde nach einem Bekämpfungsmittel gesucht.
2. Es wird an die neuen Lehrmethoden erinnert.
3. Es wird für die Erhaltung der amphibischen Landschaft plädiert.
4. Es wurde nach der genetischen Kontrolle gefragt.
5. Es wird auf den Bus gewartet.

READING

Studium in Deutschland

Die Universitäten spielen schon seit langem eine bedeutende Rolle im Erziehungssystem Deutschlands. Die erste Universität in Deutschland war Heidelberg (1386), dann kamen Köln (1388) und Erfurt (1392). Diese ersten

BUNDESBILDSTELLE BONN

Universität München

DREIHUNDERTSECHSUNDZWANZIG

Universitäten waren noch verhältnismäßig klein. Bis in das 17. Jahrhundert hinein
hatte eine Universität durchschnittlich nicht mehr als 200 Studenten. 5

Das Lehrsystem der damaligen Universitäten kann man nicht mehr mit dem
heutigen vergleichen. Im Mittelalter gab es zum Beispiel nur die traditionellen vier
klassischen Fakultäten: Theologie, Jurisprudenz, Medizin und Philosophie. Im 19.
Jahrhundert änderte man das Universitätssystem. Viele Anregungen für diese Ver-
änderung gehen auf den deutschen Sprachwissenschaftler, Diplomaten und Politiker 10
Wilhelm von Humboldt zurück. Humboldt war Leiter der preußischen Kulturpolitik
(1809/1810) und gründete die Universität Berlin. Humboldts Beitrag zum
Bildungssystem Deutschlands besteht darin, daß er die Prinzipien wissenschaft-
licher Tätigkeit formulierte. Dabei ist entscheidend, daß nach Humboldt sowohl der
Professor als auch der Student selbständige Individuen sind. Im Vordergrund des 15
Lernens steht nicht das Maß an Wissen, das jemand beherrscht, sondern die
Einstellung zum Lernen, d.h. der Drang zum Wissen und zur Erkenntnis. Für
Humboldt war das Streben nach Erkenntnis ein unendlicher Prozeß.

VOCABULARY

die **Universität, -en**	university
spielen	to play
schon seit langem	for a long time
spielen schon seit langem	have been playing for a long time
die **Rolle, -n**	role
die **Erziehung**	education
verhältnismäßig	relatively
bis . . . hinein	up into
das **Lehrsystem, -e**	educational system
vergleichen (vergleicht), verglich, verglichen	to compare
traditionell	traditional
klassisch	classical
die **Fakultät, -en**	faculty
die **Medizin**	medicine (science of)
ändern	to change
die **Anregung, -en**	stimuli, impulse
die **Veränderung, -en**	change
zurück-gehen (geht zurück), ging zurück, ist zurückgegangen	to go back
zurückgehen (auf)	to be traced back (to)
der **Sprachwissenschaftler**	philologist, linguist
der **Diplomat, -en**	diplomat

der **Politiker, -**	politician
der **Leiter, -**	director, leader
preußisch	Prussian (adj.)
die **Kulturpolitik**	cultural affairs
der **Beitrag, -̈e**	contribution
die **Bildung**	education
bestehen (besteht), bestand, bestanden	to exist
bestehen (in)	to consist (of)
die **Tätigkeit**	activity
dabei	thereby, in this case
sowohl . . . als auch	not only . . . but also
selbständig	autonomous, self-sufficient
das **Individuum, Individuen**	individual (person)
der **Vordergrund**	forefront, foreground
das **Lernen**	learning (process), study
das **Maß (an)**	amount (of)
jemand	someone, somebody

beherrschen	to command, govern	die **Erkenntnis** **unendlich**	knowledge eternal, in- finite, un- ending
nicht . . . sondern	not . . . but rather		
die **Einstellung**	attitude	der **Prozeß, -sse**	process
der **Drang**	drive, willing- ness, im- pulse, com- pulsion		

STRUCTURAL EXERCISE

Underline the attributive adjectives following definite articles or **der**-words in the above reading.

VOCABULARY EXERCISE

Give the English equivalents of the italicized words or phrases:

1. Sein Beitrag *besteht darin, daß* er die Prinzipien wissenschaftlicher Tätigkeit *for-mulierte.*
2. Dabei ist entscheidend, daß *sowohl* der Professor *als auch* der Student selbstän-dige Individuen sind.
3. *Die Universitäten spielen schon seit langem* eine bedeutende Rolle im Erziehungssystem Deutschlands.
4. Eine Universität *hatte durchschnittlich nicht mehr als* 200 Studenten.
5. Humboldt formulierte die *Prinzipien wissenschaftlicher Tätigkeit.*

STRUCTURE

5. Passive Constructions Without Subject (continued)

a. In the following examples, **es** substitutes for a missing sentence element. Al-though it functions as grammatical subject, **es** is not the true subject of the German sentence:

Es wurde laut gelacht.
Es wird sonntags nicht gearbeitet.

b. The English equivalent usually starts with *there is . . ., there was . . ., there are . . ., there were . . .,* while transforming the German verb into a noun in English:

Es wurde laut gelacht. *(There was loud laughter.)*
Es wird sonntags nicht gearbeitet. *(There is no work [done] on Sundays.)*

DREIHUNDERTACHTUNDZWANZIG

Note that when another element opens the passive construction **es** is omitted:

Es | **wird** | **sonntags nicht gearbeitet.**
Sonntags | **wird** | **nicht gearbeitet.**

Even though **es** has been eliminated from the second example, the verb retains its form (third person singular) because **es** is still the implied subject.

c.   The meaning of the German sentence is not affected by the absence of **es.**

Sonntags wird nicht gearbeitet. *(There is no work [done] on Sundays.)*

SELF-PREPARATORY EXERCISE

Give the English equivalents:

Es wurde bis spät abends getanzt.	
Es wurde im Zimmer nicht geraucht.	There was dancing (going on) until late at night.
Es wird im Labor experimentiert.	There was no smoking in the room.
Es wurde auf der Party viel gesungen.	There are experiments (going on) in the lab.
Es wurde nach einer Lösung des Problems gesucht.	There was lots of singing at the party.
	There was a search for the solution to the problem.

EXERCISES

A.   *Form passive sentences with the following elements; use* **es** *to start the sentence; follow the model:*

MODEL: / die ganze Nacht / tanzen.   (present)
Es wird die ganze Nacht getanzt.

1.   / während des Semesters / viel / arbeiten.   (present)
2.   / hier / nicht / rauchen.   (present)
3.   / nachmittags / nicht / studieren.   (past)
4.   / nach einer Lösung / suchen.   (past)
5.   / in der Chemie / viel / experimentiert.   (present)

B.   *Give the English equivalents:*

1.   Es wurde nachmittags nicht gearbeitet.
2.   Es wurden viele Aufgaben behandelt.

DREIHUNDERTNEUNUNDZWANZIG

3. Es wurde kein Licht benutzt.
4. Es wird während der Semesterferien nicht gelernt.
5. Es wird heute im Labor nicht analysiert.

6.   Agent in the Passive Voice

a.   The agent or the cause of an action (= the subject in the active construction) may be expressed in a passive construction by using:

von
durch } = *by*

b.   Personal agent: **von** = *by:*

Das Experiment wurde **von dem Chemiker** durchgeführt.
The experiment was carried out by the chemist.

c.   Personal mediator: **durch** = *by:*

Die Nachricht vom Sieg über die Perser wurde **durch einen Boten** überbracht.
The news of the victory over the Persians was delivered by a messenger.

d.   Tool, instrument, or cause of an action: **durch** = *by:*

Das Haus wurde **durch das große Feuer** zerstört.
The house was destroyed by the big fire.
Die Stadt wurde **durch Bomben** vernichtet.
The city was demolished by bombs.

EXERCISE

Give the English equivalents:

1. Es ist bekannt, daß die Röntgenstrahlen von Wilhelm Röntgen entdeckt wurden.
2. Man behauptet, daß der Regenwald am Amazonas durch Eingriffe zerstört wird.
3. Das Klima ist durch den Golfstrom beeinflußt worden.
4. Der photoelektrische Effekt ist von Einstein untersucht worden.
5. Die Strömungsgeschwindigkeit wurde durch das Rauchen vermindert.

READING

Studium in Deutschland (2)

Der Begriff der akademischen Freiheit wurde durch Humboldts Konzept ,,vom unendlichen Lernprozeß'' beeinflußt. Für Humboldt war die akademische Freiheit eine
wichtige Voraussetzung, die diesen unendlichen Lernprozeß garantieren sollte.
Dieser Begriff umschreibt die uneingeschränkte Freiheit der Forschung, der Lehre
und des Lernens. Die akademische Freiheit betrifft die Professoren und die   5

DREIHUNDERTDREISSIG

Studenten. Der Professor lehrt und forscht nicht nach vorgeschriebenen Prinzipien, sondern bestimmt die Themen der Kurse und die Bereiche der Forschung selbständig. Der Student bestimmt seinen Studienverlauf selbst und macht seine Abschlußprüfung, wenn er seiner Meinung nach dazu bereit ist.

Das Universitätssystem der Bundesrepublik hat viele Prinzipien der früheren Ent- 10 wicklungsstufen beibehalten. Seit dem 19. Jahrhundert gibt es nicht mehr nur die vier klassischen Fakultäten, sondern auch naturwissenschaftliche, landwirtschaftliche, forstwirtschaftliche und tierärztliche Disziplinen. An den technischen Hochschulen gibt es Fakultäten für allgemeine Wissenschaften, Bauwesen, Maschinenwesen, Elektrotechnik, Bergbau und Hüttenwesen. 15

An der Spitze der Fakultät steht der Dekan. Die Fakultät besteht aus Professoren, Dozenten, Räten und Wissenschaftlern mit Lehrauftrag.

Die Lernbedingungen und Lernzwecke von heute kann man nicht mehr mit denen von 1810 vergleichen. In den letzten Jahren haben die westdeutschen Universitäten Reformprogramme eingeleitet, aber nicht immer vorangetrieben und durchgeführt. 20 Heute wollen zu viele Studenten studieren, aber die Universitäten verfügen über ungenügende Studienplätze.

VOCABULARY

der	**Begriff, -e**	concept, idea
	akademisch	academic
die	**Freiheit**	freedom, liberty
die	**Vorausset-**	
	zung, -en	prerequisite
	garantieren	to guarantee
	umschreiben	to designate,
	(umschreibt),	specify, de-
	umschrieb,	scribe
	umschrieben	
	uneingeschränkt	unlimited, un-
		bounded
	betreffen (betrifft),	
	betraf, betroffen	to affect, concern
	lehren	to teach, in-
		struct
	forschen	to research
	vorgeschrieben	prescribed, pre-
		determined
das	**Thema, Themen**	subject, topic,
		theme
der	**Kurs, -e**	course
der	**Bereich, -e**	field, scope,
		realm
der	**Verlauf**	course
der	**Studienverlauf**	course of study,
		curriculum
	selbst	-self; here:
		himself

die	**Abschlußprüfung**	final exam
die	**Abschlußprüfung**	to take the final
	machen	exam
die	**Meinung, -en**	opinion
	seiner Meinung	
	nach	in his opinion
	dazu	for it
	bereit	ready
die	**Entwicklungs-**	evolutionary
	stufe, -n	steps
	bei-behalten	
	(behält bei),	
	behielt bei,	
	beibehalten	to retain, keep
	landwirtschaftlich	agricultural
	forstwirtschaftlich	forest, forestry
	tierärztlich	veterinary
	allgemein	general
das	**Bauwesen**	building, archi-
		tectural engi-
		neering
die	**Elektrotechnik**	electrical engi-
		neering
der	**Bergbau**	mining
das	**Hüttenwesen**	metallurgy
die	**Spitze, -n**	top
der	**Dekan, -e**	dean
der	**Dozent, -en**	lecturer (at a
		university)

der	**Rat, ⸚e**	instructors	**voran-treiben** to push, propel,
der	**Lehrauftrag, ⸚e**	teaching assignment, teaching appointment	**(treibt voran),** advance **trieb voran, vorangetrieben**
die	**Bedingung, -en**	condition	**durch-führen** to carry out
der	**Lernzweck, -e**	educational goal	**verfügen (über)** to have at one's
	westdeutsch	West German	disposal
das	**Reform-**	university reform	**ungenügend** insufficient
	programm, -e	program	der **Studienplatz, ⸚e** place to study
	ein-leiten	to introduce, start	(in a field)

STRUCTURAL EXERCISE

Underline all verbs with separable prefixes in the above reading.

VOCABULARY EXERCISE

Give the English equivalents of the italicized words or phrases:

1. Der Begriff der akademischen Freiheit *wurde von Humboldt beeinflußt.*
2. *An der Spitze der Fakultät steht der Dekan.*
3. *In den letzten Jahren haben die westdeutschen* Universitäten Reformprogramme *eingeleitet.*
4. Das Universitätssystem *hat viele Prinzipien der früheren Entwicklungsstufen beibehalten.*
5. Der Begriff der akademischen Freiheit *umschreibt die uneingeschränkte Freiheit der Forschung, der Lehre und des Lernens.*

esson 30

STRUCTURE

1. Statal Passive

a. The statal passive describes the condition of the subject after something has happened to it. It states the result of an action rather than the action itself:

Die Tür **ist geschlossen.** *(The door is closed.)*
Das Experiment **ist beendet.** *(The experiment is finished.)*

b. The statal passive uses **sein** + past participle:

Der Knochen **ist gebrochen.** *(The bone is broken.)* (present)
Der Knochen **war gebrochen.** *(The bone was broken.)* (past)

c. A statal passive (**sein** + past participle) cannot have an agent.

EXERCISES

A. *Form sentences in the statal passive with the following elements. Use the present tense:*

1. Das Haus _____ _____. (verkaufen)
2. Der Wagen _____ _____. (waschen)
3. Das Ökosystem _____ _____. (zerstören)
4. Die Arbeit _____ _____. (beenden)
5. Die Krankheit _____ weit _____. (verbreiten)

B. *Give the English equivalents:*

1. Die tropischen Tiere sind bedroht.
2. Die Übersetzung der Bibel ist beendet.

DREIHUNDERTDREIUNDDREISSIG

3. Der Rhein ist stark verschmutzt.
4. Der Wagen ist verkauft.
5. Die Krankheit ist weit verbreitet.

2.   Passive Voice Substitution I

a.   There are other grammatical structures which may take the place of passive constructions in German.

b.

| Active construction with reflexive verb |

PASSIVE	REFLEXIVE VERB: ACTIVE CONSTRUCTION
Die Tür wird geöffnet.	**Die Tür öffnet sich.**
The door is being opened.	*The door opens / is being opened.*

c.   In both sentences above the agent or cause of the occurrence (the person opening the door) remains unnamed.

d.   The English meaning of the passive sentence is the same as that of the active sentence with a reflexive verb.

EXERCISES

A.   *Change the following sentences to active sentences with a reflexive verb:**

EXAMPLE: Die Tür wird geöffnet.
Die Tür öffnet sich.

1. Die Strömungsgeschwindigkeit wird vermindert.
2. Die Verfassung wird geändert.
3. Die Hoffnung wird bestätigt.
4. Die Regierung wird aufgelöst.
5. Wasserstoffionen werden abgespalten.

B.   *Give the English equivalents:*

1. Der Säurerest wird gebunden. Der Säurerest bindet sich.
2. Die Methode wird geändert. Die Methode ändert sich.
3. Die Monarchie wird aufgelöst. Die Monarchie löst sich auf.
4. Das Schönheitsideal wird im Prunk ausgedrückt. Das Schönheitsideal drückt sich im Prunk aus.
5. Die Infektionskrankheit wird verbreitet. Die Infektionskrankheit verbreitet sich.

DREIHUNDERTVIERUNDDREISSIG

3.   Passive Voice Substitution II

a. | Active construction with **sich lassen** |

Das Experiment **läßt sich** leicht **beschreiben.**
The experiment can be described easily.

b.   This structure corresponds to a passive construction with the modal verb **können:**

Das Experiment **kann** leicht **beschrieben werden.**
The experiment can be described easily.

c.   The equivalent English forms of both structures are *can* (present) and *could* (past) plus *be* and the past participle of the main verb:

Examples in past tense:

Dieser Unfall **ließ sich nicht vermeiden.**
This accident could not be avoided.
Dieser Unfall **konnte nicht vermieden werden.**
This accident could not be avoided.

EXERCISES

A.   *Change the following passive sentences to active sentences with the verb* **sich lassen:***

EXAMPLE: Das Experiment kann leicht beschrieben werden.
Das Experiment läßt sich leicht beschreiben.

1.   Die Strömungsgeschwindigkeit kann schnell vermindert werden.
2.   Eine höhere Ernte kann nicht erzielt werden.
3.   Die Proteinstrukturen können durch bestimmte Verfahren analysiert werden.
4.   Eine Fremdsprache kann gelernt werden.
5.   Infektionskrankheiten können vermieden werden.

B.   *Give the English equivalents:*

1.   Baumwolle kann zu Garn gesponnen werden.
Baumwolle läßt sich zu Garn spinnen.
2.   Die Blutzirkulation konnte gemessen werden.
Die Blutzirkulation ließ sich messen.
3.   Das Ergebnis konnte ermittelt werden.
Das Ergebnis ließ sich ermitteln.
4.   Das Brechungsmuster kann registriert werden.
Das Brechungsmuster läßt sich registrieren.
5.   Die Molekularstruktur konnte errechnet werden.
Die Molekularstruktur ließ sich errechnen.

DREIHUNDERTFÜNFUNDDREISSIG

Wilhelm Busch

DREIHUNDERTSECHSUNDDREISSIG

READING

Humor: Wilhelm Busch (1832–1908)

Es sitzt ein Vogel auf dem Leim,
Er flattert sehr und kann nicht heim.
Ein schwarzer Kater schleicht herzu,
Die Krallen scharf, die Augen gluh.
Am Baum hinauf und immer höher   5
Kommt er dem armen Vogel näher.

Der Vogel denkt: Weil das so ist
Und weil mich doch der Kater frißt,
So will ich keine Zeit verlieren,
Will noch ein wenig quinquillieren   10
Und lustig pfeifen wie zuvor.
Der Vogel, scheint mir, hat Humor.

VOCABULARY

der **Humor**	humor	**am Baum hinauf**	up the tree
der **Leim**	trap, lime, glue	**kommen (kommt),**	
flattern	to flutter, beat its wings	**kam, ist**	
		gekommen	to come
heim	home; here: fly home	**näher**	closer
		doch	anyway, after all, surely
schwarz	black		
der **Kater**	(male) cat, tom cat	**verlieren (verliert), verlor, verloren**	to lose
schleichen (schleicht), schlich, ist geschlichen	to sneak up	**ein wenig**	a little
		quinquillieren	to warble, sing
schleicht . . . herzu	sneaks up to	**lustig**	merrily, happily
die **Kralle, -n**	claw	**pfeifen (pfeift), pfiff, gepfiffen**	to sing, to whistle
scharf	sharp		
das **Auge, -n**	eye	**wie**	as, like
gluh (from **glühen;** poetic license)	glowing	**zuvor**	before
		scheinen (scheint), schien, geschienen	to seem, to appear
der **Baum, ̈-e**	tree		

STRUCTURE

4. Passive Voice Substitution III

a. | **sein** + **zu** + infinitive of the main verb |

Example:

Das Problem **ist zu lösen.** *(The problem can be solved.)*

b. The preceding structure also replaces a passive construction with the modal **können:**

Das Problem **kann gelöst werden.** *(The problem can be solved.)*

c. The English meaning of the **sein** + **zu** + infinitive structure may occur in two ways:

1. *can be* + past participle (present)
   could be + past participle (past)

2. *is / are* + adjective (present)
   was / were + adjective (past)

   Examples:

   Das Problem **kann gelöst werden.**   *(The problem can be solved.)*
   Das Problem **ist zu lösen.**   *(The problem is solvable.)*

EXERCISES

A. *Change the following passive sentences to active sentences with* **sein** + **zu** + *infinitive:**

EXAMPLE: Das Problem kann gelöst werden.
             Das Problem ist zu lösen.

1. Die Existenz Gottes kann nicht bewiesen werden.
2. Das System kann nicht mehr geändert werden.
3. Ein hoher Preis konnte nicht erzielt werden.
4. Die Aufgabe kann einfach nicht erklärt werden.
5. Die traditionellen Erklärungen können verwendet werden.

B. *Give the English equivalents:*

1. Die Einheit des Landes konnte nicht erreicht werden.
   Die Einheit des Landes war nicht zu erreichen.
2. Die Degeneration der Knochen kann verhindert werden.
   Die Degeneration der Knochen ist zu verhindern.
3. Die Naturkatastrophe konnte nicht vermieden werden.
   Die Naturkatastrophe war nicht zu vermeiden.
4. Das Ergebnis konnte nicht erklärt werden.
   Das Ergebnis war nicht zu erklären.
5. Das Molekül konnte nicht gesehen werden.
   Das Molekül war nicht zu sehen.

DREIHUNDERTACHTUNDDREISSIG

READING

Die drei Einheiten

Darunter versteht man die Einheit der Handlung, des Ortes und der Zeit. Aristoteles fordert in seiner Poetik für das Drama die Einheit der Handlung, d.h. die Durchführung eines Grundmotivs ohne Episoden. Die Einheit der Zeit ist in der griechischen Trägodie ein Sonnentag; die Handlungsdauer und die Aufführungsdauer sind meist identisch. Die Einheit des Ortes ist ohnehin durch die ständige Anwesenheit des Chores auf der Bühne gegeben.

Die Poetiken der Renaissance und der französischen Klassik fordern die Wahrung der drei Einheiten fürs Drama. Lessing, ein deutscher Dramatiker und Kritiker (1729–1781), legt in seiner „Hamburgischen Dramaturgie" den Hauptakzent auf die Einheit der Handlung.

VOCABULARY

die	**Einheit, -en**	unit		**identisch**	identical
	darunter	thereby, by that		**ohnehin**	anyway, anyhow, all the
die	**Handlung, -en**	action, plot			same
der	**Ort, -e**	place, location		**ständig**	constant
	Aristoteles	Aristotle	der	**Chor, ⁻e**	chorus
	fordern	to demand, require		**ist . . . gegeben**	
die	**Poetik, -en**	poetics, theory of poetry		**(durch)**	is achieved (by)
das	**Drama, -en**	drama	die	**Bühne, -n**	stage
die	**Durchführung**	execution, production, instrumentation	die	**Klassik**	classicism
			die	**Wahrung**	preservation, maintenance
die	**Episode, -n**	episode	der	**Dramatiker, -**	dramatist, playwright
die	**Tragödie, -n**	tragedy	der	**Kritiker, -**	critic
der	**Sonnentag, -e**	day (by the sun), dawn to dusk	die	**Dramaturgie**	poetics, dramatic theory
die	**Aufführung, -en**	performance, production	der	**Hauptakzent, -e**	main accent, emphasis

STRUCTURAL EXERCISE

Underline all definite articles used in the genitive case in the above reading.

VOCABULARY EXERCISE

Give the English equivalents of the italicized words or phrases:

1. *Aristoteles fordert in seiner Poetik für das Drama die Einheit der Handlung.*
2. *Die Einheit der Handlung ist in der griechischen Tragödie ein Sonnentag.*
3. *Darunter versteht man die Einheit der Handlung, des Ortes und der Zeit.*
4. *Lessing legt den Hauptakzent auf die Einheit der Handlung.*
5. *Die Einheit des Ortes ist ohnehin durch die ständige Anwesenheit des Chores gegeben.*

DREIHUNDERTNEUNUNDDREISSIG

STRUCTURE

5. Passive Voice Substitution IV

a.

sein + adjective derived from a verb

Example:

Das Problem **ist lösbar.** *(The problem is solvable / can be solved.)*

b. The substitution is equivalent to a passive construction with the modal verb **können:**

Das Problem **kann gelöst werden.**
The problem can be solved (is solvable).

c. The most common adjective suffixes in this construction are:

-lich   **verkäuflich** *(saleable)*
-bar   **lösbar** *(solvable)*

The suffixes **-bar** and **-lich** are attached to the infinitive stem of the verb. Some verb stems have an umlaut when combined with the adjective suffixes:

erreichen	**erreichbar**	*(attainable)*
verkaufen	**verkäuflich** (umlaut)	*(saleable)*

EXERCISE

Change the following passive sentences to active sentences, using **sein** + *adjective derived from the main verb; the suffix of the adjective is indicated in parentheses:**

EXAMPLE: Das Problem kann gelöst werden.
                      Das Problem ist lösbar.

1. Diese Methode kann nicht verwendet werden.   (-bar)
2. Solche Programme können nicht durchgeführt werden.   (-bar)
3. Die verschiedenen Lehrsysteme können verglichen werden.   (-bar)
4. Das Rätsel kann gelöst werden.   (-bar)
5. Die Existenz Gottes kann bewiesen werden.   (-bar)

6. Passive Voice Substitution V

a.

Active construction: **man** + $\left\{ \begin{array}{l} \textbf{kann} \\ \textbf{konnte} \end{array} \right\}$ + infinitive of the main verb

Example:

Man kann das Problem **lösen.**
One can solve the problem. (The problem can be solved.)

DREIHUNDERTVIERZIG

b. This structure corresponds to a passive construction with the modal verb **können:**

Das Problem **kann gelöst werden.** *(The problem can be solved.)*

7. Passive Voice Substitutions (summarized)

The various substitute constructions for German passive constructions show that the same sentence may appear in several different ways:

Das Problem **kann gelöst werden.**

SUBSTITUTE CONSTRUCTIONS:

Das Problem **läßt sich lösen.**
Das Problem **ist zu lösen.**
Das Problem **ist lösbar.**
Man kann das Problem **lösen.**

The problem can be solved.
The problem is solvable.
One can solve the problem.

EXERCISES

A. *Give the various substitution possibilities for the following sentence:* **Diese Methode kann verwendet werden.**

1. construction with **sich lassen**
2. **sein** + **zu** + infinitive
3. **sein** + adjective (suffix **-bar**)
4. active construction with **man**

B. *Give the English equivalents:*

1. Der Lernzweck ist definierbar.
2. Das Resultat ist nicht erklärbar.
3. Das Niveau ist erreichbar.
4. Der Einfluß auf die folgenden Generationen ist bestimmbar.
5. Das heutige Zeitalter ist ohne die Mathematik nicht denkbar.

C. *Give the English equivalents:*

1. Der Magnetismus kann durch die Rotation der Flüssigkeit im Erdinnern erzeugt werden.
2. Der gotische Stil ist an den Spitzbogen der Fenster und Türen erkennbar.
3. War die Lebensauffassung im Zeitalter des Barocks vergleichbar mit der Lebensauffassung des Mittelalters?
4. Konnte der Bürgerkrieg verhindert werden?
5. Die verschiedenen Teilgebiete der Biologie lassen sich trennen.

D. *Use the substitute constructions indicated for the following sentences:*

1. Der Magnetismus kann durch die Rotation erzeugt werden.
   a. construction with **sich lassen**
   b. active construction with **man**

2. Der gotische Stil ist an dem Spitzbogen der Fenster und Türen erkennbar.
   a. construction with **sich lassen**
   b. active construction with **man**
   c. **können** + passive construction
   d. **sein** + **zu** + infinitive
3. War die Lebensauffassung des Barocks vergleichbar mit der des Mittelalters?
   a. construction with **sich lassen**
   b. **sein** + **zu** + infinitive
   c. active construction with **man**
   d. **können** + passive construction
4. Konnte der Bürgerkrieg verhindert werden?
   a. **sein** + **zu** + infinitive
   b. construction with **sich lassen**
   c. construction with **man**
5. Die verschiedenen Teilgebiete der Biologie lassen sich trennen.
   a. construction with **man**
   b. **können** + passive construction
   c. **sein** + adjective (suffix **-bar**)

READING

Studium in Deutschland (3)

Da es mehr Studenten als Studienplätze gibt, hat man an den westdeutschen Universitäten Zulassungsbeschränkungen eingeführt. Dieses System nennt man auch ,,numerus clausus". Es wird nur eine bestimmte Anzahl von Studenten für jede Fachrichtung zugelassen. Die Verteilung geschieht in einer zentralen Stelle, die die Bewerbung eines Studenten prüft. Eine entscheidende Zulassungsbedingung sind   5
die Zensuren vom Gymnasium. Da heute für fast alle Fächer der ,,numerus clausus" besteht, muß der Student gute Zensuren haben, um sofort studieren zu können. Wer keinen Studienplatz bekommt, muß oft lange warten oder kann das gewünschte Fach überhaupt nicht studieren.

   Der Student, der einen Studienplatz bekommen hat, fängt schon im ersten   10
Semester mit dem Fachstudium an. Dennoch kann der Student in vielen Fächern selbst entscheiden, welches Fach er bei welchem Professor studieren will. In einigen Fächern nimmt man dem Studenten auch diese Freiheit, weil Lehrpläne und Zwischenprüfungen einen bestimmten Studienverlauf festlegen. In den Geisteswissenschaften hat der Student an einer westdeutschen Universität gewöhnlich zwölf bis   15
fünfzehn Stunden in der Woche, die er in Vorlesungen, Übungen oder Seminaren zubringt. Unter Seminaren versteht man Arbeitsgruppen, die unter der Leitung eines Professors stattfinden. Im Durchschnitt rechnet man 12 Semester (= 6 Jahre) als Studiumsdauer. Das akademische Jahr dauert etwa sieben Monate. In den Semesterferien bereiten die Studenten Referate vor oder sie lernen für Prüfungen. Viele   20
Studenten arbeiten als Werkstudenten während der Ferien, weil sie Geld für den Le-

bensunterhalt brauchen. Das Studium ist an allen Universitäten und Hochschulen gebührenfrei. Viele deutsche Studenten erhalten aber auch Stipendien von dem Staat.

VOCABULARY

	da	since
die	**Zulassung, -en**	admission
die	**Beschränkung, -en**	limitation
	ein-führen	to introduce
	numerus clausus	*(Latin)* closed numbers *(limited number of students are admitted to each field to study)*
	bestimmt	certain, limited, definite
die	**Richtung, -en**	direction
das	**Fach, ¨er**	subject
die	**Fachrichtung, -en**	field of study, curriculum
	zu-lassen (läßt zu) ließ zu, zugelassen	to admit
die	**Verteilung**	distribution, allotment
	zentral	central
die	**Stelle, -n**	department, office, authority
die	**Bewerbung, -en**	application
	prüfen	to check, test, analyze
die	**Zensur, -en**	grade, mark
	sofort	immediately, right away, at once
	einen Studienplatz bekommen	to be accepted for university study
	lange	for a long time
	warten	to wait
	gewünscht	desired
	überhaupt nicht	not at all
das	**Fachstudium**	major area of study
	dennoch	nevertheless, yet, still
	nehmen (nimmt), nahm, genommen	to take (away)
der	**Lehrplan, ¨e**	curriculum, course of study

die	**Zwischenprüfung, -en**	intermediate examination
der	**Studienverlauf**	course of study, progress in studies
	fest-legen	to determine; to prescribe
die	**Geisteswissenschaften** (pl.)	liberal arts, humanities
	gewöhnlich	usually
die	**Vorlesung, -en**	lecture
die	**Übung, -en**	exercise, laboratory
das	**Seminar, -e**	seminar
	zu-bringen (bringt zu), brachte zu, zugebracht	to spend, pass the time in
	verstehen (versteht), verstand, verstanden	to understand; to mean
die	**Arbeitsgruppe, -n**	work group
die	**Leitung**	direction, leadership
	statt-finden (findet statt), fand statt, stattgefunden	to take place, occur
der	**Durchschnitt**	average
	rechnen	to count, calculate, figure
	vor-bereiten	to prepare
das	**Referat, -e**	report, lecture
der	**Werkstudent, -en**	*student who earns money during semester break*
das	**Geld**	money
der	**Lebensunterhalt**	livelihood, subsistence, living
	brauchen	to need
	gebührenfrei	free of charge, tuition free
das	**Stipendium, Stipendien**	stipend, fellowship, scholarship
der	**Staat**	state, government

STRUCTURAL EXERCISE

Underline all verbs with separable prefixes in the above reading.

VOCABULARY EXERCISE

Give the English equivalents of the italicized words or phrases:

1. *Es wird nur eine bestimmte Anzahl* von Studenten für jede Fachrichtung *zuge-lassen.*
2. Der Student muß gute Zensuren haben, *um sofort studieren zu können.*
3. *Im Durchschnitt* rechnet man 12 Semester als Studiumsdauer.
4. *Wer keinen Studienplatz bekommt,* muß oft lange warten.
5. Während der Ferien arbeiten viele Studenten, *weil sie Geld brauchen.*

Vielfalt, die sich nicht kopieren läßt.

Lesson 31

STRUCTURE

1. Question Word <u>wer</u>

a. **Wer** asks questions about persons, **was** about things (see pages 83–84):

Wer ist die Frau?　**Was braucht er?**
Who is the woman?　*What does he need?*

b. The question word **wer** (nominative) has equivalent forms in the other cases when referring to persons:

NOM.	**wer**	*who*
GEN.	**wessen**	*whose*
DAT.	**wem**	*whom, to whom*
ACC.	**wen**	*whom*

c. Application:

Genitive — possession:　**Wessen Buch ist das?**
Whose book is that?

Dative — indirect object:　**Wem hast du das Buch gegeben?**
To whom did you give the book? Whom did you give the book to?

Accusative — direct object:　**Wen hast du in Berlin gesehen?**
Whom did you see in Berlin?

Object of Preposition:　**An wen hast du gedacht?**
Whom did you think of?

DREIHUNDERTFÜNFUNDVIERZIG

EXERCISES

A. *Give the English equivalents of the question words:*

1. Wessen Buch ist das?
2. Wen hast du gesehen?
3. Auf wen hat sie gewartet?

4. Mit wem hat er gesprochen?
5. Wer hat das Geld geraubt?

B. *Give the case of the question words:*

1. Nach wem hat er gefragt?
2. Wen kennen Sie, Herr Hansen?
3. Wessen Auto steht dort?

4. Für wen hat sie gearbeitet?
5. Wer war in dem Labor?

C. *Give the English equivalents:*

1. Wer hat ihn gesehen?
2. Wen hat er gesehen?
3. Wessen Vater ist in Deutschland?
4. Mit wem spielt das Kind?
5. Wem wollte sie helfen?

2. Wo-Compounds

a. The question word **wer** and its other forms **(wessen, wem, wen)** are used to introduce questions about persons.

b. The question words **wem** and **wen** usually function as objects of the verb:

Wem hat er es gesagt?   (dative verb)
To whom did he say it?
Wen hast du gesehen?   (accusative verb)
Whom did you see?

c. They also may be used as objects of prepositions in questions about persons:

Nach wem hat er gefragt?   (dative preposition)
Whom did he ask about?
Auf wen hast du gewartet?   (preposition requiring accusative)
Whom did you wait for?

d. If the object of the preposition is a thing, a **wo**-compound is used. **Wo**-compounds are formed by combining **wo** with a preposition:

Wonach hat er gefragt?   **Worauf** hat er gewartet?
What did he ask about?   *What did he wait for?*

DREIHUNDERTSECHSUNDVIERZIG

e. Compare questions about persons and questions about things:

PERSONS	THINGS
Nach wem hat er gefragt? (Preposition + form of **wer**)	**Wonach** hat er gefragt? (**Wo** + preposition)

f. **Wo** is used with prepositions beginning with consonants:

womit   **wonach**   **wobei**   **wofür**

g. **Wor** is used with prepositions beginning with vowels:

worüber   **woraus**   **woran**   **worauf**

h. **Wer**-clauses may also function as subordinate clauses:

Wer ist das?   (independent clause)
Wissen Sie, **wer das ist?**   (subordinate clause: subordinate word order)

i. **Was** and **wo**-clauses also function as subordinate clauses:

Er wußte nicht, **was er sagte.**
He didn't know what he was saying.
Wissen Sie, **wonach er gefragt hat?**
Do you know what he asked about?

SELF-PREPARATORY EXERCISES

A. *Supply the correct form of the question word:*

Nach _____ hat er gefragt? *(whom)*	
Auf _____ wartet er? *(whom)*	Nach wem hat er gefragt?
An _____ denkst du? *(whom)*	Auf wen wartet er?
Mit _____ geht er aus? *(whom)*	An wen denkst du?
Für _____ arbeitet er? *(whom)*	Mit wem geht er aus?
	Für wen arbeitet er?

B. *Supply the correct form of the* **wo**-*compound:*

_____ wartet er? *(for what)*	
_____ hat er gefragt? *(about what)*	Worauf wartet er?
_____ denkt er? *(about what)*	Wonach hat er gefragt?
_____ spricht er? *(about what)*	Woran denkt er?
	Worüber spricht er?

EXERCISES

A. *Supply the correct form of the question word* **wer** *or the* **wo**-*compound:*

1. Ich weiß, _____ der Lehrer ist. *(who)*
2. _____ geht das deutsche Universitätssystem zurück? *(to what)* (auf)
3. _____ kann man Salze und Laugen erkennen? *(by what)* (an)
4. _____ Uhr liegt dort? *(whose)*
5. _____ kommt der Halogenwasserstoff zustande? *(through what)* (durch)

B. *Give the English equivalents:*

1. Woran kann sich Mackie Messer nicht erinnern?
2. Wodurch wurde die Handelsbilanz ausgeglichen?
3. Mit wem will sie nach New York fahren?
4. Wonach suchen die Wissenschaftler im Weltall?
5. Woran hat Schliemann mitgewirkt?

READING

Bank

Bank ist ein Wort, das aus dem Italienischen stammt. Es bedeutete ursprünglich Sitzbank oder Ladentisch. Heute versteht man darunter auch:

1. ein Unternehmen, das Geldeinlagen gegen Zinsen übernimmt, Geld gegen
   Zinsen ausleiht (Kredit), Geldwechsel und Zahlungsverkehr betreibt, Wertpapiere und ausländisches Geld für seine Kunden an- und verkauft sowie   5
   Wertgegenstände im Safe aufbewahrt;
2. eine Sand- oder Gesteinsablagerung, angeschwemmt durch die Strömung, im
   Meer oder in Flüssen;
3. eine Spielbank. In Spielbanken kann man an Glücksspielen, wie Roulett oder
   Poker usw., teilnehmen und dabei versuchen, sein eingesetztes Geld zu verviel-   10
   fachen. Auf die Dauer gewinnt jedoch stets die Spielbank.

DREIHUNDERTACHTUNDVIERZIG

VOCABULARY

die	**Bank, -en**	bank
	stammen	to come from, originate
	ursprünglich	originally
die	**Sitzbank, ⸚e**	bench, seat
der	**Tisch, -e**	table
der	**Ladentisch, -e**	counter
das	**Unternehmen**	enterprise, undertaking, company
die	**Einlage, -n**	deposit, investment
der	**Zins, -en**	interest
	übernehmen (übernimmt), übernahm, übernommen	to accept, receive
	aus-leihen (leiht aus), lieh aus, ausgeliehen	to loan
der	**Kredit, -e**	credit, loan
der	**Geldwechsel**	monetary exchange
der	**Zahlungsverkehr**	financial transaction
	betreiben (betreibt), betrieb, betrieben	to manage; to carry on, pursue

das	**Wertpapier, -e**	share, bond, security
	ausländisch	foreign
der	**Kunde, -n**	customer
	an-kaufen	to buy (up)
	verkaufen	to sell
die	**Wertgegenstände** (pl.)	valuables, precious objects
der	**Safe**	vault
	auf-bewahren	to keep, store
der	**Sand**	sand
das	**Gestein**	rock(s)
die	**Ablagerung, -en**	deposit
	angeschwemmt (durch)	washed up (by)
die	**Spielbank, -en**	gambling casino
das	**Glücksspiel, -e**	game of chance
	usw. (und so weiter)	etc.
	eingesetzt	wagered, bet
	vervielfachen	to multiply, increase
	auf die Dauer	in the long run
	gewinnen (gewinnt), gewann, gewonnen	to win; to gain
	stets	always

STRUCTURE

3. Imperatives

a. German employs three command forms:

INFINITIVE: **vergessen** *(to forget)*

du-form: **Vergiß** das nicht, Richard!
ihr-form: **Vergeßt** das nicht, Hermann und Dorothea!
Sie-form: **Vergessen Sie** das nicht, Herr Schmidt!

All commands are followed by an exclamation mark (**!**).

b. **du**-form

The verb stem is used for the **du** command form. The present-tense vowel shifts (except for umlauts) also occur in the imperative. Verbs with stems ending in **-d** or **-t** add **-e**:

vergiß!	*(forget)*	**schlaf!**	*(sleep)*	**warte!**	*(wait)*
lies!	*(read)*	**fahr!**	*(drive)*	**antworte!**	*(answer)*
komm!	*(come)*				

c.   **ihr**-form

The **ihr**-form of the imperative is the same as the **ihr**-form of the present tense:

vergeßt!	*(forget)*	**kommt!**	*(come)*
lest!	*(read)*	**schlaft!**	*(sleep)*

d.   **Sie**-form

The infinitive comes first and is followed by the pronoun **Sie:**

Kommen Sie mit, Frau Braun! *(Come along, Mrs. Braun.)*
Bleiben Sie in Kalifornien, Herr Niessen! *(Stay in California, Mr. Niessen.)*

SELF-PREPARATORY EXERCISE

Supply the imperative forms:

_____ es nicht, Herr Schmidt! (vergessen)	
_____ zu Hause, Richard! (bleiben)	Vergessen Sie es nicht, Herr Schmidt!
_____ gut, Kinder! (schlafen)	Bleib zu Hause, Richard!
_____ den Text, Studenten! (lesen)	Schlaft gut, Kinder!
_____ ein gutes Buch, Christa! (lesen)	Lest den Text, Studenten!
	Lies ein gutes Buch, Christa!

EXERCISES

A.   Use the elements given to form commands:*

1. vergessen / es / nicht / Georg
2. gehen / nach Hause / Kinder
3. geben / mir / das Buch / Johann
4. kaufen / nicht zu viel / Kinder
5. schlafen / gut / Hans und Inge

B.   Give the English equivalents:

1. Kommen Sie mit, Herr Braun!
2. Bleibt in Kalifornien!
3. Mach das nicht, Heinrich!
4. Frag den Chef!
5. Arbeitet!

DREIHUNDERTFÜNFZIG

READING

Zitat ohne Kommentar: Die NSDAP als einzige Partei

Wer es unternimmt, den organisatorischen Zusammenhalt einer anderen politischen Partei aufrechtzuerhalten oder eine neue politische Partei zu bilden, wird, sofern nicht die Tat nach anderen Vorschriften mit einer höheren Strafe bedroht ist, mit Zuchthaus bis zu drei Jahren oder mit Gefängnis von sechs Monaten bis zu drei Jahren bestraft. (Gesetz gegen die Neubildung von Parteien vom 14. Juli 1933)

VOCABULARY

das **Zit<u>at</u>, -e**	quote, quotation	die **Vorschrift, -en**	rule, order, regulation
der **Kommen<u>ta</u>r, -e**	commentary	
einzig	sole, only	die **Strafe, -n**	punishment, penalty
organisat<u>o</u>risch	organizational	
der **Zusammenhalt**	unity, cohesiveness	das **Zuchthaus, ˸er**	penitentiary
aufrecht-erhalten	to maintain, to	das **Gefängnis, -se**	prison
(erhält aufrecht),	preserve	**bestrafen**	to punish
erhielt aufrecht,		das **Gesetz, -e**	law
aufrechterhalten		die **Neubildung, -en**	new formation, new establishment
sof<u>e</u>rn	as far as	
die **Tat, -en**	action, deed, act	

das **Zit<u>at</u>, -e** — quote, quotation
der **Kommen<u>ta</u>r, -e** — commentary
einzig — sole, only
organisat<u>o</u>risch — organizational
der **Zusammenhalt** — unity, cohesiveness
aufrecht-erhalten (erhält aufrecht), erhielt aufrecht, aufrechterhalten — to maintain, to preserve
sof<u>e</u>rn — as far as
die **Tat, -en** — action, deed, act

die **Vorschrift, -en** — rule, order, regulation
die **Strafe, -n** — punishment, penalty
das **Zuchthaus, ˸er** — penitentiary
das **Gefängnis, -se** — prison
bestrafen — to punish
das **Gesetz, -e** — law
die **Neubildung, -en** — new formation, new establishment

STRUCTURE

4. Weak Nouns

a.   Some German nouns end in **-en** or **-n** in singular cases (except for the nominative) as well as in all plural cases. These nouns are called weak nouns:

	SINGULAR	PLURAL
NOM.	der Mensch	die Menschen
GEN.	des Menschen	der Menschen
DAT.	dem Menschen	den Menschen
ACC.	den Menschen	die Menschen

b.   Other weak nouns are:

der Student	*student*	**der Soldat**	*soldier*
der Junge	*boy*	**der Kunde**	*customer*
der Patient	*patient*	**der Geselle**	*companion, journeyman*
der Polizist	*policeman*	**der Diplomat**	*diplomat*

DREIHUNDERTZWEIUNDFÜNFZIG

c.   Exception:

der Herr   *gentleman, mister, sir*

	SINGULAR	PLURAL
NOM.	der Herr	die Herren
GEN.	des Herrn	der Herren
DAT.	dem Herrn	den Herren
ACC.	den Herrn	die Herren

SINGULAR: add **-n** (except for nominative)
PLURAL: add **-en**

EXERCISES

A.   *Complete the sentences in accordance with the cues:*

1. Wo ist d_____ Student?   *(Where's the student?)*
2. Wo sind d_____ Studenten?   *(Where are the students?)*
3. Zeig es d_____ Soldat_____!   *(Show it to the soldiers.)*
4. Ich sehe k_____ Polizist_____.   *(I don't see any policeman.)*
5. Gib es d_____ Herr_____!   *(Give it to the gentlemen.)*

B.   *Give the plural forms of the definite articles and nouns, changing verb forms when required:**

1. Wo ist der Junge?   4. Siehst du den Polizisten?
2. Der Student arbeitet wenig.   5. Der Junge läuft schnell.
3. Gib es dem Herrn!

5. Dates

a.   Ordinal numbers are used for giving dates in German:

Heute ist **der fünfundzwanzigste Juni.** *(Today is the 25th of June.)*

b.   Ordinal numbers add adjective endings depending on the case in which they are used:

Am 25. Juni: Am fünfundzwanzigsten Juni

Note that the date in numerals is always followed by a period to indicate the use of an ordinal number.

c.   There are two ways to ask for the date:

Der wievielte ist heute?   **Heute ist der zehnte Mai.**
What day is today?   *Today is May 10th.*

Den wievielten haben wir heute?   **Heute haben wir den 31. Januar.**
What is the date today?   *Today is January 31st.*

d.   The date on letters is usually written this way:

Hamburg, den 17. September 1979

e.   Examples of other uses of dates:

Herr Mahler wurde am 18. 5. 1923 geboren.
(Herr Mahler wurde am achtzehnten, fünften, neunzehnhundertdreiund-
  zwanzig geboren.)
Mr. Mahler was born on May 18, 1923.

Ich bestätige Ihren Brief vom 6. April.
I am confirming your letter of April 6.

EXERCISE

Write out the following dates:

1.   Heute ist der 12. 4. 1982.
2.   Mein Freund kommt am 29. August.
3.   Die Bank verkaufte die Wertpapiere am 13. 3. 1967.
4.   München, den 31. März, 1888.
5.   Am wievielten will dein Bruder kommen? — Er will am 26. hier sein.

READING

Die Deutsche Demokratische Republik (DDR)

Als Folge des 2. (zweiten) Weltkrieges entstanden auf dem Gebiet des früheren
Deutschen Reiches zwei neue Staaten. Im Westen kam die Bundesrepublik Deutschland zustande, im Osten die Deutsche Demokratische Republik. Beide Staaten gingen
aus ehemaligen Besatzungszonen hervor. Die Bundesrepublik bestand nach 1945
zunächst aus drei Besatzungszonen (amerikanische, britische und französische   5
Zone). Die Deutsche Demokratische Republik entstand auf dem Gebiet der früheren
russischen Besatzungszone.
  Auf Betreiben der Sowjetunion errichtete die SED (Sozialistische Einheitspartei
Deutschlands) im Jahre 1949 die DDR. Die SED ist die Staatspartei der DDR und
besteht seit 1946, als man die SPD (Sozialdemokratische Partei Deutschlands) und   10
die KPD (Kommunistische Partei Deutschlands) in der neuen SED vereinigte. Die
DDR besteht heute aus 14 Landesbezirken, die aus den früheren Ländern Brandenburg, Mecklenburg, Sachsen-Anhalt, Thüringen und Sachsen entstanden. In der
DDR wohnen heute rund 17 Millionen Einwohner auf einer Fläche von ungefähr
108 000 km² (Quadratkilometer).   15

Die Verfassung der DDR kennt nur das Primat der Gemeinschaft, nicht dagegen die
Freiheit des einzelnen um des einzelnen willen. Das Parlament, die Volkskammer,
hat 400 Abgeordnete. Es beschließt Gesetze, wählt und entläßt die Mitglieder des
Obersten Gerichtshofes und den Generalstaatsanwalt und bestellt und entläßt die
Regierung. Die Regierung der DDR, der Ministerrat, arbeitet nach dem Prinzip des   20
„Demokratischen Zentralismus", d.h., daß alle untergeordneten Organe an die
Weisungen des Ministerrats gebunden sind. Besonders offensichtlich treten die
zentralistischen Tendenzen in der Wirtschaftsverwaltung hervor, wo der Volkswirtschaftsrat und die Plankommission seit 1961 eine straffe Kontrolle ausüben. Alle
staatliche Verwaltung unterliegt der Lenkung und Kontrolle durch die SED. Die   25
größte Zahl der Produktionseinrichtungen sind im Besitz des Staates. Die DDR ist
Mitglied der COMECON (Council for Mutual Economic Aid) und damit in die Wirtschaft des gesamten Ostblocks eingegliedert. Der größte Teil der Landwirtschaft
besteht aus staatlichen Produktionsgenossenschaften. Auch der Groß- und
Einzelhandel gehört zum großen Teil der staatlichen Handelsorganisation an. Die in-   30
dustriellen Betriebe sind meistens sogenannte „Volkseigene Betriebe" (VEB), die
der Staat kontrolliert. Das Erziehungs- und Ausbildungssystem der DDR besteht aus
allgemeinen polytechnischen Oberschulen (10 Jahre), erweiterten polytechnischen
Oberschulen (12 Jahre), Sonderschulen für körperlich benachteiligte Kinder, Fachschulen, Hochschulen und Universitäten. Die Absolventen der erweiterten Ober-   35
schule müssen während der Schulzeit einen praktischen Beruf lernen oder vor dem
Studium ein einjähriges Praktikum ableisten.

VOCABULARY

zustande-kommen (kommt zustande), kam zustande, ist zustande-gekommen	to come about, come into being	vereinigen	to unite, to unify
		der Landesbezirk, -e	district (of the state)
hervor-gehen (geht hervor), ging hervor, ist hervor-gegangen (aus)	to result; to proceed (from)	Sachsen	Saxony
		Thüringen	Thuringia
		wohnen	to live
		ungefähr	approximately, about
ehemalig	former, previous	das Primat	primacy
		die Gemeinschaft	community
		dagegen	on the other hand
entstehen (entsteht), entstand, ist entstanden	to arise, originate	um des einzelnen willen	for the sake of the individual
		die Volkskammer	peoples' chamber, house of peoples' representatives
das Betreiben	urging, instigation		
errichten	to establish	beschließen (beschließt), beschloß, beschlossen	to determine, decide
bestehen (besteht), bestand, bestanden	to exist		
bestehen (aus)	to consist (of)	wählen	to elect

DREIHUNDERTEINUNDFÜNFZIG

	entlassen (entläßt), entließ, entlassen	to release, dismiss	
das	Mitglied, -er	member	
der	Oberste Gerichtshof	highest court	
der	Staatsanwalt, ⁻e	public prosecutor	
	bestellen	to appoint	
der	Ministerrat	cabinet counsel	
der	Zentralismus	centralism	
	untergeordnet	subordinate	
die	Weisung, -en	direction, order	
	hervor-treten (tritt hervor), trat hervor, ist hervorgetreten	to appear, come forth	
	offensichtlich	obvious	
	zentralistisch	centralist	
die	Tendenz, -en	tendency, propensity, inclination	
der	Volkswirtschaftsrat	peoples' economic council	
die	Plankommission	planning commission	
	straff	strict, tight	
	aus-üben	to exercise, exert, carry out	

	unterliegen (unterliegt), unterlag, unterlegen	to be subordinate to
die	Lenkung	direction, control, guidance
die	Kontrolle, -n	supervision, control
die	Einrichtung, -en	institution
der	Besitz	possession
	ein-gliedern	to incorporate
die	Genossenschaft, -en	cooperative
der	Großhandel	wholesale trade
der	Einzelhandel	retail business
der	Betrieb, -e	factory, industry, works
	volkseigen	owned by the people
	erweitern	to expand
	erweitert	expanded
	sonder-	special
	körperlich	physically
	benachteiligt	handicapped
die	Fachschule, -n	technical school, trade school
der	Absolvent, -en	graduate
das	Praktikum	practical work
	ab-leisten	to serve, pass

STRUCTURAL EXERCISE

Underline all verbs with separable prefixes in the above reading.

VOCABULARY EXERCISE

Give the English equivalents of the italicized words or phrases:

1. Zwei neue Staaten entstanden *auf dem Gebiet des früheren Deutschen Reiches.*
2. *Die Bundesrepublik bestand zunächst aus* drei Besatzungszonen.
3. Siebzehn Millionen Einwohner *wohnen auf einer Fläche von* 108 000 km².
4. Wer es unternimmt, *eine neue Partei zu bilden,* wird bestraft.
5. *Bank ist ein Wort,* das aus dem Italienischen stammt.

Bevor Sie kaufen, prüfen Sie Angebote.

esson 32

STRUCTURE

1. Comparative and Superlative

a. The German word **laut** may function in three different ways:

1. As an adverb modifying a verb:

   Der Pastor spricht **laut.** *(The pastor speaks loudly.)*

   Here **laut** describes the manner of the pastor's speaking, that is, it modifies the verb **sprechen** and not the noun subject **der Pastor.**

2. As a predicate adjective:

   Die Musik ist **laut.** *(The music is loud.)*

   The predicate adjective modifies the subject and is separated from the subject by a verb (usually **sein**). A predicate adjective has no endings.

3. As an attributive adjective:

   Das ist ein **lautes** Instrument. *(That's a loud [noisy] instrument.)*

   An attributive adjective also modifies a noun, but it stands directly before that noun and takes the usual adjective endings.

b. In English and German, there are three levels of comparison for adjectives and adverbs:

POSITIVE:	*large*	basic, dictionary form
COMPARATIVE:	*larger*	compares two unlike objects
SUPERLATIVE:	*largest*	maximum level of comparison

Examples:

POSITIVE: This tree is large.
COMPARATIVE: This tree is larger (than that tree).
SUPERLATIVE: This tree is largest (of all trees).

English adds **-er** and **-est** (or *more* or *most* when the adjective is of two or more syllables) to form the comparative and superlative.

c.   German adds **-er** to form the comparative and **-st** to form the superlative:

POSITIVE:	**billig**	*inexpensive, cheap*
COMPARATIVE:	**billiger**	*cheaper*
SUPERLATIVE:	**billigst**	*(the) cheapest*

d.   Attributive adjectives (before a noun) take the appropriate adjective endings:

Er hat das **billige** Buch.   *(He has the cheap book.)*
Er hat das **billigere** Buch.   *(He has the cheaper book.)*
Er hat das **billigste** Buch.   *(He has the cheapest book.)*

e.   In the superlative forms of predicate adjectives and adverbs, German adds the following: **am** + adjective + **-sten**:

am billigsten *(the cheapest)*

Example of a predicate adjective in the positive, comparative, and superlative:

Dieser Wein ist **billig.**   (Positive)
This wine is cheap.

Dieser Wein ist **billiger.**   (Comparative)
This wine is cheaper.

Dieser Wein ist **am billigsten.**   (Superlative)
This wine is the cheapest.

SELF-PREPARATORY EXERCISE

Give the comparative and superlative forms of the following predicate adjectives and adverbs:*

schnell *(fast)*	
klein *(small)*	schneller, am schnellsten
dick *(thick, heavy)*	kleiner, am kleinsten
einfach *(simple)*	dicker, am dicksten
freundlich *(friendly)*	einfacher, am einfachsten
	freundlicher, am freundlichsten

EXERCISES

A. *Give the comparative forms:**

    1. unendlich   3. glücklich   5. reich
    2. anständig   4. wichtig

B. *Give the superlative forms (use* **am** + *adjective* + **-sten***):**

    1. hell   3. riesig   5. mächtig
    2. flach   4. langsam

READING

Wie entsteht Deflation?

Die Ursachen einer Deflation können aus dem Zusammenwirken vieler Verhaltensweisen hervorgehen, ohne daß jemand die Deflation will.

   Die Störungen im Verhältnis von Gesamtangebot in Gütern und Gesamtnachfrage
in Geld können von beiden Seiten ausgehen. Das Güterangebot kann durch
Steigerungen der Produktivität, durch plötzliches Angebot großer Warenbestände
aus staatlichen Vorräten, etwa bei einer Demobilisierung, und aus anderen Gründen   5
ansteigen. Die Gesamtnachfrage kann z.B. nachlassen, wenn die Konsumenten ihre
Ausgaben einschränken; wenn die Banken ihr Kreditvolumen einschränken, und aus
anderen Gründen. Gewöhnlich wirken mehrere Ursachen zusammen.

VOCABULARY

entstehen (entsteht), entstand ist entstanden	to arise, originate	aus-gehen (geht aus), ging aus, ist ausgegangen (von)	to start, proceed (from)
die **Deflation**	deflation	an-steigen (steigt an), stieg an, ist angestiegen (durch)	to rise, climb; to increase (because of)
das **Zusammenwirken**	working together, acting together		
		die **Steigerung**	increase
		die **Produktivität**	productivity
die **Ursache, -n**	cause	**plötzlich**	suddenly
ohne daß	without + (verb + -ing)	die **Ware, -n**	goods, articles, commodity
ohne daß . . . will	without anyone wanting the deflation	der **Bestand, ⁀e**	stock, supply
		der **Vorrat, ⁀e**	reserve
die **Störung**	disturbance, disruption	die **Demobilisierung**	demobilization
		nach-lassen (läßt nach), ließ nach, nachgelassen	to decrease, let up
gesamt	total, entire		
das **Angebot, -e**	supply, offer		
die **Güter** (pl.)	goods	der **Konsument, -en** (weak noun)	consumer, user
die **Nachfrage**	demand		
die **Seite, -n**	side		

DREIHUNDERTACHTUNDFÜNFZIG

die **Ausgabe, -n**	expenses, out-lay, expend-iture	**gewöhnlich**	usually
		zusammen-wirken	to work to-gether, act to-gether
ein-schränken	to limit, cut back		
das **Volumen**	volume, ca-pacity		

STRUCTURAL EXERCISE

Underline all verbs with separable prefixes in the above reading.

VOCABULARY EXERCISE

Give the English equivalents of the italicized words or phrases:

1. *Das Güterangebot kann durch Steigerung der Produktivität ansteigen.*
2. *Die Gesamtnachfrage kann nachlassen.*
3. *Gewöhnlich wirken mehrere Ursachen zusammen.*
4. Eine Deflation kann entstehen, *ohne daß jemand die Deflation will.*
5. Die Ursachen einer Deflation *können aus dem Zusammenwirken vieler Verhaltensweisen hervorgehen.*

STRUCTURE

2. Comparative and Superlative (continued)

a. Adjectives ending in **-e** add only **-r** in the comparative:

POSITIVE: **leise** *(soft)*
COMPARATIVE: **leiser**
SUPERLATIVE: **(am) leisest(en)**

b. Adjectives ending in **-el** drop the **-e-** in the comparative:

POSITIVE: **dunkel** *(dark)*
COMPARATIVE: **dunkler**
SUPERLATIVE: **(am) dunkelst(en)**

c. Adjectives ending in **-d, -t,** or **-s**-sounds (**s, ß, ss, tz, z**) add an additional **-e** before the **-st** in the superlative:

POSITIVE: **laut** *(loud)*
COMPARATIVE: **lauter**
SUPERLATIVE: **(am) lautest(en)**

d.   Forms of **hoch-**

The adjective **hoch** *(high, tall)* has two stems — **hoch** and **hoh-**. These stems are used in the following way:

	ATTRIBUTIVE ADJECTIVE	PREDICATE ADJECTIVE	ADVERB
POSITIVE	**hoh-**	**hoch**	**hoch**
COMPARATIVE	**höher-**	**höher**	**höher**
SUPERLATIVE	**höchst-**	**am höchsten**	**am höchsten**

Examples:

Der **hohe** Berg.   (attributive adjective)
The high mountain.

Der Berg ist **hoch.**   (predicate adjective)
The mountain is high.

Das Flugzeug fliegt **hoch.**   (adverb)
The airplane is flying high.

e.   Irregular forms

groß   *(big, tall)*
größer
(am) größt(en)

gut   *(good)*
besser
(am) best(en)

viel   *(many, a lot)*
mehr
(am) meist(en)

gern   *(to like)* (used adverbially)
lieber   *(to prefer)* (used adverbially)
(am) liebst(en)   *(to like best [of all])*

Examples:

Der Karpfen frißt **gern** Würmer. *(The carp likes to eat worms.)*
Sie spielt **lieber** Tennis. *(She prefers to play tennis.)*
Er trinkt **am liebsten** Wein. *(He likes to drink wine best of all.)*

EXERCISES

A.   *Give the comparative forms:* *

   1.   bekannt   3.   groß   5.   hoch
   2.   rasch   4.   gut

DREIHUNDERTSECHZIG

B. *Give the superlative forms (use **am** . . .):**
1. wenig   3. groß   5. gern
2. dunkel   4. viel

C. *Give the English equivalents of the following sentences:*
1. Das höchste Gebäude der Welt steht in New York.
2. Kalifornien hat das beste Klima.
3. Die meisten Häuser in Deutschland sind aus Stein.
4. Er trinkt Bier am liebsten.
5. Die Ernte erzielte höhere Preise.

D. *Change the adjectives or adverbs to superlative:**
1. Das Buch ist interessant.
2. Das Studium der Biologie ist leicht.
3. Die Erträge waren niedrig.
4. Dieser Stein wiegt mehr.
5. Die Wassertemperatur war kühl.

READING

Wie entsteht Deflation? (2)

Die einzelnen Ursachen können sich wechselseitig steigern und damit kumulativ
wirken: fehlende Nachfrage läßt die Preise sinken. Sinkende Preise veranlassen die
Unternehmer, mit Investitionen zurückzuhalten. Die Unternehmen können bei den
sinkenden Preisen Verluste erleiden; sie müssen Arbeitskräfte entlassen. Da die
Einkommen der Entlassenen stark zurückgehen, sinkt die Gesamtnachfrage nun erst   5
recht. So kann Deflation in einem circulus vitiosus wie in den Jahren 1929 bis 1932
zu Massenarbeitslosigkeit und schwerster Wirtschaftskrise führen.

   Die Krise hat Hitlers Aufstieg zur Macht begünstigt und insofern mittelbar
schließlich den Zweiten Weltkrieg herbeigeführt. Ihre vielfältigen Ursachen wurden
damals nicht durchschaut. Deshalb wirkten die staatlichen Maßnahmen zum großen   10
Teil verschlimmernd statt heilend. Erst von 1932 ab erkannte man, daß den Konsumenten neue Kaufkraft zugeführt werden muß, z.B. durch staatliche Arbeitsbeschaf-
fung, um die Deflation zu überwinden, und handelte nach dieser Erkenntnis. Die
heutige Wirtschaftspolitik hat aus den damaligen Erfahrungen gelernt und versucht,
schon bei den ersten Anzeichen einer Krise durch gezielte staatliche Maßnahmen   15
Nachfrage und Konjunktur zu beleben.

VOCABULARY

wechselseitig	reciprocally, mutually	**damit**	thereby
sich steigern	to increase, mount	**kumulativ**	cumulative
		wirken	to act; to work; to operate

	fehlen	to lack, miss		mittelbar	indirectly
	fehlend	lacking		schließlich	finally, ulti-
	sinkend	sinking			mately
	veranlassen	to cause	der	Zweite Weltkrieg	Second World
der	Unternehmer, -	entrepreneur,			War
		factory		herbei-führen	to cause, bring
		owner			about
die	Investition, -en	investment		vielfältig	various, mani-
	zurück-halten	to hold back,			fold
	(hält zurück),	curb		durchschauen	to see through,
	hielt zurück,				understand, grasp
	zurückgehalten		die	Maßnahmen (pl.)	measure(s)
der	Verlust, -e	loss		verschlimmern	to worsen,
	erleiden (erleidet),				aggravate
	erlitt, erlitten	to suffer		heilen	to heal
die	Arbeitskräfte (pl.)	work force, labor,		erst	only, not until
		workers		von . . . ab	beginning with
	entlassen (entläßt),	to release, dis-	die	Kaufkraft, ⸚e	buying power,
	entließ, entlassen	charge			purchasing
das	Einkommen, -	income			power
der	Entlassene, -n	released or		zu-führen	to give, pro-
		discharged			cure
		person	die	Beschaffung	procurement,
	zurück-gehen,	to decline,			providing
	(geht zurück),	diminish		überwinden	
	ging zurück, ist			(überwindet),	
	zurückgegangen			überwand,	
	nun	now		überwunden	to overcome
	erst recht	more than ever,		handeln (nach)	to act (accord-
		all the			ing to)
		more	die	Erkenntnis, -se	knowledge
	circulus vitiosus	(Latin) vicious	das	Anzeichen, -	sign, indication,
		circle			symptom
die	Masse, -n	mass		gezielt	directed, aimed,
die	Arbeitslosigkeit	unemployment			special
	arbeitslos	unemployed	die	Konjunktur	state of business,
die	Krise, -n	crisis			boom
die	Wirtschaftskrise, -n	economic crisis		beleben	to revive, in-
	begünstigen	to favor; to help			vigorate
	insofern	insofar, to that			
		extent			

STRUCTURAL EXERCISE

Underline all infinitive phrases with **zu** in the above reading.

VOCABULARY EXERCISE

Give the English equivalents of the italicized words or phrases:

1. *Fehlende Nachfrage läßt die Preise sinken.*
2. *Die einzelnen Ursachen können sich wechselseitig steigern.*
3. Die Unternehmer *müssen Arbeitskräfte entlassen.*

DREIHUNDERTZWEIUNDSECHZIG

4. *Da die Einkommen der Entlassenen stark zurückgehen, sinkt die Gesamt-nachfrage.*

5. *So kann Deflation zu einer schweren Wirtschaftskrise führen.*

STRUCTURE

3. Comparative and Superlative (continued)

Most one-syllable adjectives with stem vowels **a** and **u** add umlaut in the comparative and superlative forms:

POSITIVE: **alt**
COMPARATIVE: **älter**
SUPERLATIVE: **(am) ältest(en)**

SELF-PREPARATORY EXERCISE

*Give the comparative and superlative forms:**

alt	
jung	älter, am ältesten
stark	jünger, am jüngsten
lang	stärker, am stärksten
kurz	länger, am längsten
warm	kürzer, am kürzesten
	wärmer, am wärmsten

jung = young

EXERCISES

A. *Give the comparative forms:**

1. jung   3. warm   5. lang
2. kalt   4. alt

B. *Give the superlative forms (use* **am** *+ adjective +* **-sten***):**

1. kurz   3. lang   5. stark
2. alt   4. jung

C. *Change the following sentences to comparative:**

1. Das Mädchen ist jung.
2. Der Winter war kalt.
3. Die Nacht war kurz.
4. Das Wasser ist warm.
5. Die Straße ist lang.

D. *Give the English equivalents of the following sentences:*

1. Seine Haare sind am kürzesten.
2. Ihr Bruder ist am jüngsten.
3. Das Studium der Chemie dauert am längsten.
4. Im Sommer ist es am wärmsten in Europa.
5. Wann war es am kältesten?

READING

Logarithmen

Der Logarithmus ist der Exponent (n), mit dem man die Basis (a) potenziert, um den Numerus (b) zu erhalten. Man kann als Basis außer 0 und 1 jede Zahl verwenden; die Wissenschaft verwendet die sogenannten „natürlichen" Logarithmen mit der Basis e, Abkürzung ln; für praktische Rechnungen benutzt man die „dekadischen" Logarithmen (Zehnerlogarithmen); sie heißen auch gewöhnliche oder „Briggsche Logarithmen". Sie haben die Basis 10 und sind in den Logarithmentafeln zusammengestellt. Um die Schreibweise zu vereinfachen, läßt man die Basis 10 weg und kürzt meist lg ab.

$$\log_a b = n$$

a = Logarithmenbasis
b = Numerus
n = Logarithmus

5

10

VOCABULARY

der **Logarithmus, Logarithmen**	logarithm	**Briggsche**	Brigg's *(name used as adjective)*
der **Exponent, -en** *(weak noun)*	exponent	die **Tafel, -n**	table, board
die **Basis**	base	**zusammen-stellen**	to compile, put together
potenzieren	to raise to higher power	die **Schreibweise**	writing, style
der **Numerus**	number, antilogarithm	**weg-lassen (läßt weg), ließ weg, weggelassen**	to leave off, eliminate
die **Abkürzung, -en**	abbreviation	**ab-kürzen**	to abbreviate, shorten
praktisch	practical		
dekadisch	decade	**meist**	generally, usually
der **Zehnerlogarithmus, . . .men**	base ten logarithm		

STRUCTURAL EXERCISE

Underline all infinitive phrases using the **zu**.

VOCABULARY EXERCISE

Give the English equivalents of the italicized words or phrases:

1. Der Logarithmus ist der Exponent, *mit dem* man die Basis potenziert.

DREIHUNDERTVIERUNDSECHZIG

2. Die „Briggschen Logarithmen" *sind* in den Logarithmentafeln *zusammengestellt.*
3. Man *läßt* die Basis 10 *weg* und *kürzt* meist lg *ab.*

STRUCTURE

4. Attributive Adjectives

a. Predicate adjectives and adverbs take the following comparative and superlative endings:

POSITIVE:	**-**	**klein**
COMPARATIVE:	**-er**	**kleiner**
SUPERLATIVE:	**-(e)st**	**am kleinsten**

b. Attributive adjectives (before a noun) take the appropriate adjective endings:

POSITIVE: **klein( )**
COMPARATIVE: **kleiner( )**
SUPERLATIVE: **kleinst( )**

Examples:

POSITIVE: Das ist der **kleine** Wagen.
COMPARATIVE: Das ist der **kleinere** Wagen.
SUPERLATIVE: Das ist der **kleinste** Wagen.

SELF-PREPARATORY EXERCISE

Give the comparative and superlative forms of the following attributive adjectives:*

die kleine Wohnung	
die alte Frau	die kleinere Wohnung die kleinste Wohnung
das große Kind	die ältere Frau die älteste Frau
der neue Wagen	das größere Kind das größte Kind
mit dem neuen Wagen	der neuere Wagen der neueste Wagen
für den alten Mann	mit dem neueren Wagen mit dem neuesten Wagen
	für den älteren Mann für den ältesten Mann

EXERCISES

A. *Supply the correct form of the adjective:*

    1. Er ist mein _____ Freund. *(best)*
    2. Es ist das _____ Haus. *(oldest)*
    3. Haben Sie keine _____ Bücher? *(cheaper)*
    4. Das ist seine _____ Schwester. *(younger)*
    5. Er trinkt nur _____ Bier. *(cold)*

B. *Give the English equivalents of the following sentences:*

    1. Die höchsten Berge sind in den Alpen.
    2. Wie heißt Ihre jüngste Tochter, Frau Robinson?
    3. Die romanische Kirche hat die stärksten Mauern.
    4. Afrika ist der drittgrößte Erdteil.
    5. Der meiste Schnee fällt in den Gebirgen.

READING
Logarithmieren

Der Logarithmus eines Produktes ist gleich der Summe der Logarithmen der Faktoren:

$$\lg(ab) = \lg a + \lg b.$$

Der Logarithmus eines Quotienten (eines Bruches) ist gleich der Differenz der Logarithmen des Zählers und des Nenners:

$$\lg \frac{a}{b} = \lg a - \lg b. \qquad 5$$

Der Logarithmus einer Potenz ist gleich dem Produkt aus dem Potenzexponenten und dem Logarithmus der zu potenzierenden Zahl:

$$\lg(a^n) = n \lg a.$$

Der Logarithmus einer Wurzel ist gleich dem Quotienten aus dem Logarithmus des Radikanden und dem Wurzelexponenten:

$$\lg \sqrt[n]{a} = \frac{1}{n} \lg a. \qquad 10$$

VOCABULARY

logarithmieren	to determine the logarithm of	der **Zähler**	*here:* numerator
das **Produkt, -e**	product, result	der **Nenner**	denominator
die **Summe, -n**	sum	die **Potenz**	power
gleich der **Summe**	equals the sum (of)	**der zu**	of the number to be
der **Quotient, -en**	quotient	**potenzierenden**	raised to a higher
der **Bruch, ⁔e**	fraction; fracture, break	**Zahl**	power
die **Differenz, -en**	difference	die **Wurzel**	root
		der **Radikant**	radical

STRUCTURAL EXERCISE

Underline all definite articles in the genitive case in the above reading.

DREIHUNDERTSECHSUNDSECHZIG

VOCABULARY EXERCISE

Give the English equivalents of the italicized words or phrases:

1. Der *Logarithmus* eines Produktes *ist gleich der Summe der Logarithmen der Faktoren.*
2. *Der Logarithmus eines Quotienten* ist gleich der Differenz der Logarithmen des Zählers und des Nenners.
3. *Um die Schreibweise zu vereinfachen,* läßt man die Basis 10 weg.

STRUCTURE

5. Expressions with Positive and Comparative

a. Positive

> **so . . . wie** = *as . . . as*

Er liest **so schnell wie du.** *(He reads as fast as you.)*

b. Comparative

    1. Comparative with **als:**

        Er liest **immer schneller.** *(He reads faster and faster [faster all the time].)*

    2. Comparative with **immer:**

        Er liest **immer schneller.** *(He reads faster and faster.)*

    3. Comparative with **je . . . desto:**

        Je mehr, desto besser. *(The more the better.)*

SELF-PREPARATORY EXERCISE

Give the English equivalents:

Je mehr, desto besser.	
Er singt immer besser.	The more the better.
Sie singt besser als du.	He sings better all the time.
Je mehr er arbeitet, desto mehr Geld bekommt er.	She sings better than you.
Sie ist schöner, als ich dachte.	The more he works the more money he gets.
Sie sind nicht so gut, wie ich dachte.	She is prettier than I thought.
	You (they) aren't as good as I thought.

EXERCISES

A. *Complete:*

1. Es ist nicht _____ damals. *(as warm as)*
2. _____ er trinkt, _____ wird er. *(The more he drinks, the louder . . .)*
3. Sie spielt _____ du. *(better than)*
4. Er läuft _____. *(faster all the time)*
5. Nichts ist _____ das. *(easier than)*

B. *Give the English equivalents:*

1. Sie spricht besser als du.
2. Es wird immer besser.
3. Sie ist jünger, als ich dachte.
4. Es ist nicht so kalt wie damals.
5. Je mehr, desto besser.

READING

Wein

Ausgangsstoff zur Weinbereitung sind die Trauben des Weinstocks (Vitis vinifera).
Auf die Beschaffenheit des Weins sind nicht nur die Art der Rebe, sondern auch der
Boden, das Klima und die Witterungsverhältnisse von ausschlaggebendem Einfluß.
Warmes sonniges Wetter im allgemeinen, trockene Witterung besonders zur Blüte-
zeit und große Wärme bis zur Reife sind die Voraussetzung für eine gute Weinernte.   5
Der Boden muß reich an Kali, Kalk, Phosphorsäure und Eisen sein. Der Saft der
Trauben enthält Glukose (Traubenzucker) und Fruktose (Fruchtzucker), Weinsäure,
Apfelsäure und geschmacksbildende Stoffe („Bukettstoffe"). In den Schalen und
Kernen befindet sich Gerbsäure; die Schalen enthalten außerdem den Farbstoff der
Beeren.   10

Ende August beginnen die anfänglich harten und sauren Beeren weich und süß zu
werden. Hierbei wird die Weinsäure gebunden, die Apfelsäure nimmt im Gehalt ab
und der Zucker nimmt mengenmäßig zu. An der Bildung der Bukettstoffe ist der Pilz
des Traubenschimmels („Edelfäule") maßgebend beteiligt. Er ist daher auf den
Trauben sehr erwünscht.   15

VOCABULARY

der **Ausgangsstoff, -e**	basic material, primary substance		die **Rebe, -n**	vine, grape tendril
die **Weinbereitung**	wine production		die **Witterung**	weather
			die **Witterungsverhältnisse** (*pl.*)	weather conditions
die **Traube, -n**	grape		**ausschlaggebend**	decisive
der **Weinstock, ⸚e**	vine		der **Einfluß (auf)**	influence (on)
die **Beschaffenheit**	condition		**sonnig**	sunny

das	**Wetter**	weather	**weich**	soft
	im allgemeinen	in general	**süß**	sweet
	trocken	dry	**hierbei**	thereby, during that time
die	**Blüte, -n**	blossom		
die	**Reife**	maturity	**binden (bindet),**	
das	**Kali**	potash	**band, gebunden**	to bind
der	**Kalk**	lime, chalk, calcium	**ab-nehmen (nimmt ab), nahm ab,**	
der	**Saft, ⁻e**	juice, sap	**abgenommen**	to decrease
die	**Glukose**	glucose	der **Gehalt**	content
der	**Zucker**	sugar	**zu-nehmen (nimmt zu),**	
die	**Frucht, ⁻e**	fruit	**nahm zu,**	
die	**Weinsäure**	tartaric acid	**zugenommen**	to increase
die	**Apfelsäure**	malic acid	**mengenmäßig**	quantitatively
der	**Geschmack**	taste	der **Pilz, -e**	fungus, mushroom
das	**Bukett**	aroma		
der	**Kern, -e**	seed, pip	der **Schimmel**	mould, mildew
	sich befinden (befindet), befand, befunden	to be; to be found; to be present	die **Edelfäule**	"noble rot" *(ashgray mildew)*
die	**Gerbsäure**	tannic acid	**maßgebend**	decisively, influentially
	außerdem	besides, in addition	**beteiligt sein (an)**	to participate (in), be part (of), be involved (in)
der	**Farbstoff, -e**	pigment		
die	**Beere, -n**	berry		
	anfänglich	initially		
	hart	hard	**erwünschen**	to desire

STRUCTURAL EXERCISE

A. *Underline all verbs with inseparable prefixes in the above reading.*

B. *Give the English equivalents of the following adverbs:*

1. anfänglich 3. mengenmäßig 5. besonders
2. außerdem 4. maßgebend

VOCABULARY EXERCISE

Give the English equivalents of the italicized words or phrases:

1. In den Schalen und Kernen *befindet sich* Gerbsäure.
2. *Nicht nur* die Art der Rebe, *sondern auch* der Boden ist wichtig.
3. Der Boden *muß reich an* Kali und Eisen *sein.*
4. Die Apfelsäure *nimmt* im Gehalt *ab,* der Zucker *nimmt* mengenmäßig *zu.*
5. Die Witterungsverhältnisse *sind von ausschlaggebendem Einfluß.*

Je weiter - um so besser.

esson **33**

STRUCTURE

1. Present Participle

a. So far, the function of the verb in a clause has been limited to the predicate:

Der Mann **baut** das Haus. *(The man builds the house.)*

b. The verb may also assume other functions in a sentence, for instance, as a participle. There are two forms of the participle in German:

Present participle   Past participle

c. The present participle is formed by adding **-d** to the infinitive stem:

gehen	**gehend**	*(going)*
laufen	**laufend**	*(running)*
warten	**wartend**	*(waiting)*
spielen	**spielend**	*(playing)*
studieren	**studierend**	*(studying)*

d. The present participle may be used as an attribute to a noun:

der **experimentierende** Chemiker *(the experimenting chemist)*
ein **spielendes** Kind *(a playing child)*

e. As an attribute of a noun, the present participle adds the appropriate adjective endings.

DREIHUNDERTSIEBZIG

EXERCISES

A. *Supply the adjective endings for the following present participles:*

1. das fahrend_____ Auto
2. ein arbeitend_____ Mann
3. eine schreibend_____ Studentin
4. die spielend_____ Kinder
5. einem singend_____ Mann

B. *Supply the adjective endings for the following present participles:*

1. mit einem fahrend_____ Auto
2. für einen arbeitend_____ Mann
3. zu der schreibend_____ Studentin
4. zwischen den spielend_____ Kindern
5. neben einem singend_____ Mann

C. *Translate into English:*

1. der fragende Student
2. mit einem spielenden Radio
3. durch seinen singenden Vogel
4. neben einem schlafenden Schüler
5. für einen arbeitenden Arzt

READING

Wein (2)

Zur Herstellung von Weißwein werden ganze Trauben oder Beeren zerquetscht, die von den Stielen gelöst worden sind. Man läßt den Brei mehrere Tage stehen, damit die Bukettstoffe, die in den Schalen enthalten sind, in den Saft übergehen können. Dann preßt man den Saft ab (= Kelterung), der als trübe, sehr süß schmeckende Flüssigkeit abläuft.   5

Bei der Herstellung von Rotwein wird der Saft nicht abgepreßt, sondern die zerquetschten Trauben mit Schalen, Kernen und Stielen unmittelbar vergoren. Die Gerbsäure geht dann in die Flüssigkeit über, ebenso der Farbstoff der Schalen, weil sich dieser in den Säuren leicht löst, wenn Alkohol zugegen ist.

VOCABULARY

weiß	white	**über-gehen**	
der **Weißwein**	white wine	**(geht über),**	
stehen-lassen	to leave un-	**ging über,**	
(läßt stehen),	touched	**ist übergegangen**	to pass over into
ließ stehen,		**ab-pressen**	to squeeze out,
stehengelassen			press out
der **Stiel, -e**	stem	die **Kelterung**	pressing
lösen	*here:* to remove	**trüb**	opaque, turbid
zerquetschen	to crush, squash	**schmecken**	to taste
der **Brei**	mash, pulp	die **Flüssigkeit, -en**	liquid

DREIHUNDERTEINUNDSIEBZIG

ab-laufen		**unmittelbar**	immediately
(läuft ab),		**vergären (vergärt),**	
lief ab,		**vergor,**	
ist abgelaufen	to run off	**ist vergoren**	to ferment
der **Rotwein**	red wine	**sich lösen**	to dissolve
zerquetscht	crushed, squashed	**zugegen sein**	to be present

STRUCTURE

2. Present Participle as Noun

a.   The present participle may also be used as a noun:

der Schlafende   **eine Reisende**
the sleeping (man)   *a traveler (woman)*

b.   When the present participle is used as a noun, it assumes adjective endings:

Im Bahnhof sah ich **die Reisenden.** *(I saw the travelers in the railroad station.)*

The adjectival noun **die Reisenden** means "people who are traveling":

die reisenden Leute *(the traveling people)*
die Reisenden *(the travelers)*

An adjective that functions as a noun is capitalized.

c.   A noun derived from a present participle retains the adjective endings as if the implied noun (for example, **Leute**) were still present.

d.   Nouns formed from present participles (adjectival nouns) refer only to humans.

EXERCISE

Form adjectival nouns:

EXAMPLE: *the traveling man* / reisen /
                  der Reisende

1. *the drinking man* / trinken /   4. *the fleeing people* / fliehen /
2. *a studying woman* / studieren /   5. *a suffering woman* / leiden /
3. *a sleeping boy* / schlafen /

READING

Glutaminsäure

Glutaminsäure, schon vor ein paar Jahren als „Intelligenztablette" im Gespräch, dann aber ebenso schnell wieder in der Versenkung verschwunden, scheint doch auf die Nervenreaktionsgeschwindigkeit geistig behinderter Kinder zu wirken. Ein

DREIHUNDERTZWEIUNDSIEBZIG

großangelegter Versuch in England soll beweisen, daß man bei Lerngestörten durch Glutaminsäure ein biochemisches Defizit in der Übertragung von Nervenende zu Nervenende beheben kann.

5

VOCABULARY

das **Glutamin**	glutamine	
vor	ago	
ein paar Jahren	a few years	
die **Tablętte, -n**	tablet, pill	
das **Gespräch, -e**	talk, discussion	
ebenso schnell	just as fast	
die **Versenkung**	hollow, depression	
in der Versenkung verschwinden	to disappear from sight, cease to exist	
verschwinden (verschwindet), verschwand, ist verschwunden	to disappear	
die **Reaktion, -en**	reaction	

geistig	mental(ly)
behindert	retarded
wirken	to effect, act upon
großangelegt	large scale
der **Versuch, -e**	experiment
beweisen (beweist), bewies, bewiesen	to prove, show
der **Lerngestörte, -n**	person with learning disability
das **Defizit**	lack, shortage, deficit
die **Übertragung**	transmission
beheben (behebt), behob, behoben	to remove; to relieve; to remedy

VOCABULARY EXERCISE

Give the English equivalents of the italicized words or phrases:

1. *Schon vor ein paar Jahren hat man über Glutaminsäure gesprochen.*
2. *Man kann ein Defizit in der Übertragung von Nervenende zu Nervenende beheben.*
3. *Glutaminsäure scheint auf die Nervenreaktionsgeschwindigkeit geistig behinderter Kinder zu wirken.*

STRUCTURE

3.   <u>zu</u> + Present Participle

a.   The preposition **zu** may be combined with a present participle:

Er beschreibt die **zu destillierende** Flüssigkeit.
He describes the liquid (that is) to be distilled.

b.   **zu destillierende** offers three possibilities of interpretation:

$$\text{is to be} \begin{cases} \textit{will be} & \textit{(future)} \\ \textit{can be} & \textit{(ability)} \\ \textit{must be} & \textit{(compulsion)} \end{cases} \textit{distilled}$$

c.   **zu** plus present participle may also express a negative aspect:

Das ist eine **nicht zu öffnende** Tür.
That is a door which cannot be opened.

The idea conveyed in the preceding example may also be expressed by a relative clause:

Das ist eine Tür, **die nicht geöffnet werden kann.**

d.   The following words may show the negative aspect of **zu** + present participle:

> **kaum**
> **nicht**
> **schwer**

SELF-PREPARATORY EXERCISE

Give the English equivalents:

eine zu vermeidende Wirkung	
das nicht zu erwartende Ergebnis	an effect which is to be avoided
der aufzulösende Stoff	the result which is not to be expected
	the material to be dissolved

EXERCISE

Give the English equivalents of the following sentences:

1. Das ist ein zu behebendes Defizit.
2. Das war eine kaum zu glaubende Reaktion.
3. Man hatte ein schwer zu lösendes Rätsel.
4. Es ist ein nicht zu lösendes Problem.
5. Es ist eine schwer zu durchschauende Krise.

4.   <u>sein</u> + <u>zu</u> + Infinitive

a.   From the discussion of the passive voice substitutes, we know that the **können** + past participle + **werden** construction is similar in meaning to

> **sein** + **zu** + infinitive

Example:

Das ist eine Tür, **die nicht geöffnet werden kann.**
Das ist eine Tür, **die nicht zu öffnen ist.**
That is a door which cannot be opened.

DREIHUNDERTVIERUNDSIEBZIG

b. It is also possible to substitute **sein + zu +** infinitive for **zu** + present participle:

Das ist eine **nicht zu öffnende** Tür. (present participle)
Das ist eine Tür, **die nicht zu öffnen ist.** (infinitive)

c. The following five sentences have the same English meaning:

Das ist eine **nicht zu öffnende** Tür.
Das ist eine Tür, **die nicht geöffnet werden kann.**
Das ist eine Tür, **die nicht zu öffnen ist.**
Das ist eine Tür, **die sich nicht öffnen läßt.**
Das ist eine Tür, **die man nicht öffnen kann.**
That is a door which cannot be opened.

EXERCISES

A. *Change the following sentences using* **sein + zu +** *infinitive:**

 EXAMPLE: Das ist eine **kaum zu glaubende** Geschichte.
     Das ist eine Geschichte, **die kaum zu glauben ist.**

 1. Das ist ein nicht zu behebendes Defizit.
 2. Es war eine kaum zu vermeidende Katastrophe.
 3. Es war eine schwer zu durchschauende Krise.
 4. Es ist ein schwer zu beherrschendes Volk.
 5. Es war eine schwer zu verstehende Aufführung.

B. *Supply the four possible substitutions for the following sentence; then give the English equivalents:*

Das ist ein nicht zu behebendes Defizit.

 1. Passive construction.
 2. **sein + zu +** infinitive.
 3. **sich lassen** construction.
 4. **man** construction.
 5. English equivalent.

C. *Give the English equivalents of the following sentences:*

 1. Es war eine kaum zu vermeidende Katastrophe.
 2. Es ist ein schwer zu beherrschendes Volk.
 3. Es war eine schwer zu verstehende Aufführung.
 4. Es war eine kaum zu glaubende Leistung.
 5. Es ist ein schwer zu vergleichendes Lehrsystem.

DREIHUNDERTFÜNFUNDSIEBZIG

READING

Die Schildbürger[1] wollen ein Rathaus bauen

Die Schildbürger wollten ein neues Rathaus bauen. Sie beschlossen, das Rathaus auf einem Berg zu bauen, der nicht weit von der Stadt lag. Auf dem Berg war aber ein Wald; den mußten sie zuerst abholzen. Sie fällten also die Bäume und trugen die Stämme den Berg hinunter. Es war ein heißer Tag und die Arbeit war schwer; denn sie hoben jeden Stamm auf die Schulter und trugen ihn dann den Berg hinunter. Sie 5 schwitzten und ächzten und stöhnten.

Als sie den letzten Stamm auf die Schulter heben wollten, entglitt er ihren Händen und rollte von selbst den Berg hinunter. Da standen sie mit offenen Mäulern. ,,Wie dumm waren wir!`` sagten sie zu dem Bürgermeister, der am Fuße des Berges stand. ,,Warum haben wir das nicht mit allen Stämmen gemacht?`` 10

Der Bürgermeister war der klügste Mann unter den Schildbürgern. ,,Nun``, sagte er, ,,es ist noch nicht zu spät dazu. Wir sind nicht so dumm, wie wir aussehen. Ich schlage vor, daß wir die Stämme wieder auf den Berg hinauftragen und sie dann herunterrollen lassen.``

Die guten Schildbürger waren mit diesem Rat ihres klugen Bürgermeisters sehr zu- 15 frieden. Sie schleppten die Stämme den Berg hinauf and waren hocherfreut zu sehen, wie die Stämme von selbst herunterrollten.

VOCABULARY

der **Bürger, -**	citizen	
das **Rathaus, ⸚er**	city hall	
bauen	to build	
beschließen (beschließt), beschloß, beschlossen	to decide	
weit	far	
ab-holzen	to clear of wood	
fällen	to fell, cut down	
hinunter	down	
hinunter-tragen (trägt hinunter), trug hinunter, hinuntergetragen	to carry (down)	
der **Stamm, ⸚e**	trunk, stem	

heben (hebt), hob, gehoben (auf)	to lift (onto)	
die **Schulter, -n**	shoulder	
schwitzen	to sweat	
ächzen	to groan, moan	
stöhnen	to groan, moan	
entgleiten (entgleitet), entglitt, ist entglitten	to slip from	
rollen	to roll	
von selbst	by itself, by themselves	
offen	open	
das **Maul, ⸚er**	mouth (referring to animals)	

1. **Schildbürger = Bürger von Schilda.** Schilda is a village in Saxony. The legend about the "Schildbürger" stems from a book of the 16th century in which the foolishness of the citizens of Schilda is depicted. The English equivalent is Gotham, a village near Nottingham. Its inhabitants, the "wise men of Gotham," were, according to the legend, of similar distinction.

DREIHUNDERTSECHSUNDSIEBZIG

	dumm	dumb			hinauf	up
der	**Bürgermeister**	mayor	der	**Rat**		advice
der	**Fuß, ⁻e**	foot			**zufrieden sein (mit)**	to be content
	am Fuße (+ gen.)	at the bottom				(with), be
		(of)				happy (with)
	klug	smart			**schleppen**	to drag
	spät	late			**hinauf-schleppen**	to drag up
	dazu	for it, for that			**hocherfreut**	elated, de-
	vor-schlagen	to propose,				lighted
	(**schlägt vor**),	suggest				
	schlug vor,					
	vorgeschlagen					

STRUCTURAL EXERCISE

Underline all verbs with separable prefixes in the above reading.

VOCABULARY EXERCISE

Give the English equivalents of the italicized words or phrases:

1. Wir sind nicht *so dumm wie wir aussehen.*
2. Mit diesem *Rat waren sie sehr zufrieden.*
3. Sie beschlossen, *das Rathaus auf einem Berg zu bauen.*

STRUCTURE

5. Past Participle as Attributive Adjective

a. The past participle is one of the principal parts of a verb. For example, the past
participle of the verb **machen** is: **ge — mach — t.**

b. German differentiates between weak and strong verbs. Consequently, there are
two kinds of past participles:

WEAK: **ge — mach — t**   STRONG: **ge — komm — en**

c. We have used the past participle frequently in previous lessons:

PRESENT PERFECT TENSE   PAST PERFECT TENSE

er hat gemacht   **er hatte gemacht**
er ist gekommen   **er war gekommen**

d. We have made use of the past participle to form all tenses of the passive voice.
The basic structure of the passive consists of:

> **werden** + past participle

Example:

Das Haus **wird gebaut.** *(The house is [being] built.)*

e. The statal passive used the past participle with the helper verb **sein:**

> **sein** + past participle

Example:

Das Haus **ist gebaut.** *(The house is built.)*

f. The past participle may also function as an attributive adjective:

der **verlorene** Kontinent *(the lost continent)*

Remember: The past participle describes a condition or an action which is already concluded.

g. As an attributive adjective, the past participle adds adjective endings:

der **verlorene** Kontinent   von einem **verlorenen** Kontinent
ein **verlorener** Kontinent   die **verlorenen** Kontinente

EXERCISES

A. *Add the correct endings to the following past participles used as attributive adjectives:*

1. Die gefällt_____ Stämme rollten den Berg hinunter.
2. Auf Grund des eingeschränkt_____ Kreditvolumens kam eine Deflation zustande.
3. Durch gezielt_____ Maßnahmen kann man die Konjunktur beleben.
4. Die gefordert_____ Einheit des Landes war politisch nicht durchzuführen.
5. Die gebunden_____ Metallionen stammen von den Basen.

B. *Give the English equivalents of the following sentences:*

1. Die abgespaltenen Wasserstoffionen stammen von Säuren.
2. Man verkauft den erzeugten Weizen nach Europa.
3. Die Republik Österreich entstand aus der zusammengebrochenen Donaumonarchie.
4. Den Bauhausstil erkennt man an den zusammengefaßten Fenster- und Türreihen.
5. Der beendete Versuch hat bewiesen, daß das biochemische Defizit behoben werden kann.

READING

Gibs auf! (Von Franz Kafka, 1883–1924)

Es war sehr früh am Morgen, die Straßen rein und leer, ich ging zum Bahnhof. Als ich eine Turmuhr mit meiner Uhr verglich, sah ich, daß es schon viel später war, als ich geglaubt hatte, ich mußte mich sehr beeilen, der Schrecken über diese Ent-

Franz Kafka

deckung ließ mich im Weg unsicher werden, ich kannte mich in dieser Stadt noch
nicht sehr gut aus, glücklicherweise war ein Schutzmann in der Nähe, ich lief zu ihm   5
und fragte atemlos nach dem Weg. Er lächelte und sagte: „Von mir willst du den Weg
erfahren?" „Ja", sagte ich, „da ich ihn selbst nicht finden kann." „Gibs auf, gibs
auf!", sagte er und wandte sich mit einem großen Schwunge ab, so wie Leute, die mit
ihrem Lachen allein sein wollen.

VOCABULARY

auf-geben (gibt auf), gab auf, aufgegeben	to give up, re-sign, quit	**glücklicherweise**	luckily, fortunately
gibs auf!		der **Schutzmann, -er**	policeman
(gib es auf!)	give up! quit!	die **Nähe**	vicinity
früh	early	**in der Nähe**	nearby, in the vicinity
der **Morgen**	morning	**fragen (nach)**	to ask (about, concerning)
am Morgen	in the morning		
rein	clean, pure	**atemlos**	out of breath
leer	empty	**lächeln**	to smile
der **Bahnhof, -e**	train station, rail-road station	**sich ab-wenden (wendet sich ab), wandte sich ab, sich abgewandt**	to turn away
sich beeilen	to hurry		
der **Schrecken**	shock, fright	der **Schwung**	bound, swing
die **Entdeckung**	discovery	**mit einem Schwunge**	with a motion, with a bound
lassen	*here:* to cause, make someone		
		so wie	just like
unsicher	uncertain, insecure	die **Leute** *(pl.)*	people
		das **Lachen**	laughter
sich aus-kennen (kennt sich aus), kannte sich aus, sich ausgekannt	to know one's way around	**allein**	alone

STRUCTURAL EXERCISE

Underline all strong verbs in the above reading.

VOCABULARY EXERCISE

Give the English equivalents of the italicized words or phrases:

1. Es war schon viel später, *als ich geglaubt hatte.*
2. *Ich mußte mich sehr beeilen.*
3. *Ich kannte mich in dieser Gegend noch nicht sehr gut aus.*
4. *Glücklicherweise* war ein Schutzmann in der Nähe.
5. *Der Schrecken über diese Entdeckung ließ mich im Weg unsicher werden.*

DREIHUNDERTACHTZIG

STRUCTURE

6.   Past Participles as Nouns

a.   The past participle may also be used as a noun:

Examples:

das Geschriebene   (past participle of **schreiben**   *to write*)
the written (line, book, letter, etc.), that which is written

der Gerettete   (past participle of **retten**   *to save, rescue*)
the saved (person, man, boy), the man who was rescued

b.   When the past participle is used as a noun, it assumes adjective endings:

Er zeigte ihnen **das Geschriebene.**
He showed them the written (material, letter, etc.).
Man sah **den Geretteten** auf dem Bild.
One saw the rescued (person, man, boy) in the picture.
Man sah **die Gerettete** auf dem Bild.
One saw the rescued (person, woman, girl) in the picture.

c.   Adjectival nouns refer to objects or people, with the original nouns omitted.
The past participle **(gerettet, geschrieben)** becomes a noun and is capitalized:

Ich kenne **den Geretteten.**
I know the saved ([male] person).
Ich kenne **eine Gerettete.**
I know a saved ([female] person).
Er zeigte mir **etwas Geschriebenes.**
He showed me something written (written material).

d.   Some past participles are almost always used as nouns:

der Bekannte	*acquaintance, friend (male)*
die Bekannte	*acquaintance, friend (female)*
die Bekannten	*friends, acquaintances*
der Verwandte	*relative (male)*
die Verwandte	*relative (female)*
die Verwandten	*relatives*

EXERCISE

Form nouns from past participles:

1.   *that which has been said* / sagen /
2.   *the man who is injured* / verletzen /

3. *that which has been found* / finden /
4. *that which has been explained* / erklären /
5. *something which has been mentioned* / erwähnen /

7. Adjectives and Adverbs

a. Adjectives may appear as predicate adjectives:

Der Mann ist **alt.**   Der Film ist **aufregend.** (**aufregend** = present participle)
The man is old.   *The film is exciting.*

b. They may also appear as attributive adjectives:

der **junge** Student   der **aufregende** Film
the young student   *the exciting film*

c. Adjectives and adverbs may appear together. In such situations, adverbs are easy to recognize because they have no declensional endings and precede adjectives. Attributive adjectives, however, precede nouns and take adjective endings:

das **sehr wichtige** Gebiet *(the very important area)*

wichtig is an adjective with the ending **-e; sehr** is an adverb modifying **wichtig.**

dieser **höchst charakteristische** Zustand *(this highly characteristic state)*

charakteristisch is an adjective with the ending **-e; höchst** is an adverb modifying **charakteristisch.**

d. Typical adverbial endings in German are:

-lich		-ig	
schließlich	*finally, ultimately*	**geistig**	*mentally*
plötzlich	*suddenly*	**ständig**	*constantly*
täglich	*daily*	**lustig**	*happily*
ursprünglich	*originally*		
anfänglich	*initially*		
ziemlich	*fairly, relatively*		

-weise	
glücklicherweise	*luckily, fortunately*
teilweise	*partially*

DREIHUNDERTZWEIUNDACHTZIG

EXERCISES

A. *In the following sentences identify adjectives and adverbs:*

1. Das sehr langsam fahrende Auto war alt.
2. Die äußerst schnell lesende Studentin heißt Maria Flink.
3. Das billige neue Buch ist für Studenten und Erwachsene.
4. Er hat eine ziemlich schwere Prüfung in der Schule.
5. Der Schutzmann wandte sich mit einem äußerst schnellen Schwunge ab.

B. *Give the English equivalents:*

1. Das war eine ziemlich lange Ausbildung.
2. Er mußte die äußerst schwere Prüfung wiederholen.
3. Im Alter von 16 Jahren kann man eine weiterführende dreijährige Lehre machen.
4. Er zeigte eine sehr schnelle Reaktion.
5. Sie sah das langsam laufende Kind.

C. *Give the English equivalents*

1. Die geistig behinderten Kinder gehen in eine Sonderschule.
2. Die plötzlich eingetretene Wirtschaftskrise verschlimmerte die Arbeitslosigkeit.
3. Das anfänglich sehr schnelle Auto wurde immer langsamer.
4. Die täglich erscheinende Zeitung heißt ,,Die Neue Welt".
5. Die ursprünglich wirtschaftliche Vereinigung ist jetzt eine politische Vereinigung.

READING

Die sittlichen Grundlagen des Arzt-Berufes

Schon vor mehr als 2 000 Jahren hat der griechische Arzt Hippokrates seine Schüler gelehrt, wie ein guter Arzt denken und handeln soll. Wer damals Arzt werden wollte, mußte einen feierlichen Eid leisten, den Eid des Hippokrates. Die Grundsätze dieses Eides gelten noch heute für die Ärzte aller Kulturstaaten. Sie lauten:

,,Bei meiner Aufnahme in den ärztlichen Berufsstand gelobe ich feierlich, mein 5 Leben in den Dienst der Menschlichkeit zu stellen.

Ich werde meinen Beruf mit Gewissenhaftigkeit und Würde ausüben. Die Erhaltung und Wiederherstellung der Gesundheit meiner Patienten soll oberstes Gebot meines Handelns sein.

Ich werde alle mir anvertrauten Geheimnisse wahren. Ich werde mit allen meinen 10 Kräften die Ehre und die edle Überlieferung des ärztlichen Berufes aufrechterhalten und mich in meinen ärztlichen Pflichten nicht durch Religion, Nationalität, Rasse, Parteipolitik oder soziale Stellung beeinflussen lassen. Ich werde jedem Menschen-

leben von der Empfängnis an Ehrfurcht entgegenbringen und selbst unter
Bedrohung meine ärztliche Kunst nicht in Widerspruch zu den Geboten der   15
Menschlichkeit anwenden.

Ich werde meinen Lehrern und Kollegen die schuldige Achtung erweisen. Dies
alles verspreche ich feierlich auf meine Ehre."

VOCABULARY

	sittlich	ethical	
die	Grundlage, -n	basis, principle	
der	Beruf, -e	profession, job	
	handeln	to act, to behave	
	feierlich	solemn	
der	Eid, -e	oath	
	einen Eid leisten	to take an oath	
	gelten	to be valid	
der	Kulturstaat, -en	civilized country	
	lauten	to read as follows	
die	Aufnahme	admission	
	ärztlich	medical	
der	Berufsstand, ⁻e	profession	
	geloben	to vow, to profess	
der	Dienst	service	
die	Menschlichkeit	humanity	
	stellen	to put, to place	
die	Gewissenhaftigkeit	conscientiousness	
die	Würde	dignity	
	aus-üben	to carry out, exercise	
die	Erhaltung	preservation	
die	Wiederherstellung	restoration	
der	Patient, -en	patient	
	oberst	highest	
das	Gebot, -e	precept, maxim, rule, commandment	

	an-vertrauen	to entrust	
das	Geheimnis, -se	secret	
	wahren	to preserve, to keep	
die	Ehre, -n	honor	
	edel, edle	noble	
die	Überlieferung	tradition	
	aufrecht-erhalten (erhält aufrecht), erhielt aufrecht, aufrechterhalten	to maintain, preserve	
die	Pflicht	duty	
die	Nationalität	nationality	
die	Rasse, -n	race	
die	Stellung	position	
	von . . . an	beginning with	
die	Empfängnis	conception	
die	Ehrfurcht	respect, reverance	
	entgegen-bringen (bringt entgegen), brachte entgegen, entgegengebracht	to show, manifest, bring forth	
die	Bedrohung, -en	threat, menace	
der	Widerspruch, ⁻e	contradiction	
	an-wenden (wendet an), wandte an, angewandt	to use, make use of	
	schuldig	deserved	
die	Achtung	respect, esteem	
	erweisen (erweist), erwies, erwiesen	to show, prove	
	versprechen (verspricht), versprach, versprochen	to promise	

STRUCTURAL EXERCISE

Underline all verbs used in the future tense in the above reading.

DREIHUNDERTVIERUNDACHTZIG

VOCABULARY EXERCISE

Give the English equivalents of the italicized words or phrases:

1. *Wer damals Arzt werden wollte,* mußte einen feierlichen Eid leisten.
2. Ich werde mich in meinen ärztlichen Pflichten *nicht beeinflussen lassen.*
3. Die Grundsätze *gelten noch heute.*
4. Der griechische Arzt Hippokrates lehrte *vor mehr als 2 000 Jahren.*
5. *Bei meiner Aufnahme in den Berufsstand* gelobe ich, mein Leben in den Dienst der Menschlichkeit zu stellen.

STRUCTURE

Extended Adjective Constructions

a. English usage allows only certain kinds of elements to precede a noun, and these elements are generally few in number. Additional modifying elements must follow the noun being described:

The new business *that opened on Friday* closed again on Monday.

b. Both English and German make use of relative clauses to provide information about the noun:

Das neue Buch, **das im letzten Monat erschienen ist,** war ein Erfolg.
The new book which was published last month was a success.

c. German can express the last example differently, using an extended adjective construction:

Das neue **im letzten Monat erschienene** Buch war ein Erfolg.

The German sentence has replaced the relative clause of the first example with a modified version. The past participle **(erschienen)** has been changed into an adjective **(erschienene)** modifying the noun **(das Buch)** directly.

d. In English, the relative clause can not normally be expressed by an extended adjective construction. The German extended adjective constructions are best rendered in English as relative clauses.

f.   Follow these steps to recognize and render extended adjective constructions:

1.   Identify the noun to which the entire extended adjective is related and locate the noun's definite or indefinite article (**der-**word or **ein-**word, possessive adjective, or indefinite pronouns [**viel, alle,** etc.]) if present.

2.   Identify the adjective that modifies the noun (adjective ending).

3.   Identify the elements which "extend" the adjective.

Example:

Die ([bei geistig behinderten Kindern] auftretenden) Lernprobleme können durch Glutaminsäure behoben werden.

STEP 1:   Identify noun + article: **Die ... Lernprobleme ...**

STEP 2:   Identify adjective: **... auftretenden ...**

STEP 3:   Identify expansion elements: **. . . bei geistig behinderten Kindern . . .**

After you have identified these three steps, proceed to render the expansion elements in a relative clause. Remember that the adjective can in most cases be traced back to a verb. Use this verb in the relative clause:

... auftretenden ... = auftreten

STEP 4:   Reconstruction: Die Lernprobleme, **die bei geistig behinderten Kindern auftreten,** können durch Glutaminsäure behoben werden.
The learning problems which appear in mentally retarded children can be relieved by glutamic acid.

g.   For the analysis of extended adjective constructions, it is important to remember the various kinds of adjectives that may precede the noun in Step 2 of the above analysis:

ordinary descriptive adjectives (attributive adjectives)
present participles
past participles
zu + present participle

DREIHUNDERTSIEBENUNDACHTZIG

EXERCISES

A. *Identify the three elements in the extended adjective constructions; each level corresponds to a step which will help reconstruct the German extended adjective construction into a relative clause:*

EXAMPLE: **Das im Jahre 1934 von den Nazis aufgelöste Bauhaus** wurde in Chicago neu gegründet.

Level I: noun + definite article
Level II: adjective
Level III: expansion level

Level I	Das			Bauhaus
Level II			aufgelöste	
Level III		im Jahre 1934 von den Nazis		

1. **Die durch sinkende Preise erlittenen Verluste** veranlaßten die Unternehmer, mit Investitionen zurückzuhalten.

Level I				
Level II				
Level III				

2. **Alle an den Ausgrabungen von Troja mitwirkenden Forscher** waren entweder Laien, Autodidakten oder Liebhaber.

Level I				
Level II				
Level III				

3. **Bei dieser besonders zur Veröffentlichung geeigneten Geschichte** handelt es sich um ein Märchen.

Level I				
Level II				
Level III				

DREIHUNDERTACHTUNDACHTZIG

4. **Das erste im Weltraum gefundene organische Molekül** ist ein Vinylcyanid.

Level I				
Level II				
Level III				

5. **Das aus dem Italienischen stammende Wort** Bank bedeutete ursprünglich Sitzbank oder Ladentisch.

Level I				
Level II				
Level III				

B. *Write out the three levels of the elements in the extended adjective constructions in the following sentences:*

EXAMPLE: Die bei geistig behinderten Kindern auftretenden Lernprobleme. . . .

　　　　　Level I:　　Die . . . Lernprobleme . . .
　　　　　Level II:　　. . . auftretenden . . .
　　　　　Level III:　　. . . bei geistig gestörten Kindern . . . .

1. Alle auf eine weiterführende Fachschule gehenden Schüler können später als Facharbeiter arbeiten.
   Level I:
   Level II:
   Level III:

2. Diese aus dem Unbewußten stammenden Antriebe wurden von Sigmund Freud als Hauptantriebe des menschlichen Verhaltens dargestellt.
   Level I:
   Level II:
   Level III:

3. Die die Renaissance ablösende Kunstepoche heißt Barock.
   Level I:
   Level II:
   Level III:

4. Die von Aristoteles in seiner Poetik geforderten drei Einheiten wurden in der Renaissance und in der französischen Klassik gewahrt.
   Level I:
   Level II:
   Level III:

5. Die von Basen stammenden Metallionen sind an den jeweiligen Säurerest gebunden.
   Level I:
   Level II:
   Level III:

C. *Change the following extended adjective constructions to relative clauses:*

EXAMPLE: Das im Jahre 1934 von den Nazis aufgelöste Bauhaus . . . .

    Level I: Das . . . . Bauhaus . . . .
    Level II: . . . . aufgelöste . . . .
    Level III: . . . . im Jahre 1934 von den Nazis . . .

    Relative clause: Das Bauhaus, das im Jahre 1934 von den Nazis
                     aufgelöst wurde, . . .

1. Bei dieser besonders zur Veröffentlichung geeigneten Geschichte handelt es sich um ein Märchen.

   Bei dieser Geschichte, _____ geeignet ist, handelt es sich um ein Märchen.

2. Das aus dem Italienischen stammende Wort Bank bedeutete ursprünglich Sitzbank oder Ladentisch.

   Das Wort Bank, _____ stammt, bedeutete ursprünglich Sitzbank oder Ladentisch.

3. Alle an den Ausgrabungen von Troja mitwirkenden Forscher waren entweder Laien, Autodidakten oder Liebhaber.

   Alle Forscher, _____ mitgewirkt haben, waren entweder Laien, Autodidakten oder Liebhaber.

4. Diese aus dem Unbewußten stammenden Antriebe wurden von Sigmund Freud als die Hauptantriebe des menschlichen Verhaltens dargestellt.

   Diese Antriebe, _____ stammen, wurden von Siegmund Freud als die Hauptantriebe des menschlichen Verhaltens dargestellt.

5. Die von Aristoteles in seiner Poetik geforderten drei Einheiten wurden in der Klassik und in der Renaissance gewahrt.

   Die drei Einheiten, _____ gefordert wurden, wurden in der Klassik und in der Renaissance gewahrt.

D. *Give the English equivalents of the extended adjective constructions in Exercise C.*

READING

Physik

Die Physik ist ein Zweig der Naturwissenschaft und befaßt sich mit den materiellen Kräften sowie deren Auswirkungen. Wir gliedern sie in die Teilgebiete Mechanik, Akustik sowie Lehre der elektromagnetischen Wellen, wobei jedes Gebiet in sich eine weitere Unterteilung erfährt: die Mechanik in Statik (Lehre von den ruhenden Kräften, also vom Gleichgewicht) und Dynamik (Lehre von den Bewegungen, die   5 man durch Kräfte erzeugt); die Akustik in die Lehre vom Schall, von den Schwingungen und Wellen der Materie; die Lehre der elektromagnetischen Wellen in Magnetismus, Elektrizität (Elektrostatik und Elektrodynamik), Kalorik (Lehre von der Wärme) und Optik (Lehre vom Licht).

Bei den alten Griechen war die Physik noch ein Bestandteil der Philosophie und   10
man behandelte sie spekulativ (nur durch Nachdenken) wie die Philosophie. Diese „Naturphilosophie", die auf unbestimmte Vorstellungen begründet war, verhinderte eine wesentliche Erweiterung der Naturerkenntnis. Aristoteles (384 bis 322 v. Chr.) jedoch erzielte durch empirische (auf Erfahrung gegründete) Denkungsart bedeutende Erfolge über die Erkenntnisse vom Schall und Licht. Nach ihm entdeckte   15
Archimedes (287 bis 212 v. Chr.) den Auftrieb der Flüssigkeiten, das Hebelgesetz und die Mechanik des Flaschenzuges, wie er auch die Wasserschraube erfand.

VOCABULARY

die **Physik**	physics	der **Bestandteil, -e**	component, part
der **Zweig, -e**	branch		
die **Naturwissenschaft, -en**	natural sciences	**nach-denken (denkt nach) dachte nach, nachgedacht**	to think, reflect, ponder
sich befassen (mit)	to deal (with), be occupied (with)	**unbestimmt**	indefinite, undetermined, uncertain
die **Kraft, -̈e**	power, force		
die **Auswirkung, -en**	effect	die **Vorstellung, -en**	conception, idea
die **Mechanik**	mechanics		
die **Akustik**	acoustics	**begründen**	to base, found
wobei	by which, whereby	die **Erweiterung**	expansion, extension
in sich	per se, in itself		
weiter	further	**erzielen**	to attain, to achieve
die **Unterteilung, -en**	subdivision		
erfahren (erfährt), erfuhr, erfahren	to experience, undergo	die **Denkungsart**	way of thinking, process of thinking
die **Statik**	statics	der **Erfolg, -e**	success
ruhen	to rest; to repose	der **Auftrieb, -e**	buoyancy, lift, raising, impetus
das **Gleichgewicht, -e**	equilibrium		
das **Gewicht, -e**	weight	der **Hebel, -**	lever
die **Dynamik**	dynamics	der **Flaschenzug**	set of pulleys
die **Schwingung, -en**	vibration, oscillation	die **Schraube, -n**	screw
		erfinden (erfindet), erfand, erfunden	to invent
die **Kalorik**	study of heat		
die **Optik**	optics		

STRUCTURAL EXERCISE

Underline all weak verbs with inseparable prefixes in the above reading.

VOCABULARY EXERCISE

Give the English equivalents of the italicized words or phrases:

1. Die Physik *befaßt sich mit* den materiellen Kräften.
2. Man *behandelte* die Physik spekulativ wie die Philosophie.
3. *Diese Naturphilosophie war auf unbestimmte Vorstellungen begründet.*
4. *Aristoteles erzielte bedeutende Erfolge über* die Erkenntnisse von Schall und Licht.
5. Man gliedert die Physik in Teilgebiete, *wobei jedes Gebiet in sich eine weitere Unterteilung erfährt.*

esson **35**

STRUCTURE

1. Conditional Sentences

a. The following is a conditional sentence:

Speaker: "If he needs money, (then) I will give it to him."

b. The "If . . . (then)" pattern connects two statements:

He needs money.
I will give it to him.

This connection between the two statements establishes a conditional relationship.

c. Note that the word *then* does not have to appear in the clause but may be implied. Also, the order of the "If . . . (then)" pattern may be reversed: "I will give him the money if he needs it."

d. The conditional sentence is made up of two clauses:

CONDITION: **Wenn er Geld braucht,**
If he needs the money,

RESULT: **(dann) gebe ich es ihm.**
(then) I will give it to him.

e. The German conditional clause usually starts with the conjunction **wenn:**

Wenn er das Buch findet, (dann) kann er es lesen.
If he finds the book, (then) he can read it.

Note that **dann** does not have to introduce the result clause. The result clause may also be in first position:

Er kann es lesen, wenn er das Buch findet.

f.   Word order:

1.   The **wenn**-clause is always a subordinate clause, with the conjugated verb in last position:

Wenn er des Buch **findet,** . . .

The result clause is introduced by the conjugated verb when it follows the conditional clause:

. . . . **kann er** es lesen.

2.   When the result clause comes first, the conjugated verb remains in its normal second position:

Er **kann** es lesen, wenn er. . . .

EXERCISES

A.   *Connect the following pairs of sentences to form conditional sentences. Pay attention to the word order:**

EXAMPLE: Er braucht Geld. Ich gebe es ihm.
                      Wenn er Geld braucht, gebe ich es ihm.

1.   Er führt das Experiment durch. Er muß allein sein.
2.   Das Pflanzenschutzmittel gelangt ins Wasser. Es ruft eine Degeneration der Knochen hervor.
3.   Ein Student will in Deutschland studieren. Er muß das Gymnasium beendet haben.
4.   Man gibt Lerngestörten Glutaminsäure. Das biochemische Defizit läßt sich beheben.
5.   Man verwendet DDT zur chemischen Bekämpfung. Die Insekten entwickeln schnell Resistenz gegen dieses Insektizid.

B.   *Give the English equivalents of the following conditional sentences:*

1.   Wenn eine Tageszeitung aktuell sein will, dann muß sie stets das Neueste bringen.
2.   Wenn man eine neue Getreidesorte auf den Markt bringen will, muß man sie erprobt haben.
3.   Wenn Touristen nach Italien kommen, können sie die Ursprünge der europäischen Barockkunst sehen.
4.   Wenn die Schüler die Hauptschule beendet haben, können sie mit einer Berufsausbildung anfangen.
5.   ,,Wenn wir die Macht bekommen, dann werden wir sie behalten.``

DREIHUNDERTVIERUNDNEUNZIG

READING

Philosophie

Der Name Philosophie stammt aus dem Griechischen und bedeutet: Liebe zur Weisheit. Der Philosoph hob sich von einem Weisen (sophos) ab und bezeichnete sich als einen Freund (philos) des Weisen, somit auch der Weisheit. Im alten Griechenland ist der Ursprung der Philosophie zu suchen. Sie war dort aber nicht ein Fach oder eine Beschäftigung neben anderen Fächern — der Philosoph in der abendländischen 5 Prägung taucht erst kurz vor dem Untergang Griechenlands auf —, denn in der großen griechischen Zeit gab es keine „Philosophen", wohl aber Weise und große Denker. Die Worte der Sieben Weisen (Kleobulus aus Lindos, Solon aus Athen, Chilon aus Sparta, Thales aus Milet, Pittakos aus Lesbos, Bias aus Pirene und Periander aus Korinth) standen in goldenen Buchstaben an den Tempelwänden zu 10 Delphi: „Maßhalten ist das beste!" „Nichts zu sehr!" „Erkenne dich selbst!" „Schwer ist es, edel zu sein!" „Die meisten Menschen taugen nichts!" „Müh dich um das Ganze!"

VOCABULARY

die	**Liebe**	love	der	**Untergang**	demise, fall
	sich ab-heben	to distinguish itself	das	**Wort, -e**	word
	(hebt sich ab),	or oneself	der	**Tempel, -**	temple, place of worship, sanctuary
	hob sich ab,				
	sich abgehoben			**stehen (steht),**	
der	**Weise, -n**	wise person		**stand, gestanden**	to be written, stand
	sich bezeichnen	to designate		**golden**	golden
		oneself, describe	der	**Buchstabe, -n**	letter
		oneself		**maßhalten**	to be moderate
der	**Freund, -e**	friend		**edel**	noble, high-minded
die	**Weisheit, -en**	wisdom		**die meisten**	most of the, most
der	**Ursprung, ̈e**	source, origin		**taugen**	to be worth, to be of value
die	**Beschäftigung**	occupation			
	abendländisch	occidental, Western		**sich mühen (um)**	to strive (for), to
die	**Prägung, -en**	character, designation			make an effort (for)
	auf-tauchen	to appear, emerge	das	**Ganze**	totality, whole
	kurz	shortly			

STRUCTURAL EXERCISE

Underline all reflexive verbs used in the above reading.

VOCABULARY EXERCISE

Give the English equivalents of the italicized words or phrases:

1. Im alten Griechenland *haben wir* den Ursprung der Philosophie zu suchen.
2. Der Philosoph in der abendländischen Prägung taucht *erst kurz vor* dem Untergang Griechenlands auf.

DREIHUNDERTFÜNFUNDNEUNZIG

3. *Erkenne dich selbst!*
4. *Müh dich um das Ganze!*
5. *Die Worte standen in goldenen Buchstaben* an den Tempelwänden in Delphi.

STRUCTURE

2.   Mood, Conditional Sentences, and the Subjunctive

a.   In grammatical terms, mood is that linguistic aspect of a verb which expresses the speaker's attitude (personal opinion) toward the action, condition, or state of being.

b.   The indicative mood expresses an action or a state of being regarded as a fact:

Speaker: "He needs money, and I will will give it to him."

This sentence states a fact that can be verified.

c.   The indicative mood may also express conditions. Conditional sentences in the indicative mood are called open conditions:

Speaker: "If he needs money, I will give it to him."

In this sentence, the speaker indicates his readiness in the present or in the future to provide money, if the need arises. The speaker's decision depends upon something that has not yet occurred or that is not yet known to him.

d.   The subjunctive mood is used to express a condition that is contrary to fact.

Speaker: "If he needed money, I would give it to him."

Here the speaker states a hypothetical situation. The sentence implies that the money is not needed at present. Nevertheless, the speaker would be willing to provide the money if it were needed. Thus the speaker's attitude is contrary to an established fact.

e.   Open conditions are expressed in the indicative mood. Contrary-to-fact conditions are expressed in the subjunctive mood.

EXERCISE

Indicate whether each of the following statements is:

factual = (f)   open condition = (o)   contrary-to-fact = (c)

1.   He had repaired the car when I arrived.
2.   If he had bought the car, we would have driven to New Orleans.
3.   If it rains tomorrow, we won't be able to work.
4.   When it rains, I sleep a lot.

5. If it were raining now, I'd need an umbrella.
6. Had he told me that earlier, I could have done something about it.
7. Were I to write a book, I would need to devote a lot of time and work to it.
8. When(ever) I write a book, I devote a lot of effort to the project.
9. I would understand conditional sentences, if I were to study these examples.
10. If I study these examples, I'll understand conditional sentences.

READING

Neue Erfindungen

Eine Erfindung, die Aufmerksamkeit verdient, stammt von dem französischen Biologen Dupré. Dieser Dupré, dessen Name auch manchmal wie Du Pré geschrieben
wird, obwohl man darin völlig freie Hand hat, war, außer Professor an der Sorbonne,
auch manisch-depressiv. Stimmungen großer Ausgelassenheit, in denen er sein
Glück nicht bewältigen konnte, wechselten mit Perioden tiefer Niedergeschlagenheit   5
ab. Eines Tages, als er in seinem Labor eine Anzahl Frösche eingefroren hatte, die er
einen Monat später wieder auftauen wollte, kam er auf den Gedanken, ob man diese
Weise des Konservierens auch aufs Seelenleben in Anwendung bringen könne. Er
wartete geduldig auf einen Moment nicht zu überbietender Heiterkeit und umgab
sodann sein Schädeldach mit Brocken stark unterkühlten Eises. Und voilà, durch das   10
Verlangsamen der Blutzufuhr stabilisierte sich die Stimmung der Aufgekratztheit bis
zu einer Periode von rund einem Jahr, in dem seine Kollegs von Tausenden besucht
wurden, denn sie glänzten durch Gewandtheit, unerschöpflichen Humor und einer
Menge doppelsinniger Witze, die selbst von seiner Magnifizenz kaum verstanden
wurden.   15

VOCABULARY

die **Erfindung, -en**	invention	**bewältigen**	to master, control
die **Aufmerksamkeit**	attention		
verdienen	to deserve, earn	**ab-wechseln**	to alternate
		die **Periode, -n**	period
der **Biologe, -n**	biologist	**tief**	deep
manchmal	sometimes, at times	die **Niedergeschlagenheit**	depression, dejection
völlig	completely	**eines Tages**	one day
die **Hand, ⁻e**	hand	die **Anzahl**	number
freie Hand haben	to be at total liberty	**ein-frieren (friert ein), fror ein, eingefroren**	to freeze
manisch-depressiv	manic-depressive	**auf-tauen**	to defrost, to thaw
die **Stimmung, -en**	mood, disposition		
die **Ausgelassenheit**	exuberance	**auf den Gedanken kommen**	to have the idea
das **Glück**	happiness		

	konservieren	to preserve, to conserve	unterkühlen	to chill, refrigerate, freeze
das	Seelenleben	mental life		
die	Anwendung	application, utilization	das Eis	ice
			das Verlangsamen	retardation, slowing down
	in Anwendung bringen	to use, make use (of)		
	könne (subjunctive)	could	die Zufuhr	supply
	geduldig	patiently	stabilisieren	to stabilize
	überbieten, (überbietet), überbot, überboten	to surpass, outdo, exceed	die Aufgekratztheit	excitement, mood of good humor
die	Heiterkeit	cheerfulness, gaiety, happiness	das Kolleg, -s	lecture
			glänzen	to sparkle, be brilliant
	umgeben, (umgibt), umgab, umgeben	to surround	die Gewandtheit	cleverness
			unerschöpflich	inexhaustible
	sodann	then, thereupon	der Humor	humor
			doppelsinnig	ambiguous, equivocal
der	Schädel	skull, cranium	der Witz, -e	joke, witticism
das	Schädeldach	vault of the cranium	die Magnifizenz	title for the rector of a university
der	Brocken	piece, fragment		

STRUCTURAL EXERCISE

Underline all relative clauses in the above reading.

VOCABULARY EXERCISE

Give the English equivalents of the italicized words or phrases:

1. Sein Name wird auch *manchmal* wie Du Pré geschrieben.
2. Er wartete geduldig *auf einen Moment nicht zu überbietender Heiterkeit.*
3. *Eines Tages* kam er auf einen Gedanken.
4. Man hat *darin* völlig freie Hand.
5. Eine Erfindung, *die Aufmerksamkeit verdient,* stammt von dem französischen Biologen Dupré.

STRUCTURE

3. Subjunctive in English

a. To express contrary-to-fact conditions in the present tense, English generally uses *would* + verb in the result clause and a past tense form of the verb in the conditional clause:

If he *needed* money, I *would* give it to him.

b.   Occasionally, *would* + verb is used in the conditional clause:

He could be helpful if he *would* only *do* his part.

EXERCISES

A.   *Underline the result clauses:*

1.   If I were to read a book, I would miss the party.
2.   I would understand conditional sentences if I were to study these examples.
3.   If he had bought a car, we would have driven to Denver.
4.   If he had told me that earlier, I could have done something about it.
5.   If I had more time, I would play more tennis.

B.   *Underline the conditional clauses:*

1.   She would have come to our party if it had not rained.
2.   If he needed the book, I would find it for him.
3.   I would understand the story if I read it.
4.   If she had more time, she would visit us more often.
5.   They would have been very surprised if I had arrived earlier.

4.   Forms of the Subjunctive

a.   There are three kinds of subjunctive forms in German:

Subjunctive II   **würden**-form   Subjunctive I

b.   Subjunctive II and **würden**-forms are generally identical in meaning; **würden**-forms, however, have limited application. Both forms are similar to English verb structures in the subjunctive mood.

c.   Subjunctive I forms have no structural equivalents in English and have limited application.

5.   Subjunctive II — Weak Verbs, Present Tense

German and English derive the present-tense forms of Subjunctive II from the past tense of the indicative:

PAST INDICATIVE   PRESENT SUBJUNCTIVE II

er **bezahlte** . . .   wenn er **bezahlte** . . .
He paid . . .   *if he paid* . . .

This is an example of a weak verb. The present-tense subjunctive form coincides with the past-tense indicative form of the weak verb.

Rudolf Diesel

VIERHUNDERT

EXERCISES

A. *Present subjunctive of weak verbs: change the following* **wenn**-*clauses to present Subjunctive II:**

EXAMPLE: Wenn er es kauft . . . (indicative)
            Wenn er es kaufte . . . (subjunctive)

1. Wenn wir es heute machen . . .
2. Wenn du das Buch bestellst . . .
3. Wenn ich die Tür öffne . . .
4. Wenn ihr zu Hause wohnt . . .
5. Wenn sie an der Uni studiert . . .
6. Wenn wir nicht fragen . . .
7. Wenn ihr es mir nur sagt . . .
8. Wenn ich jetzt arbeite . . .
9. Wenn es heute regnet . . .
10. Wenn du den Wagen kaufst . . .

B. *Give the English equivalents of the following sentences:*

1. Wenn man das Radio hörte . . .
2. Wenn die Mutter dem Kind antwortete . . .
3. Wenn du mehr redetest . . .
4. Wenn sie nicht täglich studierte . . .
5. Wenn er nicht so lange wartete . . .

READING

Dieselmotor

Der Dieselmotor, der nach dem deutschen Erfinder Rudolf Diesel benannt wurde, unterscheidet sich vom Benzinmotor zunächst dadurch, daß er mit dem weitaus billigeren Rohöl betrieben wird, wodurch sich seine Betriebskosten wesentlich herabsetzen. Es ist also kein Wunder, daß dieser Motor mit fortschreitender technischer Entwicklung immer mehr bevorzugt wird. Vor allem findet er große   5
Verwendung bei ortsgebundenen Kraftanlagen (z. B. Elektrizitätswerken), in Schiffen, Triebwagen der Eisenbahn sowie in Lastkraftwagen.

VOCABULARY

der **Motor, -en**	motor	**sich unterscheiden**	to differentiate
der **Erfinder, -**	inventor	**(unterscheidet sich),**	(itself),
benennen (benennt),		**unterschied sich,**	differ
benannte, benannt	to name	**sich unterschieden**	
	(after)	**weitaus**	by far

VIERHUNDERTEINS

	billig	cheap, inexpensive	**bevorzugen**	to prefer, favor

billig — cheap, inexpensive

das **Rohöl** — crude oil

vor allem — above all

betreiben (betreibt), betrieb, betrieben — to operate, drive, propel

die **Verwendung** — use, application, utilization

wodurch — whereby, through which

ortsgebunden — stationary

die **Kraftanlage, -n** — power plant

sich herab-setzen — to decrease, reduce

das **Elektrizitätswerk, -e** — (electric) power station

die **Betriebskosten** (pl.) — operating costs

das **Schiff, -e** — ship

der **Triebwagen, -** — rail car

das **Wunder** — miracle, surprise

die **Eisenbahn, -en** — railroad, train

der **Lastkraftwagen, -** — truck, lorry

fort-schreiten (schreitet fort), schritt fort, ist fortgeschritten — to progress

STRUCTURAL EXERCISE

Underline all reflexive verbs in the above reading.

VOCABULARY EXERCISE

Give the English equivalents of the italicized words or phrases:

1. *Der Dieselmotor unterscheidet sich* vom Benzinmotor *dadurch, daß* er mit weitaus billigerem Rohöl *betrieben wird.*
2. *Er wird* mit fortschreitender technischer Entwicklung *immer mehr bevorzugt.*
3. *Vor allem* findet er große Verwendung bei ortsgebundenen Kraftanlagen.

STRUCTURE

6. Subjunctive II — Strong Verbs, Present Tense

Keep in mind the following when forming the Subjunctive II of a strong verb:

a. Strong verbs use the past stem of the indicative to form the present tense of Subjunctive II:

VERB INFINITIVE	PAST-STEM INDICATIVE	PRESENT-TENSE SUBJUNCTIVE II
gehen	**ging-**	**ginge**
laufen	**lief-**	**liefe**
rufen	**rief-**	**riefe**

rufen = *to call*

b.   In Subjunctive II (present tense), the strong verbs add an umlaut (¨) to the past indicative stem whenever the stem vowel is **a, o, u:**

VERB INFINITIVE	PAST-STEM INDICATIVE	PRESENT-TENSE SUBJUNCTIVE II
kommen **ziehen**	**kam-** **zog-**	**käme** **zöge**

c.   Strong verbs add an **e** plus the past-tense personal verb endings to form Subjunctive II:

ich   käme
du   kämest
er
sie } **käme**
es
wir   kämen
ihr   kämet
sie
Sie } **kämen**

STEM   + **e** +   PERSONAL ENDINGS
(Umlaut on **a, o, u)**

EXERCISES

A.   *Change the following past-tense indicative verbs to present Subjunctive II:**

1. wir nahmen
2. ich lief
3. ihr fandet

4. der Mann blieb
5. die Leute gaben

B.   *Change the following* **wenn-***clauses to Subjunctive II, present tense:**

1. Wenn er kommt . . .
2. Wenn ich gehe . . .
3. Wenn wir nehmen . . .

4. Wenn sie ruft . . .
5. Wenn du läufst . . .

C.   *Use the following elements to form sentences in the present Subjunctive II:*

1. Wenn / ich / heute / kommen
2. Wenn / er / nach Hause / gehen
3. Wenn / wir / den Bus / nehmen
4. Wenn / die Mutter / das Kind / rufen
5. Wenn / du / jetzt / schnell / nach Hause / laufen

VIERHUNDERTDREI

D. *Express in German.*

1. If he came . . .
2. If we ran . . .
3. If the man stayed . . .

4. If the people gave . . .
5. If we took the bus . . .

E. *Weak and strong verbs mixed. Change the following* **wenn-**clauses to present Subjunctive II:*

1. Wenn ich es mache . . .
2. Wenn er nun kommt . . .
3. Wenn sie das Kind suchen . . .
4. Wenn die Leute schneller laufen . . .
5. Wenn das Auto langsamer fährt . . .

READING

Aktien

Aktien sind Wertpapiere, die man kaufen kann. Damit wird man Mitbesitzer eines Industriebetriebs. Für Aktien erhält man jedes Jahr eine Dividende, das heißt, einen Anteil am Gewinn des Unternehmens. Die Aktien ändern ihren Wert, je nachdem wie erfolgreich das Unternehmen arbeitet.

Durch den Verkauf von Aktien erhält eine Aktiengesellschaft Geld (Kapital) für 5
Vergrößerungen des Betriebs, für neue Maschinen und so weiter.

VOCABULARY

die **Aktie, -n**	share, stock	**je nachdem**	depending on, according to
kaufen	to buy		
der **Mitbesitzer, -**	co-owner	**erfolgreich**	successful
die **Dividende, -n**	dividend	der **Verkauf**	sale
der **Anteil, -e**	share, portion	die **Aktiengesellschaft**	joint stock company
der **Gewinn, -e**	profit, earnings, gain	die **Vergrößerung, -en**	expansion, enlargement
ändern	to change	**und so weiter**	
der **Wert, -e**	value	**(usw.)**	and so on (etc.)

STRUCTURE

7. Present Tense Subjunctive II — <u>haben</u> and <u>sein</u>

Haben and **sein** derive their Subjunctive II forms from the past-tense indicative stem:

VIERHUNDERTVIER

a. **haben**

PAST INDICATIVE **(a)**		PRESENT SUBJUNCTIVE II **(ä)**	
ich	**hatte** *(I had)*	ich	**hätte** *(I had)*
du	**hattest**	du	**hättest**
er sie es	**hatte**	er sie es	**hätte**
wir	**hatten**	wir	**hätten**
ihr	**hattet**	ihr	**hättet**
sie Sie	**hatten**	sie Sie	**hätten**

Subjunctive II (present tense) forms of **haben** add umlaut to the past-tense indicative forms.

b. **sein**

PAST INDICATIVE **(a)**		PRESENT SUBJUNCTIVE II **(ä)**	
ich	**war** *(I was)*	ich	**wäre** *(I were)*
du	**warst**	du	**wärest**
er sie es	**war**	er sie es	**wäre**
wir	**waren**	wir	**wären**
ihr	**wart**	ihr	**wäret**
sie Sie	**waren**	sie Sie	**wären**

In addition to changing to an umlaut form, Subjunctive II (present tense) of **sein** also adds the ending **-e** in all forms except **wir, sie,** and **Sie.**

EXERCISES

A. *Change the following indicative forms of* **haben** *to subjunctive:**

1. Wenn ich Zeit habe . . .
2. Wenn sie sein Auto hat . . .
3. Wenn wir Geld haben . . .
4. Wenn sie die Bücher haben . . .
5. Wenn ihr kein Bier habt . . .

B. *Change the following indicative forms of* **sein** *to subjunctive:**

1. Wenn ich in Berlin bin . . .
2. Wenn du Student bist . . .
3. Wenn sie alt ist . . .
4. Wenn es Sommer ist . . .
5. Wenn das Haus neu ist . . .

C.   *Give the English equivalents of the following sentences:*

1. Wenn ich Arzt wäre . . .
2. Wenn wir keinen Lehrer hätten . . .
3. Wenn mein Freund hier wäre . . .
4. Wenn das Kind größer wäre . . .
5. Wenn man mehr Geld hätte . . .

8.   Result Clauses: <u>würden</u>-Form + Infinitive

a.   Subjunctive II may be used in both conditional and result clauses:

Wenn er Geld **hätte, ginge** er ins Theater.
If he had money, he would go to the theater.

b.   The **würden**-form + infinitive may be substituted for Subjunctive II in result clauses:

Wenn er Geld **hätte, würde** er ins Theater **gehen.**
If he had money, he would go to the theater.

c.   The formation of German **würden**-forms and English *would*-forms is similar:

Conjugated form of
würden + infinitive

d.   Forms of **würden:**

ich würde . . . gehen   *(I would go)*
du würdest . . . gehen
er
sie ⎫ würde . . . gehen
es ⎭
wir würden . . . gehen
ihr würdet . . . gehen
sie ⎫ würden . . . gehen
Sie ⎭

e.   **Würden** is the subjunctive form of **werden.** It is derived from the past tense of **werden,** which is **wurden.**

f.   The **würden** forms exist only in the present tense. They are rarely used with the verbs **sein, haben, wissen,** or the modals.

VIERHUNDERTSECHS

g.   The present tense of Subjunctive II must be used in the condition-clause if the condition is contrary to fact in present time:

Wenn er Geld **hätte,** . . . *(If he had money,* . . . .*)*
Wenn sie jetzt **käme,** . . . . *(If she came now,* . . .*)*

h.   If a condition is contrary to fact in the present time, the result-clause may either be in Subjunctive II (present tense) or in the **würden-**form:

Wenn er Geld **hätte, ginge** er ins Theater.
(If he had money, he would go to the theater.)
Wenn sie jetzt **käme, würde** sie den Film **sehen.**
(If she came now, she would see the film.)

EXERCISES

A.   *Supply the* **würden** *forms of the following verbs:* *

EXAMPLE: schwimmen / ihr
                   ihr würdet schwimmen

   1.   gehen / er
   2.   sehen / es
   3.   laufen / wir
   4.   bringen / sie *(sing.)*
   5.   lesen / du
   6.   annehmen *(to accept; to assume)* / ihr
   7.   bekommen / ich
   8.   rauchen / man
   9.   abfahren / die Kinder
  10.   finden / der Chemiker

B.   *Replace the Subjunctive II forms with* **würden-***forms + infinitive:*

   1.   Ihr sähet das Haus, wenn . . .
   2.   Ich läse die Zeitung, wenn . . .
   3.   Seine Freunde führen nach Deutschland, wenn . . .
   4.   Ich kaufte das Auto, wenn . . .
   5.   Sie bliebe in Deutschland, wenn . . .

C.   *Form sentences from the given elements using* **würden:**

   1.   Die Familie / nach Wien / gehen, wenn . . .
   2.   Der Bus / in einer Stunde / abfahren, wenn   . .
   3.   Ich / eine Zigarette / rauchen, wenn . . .
   4.   Man / das Geld / annehmen, wenn . . .
   5.   Sie *(sing.)* / dir / die Zeitung / bringen, wenn . . .

READING

Bourgeois und Proletarier (Von Karl Marx, 1818–1883)

Die Geschichte aller bisherigen Gesellschaft ist die Geschichte von Klassen-
kämpfen . . .

 Die aus dem Untergang der feudalen Gesellschaft hervorgegangene moderne bür-
gerliche Gesellschaft hat die Klassengegensätze nicht aufgehoben. Sie hat nur neue
Klassen, neue Bedingungen der Unterdrückung, neue Gestaltungen des Kampfes an 5
die Stelle der alten gesetzt.

 Unsere Epoche, die Epoche der Bourgeoisie, zeichnet sich jedoch dadurch aus, daß
sie die Klassengegensätze vereinfacht hat. Die ganze Gesellschaft spaltet sich mehr
und mehr in zwei große feindliche Lager, in zwei große, einander direkt
gegenüberstehende Klassen: Bourgeoisie und Proletariat. 10

VOCABULARY

der **Bourgeois**	middle class person, bourgeois	
der **Proletarier**	proletarian	
bisherig	previous	
der **Kampf, ⸚e**	fight, strug-gle, battle	
hervor-gehen (geht hervor), ging hervor, ist hervorgegangen hervorgehen (aus)	to come from, to proceed from to emerge (from), stem (from)	
bürgerlich	middle-class, bourgeois	
der **Gegensatz, ⸚e**	contrast, anti-thesis	
auf-heben (hebt auf), hob auf, aufgehoben	to abolish, annul	
die **Bedingung, -en**	condition	

die **Unterdrückung, -en**	suppression, oppression, repression	
die **Gestaltung**	form, shape	
die **Stelle, -n**	place, site, lo-cation	
an die Stelle (+ gen.)	in the place (of)	
sich aus-zeichnen (durch)	to distin-guish (it-self) (by), mark (it-self) (by)	
sich spalten	to split, di-vide	
das **Lager, -**	camp, part, side	
einander	one another, each other	
gegenüber-stehen (steht gegenüber), stand gegenüber, gegenübergestanden	to oppose	

STRUCTURAL EXERCISE

Underline all reflexive verbs in the above reading.

VIERHUNDERTACHT

VOCABULARY EXERCISE

Give the English equivalents of the italicized words or phrases:

1. *Die aus dem Untergang der feudalen Gesellschaft hervorgegangene moderne bür-gerliche Gesellschaft* hat die Klassengegensätze nicht aufgehoben.
2. *Unsere Epoche zeichnet sich dadurch aus, daß* sie die Klassengegensätze verein-facht hat.
3. *Die ganze Gesellschaft spaltet sich mehr und mehr in zwei große feindliche Lager.*

Lesson 36

STRUCTURE

1. Würden-Form and Subjunctive II

a. Subjunctive II and **würden**-forms are equivalent in meaning in result clauses.

Wenn er Geld hätte, **ginge** er ins Theater. (Subjunctive II)
                    würde er ins Theater gehen. (**würden**-form)

b. The following verbs generally use only Subjunctive II forms:

sein and **haben**	**wäre, hätte**
wissen and the modals	**wüßte, könnte**

c. All other verbs can take the **würden** + infinitive form.

EXERCISES

A. *Form complete sentences according to the example:*

EXAMPLE: Wenn / ich / Geld / haben / , würde ich einen Wagen kaufen.
          Wenn ich Geld hätte, würde ich einen Wagen kaufen.

1. Wenn / er / Zeit / haben / , würde er nach Berlin fahren.
2. Wenn / er / Student / sein / , würde er mehr lesen.
3. Wenn / das Haus / sein / nicht so alt / , würden wir es kaufen.
4. Wenn / die Frau / keine Kinder / haben / , wäre sie glücklicher.
5. Wenn / wir / sein / in Deutschland / , würden wir nur Deutsch sprechen.

B. *Give the English equivalents of the following sentences:*

1. Wenn wir einen Wagen hätten, würden wir nach Italien fahren.
2. Wenn wir mehr Geld hätten, würden wir das Land kaufen.
3. Wenn ich mehr Zeit hätte, würde ich mehr lesen.
4. Wenn du Bier hättest, würden wir hier bleiben.
5. Wenn sie eine Studentin wäre, würde sie in einem Studentenheim wohnen.

READING

Die Brüder Grimm — Jacob Grimm: 1785–1863 — Wilhelm Grimm: 1786–1859

Beide waren Sprach- und Altertumsforscher. Beide studierten Jura und waren Professoren an der Universität Göttingen. Sie haben zusammen an der Märchensammlung gearbeitet, und sie haben die erste wissenschaftliche „Deutsche Grammatik" geschaffen.

1854 begannen sie, das „Deutsche Wörterbuch" zu schreiben. Das „Deutsche 5
Wörterbuch" ist eine Sammlung des Wortschatzes der neuhochdeutschen Sprache.
Es umfaßt 31 Bände.

VOCABULARY

der **Bruder, ⸚**	brother	der **Wortschatz**	vocabulary
die **Sammlung, -en**	collection	**umfassen**	to comprise, contain
die **Grammatik, -en**	grammar	der **Band, ⸚e**	volume
das **Wörterbuch, ⸚er**	dictionary		

STRUCTURE

2.   Past Tense — Subjunctive II

a.   The past tense of Subjunctive II is derived from the past perfect indicative:

INDICATIVE — PAST PERFECT TENSE   SUBJUNCTIVE II — PAST TENSE

Er **hatte** das Haus **gebaut.**   Er **hätte** das Haus **gebaut,** wenn . . .
He had built the house.   *He would have built the house, if . . .*
Sie **war** nach Berlin **gefahren.**   Sie **wäre** nach Berlin **gefahren,** wenn . . .
She had gone to Berlin.   *She would have gone to Berlin, if . . .*

b.   Past tense Subjunctive II:

Subjunctive II form of **haben** or **sein**	+	past participle of main verb

Brüder Grimm

VIERHUNDERTZWÖLF

EXERCISES

A. *Past Subjunctive II of verbs with* **haben.** *Change the following* **wenn***-clauses to past Subjunctive II:*

EXAMPLE: Wenn er es dir gezeigt hat . . .
             Wenn er es dir gezeigt hätte . . .

1. Wenn ich das Buch gelesen habe . . .
2. Wenn wir den Wagen gekauft haben . . .
3. Wenn wir die Arbeit geschrieben haben . . .
4. Wenn sie an der Uni studiert hat . . .

B. *Past Subjunctive II of verbs with* **sein.** *Supply the correct Subjunctive II form of* **sein:**

1. Wenn sie gelaufen . . .   4. Wenn ihr geworden . . .
2. Wenn ich gekommen . . .   5. Wenn wir gefahren . . .
3. Wenn er geflogen . . .   6. Wenn er gestorben . . .

3.   Past Subjunctive II (continued)

Form of **hätten** **wären** + past participle

The difference between the past perfect indicative and the past Subjunctive II can be seen when the forms are used in context:

Past Perfect Indicative:

Er **hatte** das Haus **gebaut,** als er genug Geld hatte.   (factual statement)
He had built the house when he had enough money.

Past Subjunctive II:

Er **hätte** das Haus **gebaut,** wenn er genug Geld **gehabt hätte.**   (contrary-to-fact)
He would have built the house if he had had enough money.

EXERCISE

The following sentences are factual statements in the indicative mood. Form conditional statements (contrary-to-fact) according to the models:

EXAMPLES: (Present Indicative):
               Wenn er es **braucht, werden** wir es ihm **geben.**
               If he needs it, we will give it to him.

               (Present Subjunctive II):
               Wenn er es **brauchte, würden** wir es ihm **geben.**
               If he needed it, we would give it to him.

(Past Subjunctive II):
Wenn er es **gebraucht hätte, hätten** wir es ihm **gegeben.**
If he had needed it, we would have given it to him.

1. Wenn Sie früher kommen, werde ich Sie abholen.
2. Wenn ich ihre Telefonnummer weiß, werde ich sie anrufen.
3. Wenn er mich fragt, werde ich es ihm sagen.

4. Past Subjunctive II of <u>haben</u> and <u>sein</u>

a. Past Subjunctive II of **haben:**

Form of   **hätten**   +   **gehabt**

Example:

er hätte gehabt *(he would have had)*

Wenn er ein Auto **gehabt hätte,** . . .
(If he had had a car, ...)

b. Past Subjunctive II of **sein:**

Form of   **wären**   +   **gewesen**

Example:

er wäre gewesen *(he would have been)*

Wenn er damals zu Hause **gewesen wäre,** . . .
(If he had been at home at that time, ...)

EXERCISE

Form contrary-to-fact sentences in the Present Subjunctive II and Past Subjunctive II:*

EXAMPLE: Wenn er ein Auto **hat, wird** er eine Reise **machen.**
Wenn er ein Auto **hätte, würde** er eine Reise **machen.**
Wenn er ein Auto **gehabt hätte, hätte** er eine Reise **gemacht.**

1. Wenn es leichter ist, wird sie es selber machen.
2. Wenn wir mehr Geld haben, werden wir länger bleiben.
3. Wenn sie wirklich klug ist, wird sie das Buch lesen.
4. Wenn ich das Geld habe, werde ich es kaufen.

READING

Die andere Möglichkeit (von Erich Kästner)

Wenn wir den Krieg gewonnen hätten,
mit Wogenprall und Sturmgebraus,

VIERHUNDERTVIERZEHN

dann wäre Deutschland nicht zu retten,
und gliche einem Irrenhaus.

Wenn wir den Krieg gewonnen hätten,   5
dann wären wir ein stolzer Staat.
Und preßten noch in unsern Betten
die Hände an die Hosennaht.

Wenn wir den Krieg gewonnen hätten,
dann wäre der Himmel national.   10
Die Pfarrer trügen Epauletten.
Und Gott wär' deutscher General.

Wenn wir den Krieg gewonnen hätten —
Zum Glück gewannen wir ihn nicht!

VOCABULARY

der **Krieg, -e**	war	
gewinnen (gewinnt),	to win, be vic-	
gewann,	torious	
gewonnen		
der **Wogenprall**	rolling roar	
das **Sturmgebraus**	clamorous clatter	
retten	to save, rescue;	
	here: (idiom)	
	nicht zu retten	
	sein to be out of	
	one's mind	
gleichen (gleicht),		
glich, geglichen	to resemble	
das **Irrenhaus, ̈-er**	insane asylum	

stolz	proud
der **Staat, -en**	state, country
pressen	to press, push
das **Bett, -en**	bed
die **Hosennaht, ̈-e**	pants' seam
der **Himmel**	heaven
national	national
der **Pfarrer, -**	pastor, minister
die **Epaulette, -n**	epaulet
wär' (= wäre)	would be
der **General**	general
zum Glück!	luckily, fortu- nately

STRUCTURE

5. Word Order in Conditional Clauses

a. The conditional clause may be in first position, or it may follow the result clause:

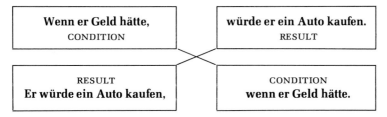

b. In the first sentence, the subordinate **(wenn)** clause precedes the result clause. The result clause therefore starts with the inflected verb (verb-subject).

c. The second sentence retains the standard word order in the result clause (subject-verb).

EXERCISE

Begin the sentences with the result clause:*

EXAMPLE: Wenn es leichter gewesen wäre, hätte sie es selber gemacht.
              Sie hätte es selber gemacht, wenn es leichter gewesen wäre.

1. Wenn wir mehr Geld hätten, würden wir länger bleiben.
2. Wenn er mich gefragt hätte, hätte ich es ihm gesagt.
3. Wenn Sie früher gekommen wären, hätte ich Sie gefragt.
4. Wenn ich das Geld hätte, würde ich es kaufen.
5. Wenn sie wirklich klug wäre, würde sie schneller arbeiten.

6.   Subjunctive II — Present Tense Modals

a. Modals add an umlaut in the present Subjunctive II if they have an umlaut in the infinitive:

INFINITIVE	PAST TENSE INDICATIVE	SUBJUNCTIVE II
dürfen	ich durfte	**ich dürfte**
können	ich konnte	**ich könnte**
müssen	ich mußte	**ich müßte**
mögen	ich mochte	**ich möchte**
But:		
sollen	ich sollte	**ich sollte**
wollen	ich wollte	**ich wollte**

b. The past tense indicative forms of **wollen** and **sollen** are identical to the Subjunctive II forms.

c. Modals have the same personal endings in the present Subjunctive II as in the past indicative:

PAST INDICATIVE	SUBJUNCTIVE II
ich konnte *(I could)*	**ich könnte** *(I could)*
du konntest	**du könntest**
er konnte	**er könnte**
sie konnte	**sie könnte**
es konnte	**es könnte**
wir konnten	**wir könnten**
ihr konntet	**ihr könntet**
sie konnten	**sie könnten**
Sie konnten	**Sie könnten**

VIERHUNDERTSECHZEHN

d. English meanings of Subjunctive II forms (present tense) of modals:

er dürfte	*he would be allowed to, he were allowed to*
er könnte	*he could, he were able to, he would be able to*
er müßte	*he would have to*
er möchte	*he would like to*
er sollte	*he should, he were supposed to*
er wollte	*he would want to, he wanted to*

EXERCISES

A. *Present subjunctive of modals; change the following **wenn-**clauses to present tense of Subjunctive II:**

EXAMPLE: Wenn ich will . . .
 Wenn ich wollte . . .

1. Wenn er es machen soll. . .
2. Wenn sie es nicht mag . . .
3. Wenn wir ins Haus gehen dürfen . . .
4. Wenn er es essen muß . . . .
5. Wenn du es schaffen kannst . . .

B. *Give the English equivalents of the following **wenn-**clauses:*

1. Wenn er die Hausaufgaben machen müßte . . .
2. Wenn er sich entschließen sollte . . .
3. Wenn du in die Stadt fahren dürftest . . .
4. Wenn sie das Buch lesen könnte. . .
5. Wenn man das machen wollte . . .

READING

Altertum

Altertum nennt man die Zeitspanne zwischen dem Beginn geschichtlicher Überlieferungen und dem Mittelalter, also von den Anfängen alt-orientalischer Hochkulturen um 4000 v. Chr. bis zum Untergang Westroms um 500 n. Chr. Völker des Altertums waren zum Beispiel die Sumerer, Babylonier, Assyrer, Meder und Perser, die Ägypter, Israeliten, Phönizier, die Griechen und Römer sowie die   5 Germanen, Kelten und Slawen in ihrer frühen Zeit. Diese Liste ist natürlich nicht vollständig, sie enthält jedoch die wichtigsten Völker aus unserem Kulturraum. Daneben muß man auch die Chinesen nennen, die eine sehr alte Kultur haben.

VIERHUNDERTSIEBZEHN

VOCABULARY

das **Altertum**	antiquity	der **Ägypter, -**	Egyptian
die **Zeitspanne**	period of time	der **Israelit, -en**	Israelite
der **Beginn**	beginning	der **Phönizier, -**	Phoenician
geschichtlich	historical	der **Römer, -**	Roman
die **Überlieferung**	tradition, transmission	der **Germane, -n**	Germanic, Teutonic
der **Anfang, -̈e**	beginning	der **Kelte, -n**	Celt
v. Chr. (= **vor Christi Geburt**)	B.C.	der **Slawe, -n**	Slav
n. Chr. (= **nach Christi Geburt**)	A.D.	die **Liste, -n**	list
		vollständig	complete
der **Sumerer, -**	Sumerian	**enthalten (enthält), enthielt, enthalten**	to contain
der **Babylonier, -**	Babylonian	der **Kulturraum**	cultural area
der **Assyrer, -**	Assyrian	**daneben**	in addition to that
der **Meder, -**	Mede	der **Chinese, -n**	Chinese
der **Perser, -**	Persian		

VOCABULARY EXERCISE

Give the English equivalents of the italicized words or phrases:

1. Völker des Altertums waren *zum Beispiel* die Sumerer und die Babylonier.
2. *Daneben muß man auch die Chinesen nennen,* die eine sehr alte Kultur haben.
3. Diese Liste *enthält* die wichtigsten Völker aus unserem Kulturraum.

STRUCTURE

7. Past Subjunctive II with Modals

a. If the modal is used with another verb, the past subjunctive II of the modal appears as follows:

Er **hätte** nach Hause **gehen sollen.** *(He should have gone home.)*

b. Remember that modals use only **haben** as helper words in the compound tenses.

c. The familiar double-infinitive construction occurs in the past subjunctive II if the modal is used with another verb.

EXERCISES

A. *Change to subjunctive II (past tense):* *

> Subjunctive II of **haben** + double infinitive

1. Ich habe gehen können.
2. Er darf ins Haus gehen.
3. Du hast fragen müssen.
4. Sie soll nach Berlin fliegen.
5. Er durfte früh abfahren.

VIERHUNDERTACHTZEHN

B.   *Form the past subjunctive II of modals plus verb:**

   1.   suchen wollen (wir)   4.   abreisen können (ihr)
   2.   wissen müssen (du)   5.   es nicht tun mögen (sie, *sing.*)
   3.   hereinkommen dürfen (Sie)

C.   *Begin the sentences with* **wenn**; *note the position of the helper verb:*

   EXAMPLE: Er hat nach Hause gehen sollen, . . .
   　　　　　 Wenn er nach Hause hätte gehen sollen, . . .

   1.   Er hat heute arbeiten müssen, . . .
   2.   Du hast früher aufstehen müssen, . . .
   3.   Wir haben viel reisen können, . . .
   4.   Das Kind hat nicht ins Haus gehen dürfen, . . .
   5.   Er hat nach Berlin fliegen wollen, . . .

8.   Subjunctive II with Wishes

Subjunctive II is used in expressing wishes, which are by nature contrary-to-fact conditions:

Er ist nicht hier.	(fact)
Wenn er nur hier wäre!	(contrary to fact) (present)
Wenn er nur hier gewesen wäre!	(contrary to fact) (past)
Ich konnte es nicht finden.	(fact)
Wenn ich es nur finden könnte!	(contrary to fact) (present)
Wenn ich es nur hätte finden können!	(contrary to fact) (past)

EXERCISES

A.   *Express wishes, contrary to fact, in present and past Subjunctive II:**

   1.   Sie kommt nicht.   4.   Du glaubst mir nicht.
   2.   Er antwortet mir nicht.   5.   Ich kann es nicht finden.
   3.   Er weiß es nicht.

B.   *Give the English equivalents of the following sentences:*

   1.   Wenn ich es nur machen könnte!
   2.   Wenn es nur nicht so schwer wäre!
   3.   Wenn ich nur mehr Zeit hätte!
   4.   Wenn wir nach Hamburg fahren dürften!
   5.   Wenn du es mir geben könntest!

9.   Subjunctive with <u>als ob</u> and <u>als wenn</u>

a.   The conjunctions **als ob** and **als wenn** (both meaning *as if*) are followed by the subjunctive:

Sie hört nichts.
Sie tut, **als ob (wenn) sie nichts hörte.**
(She acts as if she didn't hear anything.)

b.   The words **ob** and **wenn** may be omitted in German, causing a change in the word order:

Sie tut, **als hörte sie nichts.**

EXERCISES

A.   *Form sentences using* **als ob** *and* **als wenn** *in the present Subjunctive II. Start all sentences with* **Er tut, Sie tut,** *or* **Sie tun:***

EXAMPLE: Sie sieht nichts.
            Sie tut, als ob sie nichts sähe.

1.   Er kann nicht lesen.
2.   Sie weiß es nicht.
3.   Sie haben zu viel Geld.
4.   Er hat keine Zeit.
5.   Sie will nicht gehen.

B.   *Form sentences with* **als** *omitting the* **ob** *and* **wenn:***

EXAMPLE: Sie sieht nichts.
            Sie tut, als sähe sie nichts.

1.   Er kann nicht lesen.   4.   Sie weiß es nicht.
2.   Er hat keine Zeit.   5.   Sie haben zu viel Geld.
3.   Sie will nicht gehen.

C.   *Change from indicative to present and past Subjunctive II:***

1.   Wenn ich das Geld habe, kaufe ich mir das Auto.
2.   Wenn er mehr Zeit hat, liest er eine Zeitung.
3.   Wenn sie das wissen will, fragt sie ihn.
4.   Wenn er deine Nummer findet, ruft er dich an.
5.   Wenn ihr mit dem Bus fahrt, kommt ihr am frühesten an.

D.   *Give the English equivalents of the following sentences:*

1.   Wenn wir heute angekommen wären, hätte er uns die Stadt gezeigt.
2.   Wenn man das Molekül entdeckt hätte, wüßte man, ob es im Weltall Lebenskeime gibt oder nicht.
3.   Wenn man es sofort gewußt hätte, hätte man etwas dagegen tun können.

VIERHUNDERTZWANZIG

    4. Wenn sie viel studiert hätte, hätte sie die nächste Klasse erreichen können.

    5. Wenn der Bauer Chemikalien verwendet hätte, hätte er eine höhere Ernte erzielt.

E. *Restate each of the following sentences as a conjecture, first in the present, then in the past tense:*

EXAMPLES: Sie hat recht. *(She is right / correct.)*

           Es kommt mir vor, als ob sie recht hätte. (present)
           Es kommt mir vor, als ob sie recht gehabt hätte. (past)
           It seems to me as if she were / had been right.

    1. Es kommt mir vor, (sie wohnen hier)
    2.   (es interessiert ihn)
    3.   (es gefällt ihnen nicht)
    4.   (es ist nicht wahr)
    5.   (er kommt nicht)
    6.   (es geht nicht)
    7.   (sie können es nicht)
    8.   (er weiß es)

READING

Physik II

Im Mittelalter erkannte als erster der Universalgelehrte und Künstler Leonardo da Vinci (1452 bis 1519 n. Chr.) im Schall eine Wellenbewegung der Luft. Zum Begründer der Dynamik wurde Galilei (1564 bis 1642), der die Gesetze über den freien Fall, Pendel und Wurf entdeckte. Er ist auch der Erbauer der ersten Fernrohre, mit deren Hilfe er sein heliozentrisches Weltsystem (das die Sonne in den Mittel- 5 punkt stellte) aufbaute. Der englische Physiker Gilbert wurde zum Begründer der Lehre von den elektrischen und magnetischen Erscheinungen, und der deutsche Astronom Johannes Kepler entdeckte die Abnahme der Lichtstärke mit dem Quadrat der Entfernung.

    Isaac Newton (1643 bis 1727) erklärte die Begriffe Maße, Gewicht, Kraft, 10 Beschleunigung und Geschwindigkeit und stellte das Gravitationsgesetz auf, nach dem sich alle Körper einander anziehen. Das erste Quecksilberbarometer erfand 1643 der Italiener Torricelli und das erste Quecksilberthermometer stellte der deutsche Physiker Fahrenheit her. Zu Begründern der Elektrizitätslehre wurden die Italiener Galvani und Volta. Die ersten Erkenntnisse von der Erhaltung der Energie stammen 15 aus den Jahren 1842 und 1847 von den Deutschen Robert Mayer und Hermann von Helmholtz.

VOCABULARY

der	**Künstler, -**	artist	die	**Abnahme**	decrease
der	**Begründer, -**	founder	die	**Stärke**	strength, magnitude
	frei	free	das	**Quadrat, -e**	square
der	**Fall**	fall	die	**Entfernung, -en**	distance
das	**Pendel**	pendulum	die	**Beschleunigung**	acceleration
der	**Wurf, ̈e**	trajectory, projection, throw		**auf-stellen**	to advance; to lay down; to establish
der	**Erbauer, -**	builder		**an-ziehen**	
das	**Fernrohr, -e**	telescope		**(zieht an)**	
	heliozentrisch	heliocentric		**zog an,**	
der	**Mittelpunkt, -e**	center, focus, focal point		**angezogen**	to attract
				sich einander	
	stellen	to place, put		**anziehen**	to attract each other
	auf-bauen	to build, erect	das	**Quecksilber**	quicksilver, mercury
der	**Physiker, -**	physicist		**her-stellen**	to produce
die	**Erscheinung, -en**	phenomenon, appearance	die	**Erhaltung**	retention, preservation
der	**Astronom**	astronomer			

STRUCTURAL EXERCISE

Underline all reflexive verbs in the above reading.

VOCABULARY EXERCISE

Give the English equivalents of the italicized words or phrases:

1. *Zum Begründer der Dynamik wurde Galilei, der die Gesetze über den freien Fall, Pendel und Wurf entdeckte.*
2. Das erste Quecksilberthermometer *stellte* der deutsche Physiker Fahrenheit *her.*
3. Galilei ist der Erbauer der ersten Fernrohre, *mit deren Hilfe* er sein heliozentrisches Weltsystem aufbaute.
4. Isaac Newton stellte das Gravitationsgesetz auf, *nach dem sich alle Körper einander anziehen.*
5. Kepler entdeckte *die Abnahme der Lichtstärke mit dem Quadrat der Entfernung.*

STRUCTURE

10.   Subjunctive I

a.   Subjunctive I is used to express:

1.   Unreal comparison:

> Er gab das Geld aus, als **sei** er der reichste Mann auf der Erde.
> *He spent money as if he were the richest man on earth.*

2.   Indirect discourse:

In direct discourse, a statement is quoted directly:

Hans sagte: „**Ich bin krank.**"   (Indicative)
Hans said: "I am sick."

In indirect discourse, a statement is reported indirectly as a subordinate clause with or without **daß:**

Hans sagte, **daß er krank sei.**
Hans sagte, **er sei krank.**
Hans said that he was sick.

3.   Desire, request; direction:

Er lebe hoch! *(He should live a long life!)*
(A wish for good health and a long life.)

Man nehme eine Aspirin. *(Take one aspirin.)*

b.   The present tense forms of Subjunctive I are derived from:

> INFINITIVE STEM + **e** + ENDINGS

fragen:

ich	frage	wir	fragen
du	fragest	ihr	fraget

er
sie } frage
es

sie
Sie } fragen

c.   Comparison: Subjunctive I and Indicative

PRESENT INDICATIVE	PRESENT SUBJ. I	PRESENT INDICATIVE	PRESENT SUBJ. I	PRESENT INDICATIVE	PRESENT SUBJ. I
ich **nehme**	nehme	muß	müsse	habe	habe
du **nimmst**	nehmest	mußt	müssest	hast	habest
er **nimmt**	nehme	muß	müsse	hat	habe
wir **nehmen**	nehmen	müssen	müssen	haben	haben
ihr **nehmt**	nehmet	müßt	müsset	habt	habet
sie **nehmen**	nehmen	müssen	müssen	haben	haben

d.   The stem-vowel changes that occur with some verbs in the present tense are not carried over to the present Subjunctive I.

VIERHUNDERTDREIUNDZWANZIG

e.   The verb **sein** in the present Subjunctive I:

ich	sei	wir	seien
du	seiest	ihr	seiet

er }
sie } sei
es }

sie }
Sie } seien

EXERCISES

A. *Change the following sentences to Subjunctive I:* *

EXAMPLES: Er hat kein Auto.
            Er sagte, er habe kein Auto
            Er sagte, daß er kein Auto habe.

1. Er braucht mehr Zeit.
2. Er kennt das Buch nicht.
3. Er versteht die amerikanische Außenpolitik nicht.
4. Es ist nicht kalt.
5. Er hat vor, nach Deutschland zu reisen.

B. *Change the following sentences to Subjunctive I:* *

EXAMPLES: Er kann heute nicht kommen.
            Er sagte, er könne heute nicht kommen.
            Er sagte, daß er heute nicht kommen könne.

1. Er muß jetzt in die Stadt gehen.
2. Er soll es nicht sagen.
3. Er darf es nicht tun.
4. Er mag das Obst nicht.
5. Er will sie nicht mehr sehen.

11. Past Tense — Subjunctive I

The past tense of Subjunctive I is similar to the present perfect tense of the indicative:

Subjunctive I of **haben** or **sein** +	Past participle

Example:

Er **hat** ein Auto **gekauft.**	(present perfect indicative)
Er **habe** ein Auto **gekauft.**	(subjunctive I, past tense)
Er **ist** gestern **angekommen.**	(present perfect indicative)
Er **sei** gestern **angekommen.**	(subjunctive I, past tense)

VIERHUNDERTVIERUNDZWANZIG

EXERCISE

Change the following sentences to past tense Subjunctive I:*

EXAMPLE: Er ist gestern angekommen.
Er sagte, er sei gestern angekommen.
Er sagte, daß er gestern angekommen sei.

1. Er hat mehr Zeit gebraucht.
2. Es ist nicht kalt gewesen.
3. Der Bus ist zu spät angekommen.
4. Der Präsident hat die Außenpolitik formuliert.
5. Der Wissenschaftler hat das Molekül entdeckt.

READING

Schießpulver

Der Mönch Berthold Schwarz, so erzählt die Legende, habe bei alchemistischen Experimenten zufällig das Schießpulver entdeckt. Der König von Polen habe ihn später an ein Faß gebunden und in die Luft gesprengt. Wer so eine fürchterliche Sache erfinden könne, meinte der König, verdiene den Tod.

VOCABULARY

das	**Schießpulver**	gunpowder	**sprengen**	to explode, blow up
der	**Mönch, -e**	monk	**fürchterlich**	horrible, terrible
	erzählen	to tell, relate	die **Sache, -n**	thing, affair
das	**Experiment, -e**	experiment	**erfinden (erfindet),**	
	zufällig	accidentally	**erfand, erfunden**	to invent
der	**König, -e**	king	**meinen**	to think; to believe
das	**Faß, ⸚sser**	barrel, cask	**verdienen**	to deserve; to earn
das	**Pulver**	powder	der **Tod**	death

STRUCTURAL EXERCISE

Underline all verbs in Subjunctive I in the above reading.

STRUCTURE

12. Future Tense — Subjunctive I

a.   Subjunctive I uses the following forms for the future tense:

Subjunctive I of **werden**	+	Infinitive of main verb

Example:

Er **wird gehen.**   (Indicative, future tense)

Er sagte, er **werde gehen.** ⎫
Er sagt, daß er **gehen werde.** ⎬ (Subjunctive I, future tense)
He said he would go.

b.   Subjunctive I of **werden**

ich	werde	wir	werden
du	werdest	ihr	werdet

er ⎫
sie ⎬ werde
es ⎭

sie ⎫
Sie ⎬ werden

EXERCISE

Change the following sentences to future Subjunctive I:

EXAMPLE: Er kommt nicht ins Büro.
            Er sagte, er komme nicht ins Büro.
            Er sagte, er werde nicht ins Büro kommen
            He said he would not come to the office.

1. Er erzählt die Geschichte.   4. Man weiß alles.
2. Sie erarbeitet das Gebiet.   5. Er liest das Tagebuch.
3. Die Forscher finden die Ursache.

READING

Chinesisches Märchen (von Ernst Penzoldt)

Als der Krieg zwischen den beiden benachbarten Völkern unvermeidlich war, schickten die feindlichen Feldherrn Späher aus, um zu erkunden, wo man am leichtesten in das Nachbarland einfallen könnte. Und die Kundschafter kehrten zurück und berichteten ungefähr mit den gleichen Worten ihren Vorgesetzten: es gäbe nur eine Stelle an der Grenze, um in das andere Land einzubrechen. ,,Dort aber``, sagten sie, ,,wohnt ein braver kleiner Bauer in einem kleinen Haus mit seiner anmutigen Frau. Sie haben einander lieb, und es heißt, sie seien die glücklichsten Menschen auf der Welt. Sie haben ein Kind. Wenn wir nun über das kleine Grundstück ins Feindesland einmarschierten, dann würden wir das Glück zerstören. Also kann es keinen Krieg geben.`` Das sahen die Feldherren denn auch wohl oder übel ein, und der Krieg unterblieb, wie jeder Mensch begreifen wird.

5

10

VIERHUNDERTSECHSUNDZWANZIG

VOCABULARY

	benachbart	neighboring
	unvermeidlich	unavoidable
	aus-schicken	to send out
der	Feldherr, -en	field marshall, general
der	Späher, -	scout
	erkunden	to find out, ascertain, gain
	ein-fallen (fällt ein), fiel ein, ist eingefallen	to invade, attack
der	Kundschafter, -	scout, explorer
	zurück-kehren	to return
	berichten	to report
	ungefähr	approximately
	gleich	same, identical
der	Vorgesetzte, -n	superior
die	Stelle, -n	place, location
	ein-brechen (bricht ein) brach ein, ist eingebrochen	to break in, invade

	brav	honest, good
	anmutig	graceful, charming
	lieb haben	to love
	einander	each other
das	Grundstück, -e	piece of land
das	Feindesland	enemy territory
	ein-marschieren	to invade, enter, march in
	ein-sehen (sieht ein), sah ein, eingesehen	to comprehend; to concede; to realize
	wohl oder übel	willy nilly, cost what it may, like it or not
	unterbleiben (unterbleibt) unterblieb, ist unterblieben	not to take place, be discontinued, not to occur
	begreifen (begreift), begriff, begriffen	to understand, comprehend

ppendix 1

READING GERMAN TYPE

German Alphabet

ROMAN TYPE		PRONUNCIATION[1]	GERMAN TYPE (FRAKTUR)	
A	a	ah	𝔄	a
B	b	beh	𝔅	b
C	c	zeh	ℭ	c
D	d	deh	𝔇	d
E	e	eh	𝔈	e
F	f	eff	𝔉	f
G	g	geh	𝔊	g
H	h	hah	𝔥	h
I	i	ie	𝔍	i
J	j	jott	𝔍	j
K	k	kah	𝔎	f
L	l	ell	𝔏	l
M	m	emm	𝔐	m
N	n	enn	𝔑	n
O	o	oh	𝔒	o
P	p	peh	𝔓	p
Q	q	kuh	𝔒	q
R	r	err	𝔑	r
S	s	eß	𝔖	ſ,s
T	t	teh	𝔗	t
U	u	uh	𝔘	u
V	v	fau	𝔙	v
W	w	weh	𝔚	w
X	x	iks	𝔛	r
Y	y	üpsilon	𝔜	y
Z	z	zett	𝔷	z
	ß	eßzett		ß
Ä	ä	ah Umlaut	𝔄̈	ä
Ö	ö	oh Umlaut	𝔒̈	ö
Ü	ü	uh Umlaut	𝔘̈	ü

1.   Pronunciation is given in German sounds; the letters are to be pronounced in German.

LESSON 1

Der Student in Deutschland

Der Student lernt Deutsch. Der Student studiert in Deutschland. Der Student studiert Physik. Der Student lernt viel in Deutschland. Der Student bleibt ein Jahr in Deutschland.

LESSON 4

Biologie

Biologie ist das griechische Wort für die „Lehre von dem Leben". Die Biologie hat verschiedene Teilgebiete: Botanik, Zoologie und Anthropologie.

Die Botanik behandelt Pflanzen, die Zoologie behandelt Tiere, und die Anthropologie behandelt den Menschen.

Basilika

Basilika ist ein griechisches Wort. Es bedeutet Königsbau. Die Basilika hat eine rechteckige Halle. Die Halle hat Säulen und eine halbrunde Apsis. Die Basilika ist eine Urform für die christlichen Kirchen.

LESSON 7

Arithmetik

Das Wort Arithmetik stammt aus der griechischen Sprache. Die Arithmetik ist ein Teilgebiet in der Mathematik. Sie bezeichnet die Gesetze für die verschiedenen Rechenarten (Addition, Subtraktion, Division und Multiplikation).

Nahrung

Eine neue Getreidesorte erscheint auf dem Markt. Sie trägt nach einmaliger Aussaat mehrere Jahre Ähren. Die neue Roggenart spart dem Bauer viel Arbeit. Ein Forschungsinstitut in Braunschweig (Deutschland) erprobt jetzt die neue Getreidesorte.

VIERHUNDERTNEUNUNDZWANZIG

LESSON 10

Biologische Welle

500 (fünfhundert) Bauernhöfe in der Bundesrepublik Deutschland schwimmen auf der „biologischen Welle". Die Bauern verwenden nur natürliche Düngemittel. Mineraldünger und Pflanzenschutzmittel sind tabu. Die Erträge sind etwas niedriger, aber die Ernte erzielt höhere Preise.

Nur für Nichtraucher

Das Zigarettenrauchen vermindert die Strömungsgeschwindigkeit des Blutes. Sie sinkt nach einer Zigarette um 40 (vierzig) bis 60 (sechzig) Prozent. Das ist das Resultat von Ultraschallmessungen der Blutzirkulation.

LESSON 13

Unser Herz in Zahlen

Die Größe des menschlichen Herzens entspricht etwa der Größe der Faust seines Besitzers. Ein Menschenherz wiegt durchschnittlich nicht viel mehr als ein halbes Pfund. Es besteht fast ganz aus Muskulatur. Dieser Muskel hat eine große Leistungsfähigkeit. Der Herzmuskel arbeitet Tag und Nacht pausenlos. Der Hohlmuskel vollbringt an einem Tag die Leistung von 12 700 mkg. (Meterkilogramm).

Das Herz preßt mit jedem Herzschlag 60 ccm (Kubikzentimeter) Blut in das Röhrennetz des Blutgefäßsystems. Das geschieht 4 200 mal in der Stunde, am Tag 100 800 mal! Die gesamte Blutmenge des Menschen beträgt etwa 5 Liter. Das Herz befördert am Tag 5 760 Liter Blut. Der Herzschlag erteilt der Pulswelle eine Geschwindigkeit von 5 bis 6 Metern in der Sekunde.

Abitur

Das Abitur ist die Reifeprüfung an höheren Schulen. Der Schüler beendet mit dem Abitur seine Erziehung am Gymnasium. Es berechtigt zum Studium an Universitäten oder Technischen Hochschulen. Das Abitur heißt auch Matura in Österreich.

LESSON 16

Kreislaufkollaps

Die Regenwälder am Amazonas sind mit ihrer Vielfalt an Pflanzen und Tierarten ein Dorado für Wissenschaftler. Dieses äußerst komplizierte Ökosystem reagiert emp-

VIERHUNDERTDREISSIG

findlich auf Eingriffe durch die Zivilisation. Der Mensch zerstört das Ökosystem durch eine Unterbrechung des natürlichen Kreislaufs.

Ökologen plädieren für die Erhaltung der urwüchsigen amphibischen Landschaft und ihres einmaligen Innenlebens.

Abraham Lincoln

Lincoln war der 16. Präsident der Vereinigten Staaten (1861–1865). Er stammte aus einer armen Familie. Er war Advokat und Abgeordneter im Parlament von Illinois (1834–1841) und im Kongreß (1847–1849). Von 1856 an begann sein schneller Aufstieg in der Republikanischen Partei. Er vertrat eine gemäßigte Ansicht in der Sklavenfrage. Er war ein glänzender, volkstümlicher Redner und ein gewandter Parteitaktiker. Man nominierte ihn 1860 in Chicago als Präsidentschaftskandidat. Die Grundsätze seiner Politik formulierte Lincoln in seiner Rede auf dem Schlachtfeld von Gettysburg (1863): „Eine Regierung des Volkes durch das Volk für das Volk." Nach dem Ende des Bürgerkrieges zielte Lincolns Politik auf eine schnelle Wiedereingliederung der besiegten Südstaaten, aber er stieß auf den Widerstand des radikalen Segments der Partei.

Seine Gegner verhinderten jedoch nicht seine Wiederwahl (1964). Der Fanatiker J. W. Booth ermordete Lincoln im Jahre 1865.

LESSON 19

Albrecht Dürer

Albrecht Dürer war ein deutscher Maler, Graphiker und Kunsttheoretiker. Er unternahm Kunstreisen in Deutschland, nach Italien und in die Niederlande. Seine großen Werke schuf er in seiner Vaterstadt Nürnberg. Sehr bekannte Werke von ihm sind Ölgemälde („Adam und Eva"; „Die Apostel"), zahlreiche Porträts, Holzschnitte (Apokalypse"; „Ritter, Tod und Teufel") und Kupferstiche, daneben aber auch theoretische Werke über Anatomie und Perspektive.

Deutschland — Ein Überblick

Deutschland ist heute zugleich ein historischer, kultureller und geographischer Begriff. Politisch gibt es auf dem Gebiet des früheren Deutschen Reiches seit 1949 zwei deutsche Staaten: die Bundesrepublik Deutschland (BRD) und die Deutsche Demokratische Republik (DDR). Oft spricht man einfach von „Westdeutschland" und „Ostdeutschland".

Die Bundesrepublik hat ungefähr 62 Millionen Einwohner, die DDR etwa 17 Millionen. Die größte Stadt Deutschlands, Berlin, hat rund 3,2 (drei Komma zwei) Millionen Einwohner, davon 2,1 (zwei Komma eins) Millionen in West- und 1,1 (eins Komma eins) Millionen in Ost-Berlin. Dann folgt die Handels- und Hafenstadt Hamburg mit 1,8 Millionen Einwohnern. Die bayrische Hauptstadt München ist mit 1,3 Millionen Einwohnern die drittgrößte Stadt. Die Entfernung von Hamburg nach München ist ungefähr 800 Kilometer.

Geographisch gliedert man Deutschland in vier große Gebiete: die norddeutsche Tiefebene, die Mittelgebirge, das Alpenvorland, und das Hochgebirge (die Alpen). Die wichtigsten Flüsse sind der Rhein, die Weser, die Elbe, die Oder und die Donau. Der Rhein, die Weser und die Elbe fließen von Süden nach Norden in die Nordsee. Die Oder mündet in die Ostsee. Die Donau fließt von Westen nach Osten durch Österreich, Ungarn und den Balkan in das Schwarze Meer.

LESSON 22

Aktuell

Aktuell nennt man etwas, was im Augenblick wichtig oder interessant ist. Tageszeitungen müssen aktuell sein, d.h. sie müssen stets das Neueste bringen.

Neue Quellen der Energie

Die Bundesrepublik Deutschland ist das erste Land auf der Erde, für das man einen „Wärmeatlas" erstellen will. Dieser Atlas soll angeben, wo und zu welchen Zeiten im Lande man Energie verbraucht. Außerdem teilt er mit, wo im Jahre 2 000 ein Fernwärmenetz bestehen soll. Auf diese Weise kann man langfristig die Energieversorgung auf Kernenergie und andere Arten von Energie umstellen.

Renaissance — Humanismus — Reformation

Die Renaissance ist die große europäische Kulturepoche, die die Wende vom Mittelalter zur Neuzeit umfaßt. Sie überwindet das mittelalterliche Welt- und Menschenbild und die überkommene Staats- und Gesellschaftsordnung. An die Stelle des Autoritätsglaubens tritt der Geist kritischer Forschung; der Mensch wird zum Maß aller Dinge; die Staatsraison zum Prinzip der Politik. Die italienischen Fürstenhöfe — besonders das Florenz der Medici — sind beispielhaft für Europa. Byzantinische Gelehrte, die nach der Eroberung von Byzanz und Griechenland durch die Türken nach Italien geflüchtet waren, haben das Studium der antiken Literatur angeregt. Die Kunst- und Lebensauffassung der Antike gelten den Humanisten als Vorbild. Die Reformation zerstört die Einheit des Glaubens. Neben der lateinischen Dichtung der Humanisten entsteht in Deutschland ein reiches literarisches Leben. Durch den Buchdruck werden die literarischen Erzeugnisse rasch zum Gemeingut aller Gebildeten.

Vertreter der Renaissance, des Humanismus und der Reformation waren:

Johannes Reuchlin, 1455–1522   Martin Luther, 1483–1546
Erasmus von Rotterdam, 1469–1536   Ulrich von Hutten, 1488–1523

VIERHUNDERTZWEIUNDDREISSIG

LESSON 25

Die Schweiz

Die Schweiz liegt mitten in Europa. Ihre Nachbarn sind: Frankreich, Italien, Öster=
reich, Liechtenstein und Deutschland. Die Schweiz ist eine Bundesrepublik mit 41 288
km² (Quadratkilometer) Fläche und 6 Millionen Einwohnern. 74,4% der Schweizer
Bürger sprechen Deutsch, 20,2% Französisch, 4,1% Italienisch und 1% Räto=
romanisch. Neben den Amtssprachen Deutsch, Französisch, Italienisch erkennt man auch
seit 1938 Rätoromanisch als Landessprache an. Die Schweiz ist ein Bundesstaat mit
22 souveränen Kantonen. Die landwirtschaftliche Nutzung besteht aus Getreide=,
Wein= und Obstanbau. Die Schweiz hat sehr geringe Bodenschätze und exportiert einen
großen Teil ihrer Industriegüter, besonders Maschinen, Uhren, chemische Erzeugnisse,
Textil= und Nahrungsmittel. Die Handelsbilanz ist auf Grund der hohen Einfuhren
von Nahrungs= und Genußmitteln, von Spezialmaschinen, Autos und Instrumenten
stark passiv. Das Land gleicht sie jedoch durch Kapitalerträge, Gütertransit und
Fremdenverkehr aus.

Die heutige Schweiz mit ihren 22 Kantonen ist das Resultat der Bundesverfassung
von 1814, die der Wiener Kongreß bestätigte. Zugleich erkannte der Kongreß die Neu=
tralität der Schweiz und die Unverletzbarkeit ihres Gebietes an. Die Verfassung von
1814 machte die Schweiz zu einem losen Staatenbund. Dann folgten politische
Auseinandersetzungen, bis schließlich 1847 die liberalen Sieger den Staatenbund in
einen Bundesstaat umwandelten, der noch heute besteht.

Der Optimist (von Sigismund von Radecki)

Diese Geschichte ist ein Märchen und daher besonders zur Veröffentlichung geeignet.

Es waren einmal zwei Frösche, die einen Kuhstall besuchten. Der eine Frosch war
seiner seelischen Einstellung nach Optimist. Der andere Frosch war aus Natur
pessimistisch.

Mit einem riesigen Sprung sprangen beide in einen Metalleimer und plumpsten
in die Milch. Der Pessimist starrte entsetzt auf die spiegelglatten, unbekletterbaren
Metallwände, schwamm ein paar Minuten, gab endlich den hoffnungslosen Kampf auf,
sank auf den Grund und ertrank.

Der optimistische Frosch starrte ebenfalls auf die spiegelglatten Metallwände. Dann
aber faßte er sich ein Herz und ist die ganze Nacht hindurch so unverdrossen geschwom=
men, rückgeschwommen, hat gekrault und gestrampelt — daß er beim Morgengrauen
hoch oben auf einem Berg von Butter saß!

LESSON 28

Arbeiter und die Wirtschaft

Wenn die Nachfrage nach Arbeitern steigt, so steigen die Arbeiter im Preis. Wenn die
Nachfrage fällt, dann fällt sie so sehr, daß eine Anzahl von Arbeitern nicht verkäuflich

ift, d.h. „auf Lager bleiben", so bleiben sie eben liegen, und da sie vom bloßen Liegen nicht leben können, so sterben sie Hungers. . . . (Aus dem Buch von Friedrich Engels: „Die Lage der arbeitenden Klassen in England")

Säuren, Laugen und Salze

Säuren sind chemische Verbindungen, die in wäßriger Lösung Wasserstoffionen abspalten. In je größerem Umfange dies geschieht, um so stärker ist die saure Wirkung. Laugen oder Basen sind chemische Verbindungen, die in wäßriger Lösung Hydroxylionen abspalten. Säuren sind z.B. alle Wasserstoffverbindungen der Nichtmetalle (insbesondere die Halogenwasserstoffe) sowie die Verbindungen der Nichtmetalle (vor allem der Schwefel-, Stickstoff-, Chlor- und Phosphoroxide sowie des Kohlendioxids) mit Wasser. Basen sind z.B. alle Oxide und Hydroxide der Metalle (insbesondere der Alkalimetalle), sowie das Ammoniumhydroxid. Beim Zusammentreffen von Säuren und Basen entstehen unter gleichzeitiger Bildung von Wasser die Salze, bei denen statt der Wasserstoffionen Metallionen, die von den Basen stammen, an den jeweiligen Säurerest gebunden sind. An dem Namen eines Salzes kann man erkennen, auf welcher Säure und welcher Base es zustandekam.

Das Schulsystem der BRD

Es gibt verschiedene Arten von Gymnasien, darunter: das altsprachliche (Hauptsprachen: Latein und Griechisch), das neusprachliche (Hauptsprachen: Englisch und Französisch) und das mathematisch-naturwissenschaftliche Gymnasium. Ein Schüler hat pro Woche etwa 30 Stunden Unterricht in 12 bis 14 Fächern. Der Unterricht beginnt meist um 8 Uhr und endet gegen 13 Uhr. Nachmittags ist normalerweise kein Unterricht. Für die höheren Klassen finden an ein oder zwei Nachmittagen Arbeitsgemeinschaften statt. Dort soll jeder das lernen, was ihn besonders interessiert, z.B. Philosophie, Musik, Literatur, Physik oder eine zusätzliche Fremdsprache.
Die jüngeren Schüler sollen im Durchschnitt täglich ein bis zwei Stunden Hausaufgaben machen, die älteren zwei bis drei Stunden. Der Stundenplan eines 16jährigen Oberschülers in einem neusprachlichen Gymnasium sieht ungefähr so aus:

	Montag	Dienstag	Mittwoch
1	Englisch	—	Sozialkunde
2	Geschichte	Latein	Englisch
3	Kunst	Physik	Deutsch
4	Kunst	Französisch	Mathematik
5	Deutsch	Sport	Religion
6	—	Musik	—

VIERHUNDERTVIERUNDDREISSIG

	Donnerstag	Freitag	Samstag
1	Französisch	Physik	Chemie
2	Latein	Deutsch	Mathematik
3	Geschichte	Mathematik	Deutsch
4	Englisch	Erdkunde	Englisch
5	Sport	Französisch	Erdkunde
6	—	—	—

Das Schuljahr beginnt nach den Sommerferien und endet in Juni oder Juli. Im Jahr hat ein Schüler etwa drei Monate Ferien. Die Sommerferien zwischen Juli und September sind die längsten Ferien und dauern etwa sechs Wochen. Zu Weihnachten und um Ostern gibt es noch einmal kurze Ferien von zwei bis drei Wochen Dauer.

LESSON 31

Bank

Bank ist ein Wort, das aus dem Italienischen stammt. Es bedeutete ursprünglich Sitzbank oder Ladentisch. Heute versteht man darunter auch:

1. ein Unternehmen, das Geldeinlagen gegen Zinsen übernimmt, Geld gegen Zinsen ausleiht (Kredit), Geldwechsel und Zahlungsverkehr betreibt, Wertpapiere und ausländisches Geld für seine Kunden an- und verkauft sowie Wertgegenstände im Safe aufbewahrt;
2. eine Sand- oder Gesteinsablagerung, angeschwemmt durch die Strömung, im Meer oder in Flüssen;
3. eine Spielbank. In Spielbanken kann man an Glücksspielen, wie Roulett oder Poker usw., teilnehmen und dabei versuchen, sein eingesetztes Geld zu vervielfachen. Auf die Dauer gewinnt jedoch stets die Spielbank.

Zitat ohne Kommentar: Die NSDAP als einzige Partei

Wer es unternimmt, den organisatorischen Zusammenhalt einer anderen politischen Partei aufrechtzuerhalten oder eine neue politische Partei zu bilden, wird, sofern nicht die Tat nach anderen Vorschriften mit einer höheren Strafe bedroht ist, mit Zuchthaus bis zu drei Jahren oder mit Gefängnis von 6 Monaten bis zu drei Jahren bestraft. (Gesetz gegen die Neubildung von Parteien vom 14. Juli 1933)

Die Deutsche Demokratische Republik (DDR)

Als Folge des 2. (zweiten) Weltkrieges entstanden auf dem Gebiet des früheren Deutschen Reiches zwei neue Staaten. Im Westen kam die Bundesrepublik Deutsch-

VIERHUNDERTFÜNFUNDDREISSIG

land zustande, im Osten die Deutsche Demokratische Republik. Beide Staaten gingen aus ehemaligen Besatzungszonen hervor. Die Bundesrepublik bestand nach 1945 zunächst aus drei Besatzungszonen (amerikanische, britische und französische Zone). Die Deutsche Demokratische Republik entstand auf dem Gebiet der früheren russischen Besatzungszone.

Auf Betreiben der Sowjetunion errichte die SED (Sozialistische Einheitspartei Deutschlands) im Jahre 1949 die DDR. Die SED ist die Staatspartei der DDR und besteht seit 1946, als man die SPD (Sozialdemokratische Partei Deutschlands) und die KPD (Kommunistische Partei Deutschlands) in der neuen SED vereinigte. Die DDR besteht heute aus 14 Landesbezirken, die aus den früheren Ländern Brandenburg, Mecklenburg, Sachsen-Anhalt, Thüringen und Sachsen entstanden. In der DDR wohnen heute rund 17 Millionen Einwohner auf einer Fläche von ungefähr 108 000 km² (Quadratkilometer).

Die Verfassung der DDR kennt nur das Primat der Gemeinschaft, nicht dagegen die Freiheit des einzelnen um des einzelnen willen. Das Parlament, die Volkskammer, hat 400 Abgeordnete. Es beschließt Gesetze, wählt und entläßt die Mitglieder des Obersten Gerichtshofes und den Generalstaatsanwalt und bestellt und entläßt die Regierung. Die Regierung der DDR, der Ministerrat, arbeitet nach dem Prinzip des „Demokratischen Zentralismus", d.h., daß alle untergeordneten Organe an die Weisungen des Ministerrats gebunden sind. Besonders offensichtlich treten die zentralistischen Tendenzen in der Wirtschaftsverwaltung hervor, wo der Volkswirtschaftsrat und die Plankommission seit 1961 eine straffe Kontrolle ausüben. Alle staatliche Verwaltung unterliegt der Lenkung und Kontrolle durch die SED. Die größte Zahl der Produktionseinrichtungen sind im Besitz des Staates. Die DDR ist Mitglied der COMECON und damit in die Wirtschaft des gesamten Ostblocks eingegliedert. Der größte Teil der Landwirtschaft besteht aus staatlichen Produktionsgenossenschaften. Auch der Groß- und Einzelhandel gehört zum großen Teil der staatlichen Handelsorganisation an. Die industriellen Betriebe sind meistens sogenannte „Volkseigene Betriebe" (VEB), die der Staat kontrolliert. Das Erziehungs- und Ausbildungssystem der DDR besteht aus allgemeinen polytechnischen Oberschulen (10 Jahre), erweiterten polytechnischen Oberschulen (12 Jahre), Sonderschulen für körperlich benachteiligte Kinder, Fachschulen, Hochschulen und Universitäten. Die Absolventen der erweiterten Oberschule müssen während der Schulzeit einen praktischen Beruf lernen oder vor dem Studium ein einjähriges Praktikum ableisten.

LESSON 34

Physik

Die Physik ist ein Zweig der Naturwissenschaft und befaßt sich mit den materiellen Kräften sowie deren Auswirkungen. Wir gliedern sie in die Teilgebiete Mechanik, Akustik sowie Lehre der elektromagnetischen Wellen, wobei jedes Gebiet in sich eine

VIERHUNDERTSECHSUNDDREISSIG

weitere Unterteilung erfährt: die Mechanik in Statik (Lehre von den ruhenden Kräften, also vom Gleichgewicht) und Dynamik (Lehre von den Bewegungen, die man durch Kräfte erzeugt); die Akustik in die Lehre vom Schall, von den Schwingungen und Wellen der Materie; die Lehre der elektromagnetischen Wellen in Magnetismus, Elektrizität (Elektrostatik und Elektrodynamik), Kalorik (Lehre von der Wärme) und Optik (Lehre vom Licht).

Bei den alten Griechen war die Physik noch ein Bestandteil der Philosophie und man behandelte sie spekulativ (nur durch Nachdenken) wie die Philosophie. Diese „Naturphilosophie", die auf unbestimmte Vorstellungen begründet war, verhinderte eine wesentliche Erweiterung der Naturerkenntnis. Aristoteles (384 bis 322 v. Chr.) jedoch erzielte durch empirische (auf Erfahrung gegründete) Denkungsart bedeutende Erfolge über die Erkenntnisse vom Schall und Licht. Nach ihm entdeckte Archimedes (287 bis 212 v. Chr.) den Auftrieb der Flüssigkeiten, das Hebelgesetz und die Mechanik des Flaschenzuges, wie er auch die Wasserschraube erfand.

ppendix 2

SUMMARY OF FORMS

1. Articles

a. Definite article

	SINGULAR			PLURAL
	MASCULINE	FEMININE	NEUTER	ALL GENDERS
NOMINATIVE	der	die	das	die
GENITIVE	des	der	des	der
DATIVE	dem	der	dem	den
ACCUSATIVE	den	die	das	die

b. Indefinite article

	SINGULAR			PLURAL
	MASCULINE	FEMININE	NEUTER	ALL GENDERS
NOMINATIVE	ein	eine	ein	keine
GENITIVE	eines	einer	eines	keiner
DATIVE	einem	einer	einem	keinen
ACCUSATIVE	einen	eine	ein	keine

2. Prepositions

a. With the accusative

bis	*until, up to, as far as*	ohne	*without*
durch	*through, by*	um	*around, at, about*
für	*for*	wider	*against*
gegen	*against, around*		

b. With the dative

aus	*out of, from, for*	nach	*to, according to, after*
außer	*except, beside, beyond*	seit	*since*
bei	*with, at*	von	*from, by*
gegenüber	*opposite*	zu	*to, at*
mit	*with*		

VIERHUNDERTACHTUNDDREISSIG

c.   With the dative or accusative

an	on, onto, at, by	über	above, about, across
auf	on, upon	unter	under, among
hinter	behind	vor	in front of, before, ago
in	in, into	zwischen	between
neben	next to, beside		

d.   With the genitive

(an)statt	instead of	jenseits	on that side of
aufgrund	on account of, because of	trotz	in spite of, despite
außerhalb	outside of	während	during
innerhalb	inside of	wegen	on account of, because of
diesseits	on this side of		

3.   Verbs

a.   **sein**

INDICATIVE

PRESENT	PAST
ich bin	ich war
du bist	du warst
er ist	er war
sie ist	sie war
es ist	es war
wir sind	wir waren
ihr seid	ihr wart
sie sind	sie waren
Sie sind	Sie waren

PRESENT PERFECT	PAST PERFECT
ich bin gewesen	ich war gewesen
du bist gewesen	du warst gewesen
er ist gewesen	er war gewesen
sie ist gewesen	sie war gewesen
es ist gewesen	es war gewesen
wir sind gewesen	wir waren gewesen
ihr seid gewesen	ihr wart gewesen
sie sind gewesen	sie waren gewesen
Sie sind gewesen	Sie waren gewesen

FUTURE

ich werde sein
du wirst sein
er wird sein
sie wird sein
es wird sein
wir werden sein
ihr werdet sein
sie werden sein
Sie werden sein

FUTURE PERFECT

ich werde gewesen sein
du wirst gewesen sein
er wird gewesen sein
sie wird gewesen sein
es wird gewesen sein
wir werden gewesen sein
ihr werdet gewesen sein
sie werden gewesen sein
Sie werden gewesen sein

IMPERATIVE

sei!
seien wir!
seid!
seien Sie!

PAST INFINITIVE: gewesen sein

SUBJUNCTIVE

PRESENT SUBJUNCTIVE I

ich sei
du seiest
er sei
sie sei
es sei
wir seien
ihr seiet
sie seien
Sie seien

PRESENT SUBJUNCTIVE II

ich wäre
du wärest
er wäre
sie wäre
es wäre
wir wären
ihr wäret
sie wären
Sie wären

PAST SUBJUNCTIVE I

ich sei gewesen
du seiest gewesen
er sei gewesen
sie sei gewesen
es sei gewesen
wir seien gewesen
ihr seiet gewesen
sie seien gewesen
Sie seien gewesen

PAST SUBJUNCTIVE II

ich wäre gewesen
du wärest gewesen
er wäre gewesen
sie wäre gewesen
es wäre gewesen
wir wären gewesen
ihr wäret gewesen
sie wären gewesen
Sie wären gewesen

VIERHUNDERTVIERZIG

b.   **haben**

INDICATIVE

PRESENT

ich habe
du hast
er hat
sie hat
es hat
wir haben
ihr habt
sie haben
Sie haben

PAST

ich hatte
du hattest
er hatte
sie hatte
es hatte
wir hatten
ihr hattet
sie hatten
Sie hatten

PRESENT PERFECT

ich habe gehabt
du hast gehabt
er hat gehabt
sie hat gehabt
es hat gehabt
wir haben gehabt
ihr habt gehabt
sie haben gehabt
Sie haben gehabt

PAST PERFECT

ich hatte gehabt
du hattest gehabt
er hatte gehabt
sie hatte gehabt
es hatte gehabt
wir hatten gehabt
ihr hattet gehabt
sie hatten gehabt
Sie hatten gehabt

FUTURE

ich werde haben
du wirst haben
er wird haben
sie wird haben
es wird haben
wir werden haben
ihr werdet haben
sie werden haben
Sie werden haben

FUTURE PERFECT

ich werde gehabt haben
du wirst gehabt haben
er wird gehabt haben
sie wird gehabt haben
es wird gehabt haben
wir werden gehabt haben
ihr werdet gehabt haben
sie werden gehabt haben
Sie werden gehabt haben

IMPERATIVE

habe!
haben wir!
habt!
haben Sie!

PAST INFINITIVE: gehabt haben

SUBJUNCTIVE

PRESENT SUBJUNCTIVE I

ich habe
du habest
er habe
sie habe
es habe
wir haben
ihr habet
sie haben
Sie haben

PRESENT SUBJUNCTIVE II

ich hätte
du hättest
er hätte
sie hätte
es hätte
wir hätten
ihr hättet
sie hätten
Sie hätten

PAST SUBJUNCTIVE I

ich habe gehabt
du habest gehabt
er habe gehabt
sie habe gehabt
es habe gehabt
wir haben gehabt
ihr habet gehabt
sie haben gehabt
Sie haben gehabt

PAST SUBJUNCTIVE II

ich hätte gehabt
du hättest gehabt
er hätte gehabt
sie hätte gehabt
es hätte gehabt
wir hätten gehabt
ihr hättet gehabt
sie hätten gehabt
Sie hätten gehabt

c.   **werden**

INDICATIVE

PRESENT

ich werde
du wirst
er wird
sie wird
es wird
wir werden
ihr werdet
sie werden
Sie werden

PAST

ich wurde
du wurdest
er wurde
sie wurde
es wurde
wir wurden
ihr wurdet
sie wurden
Sie wurden

PRESENT PERFECT

ich bin geworden
du bist geworden
er ist geworden
sie ist geworden
es ist geworden

PAST PERFECT

ich war geworden
du warst geworden
er war geworden
sie war geworden
es war geworden

VIERHUNDERTZWEIUNDVIERZIG

wir sind geworden
ihr seid geworden
sie sind geworden
Sie sind geworden

wir waren geworden
ihr wart geworden
sie waren geworden
Sie waren geworden

FUTURE

ich werde werden
du wirst werden
er wird werden
sie wird werden
es wird werden
wir werden werden
ihr werdet werden
sie werden werden
Sie werden werden

FUTURE PERFECT

ich werde geworden sein
du wirst geworden sein
er wird geworden sein
sie wird geworden sein
es wird geworden sein
wir werden geworden sein
ihr werdet geworden sein
sie werden geworden sein
Sie werden geworden sein

IMPERATIVE

werde!
werdet!
werden Sie!

PAST INFINITIVE: geworden sein

SUBJUNCTIVE

PRESENT SUBJUNCTIVE I

ich werde
du werdest
er werde
sie werde
es werde
wir werden
ihr werdet
sie werden
Sie werden

PRESENT SUBJUNCTIVE II

ich würde
du würdest
er würde
sie würde
es würde
wir würden
ihr würdet
sie würden
Sie würden

PAST SUBJUNCTIVE I

ich sei geworden
du seiest geworden
er sei geworden
sie sei geworden
es sei geworden
wir seien geworden
ihr seiet geworden
sie seien geworden
Sie seien geworden

PAST SUBJUNCTIVE II

ich wäre geworden
du wärest geworden
er wäre geworden
sie wäre geworden
es wäre geworden
wir wären geworden
ihr wäret geworden
sie wären geworden
Sie wären geworden

VIERHUNDERTDREIUNDVIERZIG

d. Weak-verb conjugation: **lernen**

INDICATIVE

PRESENT	PAST
ich lerne	ich lernte
du lernst	du lerntest
er lernt	er lernte
sie lernt	sie lernte
es lernt	es lernte
wir lernen	wir lernten
ihr lernt	ihr lerntet
sie lernen	sie lernten
Sie lernen	Sie lernten

PRESENT PERFECT	PAST PERFECT
ich habe gelernt	ich hatte gelernt
du hast gelernt	du hattest gelernt
er hat gelernt	er hatte gelernt
sie hat gelernt	sie hatte gelernt
es hat gelernt	es hatte gelernt
wir haben gelernt	wir hatten gelernt
ihr habt gelernt	ihr hattet gelernt
sie haben gelernt	sie hatten gelernt
Sie haben gelernt	Sie hatten gelernt

FUTURE	FUTURE PERFECT
ich werde lernen	ich werde gelernt haben
du wirst lernen	du wirst gelernt haben
er wird lernen	er wird gelernt haben
sie wird lernen	sie wird gelernt haben
es wird lernen	es wird gelernt haben
wir werden lernen	wir werden gelernt haben
ihr werdet lernen	ihr werdet gelernt haben
sie werden lernen	sie werden gelernt haben
Sie werden lernen	Sie werden gelernt haben

IMPERATIVE

lerne!
lernen wir!
lernt!
lernen Sie!

PAST INFINITIVE: gelernt haben

VIERHUNDERTVIERUNDVIERZIG

SUBJUNCTIVE

PRESENT SUBJUNCTIVE I	PRESENT SUBJUNCTIVE II
ich lerne	ich lernte
du lernest	du lerntest
er lerne	er lernte
sie lerne	sie lernte
es lerne	es lernte
wir lernen	wir lernten
ihr lernet	ihr lerntet
sie lernen	sie lernten
Sie lernen	Sie lernten

PAST SUBJUNCTIVE I	PAST SUBJUNCTIVE II
ich habe gelernt	ich hätte gelernt
du habest gelernt	du hättest gelernt
er habe gelernt	er hätte gelernt
sie habe gelernt	sie hätte gelernt
es habe gelernt	es hätte gelernt
wir haben gelernt	wir hätten gelernt
ihr habet gelernt	ihr hättet gelernt
sie haben gelernt	sie hätten gelernt
Sie haben gelernt	Sie hätten gelernt

e. Strong-verb conjugation: **lesen**

INDICATIVE

PRESENT	PAST
ich lese	ich las
du liest	du lasest
er liest	er las
sie liest	sie las
es liest	es las
wir lesen	wir lasen
ihr lest	ihr last
sie lesen	sie lasen
Sie lesen	Sie lasen

PRESENT PERFECT	PAST PERFECT
ich habe gelesen	ich hatte gelesen
du hast gelesen	du hattest gelesen
er hat gelesen	er hatte gelesen
sie hat gelesen	sie hatte gelesen
es hat gelesen	es hatte gelesen

VIERHUNDERTFÜNFUNDVIERZIG

wir haben gelesen
ihr habt gelesen
sie haben gelesen
Sie haben gelesen

wir hatten gelesen
ihr hattet gelesen
sie hatten gelesen
Sie hatten gelesen

FUTURE

ich werde lesen
du wirst lesen
er wird lesen
sie wird lesen
es wird lesen
wir werden lesen
ihr werdet lesen
sie werden lesen
Sie werden lesen

FUTURE PERFECT

ich werde gelesen haben
du wirst gelesen haben
er wird gelesen haben
sie wird gelesen haben
es wird gelesen haben
wir werden gelesen haben
ihr werdet gelesen haben
sie werden gelesen haben
Sie werden gelesen haben

IMPERATIVE

lies!
lesen wir!
lest!
lesen Sie!

PAST INFINITIVE: gelesen haben

SUBJUNCTIVE

PRESENT SUBJUNCTIVE I

ich lese
du lesest
er lese
sie lese
es lese
wir lesen
ihr leset
sie lesen
Sie lesen

PRESENT SUBJUNCTIVE II

ich läse
du läsest
er läse
sie läse
es läse
wir läsen
ihr läset
sie läsen
Sie läsen

PAST SUBJUNCTIVE I

ich habe gelesen
du habest gelesen
er habe gelesen
sie habe gelesen
es habe gelesen
wir haben gelesen
ihr habet gelesen
sie haben gelesen
Sie haben gelesen

PAST SUBJUNCTIVE II

ich hätte gelesen
du hättest gelesen
er hätte gelesen
sie hätte gelesen
es hätte gelesen
wir hätten gelesen
ihr hättet gelesen
sie hätten gelesen
Sie hätten gelesen

VIERHUNDERTSECHSUNDVIERZIG

f. Strong-verb conjugation: **laufen**

INDICATIVE

PRESENT

ich laufe
du läufst
er läuft
sie läuft
es läuft
wir laufen
ihr lauft
sie laufen
Sie laufen

PAST

ich lief
du liefst
er lief
sie lief
es lief
wir liefen
ihr lieft
sie liefen
Sie liefen

PRESENT PERFECT

ich bin gelaufen
du bist gelaufen
er ist gelaufen
sie ist gelaufen
es ist gelaufen
wir sind gelaufen
ihr seid gelaufen
sie sind gelaufen
Sie sind gelaufen

PAST PERFECT

ich war gelaufen
du warst gelaufen
er war gelaufen
sie war gelaufen
es war gelaufen
wir waren gelaufen
ihr wart gelaufen
sie waren gelaufen
Sie waren gelaufen

FUTURE

ich werde laufen
du wirst laufen
er wird laufen
sie wird laufen
es wird laufen
wir werden laufen
ihr werdet laufen
sie werden laufen
Sie werden laufen

FUTURE PERFECT

ich werde gelaufen sein
du wirst gelaufen sein
er wird gelaufen sein
sie wird gelaufen sein
es wird gelaufen sein
wir werden gelaufen sein
ihr werdet gelaufen sein
sie werden gelaufen sein
Sie werden gelaufen sein

IMPERATIVE

lauf!
laufen wir!
lauft!
laufen Sie!

PAST INFINITIVE: gelaufen sein

VIERHUNDERTSIEBENUNDVIERZIG

SUBJUNCTIVE

PRESENT SUBJUNCTIVE I	PRESENT SUBJUNCTIVE II
ich laufe	ich liefe
du laufest	du liefest
er laufe	er liefe
sie laufe	sie liefe
es laufe	es liefe
wir laufen	wir liefen
ihr laufet	ihr liefet
sie laufen	sie liefen
Sie laufen	Sie liefen

PAST SUBJUNCTIVE I	PAST SUBJUNCTIVE II
ich sei gelaufen	ich wäre gelaufen
du seiest gelaufen	du wärest gelaufen
er sei gelaufen	er wäre gelaufen
sie sei gelaufen	sie wäre gelaufen
es sei gelaufen	es wäre gelaufen
wir seien gelaufen	wir wären gelaufen
ihr seiet gelaufen	ihr wäret gelaufen
sie seien gelaufen	sie wären gelaufen
Sie seien gelaufen	Sie wären gelaufen

4. Passive Voice

a. Present tense, indicative

> Form of **werden** + past participle of main verb

ich werde gesucht	wir werden gesucht
du wirst gesucht	ihr werdet gesucht
er wird gesucht	sie werden gesucht
sie wird gesucht	Sie werden gesucht
es wird gesucht	

b. Past tense, indicative

> Form of **wurden** + past participle of main verb

ich wurde gesucht	wir wurden gesucht
du wurdest gesucht	ihr wurdet gesucht
er wurde gesucht	sie wurden gesucht
sie wurde gesucht	Sie wurden gesucht
es wurde gesucht	

VIERHUNDERTACHTUNDVIERZIG

    c.   Present perfect, indicative

> Form **sein** + past participle of main verb + **worden**

ich bin gesucht worden	wir sind gesucht worden
du bist gesucht worden	ihr seid gesucht worden
er ist gesucht worden	sie sind gesucht worden
sie ist gesucht worden	Sie sind gesucht worden
es ist gesucht worden	

    d.   Past perfect, indicative

> Past tense of **sein** + past participle of main verb + **worden**

ich war gesucht worden	wir waren gesucht worde
du warst gesucht worden	ihr wart gesucht worden
er war gesucht worden	sie waren gesucht worde
sie war gesucht worden	Sie waren gesucht worde
es war gesucht worden	

    e.   Future

> Form of **werden** + past participle of main verb + **werden**

ich werde gesucht werden	wir werden gesucht werden
du wirst gesucht werden	ihr werdet gesucht werden
er wird gesucht werden	sie werden gesucht werden
sie wird gesucht werden	Sie werden gesucht werden
es wird gesucht werden	

    f.   Future perfect

> Form of **werden** + past participle of main verb + **worden** + **sein**

ich werde gesucht worden sein	wir werden gesucht worden sein
du wirst gesucht worden sein	ihr werdet gesucht worden sein
er wird gesucht worden sein	sie werden gesucht worden sein
sie wird gesucht worden sein	Sie werden gesucht worden sein
es wird gesucht worden sein	

    g.   Present tense, Subjunctive I

> Subjunctive I form of **werden** + past participle

ich werde gesucht	wir werden gesucht
du werdest gesucht	ihr werdet gesucht

VIERHUNDERTNEUNUNDVIERZIG

er werde gesucht   sie werden gesucht
sie werde gesucht   Sie werden gesucht
es werde gesucht

h.   Present tense, Subjunctive II

> Subjunctive II form of **werden** + past participle

ich würde gesucht   wir würden gesucht
du würdest gesucht   ihr würdet gesucht
er würde gesucht   sie würden gesucht
sie würde gesucht   Sie würden gesucht
es würde gesucht

i.   Past tense, Subjunctive I

> Subjunctive I form of **sein** + past participle + **worden**

ich sei gesucht worden   wir seien gesucht worden
du seiest gesucht worden   ihr seiet gesucht worden
er sei gesucht worden   sie seien gesucht worden
sie sei gesucht worden   Sie seien gesucht worden
es sei gesucht worden

j.   Past tense, Subjunctive II

> Subjunctive II form of **sein** + past participle + **worden**

ich wäre gesucht worden   wir wären gesucht worden
du wärest gesucht worden   ihr wäret gesucht worden
er wäre gesucht worden   sie wären gesucht worden
sie wäre gesucht worden   Sie wären gesucht worden
es wäre gesucht worden

k.   Future, Subjunctive II

> Subjunctive II form of **werden** + past participle + **werden**

ich würde gesucht werden   wir würden gesucht werden
du würdest gesucht werden   ihr würdet gesucht werden
er würde gesucht werden   sie würden gesucht werden
sie würde gesucht werden   Sie würden gesucht werden
es würde gesucht werden

VIERHUNDERTFÜNFZIG

l. Future perfect, Subjunctive II

> Subjunctive II form of **werden** + past participle + **worden** + **sein**

ich würde gesucht worden sein　　　wir würden gesucht worden sein
du würdest gesucht worden sein　　ihr würdet gesucht worden sein
er würde gesucht worden sein　　　sie würden gesucht worden sein
sie würde gesucht worden sein　　　Sie würden gesucht worden sein
es würde gesucht worden sein

5. Modal Verbs

a. Meanings

können	*to be able to, can*
wollen	*to want to, intend to*
müssen	*to have to, must*
mögen	*to like to, like*
dürfen	*to be permitted to, may*
sollen	*to be supposed to, ought*

b. Present tense, indicative

	können	**wollen**	**müssen**	**mögen**	**dürfen**	**sollen**
ich	kann	will	muß	mag	darf	soll
du	kannst	willst	mußt	magst	darfst	sollst
er	kann	will	muß	mag	darf	soll
sie	kann	will	muß	mag	darf	soll
es	kann	will	muß	mag	darf	soll
wir	können	wollen	müssen	mögen	dürfen	sollen
ihr	könnt	wollt	müßt	mögt	dürft	sollt
sie	können	wollen	müssen	mögen	dürfen	sollen
Sie	können	wollen	müssen	mögen	dürfen	sollen

c. Past tense, indicative

ich	konnte	wollte	mußte	mochte	durfte	sollte
du	konntest	wolltest	mußtest	mochtest	durftest	solltest
er	konnte	wollte	mußte	mochte	durfte	sollte
sie	konnte	wollte	mußte	mochte	durfte	sollte
es	konnte	wollte	mußte	mochte	durfte	sollte
wir	konnten	wollten	mußten	mochten	durften	sollten
ihr	konntet	wolltet	mußtet	mochtet	durftet	solltet
sie	konnten	wollten	mußten	mochten	durften	sollten
Sie	konnten	wollten	mußten	mochten	durften	sollten

VIERHUNDERTEINUNDFÜNFZIG

d.   Present perfect, indicative

1. | Form of **haben** + past participle of modal verb |

ich habe
du   hast
er   hat   gekonnt
sie hat   gewollt
es   hat   gemußt
wir haben   gemocht
ihr habt   gedurft
sie haben   gesollt
Sie haben

2. | Form of **haben** + infinitive of main verb + infinitive of modal |

er hat (ihn) sehen können

e.   Past perfect, indicative

1. | Past tense form of **haben** + past participle of modal verb |

er hatte gekonnt; gewollt; gemußt; gemocht; gedurft; gesollt

2. | Past tense form **haben** + infinitive of main verb + infinitive of modal verb |

er hatte (ihn) sehen können

f.   Future tense, indicative

| Form of **werden** + modal verb |

er wird können

g.   Future perfect, indicative

| Form of **werden** + past participle of modal verb + infinitive of **haben** |

er wird gekonnt haben

VIERHUNDERTZWEIUNDFÜNFZIG

h.   Present tense, Subjunctive I

ich könne	wolle	müsse	möge	dürfe	solle
du könnest	wollest	müssest	mögest	dürfest	sollest
er könne	wolle	müsse	möge	dürfe	solle
sie könne	wolle	müsse	möge	dürfe	solle
es könne	wolle	müsse	möge	dürfe	solle
wir können	wollen	müssen	mögen	dürfen	sollen
ihr könnet	wollet	müsset	möget	dürfet	sollet
sie können	wollen	müssen	mögen	dürfen	sollen
Sie können	wollen	müssen	mögen	dürfen	sollen

i.   Present tense, Subjunctive II

ich könnte	wollte	müßte	möchte	dürfte	sollte
du könntest	wolltest	müßtest	möchtest	dürftest	solltest
er könnte	wollte	müßte	möchte	dürfte	sollte
sie könnte	wollte	müßte	möchte	dürfte	sollte
es könnte	wollte	müßte	möchte	dürfte	sollte
wir könnten	wollten	müßten	möchten	dürften	sollten
ihr könntet	wolltet	müßtet	möchtet	dürftet	solltet
sie könnten	wollten	müßten	möchten	dürften	sollten
Sie könnten	wollten	müßten	möchten	dürften	sollten

j.   Past tense, Subjunctive I

> Subjunctive I form of **haben** + past participle of modal verb

er habe gekonnt; gewollt; gemußt; gemocht; gedurft; gesollt

k.   Past tense, Subjunctive II

> Subjunctive II form of **haben** + past participle of modal verb

er hätte gekonnt; gewollt; gemußt; gemocht; gedurft; gesollt

l.   Future, Subjunctive I

> Subjunctive I form of **werden** + infinitive of modal verb

er werde können

m.   Future perfect, Subjunctive I

> Subjunctive I form **werden** + past participle of modal verb + infinitive of **haben**

er werde gekonnt haben

6. Inseparable Verb Prefixes

be-, ent-, emp-, er-, ver-, zer-, ge-, miß-, wider-, voll-

7. Selective List of Strong and Irregular Verbs

INFINITIVE	3RD SING. PRES. (IF IRREGULAR)	PAST	PAST PARTICIPLE
an-fangen *(to begin)*	fängt an	fing an	angefangen
beginnen *(to begin)*		begann	begonnen
bieten *(to offer)*		bot	geboten
bitten *(to ask, request)*		bat	gebeten
bleiben *(to stay)*		blieb	ist geblieben
brechen *(to break)*	bricht	brach	(ist) gebrochen
brennen *(to burn)*		brannte	gebrannt
bringen *(to bring)*		brachte	gebracht
denken *(to think)*		dachte	gedacht
ein-laden *(to invite)*	lädt ein	lud ein	eingeladen
empfehlen *(to recommend)*	empfiehlt	empfahl	empfohlen
erschrecken *(to be frightened)*	erschrickt	erschrak	ist erschrocken
essen *(to eat)*	ißt	aß	gegessen
fahren *(to drive, go)*	fährt	fuhr	(ist) gefahren
fallen *(to fall)*	fällt	fiel	ist gefallen
finden *(to find)*		fand	gefunden
fliegen *(to fly)*		flog	(ist) geflogen
geben *(to give)*	gibt	gab	gegeben
gehen *(to go)*		ging	ist gegangen
gelingen *(to succeed)*		gelang	ist gelungen
geschehen *(to happen)*	geschieht	geschah	ist geschehen
gewinnen *(to win)*		gewann	gewonnen
haben *(to have)*	hat	hatte	gehabt
halten *(to hold)*	hält	hielt	gehalten
heißen *(to be called)*		hieß	geheißen
helfen *(to help)*	hilft	half	geholfen
kennen *(to know)*		kannte	gekannt
kommen *(to come)*		kam	ist gekommen
lassen *(to let, leave)*	läßt	ließ	gelassen
laufen *(to run)*	läuft	lief	ist gelaufen
leiden *(to suffer)*		litt	gelitten
lesen *(to read)*	liest	las	gelesen
liegen *(to lie, recline)*		lag	gelegen
nehmen *(to take)*	nimmt	nahm	genommen
nennen *(to name)*		nannte	genannt
raten *(to advise; to guess)*	rät	riet	geraten
rufen *(to call)*		rief	gerufen

INFINITIVE	3RD SING. PRES. (IF IRREGULAR)	PAST	PAST PARTICIPLE
scheinen (to seem; to shine)		schien	geschienen
schlafen (to sleep)	schläft	schlief	geschlafen
schließen (to close)		schloß	geschlossen
schneiden (to cut)		schnitt	geschnitten
schreiben (to write)		schrieb	geschrieben
schreien (to scream)		schrie	geschrien
schwimmen (to swim)		schwamm	(ist) geschwommen
sehen (to see)	sieht	sah	gesehen
sein (to be)	ist	war	ist gewesen
senden (to send)		sandte	gesandt
singen (to sing)		sang	gesungen
sitzen (to sit)		saß	gesessen
sprechen (to speak)	spricht	sprach	gesprochen
stehen (to stand)		stand	gestanden
steigen (to climb)		stieg	ist gestiegen
sterben (to die)	stirbt	starb	ist gestorben
tragen (to carry, wear)	trägt	trug	getragen
treffen (to hit, meet)	trifft	traf	getroffen
treiben (to drive)		trieb	getrieben
treten (to step; to kick)	tritt	trat	(ist) getreten
trinken (to drink)		trank	getrunken
tun (to do)		tat	getan
vergessen (to forget)	vergißt	vergaß	vergessen
vergleichen (to compare)		verglich	verglichen
verlieren (to lose)		verlor	verloren
verschwinden (to disappear)		verschwand	ist verschwunden
wachsen (to grow)	wächst	wuchs	ist gewachsen
waschen (to wash)	wäscht	wusch	gewaschen
werden (to become)	wird	wurde	ist geworden
werfen (to throw)	wirft	warf	geworfen
wissen (to know)	weiß	wußte	gewußt
ziehen (to pull; to move)		zog	(ist) gezogen

8.   Declension of Pronouns

a.   Personal pronouns

SINGULAR

NOMINATIVE	ich	du	er	sie	es
GENITIVE	(meiner)	(deiner)	(seiner)	(ihrer)	(seiner)
DATIVE	mir	dir	ihm	ihr	ihm
ACCUSATIVE	mich	dich	ihn	sie	es

PLURAL

NOMINATIVE	wir	ihr	sie	Sie *(sing. and pl.)*
GENITIVE	(unser)	(euer)	(ihrer)	(Ihrer)
DATIVE	uns	euch	ihnen	Ihnen
ACCUSATIVE	uns	euch	sie	Sie

b. Interrogative pronouns

	MASCULINE AND FEMININE	NEUTER
NOMINATIVE	wer	was
GENITIVE	wessen	—
DATIVE	wem	—
ACCUSATIVE	wen	was

c. Relative pronouns

	SINGULAR			PLURAL
	MASCULINE	FEMININE	NEUTER	ALL GENDERS
NOMINATIVE	der	die	das	die
GENITIVE	dessen	deren	dessen	deren
DATIVE	dem	der	dem	denen
ACCUSATIVE	den	die	das	die

d. Reflexive pronouns

	ACCUSATIVE		DATIVE
(ich setze)	mich	(ich schmeichle)	mir
(du setzt)	dich	(du schmeichelst)	dir
(er setzt)	sich	(er schmeichelt)	sich
(sie setzt)	sich	(sie schmeichelt)	sich
(es setzt)	sich	(es schmeichelt)	sich
(wir setzen)	uns	(wir schmeicheln)	uns
(ihr setzt)	euch	(ihr schmeichelt)	euch
(sie setzen)	sich	(sie schmeicheln)	sich
(Sie setzen)	sich	(Sie schmeicheln)	sich

9. Adjective Declensions

a. Adjectives preceded by **der**-words (weak declension):

SINGULAR:	MASCULINE	FEMININE	NEUTER
NOMINATIVE	**der** gute Mann	**die** gute Frau	**das** gute Kind
GENITIVE	**des** guten Mannes	**der** guten Frau	**des** guten Kindes
DATIVE	**dem** guten Mann	**der** guten Frau	**dem** guten Kind
ACCUSATIVE	**den** guten Mann	**die** gute Frau	**das** gute Kind

VIERHUNDERTSECHSUNDFÜNFZIG

PLURAL:	ALL GENDERS
NOMINATIVE	**die** guten Kinder
GENITIVE	**der** guten Kinder
DATIVE	**den** guten Kindern
ACCUSATIVE	**die** guten Kinder

b. Unpreceded adjectives (strong declension):

	SINGULAR			PLURAL
	MASCULINE	FEMININE	NEUTER	ALL GENDERS
NOMINATIVE	gut**er** Tee	gut**e** Milch	gut**es** Bier	gut**e** Weine
GENITIVE	gut**en** Tees	gut**er** Milch	gut**en** Bieres	gut**er** Weine
DATIVE	gut**em** Tee	gut**er** Milch	gut**em** Bier	gut**en** Weinen
ACCUSATIVE	gut**en** Tee	gut**e** Milch	gut**es** Bier	gut**e** Weine

c. Adjectives preceded by **ein**-words (mixed declension):

SINGULAR:	MASCULINE		FEMININE		NEUTER	
NOMINATIVE	**ein**	gut**er** Mann	**eine** gut**e** Frau		**ein**	gut**es** Kind
GENITIVE	**eines**	gut**en** Mannes	**einer** gut**en** Frau		**eines**	gut**en** Kindes
DATIVE	**einem**	gut**en** Mann	**einer** gut**en** Frau		**einem**	gut**en** Kind
ACCUSATIVE	**einen**	gut**en** Mann	**eine** gut**e** Frau		**ein**	gut**es** Kind

PLURAL:	ALL GENDERS
NOMINATIVE	**keine** guten Kinder
GENITIVE	**keiner** guten Kinder
DATIVE	**keinen** guten Kindern
ACCUSATIVE	**keine** guten Kinder

10. Comparison of Adjectives and Adverbs

	POSITIVE	COMPARATIVE	SUPERLATIVE
REGULAR	schön	schöner	am schönsten
	jung	jünger	am jüngsten
	groß	größer	am größten
	dunkel	dunkler	am dunkelsten
IRREGULAR	gut	besser	am besten
	viel	mehr	am meisten
	hoch	höher	am höchsten
	nah	näher	am nächsten
ADVERBS	gern	lieber	am liebsten
	bald	eher	am ehesten
	sehr	mehr	am meisten

VIERHUNDERTSIEBENUNDFÜNFZIG

11. Conjunctions

a.   Coordinating

und	*and*	aber	*but*
oder	*or*	sondern	*but*
denn	*because, for*		

b.   Subordinating

als	*when*	ob	*whether, if*
als ob	*as if*	obgleich	*although*
bevor	*before*	obwohl	*although*
bis	*until*	obschon	*although*
ehe	*before*	seitdem	*since*
da	*since, because*	sobald	*as soon as*
damit	*so that*	während	*while*
daß	*that*	weil	*because*
indem	*by . . . (-ing)*	wie	*as*
nachdem	*after*	wenn	*when, whenever*

12. Abbreviations

a.a.O.	(am angegebenen Ort)	*loc. cit.*
Abs.	(Absender)	*sender*
Abt.	(Abteilung)	*department*
A.G.	(Aktiengesellschaft)	*stock company*
Anm.	(Anmerkung)	*footnote*
Bd.	(Band)	*volume*
betr.	(betreffend, betrifft)	*concerning, referring to*
bez.	(bezüglich)	*concerning, referring to*
bzw.	(beziehungsweise)	*respectively, or*
ca.	(circa)	*about, approximately*
dgl.	(dergleichen)	*of similar kind*
d.h.	(das heißt)	*that is to say, i.e.*
geb.	(geboren)	*born*
gest.	(gestorben)	*deceased*
gez.	(gezeichnet)	*signed*
G.m.b.H.	(Gesellschaft mit beschränkter Haftung)	*company with limited liability*
lt.	(laut)	*according to*
m. E.	(meines Erachtens)	*in my opinion*
m. W.	(meines Wissens)	*as far as I know*
n. Chr.	(nach Christus)	*A. D.*
sog.	(sogenannt-)	*so-called*
s.o.	(siehe oben)	*see above*

s. S.	(siehe Seite)	*see page*
s. u.	(siehe unten)	*see below*
u.a.	(unter anderem)	*among other things*
u.ä.	(und ähnliche)	*and similar things*
usw.	(und so weiter)	*etc.*
v. Chr.	(vor Christus)	*B.C.*
vgl.	(vergleiche)	*compare, cf.*
v.H.	(vom Hundert)	*percent, %*
z. B.	(zum Beispiel)	*for instance, for example*
z. T.	(zum Teil)	*in part, partially*
z. Z.	(zur Zeit)	*at present*

Vocabularies

The German vocabulary entries refer to the text page on which words are first used. See the "Vocabulary" section in the Preface for a more complete explanation.

The English vocabulary lists words occurring in the English-German exercises. References are to pages on which the words first appear.

GERMAN VOCABULARY

ab 266
abendländisch 395
aber 71
ab-fahren 198
der Abfall, -̈e 286
der Abfallstoff, -e 286
die Abgabe, -n 286
ab-geben 287
der Abgeordnete, -n 167
sich ab-heben 395
ab-holzen 376
das Abitur 133
das Abkommen 305
ab-kürzen 364
die Abkürzung, -en 364
die Ablagerung, -en 349
ab-laufen 372
ab-leisten 355
ab-leiten 299
ab-lösen 263
die Abnahme 422
ab-nehmen 369
ab-nutzen 199
ab-pressen 371
die Abreaktion 234
ab-schließen 307
der Abschluß, -̈e 266
die Abschlußprüfung, -en 331
der Abschnitt, -e 187
absolut 156
der Absolvent, -en 355
ab-spalten 313
die Abstammung 233
die Abstimmung, -en 291
ab-wechseln 397
sich ab-wenden 380
ach 295
acht 25
die Acht 193
die Achtung 384
achtzehn 31
achtzig 54
die Addition 63
der Adel, - 193
die Adresse, -n 50
der Advokat, -en 167
ächzen 376
der Ägypter, - 418
die Ähre, -n 66
älter 319
ändern 327, 404
der Äquator 152

die Ärztin, -nen 27
ärztlich 384
äußerst 161
das Afrika 45, 51
der Agnostiker, 43
akademisch 331
die Aktie, -n 404
die Aktiengesellschaft 404
aktuell 237
die Akustik 391
die Algebra 109
das Alkali, -en 313
der Alkohol 24
alle 43
allein 380
alles 183
allgemein 331, 369
die Alliierten (pl.) 305
die Alpen 208
als 75, 167, 214, 253
also 109
als ob 137
alt 47
der Altar, -e 173
die Altarnische, -n 173
das Alter 109, 266
das Altertum 47, 418
die Altertumskunde 47
altsprachlich 319
der Amazonas 161
das Amerika 45, 51
der Amerikaner, - 50, 305
amerikanisch 197
die Aminosäure, -n 256
das Ammonium 313
amphibisch 161
das Amt, -̈er 273
die Amtssprache, -n 273
an 43, 100
die Analyse, -n 103
analysieren 103
die Anatomie 201
der Anbau 273
ander 121
an-deuten 199
an-erkennen 273
anfänglich 369
der Anfang, -̈e 418
an-fangen 266
an-geben 240
der Angebot, -e 358
angeblich 57
angeschwemmt 349

sich (etwas) anhören 265
an-kaufen 349
an-kommen 203
anmutig 427
an-nehmen 407
annektieren 306
die Anordnung, -en 104
an-regen 247
die Anregung, -en 327
der Anschlag, -̈e 191
sich (etwas) an-sehen 264, 265
die Ansicht, -en 167
die Ansiedlung, -en 251
anständig 322
ein Anständiger 322
anstatt 113, 173
anstatt . . . zu 248
an-steigen 358
der Anteil, -e 286, 404
die Anthropologie 31
antik 247
die Antike 247
der Antisemit, -en 213
der Antisemitismus 213
der Antrieb, -e 234
antworten 43
an-vertrauen 384
an-wenden 384
die Anwendung, -en 291, 398
die Anzahl 310, 397
das Anzeichen, - 362
an-ziehen 422
sich an-ziehen 422
der Anzug, -̈e 56
die Aorta 286
der Apfel, -̈e 17
die Apfelsäure 369
der Aphorismus, Aphorismen 322
die Apokalypse 201
der Apostel, - 201
der April 55
die Apsis, Apsiden 36, 173
die Arbeit 66
arbeiten 15, 19
arbeitend 310
der Arbeiter, - 267, 310
die Arbeitsgemeinschaft, -en 319
die Arbeitsgruppe, -n 343

die Arbeitskraft, ¨e 362
  arbeitslos 362
die Arbeitslosigkeit 362
der Archäologe, -n 250
die Archäologie 47
die Architektur 187
  Aristoteles 339
die Arithmetik 63
  arm 72, 167
der Arm, -e 17
die Art, -en 17, 63
die Arterie, -n 286
der Arzt, ¨e 56, 233
das Asien 45, 51
der Assyrer, - 418
der Astronom, -en 422
die Astronomie 256
  atemlos 380
der Atheismus 42
der Atheist, -en 42
der Atlantik 61
  atlantisch 226
der Atlas 240
das Atoll 57
das Atom, -e 104
die Atomanordnung, -en
  104
  auch 24, 256
  auf 66, 100
der Aufbau 266
  auf-bauen 422
  auf-bewahren 349
die Auffassung, -en 187
die Aufführung, -en 339
die Aufgabe, -n 290, 319
  auf-geben 279, 380
die Aufgekratztheit 398
  auf-heben 408
  auf-lösen 290
die Aufmerksamkeit 397
die Aufnahme, -n 229,
  286, 384
  auf-nehmen 287
  aufrecht-erhalten 351,
  384
  aufregend 382
  auf-stehen 203
  auf-stellen 422
der Aufstieg, -e 167
  aufstrebend 187
  auf-tauchen 395
  auf-tauen 397
  auf-treten 387
der Auftrieb, -e 391
  auf-zeichnen 199

das Auge, -n 337
der August 55
  aus 19, 62, 88, 213
die Ausbildung, -en 266
  aus-drücken 263
die Auseinandersetzung,
  -en 274
die Ausgabe, -n 193, 359
der Ausgangsstoff, -e 368
  aus-gehen 358
die Ausgelassenheit 397
  aus-gleichen 274
die Ausgrabung, -en 250
  aus-halten 203
  sich aus-kennen 380
  ausländisch 349
  aus-leihen 349
  aus-rechnen 199
die Aussaat 66
  aus-schicken 427
  aus-sehen 266, 319
  außer 250
  außerdem 240, 369
  außerhalb 113
das Australien 45, 51
  australisch 256
  aus-üben 355, 384
die Auswirkung, -en 391
  sich aus-zeichnen 408
das Auto, -s 44, 64
der Autodidakt, -en 251
die Autorität 245
der Autoritätsglauben 247

der Babylonier, - 418
  babylonisch 193
der Backofen, - 25
der Badeanzug, ¨e 56
  baden 56
der Bäcker, - 55
der Bahnhof, ¨e 380
der Balkan 208
die Banane, -n 153
der Band, ¨e 299, 411
die Bank, ¨e 121
die Bank, -en 267, 349
das Barock 263
der Bart, ¨e 322
der Basalt 55
die Base, -n 313
die Basilika 36
die Basis 364
der Bau 36
  bauen 290, 376
der Bauer, -n 66

das Bauernhaus, ¨er 82
der Bauernhof, ¨e 94
die Bauform, -en 82
das Bauhaus 290
der Baukörper, - 88
die Baukunst 28
das Baumaterial 291
der Baustein, -e 104, 256
die Bauweise, -n 82
der Baum, ¨e 337
die Baumwolle 51
der Baumwollstrauch, ¨er
  51
das Bauwesen 331
  Bayern 88
  bayrisch 208
  bedeuten 36, 188
  bedeutend 250
die Bedingung, -en 332,
  408
  bedrohen 180, 188
die Bedrohung, -en 384
  sich beeilen 261, 380
  beeindrucken 299
  beeinflussen 82, 291
  beenden 115, 188
die Beere, -n 369
  sich befassen 391
  sich befinden 369
  befördern 128, 188
die Befreiung, -en 251
der Befund, -e 234
der Beginn 191, 418
  beginnen 121
  begreifen 427
der Begriff, -e 28, 207, 290
  begründen 391
der Begründer, - 299, 422
  begünstigen 362
  behalten 282
  behandeln 31, 188
die Behandlung, -en 234
  behaupten 234
  beheben 373
  beherrschen 328
  behindert 373
  bei 65, 269
  bei-behalten 331
  beide 279
das Beispiel, -e 266
  beispielhaft 247
  bei-stehen 203
  bei-stimmen 199
der Beitrag, ¨e 327
die Bekämpfung, -en 180

gegossen **140**
der Gehalt 369
das Geheimnis, -se 384
gehen 19, 206, 299
das Gehirn, -e 286
gehören 104
der Geist 247
die Geisteswissenschaften
(pl.) 343
geistig 373
gelangen 229
das Geld 343
das Geldwechsel 349
der Gelehrte, -n 247
geloben 384
gelten 247, 384
das Gemälde, - 201
gemäßigt 146
das Gemeingut, ̈er 247
gemeinsam 256
die Gemeinschaft, -en 354
das Gemisch 36
genau 104
der General, -e; ̈e 415
die Generation, -en 140
genetisch 181
genieren 261
die Genossenschaft, -en
355
der Genuß, ̈e 274
das Genußmittel, - 274
geographisch 207
die Geologie 121
die Geometrie 109
die Gerade 239
die Gerbsäure 369
der Gerette, -n 381
die Gerette, -n 381
gering 146
der Germane, -n 418
gern 360
die Gerste 24
gesamt 128, 193
die Gesamtausgabe, -n
193
die Gesamtblutmenge 286
geschehen 128, 313
die Geschichte, -n 214
geschichtlich 418
geschlossen 87
der Geschmack 369
das Geschriebene 381
die Geschwindigkeit 98
der Geselle, -n 351
die Gesellschaft, -en 245

die Gesellschaftsordnung
245
das Gesetz, -e 63, 351
das Gesicht, -er 295
das Gespräch 373
gestaltend 290
die Gestaltung, -en 173,
408
das Gestein 349
gestorben 115
geteilt durch 145
das Getreide 66
die Getreidesorte, -n 66
das Gewächs 51
gewährleisten 286
das Gewässer 70
gewandt 167
die Gewandtheit 398
das Gewebe 36, 286
das Gewicht, -e 391
der Gewinn, -e 404
gewinnen 348, 415
die Gewissenhaftigkeit
384
gewöhnlich 24, 263
das Gewölbe, - 173, 187
gewünscht 343
gezielt 362
der Giebel, - 173
gießen **140**
der Gips 56
glänzen 398
glänzend 167
das Glas, ̈er 42
glatt 279
glauben 42, 43
der Glauben 43, 247
das Glaubensbekenntnis,
-se 43
gleich 146, 427
gleichen 415
das Gleichgewicht 391
die Gleichung, -en 109
gleichzeitig 313
gliedern 208
die Gliederung, -en 171
das Glück 397, 415
glücklich 72, 322
glücklicherweise 380
das Glücksspiel 348
gluh 337
die Glukose 369
das Glutamin 373
der Gneis 55
das Gold 18, 35, 153

golden 395
der Golf, -e 146
der Golfstrom 146
die Gotik 173
der Gott, ̈er 42, 282
die Gottesleugnung 42
die Gottlosigkeit 42
der Graben 251
der Grad, - 133
die Grammatik, -en 411
der Granit 55
die Graphik 28
der Graphiker, - 201
der Graphit 306
grau 70
das Graue 239
der Greis, -e 296
die Grenze, -n 222
Griechenland 247
griechisch 31
das Griechisch 319
die Größe, -n 109, 263
größer 256
größt 207
groß 128
großangelegt 373
der Großhandel 355
die Großzügigkeit 263
gründen 290
der Grundbaustein, -e 256
das Grundstück 427
das Grüne 239
der Grund, ̈e 213, 256,
273, 279
die Grundform, -en 82
die Grundlage, -n 104, 384
der Grundriß 173
der Grundsatz, ̈e 167
die Güter (pl.) 358
der Gütertransit 274
gut 64, 360
das Gut, ̈er 273
das Gute 239
das Gymnasium,
Gymnasien 134

das Haar, -e 51
die Haargefäße (pl.) 286
haben 22, 36
das Hab und Gut 214
hängen 125
häufig 171
der Hafen, ̈ 208
die Hafenstadt, ̈e 208
der Hagel 55

der Januar 55
je 173, 404
jed- 75, 105
jeder 319
jedoch 168, 274
jemand 327
jen- 105
jenseits 113
das Jenseits 187
jetzt 66
je . . . um so (desto) 313
jeweilig 313
das Joch, -e 173
der Jude, -n 213
jüdisch 233
jünger 319
Jugoslawien 306
der Juli 55
jung 363
der Junge, -n 351
der Juni 55
die Jura (pl.) 299

der Käfer 56
der Kaffee 153
der Kaiser, - 115
das Kali 369
das Kalium 35
der Kalk 369
die Kalorik 391
das Kalzium 35
der Kakao 153
kalt 133, 206
das Kambrium 45
sich kämmen 265
die Kammer, -n 286
der Kampf, ⸚e 251, 408
der Kandidat, -en 167
kanonisch 191
der Kanton, -e 273
die Kapillare, -n 287
das Kapital 273
der Kapitalertrag, ⸚e 273
der Karpfen 70
die Karriere 299
die Karte, -n 50
die Katastrophe 226
der Kater 56, 337
kathartisch 234
kaufen 59, 404
sich (etwas) kaufen 265
die Kaufkraft, ⸚e 362
kaufmännisch 267

der Kautschuk 153
der Keim, -e 173, 256
die Keimzelle 173
kein(e) 82, 142
der Kelte, -n 418
die Kelterung 371
kennen 70, 125
der Kenner, - 55
der Kern, -e 240, 369
die Kernenergie 240
die Kette, -n 322
der Kiesel 56
das Kind, -er 11, 266
die Kirche, -n 36
klar 290
die Klasse, -n 267
die Klassik 339
klassisch 327
klein 171
Kleinasien 251
das Klima 82
klopfen 206
klug 377
der Knirps 56
der Knochen 229
Köln 222
der König, -e 36, 425
der Königsbau 36
können 215
der Körper, - 88
körperlich 355
die Körperschlagader 286
das Kohlendioxid 286
der Kollaps 160
das Kolleg, -s 398
der Kollege, -n 256
das Komma 208
kommen 62, 214, 337
der Kommentar, -e 351
kommunistisch 299
kompliziert 161, 256
der Kongreß, -e 167
die Konjunktur 362
konservieren 398
der Konsument, -en 358
der Kontinent, - 152
kontiental 146
die Kontrolle, -n 181, 355
das Konzept, -e 291
die Kostenrechnung 121
die Kraft, ⸚e 391
die Kraftanlage, -n 402
die Kralle, -n 337
das Krankenhaus, ⸚er 25
die Krankheit, -en 26, 180

kraulen 279
der Krebs 70
der Kredit, -e 349
der Kreis, -e 160
der Kreislauf 160, 286
das Kreuz, -e 214
der Kreuzzug, ⸚e 214
der Krieg, -e 168, 415
kriegen 322
die Krise, -n 362
der Kristall, -e 104
der Kristallograph, -e 104
die Kristallstruktur, -en 104
der Kritiker, - 339
kritisch 214
das Kubikzentimeter, - 128
kühl 146
künftig 256
der Künstler, - 422
die Kuh, ⸚e 26
der Kuhstall, ⸚e 278
die Kultur 47
kulturell 207
die Kulturpolitik 327
der Kulturraum 418
der Kulturstaat, -en 384
kumulativ 361
die Kunde 47
der Kunde, -n 349, 351
der Kundschafter, - 427
die Kunst, ⸚e 28, 201
das Kunsthandwerk 28
das Kupfer, - 35, 153
der Kupferstich, -e 201
der Kurs, -e 331
kurz 319, 395

das Labor 17, 19
das Lachen 380
der Ladentisch, -e 349
lächeln 380
längst- 319
lärmen 206
die Lage, -n 310
das Lager, - 310, 408
der Laie, -n 251
die Lampe, -n 11
das Land, ⸚er 42, 75, 121
der Landesbezirk, -e 354
die Landessprache, -n 273
die Landschaft, -en 82
die Landschaftsform, -en 82
Landshut 121

das Metall, -e 279
der Meter, - 51
die Methode, -n 104
mich 275
die Milch 256
die Milchkanne 25
die Milchstraße 256
die Million, -en 75
mindestens 266
das Mineral, -ien 94
der Mineraldünger 94
der Ministerrat 355
minus 145
die Minute, -n 279, 286
mir 284
mit 56, 62
der Mitarbeiter 299
der Mitbesitzer 404
der Mitglied, -er 355
mit-nehmen 203
die Mitte 251
mit-teilen 199, 240
mittel- 208
das Mittel, - 94, 180
das Mittelalter 214
mittelalterlich 245
mittelbar 362
der Mittelbau 173
mitteldeutschland 87
das Mittelgebirge 208
der Mittelpunkt, -e 422
mitten 152
die mittlere Reife 267
der Mittwoch 55
mit-wirken 250
die Moderne 239
mögen 215
möglich 140
möglicherweise 256
die Möglichkeit 181
der Mönch, -e 425
das Molekül, -e 104
die Molekularstruktur,
-en 104
die Monarchie 306
der Monat, -e 319
der Monsun 95
der Montag 19, 55
morgen (adj.) 210
der Morgen 380
das Morgengrauen 279
die Moritat 295
die Mosel 299
das Motiv, -e 263
der Motor, -en 401

die Mücke, -n 180
sich mühen 395
multipliziert mit 145
München 208
münden 208
müssen 215
die Multiplikation 63
die Musik 319
der Muskel, -n 128
die Muskulatur, -en 128
das Muster, - 104
die Mutter, - 26, 40
die Muttersprache, -n 75
Mykena 250

nach 62, 66, 104, 132,
278
der Nachbar, -n 273
nachdem 212, 404
nach-denken 203, 391
die Nachfrage 310, 358
nach-lassen 358
nachmittags 319
der Nachmittag, -e 319
nach-prüfen 199
die Nacht, -e 128, 279
die Nähe 380
näher 337
der Nährstoff, -e 286
der Name, -n 57
die Nation 193
national 415
die Nationalität 384
das Natrium 35, 45
natürlich 94
die Natur 26, 226, 278
die Naturwissenschaft,
-en 391
naturwissenschaftlich
319
der Nazi 213
n. Chr. (nach Christi
Geburt) 418
neben 100, 247
der Neckar 146
nehmen 136, 343
nennen 47
der Nenner 366
das Neon 36
der Nerv, -en 233
der Nervenarzt, -e 233
das Netz, -e 128, 240
neu 66
die Neubildung, -en 351
das Neueste 237

neun 25
neunjährig 267
neunzehn 31
neunzig 54
neusprachlich 319
die Neutralität 274
die Neuzeit 245
nicht 43, 69
nicht mehr 282
das Nichtmetall, -e 313
nichts 183, 296
nicht . . . sondern
328
niederdeutsch 82
die Niedergeschlagenheit
397
die Niederlande 201
Niedersachsen 82
niedrig(er) 94
die Niere, -n 286
die Nische, -n 173
das Niveau 153
der Nobelpreis 115
noch 197
noch einmal 319
noch heute 251, 291
noch nicht 153
noch wenig 251
nominieren 167
nord 146, 207
der Norden 55, 208
der Nordosten 55
die Nordsee 208
normalerweise 267,
319
der November 55
Nürnberg 201
die Null, -en 25, 156
der Nullpunkt 156
der Numerus 364
numerus clausus 343
nun 362
nur 19, 229
die Nutzung 273

ob 137
der Oberbau 88
oberdeutsch 88
der Oberschüler 319
oberst 384
der Oberste Gerichtshof
355
die Oberstufe 266
das Obst 266
obgleich 149

schreiben 163
der Schreibtisch, -e 35
die Schreibweise 364
die Schrift, -en 299
der Schritt, -e 256
der Schüler, - 50
schuldig 384
die Schule, -n 115, 266
das Schuljahr 319
die Schulter, -n 376
die Schulzeit 267
der Schutz 94
der Schutzmann, ¨er 380
schwarz 88, 337
das Schwarze Meer 208
der Schwarzwald 88, 222
der Schwefel 36, 313
die Schweiz 45, 75, 222
schwer 19
die Schwester 15, 27
schwimmen 94, 279
die Schwingung, -en 391
schwitzen 376
der Schwung 380
sechs 25
sechzehn 31
sechzig 54
seelisch 234
das Seelenleben 398
das Segment, -e 168
sehen 30, 295
sich sehnen 261
sehr 24
sein (adj.) 134, 143
sein (verb) 21
seit 62, 180
seitdem 212
die Seite, -n 140, 173, 358
das Seitenschiff, -e 173
der Seitenturm, ¨e 173
seither 214
die Sekunde, -n 128
selbst 331
selbstständig 306, 327
das Seminar, -e 343
senkrecht 187
die Senkrechte 239
der September 55
setzen 260
sich setzen 260
das Sextett 45
in sich 391
sie 15, 63
Sie 275
sieben 25

siebt 244
siebzehn 31
siebzig 54
der Sieger, - 274
das Silber 35
die Sinfonie 26
singen 11, 12
der Singvogel, ¨ 35
sinken 98, 226
sinkend 362
der Sisal 153
sittlich 384
die Sitzbank, ¨e 349
sitzen 279
sitzen-bleiben 267
das Skelett, -e 286
skeptisch 43
der Sklave, -n 167
der Slawe, -n 418
sodann 398
sofern 351
sofort 343
sogar 256
sogenannt 104
der Sohn, ¨e 18, 56
solch 105, 144
der Soldat, -en 351
sollen 215
der Sommer, - 55, 146
die Sommerferien (pl.) 319
die Sonde, -n 197
sonder 355
sondern 71, 72
der Sonnentag, -e 339
sonnig 368
der Sonntag 55, 296
die Sorte 66
souverän 273
die Souveränität 305
sowie 313, 380
sowohl . . . als auch 327
der Sozialismus 299
die Sozialkunde 319
der Späher, - 427
spät 173, 377
später 173
die Spätgotik 187
die Spalte, -n 140
sich spalten 408
das Spanien 45, 214
sparen 66
der Speicher, - 88
der Speicherraum, ¨e 88

spezial 274
der Spiegel, - 279
spiegelglatt 279
die Spielbank 348
spielen 12, 327
spinnen 51
der Spitzbogen 187
die Spitze, -n 173, 331
der Sport 319
die Sprache, -n 47
der Sprachwissenschaftler 327
sprechen 30
sprengen 425
springen 279
der Sprung, ¨e 279
der Staat, -en 168, 245, 415
der Staatenbund 274
staatlich 266
der Staatsanwalt, ¨e 355
die Staatsordnung 245
die Staatsraison 247
stabilisieren 398
die Stadt, ¨e 191
ständig 339
die Stärke 422
stärker 313
der Stahl 36
der Stall, ¨e 82
der Stamm, ¨e 376
stammen 63, 167, 349
stand-halten 214
stark 171, 274
stark passiv 274
starren 279
die Statik 391
die Station 26
statt 113, 313
statt . . . zu 248
statt dessen 299
statt-finden 319, 343
stechen 180
die Stechmücke 180
stehen 11, 12, 87, 371, 395
steigen 310
sich steigern 361
die Steigerung, -en 358
der Stein, -e 88
die Stelle, -n 245, 343, 408
stellen 260, 384, 422
sich stellen 260
die Stellung, -en 384
sterben 115, 310
die Stereometrie 110

stets 173, 237, 348
der Steuer, -n 121
der Stich, -e 201
der Stichstoff 313
der Stiel, -e 371
stiften 193
der Stil, -e 171, 263
die Stimmung, -en 397
das Stipendium, Stipendien 343
stöhnen 376
die Störung, -en 358
der Stoff, -e 57
stolz 415
stossen 168
die Strafe, -n 351
straff 355
der Strahl, -en 104
strampeln 279
die Straße, -n 256
der Strauch, ̈er 51
das Streben 187
die Strecke, -n 110
die Streuung, -en 104
die Strömung, -en 98
der Strom, ̈e 146
die Struktur, -en 103
der Student, -en 13
das Studentenheim 290
die Studentin, -nen 27
der Studienbeginn 191
der Studienplatz, ̈e 332, 343
der Studienverlauf 331
studieren 11, 13
das Studium 19
das Sturmgebraus 415
die Stütze 263
die Stufe, -n 173
stufenförmig 173
die Stunde, -n 104, 319
der Stundenplan 319
die Subtraktion 63
die Suche 256
suchen 180
sich (etwas) suchen 265
der Suchgraben 251
süd 57
der Süden 55, 208
südöstlich 222
der Südpazifik 57
der Südstaat, -en 168
der Südwesten 55
süß 369

die Süßigkeit, -en 266
die Suggestion 234
der Sumerer, - 418
die Summe, -n 322, 366
das System 161, 266

die Tablette 373
tabu 94
täglich 319
die Tätigkeit 327
die Tafel, - 364
der Tag, -e 39, 128
das Tagebuch, ̈er 251
eines Tages 397
die Tageszeitung, -en 237
der Taifun 55
der Taktiker, - 167
die Tante, -n 27
die Tat, -en 351
taugen 395
tausend 65
technisch 109
der Teil, -e 31, 273
das Teilgebiet 31
teil-nehmen 250
teilweise 306
der Tempel, - 395
die Temperatur 146
die Tendenz, -en 355
das Tennis 21, 74
das Testament, -e 193
der Teufel, - 193
textil 51
der Textilrohstoff 51
das Theater 61
das Thema, (Themen) 331
die Theologie 191
der Theoretiker, - 201
theoretisch 115, 201
die Theorie, -n 115
die These, -n 191
Thüringen 354
tief 156, 208, 397
die Tiefebene 208
die Tiefsee 35
das Tier, -e 31
tierärztlich 331
Tiryns 250
der Tisch, -e 11, 349
die Tochter, ̈ 15, 26, 79
der Tod 193, 425
tot 296
der Tourist, -en 222
traditionell 327
tragen 66, 173

die Tragödie, -n 339
transportieren 286
die Traube, -n 368
traumatisch 234
treiben 233
trennen 88
die Trennwand, ̈e 88
treten 229, 247
der Trieb, -e 234
der Triebwagen, - 402
die Trigonometrie 110
trinken 182
trocken 369
Troja 250
trojanisch 251
tropisch 152, 180
trotz 113, 153
trüb 371
die Tschechoslowakei 45, 306
tschechoslowakisch 222
die Tür, -e 187
der Türke, -n 247
die Tüte 266
tun 322
die Turkei 45
der Turm, ̈e 171
die Turmspitze, -n 171

über 19, 100, 287
überbieten 398
der Überblick 207
übergehen 371
überhaupt 42, 343
überkommen 245
die Überlieferung, -en 384, 418
über-nehmen 349
die Überprüfung 214
die Übersetzung, -en 193
die Übertragung, -en 373
überwinden 245, 362
die Überzeugung, -en 322
die Übung, -en 343
das Ufer, - 222
die ̈r, -en 133, 273
̈ 115
̈ra 98
der Ultraschall 98
die Ultraschallmessung, -en 98
um 33, 87, 132, 319
der Umfang, ̈e 313
umfassen 245, 411

ENGLISH VOCABULARY

Index to Structure

VIERHUNDERTSECHSUNDACHTZIG

# Index to Readings